FamilyFun

VACATION GUIDE

Mid-Atlantic

By Alice Lecesse Powers, Denise Weldon-Siviy,
Rich Mintzer, Elisa Gallaro, and the
experts at **FamilyFun** Magazine

DISNEP

EDITIONS
New York

FamilyFun
VACATION GUIDE
Mid-Atlantic

Editorial Director
Lois Spritzer

Design & Production
IMPRESS, INC.
Hans Teensma
Pam Glaven
Katie Craig
Lisa Newman
James McDonald
Katie Winger

Disney Editions and *FamilyFun*

Book Editors
Alexandra Kennedy
Wendy Lefkon
Lisa Stiepock

Research Editor
Beth Honeyman

Contributing Editors
Jon Adolph
Rani Arbo
Duryan Bhagat
Jodi Butler
Jaqueline Cappuccio
Deanna Cook
Tony Cuen
Ann Hallock
Jessica Hinds
Martha Jenkins
Rich Mintzer
Jody Revenson
David Sokol
Deborah Way

Copy Editors
Diane Hodges
Jenny Langsam
Monica Mayper
Jill Newman

Editorial Assistants
Laura Gomes
Jean Graham

Production
Janet Castiglione
Sue Cole

This book is dedicated to our *FamilyFun* readers, and contributors, and to traveling families everywhere.

WRITERS
Alice Lecesse Powers (Washington, D.C., Delaware, Maryland, Virginia) is the editor of the *Access Guide to Washington* and coauthor of the *D.K. Guide to Washington*. With her husband and three daughters, she has traveled to every quadrant of the U.S., as well as to Canada and many countries in Europe.

Denise Weldon-Siviy (Pennsylvania) is a mother of four who spends much of her time traveling. Between vacations, she teaches English and Computer Applications at the Gettysburg Campus of Harrisburg Area Community College.

Rich Mintzer (New York City, New Jersey), author of 30 nonfiction books, lives with his wife, Carol, and two children in Westchester, New York. Recent Mintzer family travels have included a family resort in Vermont and fun-filled visits to the Jersey Shore.

Elisa Gallaro (Upstate New York) has more than 20 years' writing experience. She enjoys traveling with her husband and two sons.

Illustrations by **Kandy Littrell**

For information address Disney Editions, 114 Fifth Avenue, New York, New York 10011-5690.

Printed in the United States of America

First Edition
1 3 5 7 9 10 8 6 4 2
Library of Congress Cataloging-in-Publication Data on file
ISBN 0-7868-5305-0

Visit www.disneyeditions.com

CONTENTS

Dear Parents,

A FRIEND OF MINE—a dad— said something recently that rang true to me. "A great childhood," he said, thinking aloud, "is really made up of a thousand small good moments." His comment prompted me to step back and take stock of what those moments might be for my own two young sons. What will be their happiest memories? Topping the list in my mind are the simple but extraordinary pleasures we've had traveling together: the hermit crabs we discovered at a Maine beach, the afternoon spent playing catch on the Mall in Washington, the thrill of a first flight, a first train ride, a first hike to a mountaintop.

As parents, we all work incredibly hard to find the time and money to take our children on vacation. We want to show them the remarkably varied American landscape and introduce them to its many cultures and histories. We want to get away from jobs, homework, and household chores long enough to enjoy one another's company uninterrupted. And most of all, we want to have fun.

The editors at *FamilyFun* and I take great pride in this book and others in the series. They are a culmination of ten years' worth of gathering for our readers' the best vacation advice out there. Traveling with children is an art—and our charge is to help with your decisions every step of the way so that you can make the most of every minute of your time away.

Alexandra Kennedy

Alexandra Kennedy
Editorial Director

How to Use This Guide

WELCOME TO THE world of *FamilyFun* magazine's new travel guide series. In our effort to present you with the finest in vacation options, we called on the best experts we know: our hardy group of writers. All are parents who travel with their kids, and all live and work in the area(s) about which they're writing. These are the people who can tell you where to find that teddy bear shop that isn't in the main mall, which restaurant has the best milk shakes, which museum will invite your toddler to roll up his sleeves and create art, and which theme park will give your preteen a good return on the price of admission. With all their recommendations comes the endorsement of their kids: our traveling children have been our best critics.

Since all of the guides in this series cover more than one state, we have divided them into easy-to-use sections. So here's a guide to the guide.

READY, SET, GO!—is a mini-encyclopedia of handy facts, practical advice, what to do/where to go/when to go/how to travel: in other words, all you need to know about planning a successful family vacation.

INTRODUCTION—will give you an overview of the states being covered in this guidebook. Read it—it will whet your appetite, and perhaps give you some new ideas for family activities.

CHAPTERS—States and chapters are presented in geographical order. Chapters represent the regions we think your family will enjoy most. We have omitted those places that we feel would not be family-friendly or are too expensive for what you get in return. We've included general maps to help orient you as you read.

FamilyFun has given each entry a rating—stars (★) that range from one to four—to guide you to our favorites. Remember, however, that this guidebook contains nothing that we do not recommend—it's just that we liked some things better than others. We've also assigned a dollar sign rating ($)—in high season for a family of four, also ranging from one to four. Check the price range at the start of each chapter as the key changes. We hope that this will help you to decide whether a hotel, restaurant, or attraction will fit in with your budget.

Typically, we start each chapter with an introduction, followed by *FamilyFun*'s Must-See List of up to ten things to try to do while visiting. We've divided attractions into two categories: "Cultural Attractions" (museums, historic sites, and so on) and "Just for Fun" (water parks, zoos, aquariums, roller coasters, and the like). Wherever possible, we've included Website information.

What more can we say? We hope that this guide helps you to fashion the best possible vacation for your family, one that is a pleasure in the planning, a delight in the doing, and one that will leave every member of your clan with memories that will last a lifetime—or at least until ninth grade.

Bon Voyage!

Mid-Atlantic

I F YOU ARE PLANNING a family vacation to one or several of the Mid-Atlantic states—Delaware, Maryland, New York, New Jersey, Pennsylvania, Virginia, or Washington, D.C.—these pages contain enough choices to fulfill your kids' fondest dreams—and yours, too.

Your family can spend a long weekend in a large, grand city or a week on one of the country's prettiest shores. If you and your kids like to hike, swim, ski, or boat, you can do all of these—and more; if your group is of a more intellectual bent, you can explore the world and expand your knowledge at a mind-boggling number of museums and historical and cultural sites. The region also boasts numerous zoos and amusement parks, as well as attractions that are simply one of a kind.

New York, you and your kids will discover, is more than towering skyscrapers and overcrowded streets.

In the Washington, D.C., chapter, you'll learn which of the usual tourist attractions are most likely to keep your campers happy.

We'll also give you the inside scoop on Baltimore, home to the

spectacular Harborplace, and Philadelphia, where, in addition to seeing the Liberty Bell, your family can enjoy one of the best kid's museums in the country.

Virginia's Historic Triangle includes Jamestown, the site of the first permanent English settlement in America; Yorktown, where the troops fought the last battle of the Revolution; and Williamsburg, the popular re-created colonial town. The region also has a wealth of historic homes and villages, art and children's museums, and science centers.

If sun, sand, and surf are essential ingredients in your family's vacation recipe, the Mid-Atlantic region has plenty of beaches to comb. New Jersey, Delaware, Maryland, and Virginia have a wide range of seaside settings, from the honky-tonk boardwalks of the Jersey Shore to the serene and pristine stretches of sand at Virginia's Assateague Island.

Natural beauty and outdoor adventures abound inland as well. Upstate New York is home to the thundering waters of Niagara Falls as well as the Adirondacks Region, site of America's largest state park outside Alaska; two of its more popular family vacation destinations are Lake Placid and Lake George. Your family can take a boat tour of Chesapeake Bay, Maryland; paddle a canoe on the Delaware Water Gap; go camping in the Pocono Mountains; or explore the caves and caverns of Pennsylvania. Much of Virginia's Shenandoah Valley is devoted to national parks.

Families who like skiing and other winter sports can head for Upstate New York, Northern New Jersey, and the Poconos of Pennsylvania.

Throughout the region are amusement parks with rides thrilling enough to make the most fearless 10-year-old shriek, and water parks that offer dramatic ways to beat the summer heat. Pennsylvania alone is home to four of the world's top ten coasters—and to Hershey Park, the only amusement park made even more enticing by the overwhelming smell of chocolate in the air.

It's all here. Bring your dreams—and your kids. We'll do the rest.

Let the fun begin!

Pack up and get going.
You're on vacation!

Ready, Set, Go!

JUST TEN YEARS AGO, *FamilyFun* was a fledgling magazine, and the family travel "industry"— now a booming, $100 billion annual trade—was as much a newcomer as we were. In a way, you could say we have grown up together.

FamilyFun was one of the first national magazines to actively research and publicize travel ideas for families with school-age children (a fun job, we must add). Over the last decade, as the numbers of traveling families increased, so did the business of family travel. These days, there are more resources, opportunities, and means for the vacationing family than ever before —which, in turn, gives *FamilyFun* the chance to be an even more valuable clearinghouse of ideas for you.

Through the years, we have been privileged to work with veteran travel writers and editors who have gone around the world with their kids. We've also taken time to listen to our readers—insightful, creative families from across the United States—and to note (and sometimes publish) their stories, recommendations, and tips on traveling as a family. A combination of those two wisdoms is what awaits you on the following pages.

Although it may not be readily apparent, a lot of trial and error underlies these pages. Each destination, before it reaches this book, undergoes a rigorous investigation, and not all make the grade.

We know that family vacations are a big investment, and we know that's why you're here. You're hoping to sidestep the pitfalls of experimentation and to locate destinations that will be a real hit with your family. Congratulations! You've come to the right place.

FIRST STEPS

At the outset, organizing a family vacation can seem as daunting as landing a probe on Mars. Better to stay home and watch the Discovery Channel, you think—maybe toast a few marshmallows in the fireplace.

The truth is that planning an adventurous vacation can be fun, especially if you prepare for it in advance and involve your kids. The onerous part is remembering all the things you have to think about.

That's where we come in. This introductory chapter covers family travel from A to Z, from deciding where to go, to getting there and making the most of your vacation. Some of this may seem like old news to you, but we want to make sure you don't forget a thing.

How much do we spend?

Chances are, you already know approximately what you have to spend on a vacation—and you've already got a modus operandi when it comes to money matters. Maybe you're a family that carefully figures a budget, then finds a vacation to fit it. Or maybe you're the type to set your heart on a once-in-a-lifetime trip, then scrimp and save until you can make it happen.

HAVE MODEM, WILL TRAVEL
For information on how to research and book travel plans on the Web, turn to page 31.

Determine the type of trip you will take. Before you even start your planning, take a moment to consider: what kind of trip are you taking? Are you splurging on a dream vacation, or conserving on a semi-annual getaway? What aspects of this trip are most important to you?

Budget carefully. Once you know what those broad parameters are, the next step is to think through your vacation budget in detail—if not at the outset of planning, then at an opportune point along the way. When you know what you have to spend, you'll make quicker and less stressful decisions en route and you'll be able to pay the bills without a grimace once you get home. You'll find lots of budget-saving tips in this introductory chapter.

When can we go?

Scheduling your vacation well can make a big difference in everyone's experience of the trip.

Consider each individual. Most likely, tight school and work schedules will decide when you travel — but if possible, aim for a time slot that allows everyone to relax. For instance, an action-packed road trip sounds exciting, but it might be just the wrong medicine for a parent who's squeezing it into a packed work schedule. End-of-summer trips may be tough for kids with back-to-school anxieties, and midyear trips that snatch kids from school sometimes cause more trouble than they're worth.

Where do we go?

In this book (and the others in this travel series), you'll find scores of winning family destinations. By all means, though, don't stop here. Doing your own research is half the fun, and these days, you have a wealth of resources at your disposal.

Make a list of destinations. What hot spots intrigue your clan? What adventures would you like to try? Draw up a big list, and don't worry about coming up with too many ideas—you can return to this list year after year. Here are a few trails you can follow: relatives, friends, and coworkers (who love to report on their own successful trips), a professional travel agent, local chambers of commerce and state tourism boards, and magazines, the Internet (see page 34 for some good family travel sites), and local hotels and outfitters in the geographic areas you're interested in.

Evaluate your family. A good vacation has to accommodate *everyone* in the family, no matter what their ages, limitations, or interests. While no destination will make everyone happy all the time, you should search vigilantly for those that offer a niche for each family member.

Involve your kids. The more involved your kids are in planning—especially during these early, brainstorming stages — the more likely they are to work to make the trip a success.

Experiment wisely. While experimentation can add spice to a trip, too much may overwhelm your kids (and you). If your child has her heart set on horseback riding, for example, make sure she tries it out at home before you put down a deposit on a dude ranch vacation.

Check the season. Be informed about travel conditions for the time of your trip and make sure you're not heading for trouble (hurricane season in Florida, for example, or black-fly season in the Adirondacks). This is especially important if you're cashing in on off-season deals.

Local Flavor on the Cheap

Don't wait till you arrive at your destination to investigate opportunities for local fun—research a few in advance:

♦ Check out a regional festival or agricultural fair. For fairs in the western U.S., visit www.fairs net.org and for festivals nationwide, visit www.festivals.com

♦ Explore a college campus (which may offer green space, bike paths, museums, observatories, and more). To find a list, go to a general Internet search engine like www.yahoo.com, click on education, and search for colleges by state. Then, call the school's information office for a map and a roster of special events.

♦ Visit a farmers' market. For a list of markets around the U.S., log on to www.ams.usda.gov/farmersmarkets/

♦ Take in an air show (they're usually free at military bases). For a list of air shows by region, see www.airshows.org

♦ Find a local nature center or Audubon preserve.

Schedule appropriately. How much time do you need to give this particular destination its due? You don't want to feel like you're rushing through things—but neither do you want to run out of activities that will interest your kids.

Should we have an itinerary?

Drawing up a travel itinerary, whether it's rough or detailed, will ensure that you travel wisely, hit the hot spots, and give everyone in your group a say in what you'll see.

Include something for everyone. No doubt, each member of your family will have his or her own list of must-sees. If a unanimous vote on itinerary stops is out of the question, ask everyone to write down top choices, then create a schedule that guarantees each person at least one or two favorites. If your children span a wide age range, remind them that there will be some patient standing by while siblings (and Mom and Dad) have their moments in the sun.

Involve the kids (again). Once you've got the basic stops down, kids can help research destinations, plan driving routes, locate pit stops, and help plan rainy-day alternatives.

Make a plan, then break it. Don't let your preplanned schedule get in the way of spontaneous delights. What if your kids want to ride that water slide for an extra three hours? One fun moment in hand is usually worth at least two on the itinerary.

Beat the crowds. Remember to head for popular attractions first thing in the morning or in late afternoon and early evening. Save the middle of the day for poolside fun or activities that take you off the beaten path and away from crowds.

Travel in tune with your family's natural rhythms. Preschoolers tend to be at their best early in the day—a good time for structured activities. Many teens, on the other hand, are pictures of grogginess before noon. Adapt your itinerary to suit ingrained family habits—including your usual meal and nap times—and you'll have smoother sailing. When visiting very popular destinations, take the time to find out in advance when their slowest periods are.

Train your own tour guides

Guided tours at historic sites and museums are often a snooze (or too sophisticated) for young kids. Instead, create your own tour—have each family member study up on a different attraction by writing or calling for brochures, surfing the Web, and visiting the library. Then, when you arrive, you'll have an expert guide on board.

GETTING THERE

As we all know, the experience of taking kids from point A to point B runs the gamut from uneventful (read: bliss) to miserable. Knowing the ins and outs of your travel options will speed you toward a sane trip.

FamilyFun READER'S TIP

Hire Some Junior Travel Agents

When we were planning a summer trip to Louisiana, I overheard one of my kids tell another that they were going to have to do everything Mom and Dad wanted to do. That's when I decided that each family member would get to plan a full day of our trip. I purchased a regional travel guide and told everyone they had $200 for one day's activities, meals, and accommodations, so they would have to budget (a useful exercise for my 10- and 12-year-olds). Every night, any money left over from that day was given to the next planner. I am proud to say that everything went well, and the kids proclaimed it the best vacation ever!

Cindy Long, Spring, Texas

15

By Plane

PROS: It's fast. And if you land a good deal, air travel can actually be affordable.

CONS: If you don't land a good deal, air travel can be prohibitively expensive, especially for a big family. Other pitfalls include flight delays, mounting claustrophobia on long trips, and strict baggage restrictions.

Look for deals. Traveling in off-peak season and taking off-peak flights (very early or very late in the day) may save you money; flying midweek and staying over Saturday night almost always will. You may also wish to research deals at different airports (for instance, T. F. Green Airport in Providence, Rhode Island, often offers cheaper fares than Boston's Logan Airport 45 minutes away). Also, remember that most sale tickets have a cutoff date—you'll have to book two, three, or four weeks ahead of your departure date to get the deal.

Consider using an agent. Booking your own airline reservations on the Web is a cinch these days (see pages 35 and 36), but there are still advantages to using a professional travel agent who knows your family's needs. First of all, for the $10 or $20 per-ticket surcharge you may pay, you'll save Web-surfing time, and you'll be spared the stress of baby-sitting the fickle airline market. Also,

an agent may be able to suggest a Plan B (such as using a smaller airport to get a better deal)—something the Web search engines can't do for you. Try to get a good agent recommendation through friends, coworkers, or relatives; if you need further help, the American Society of Travel Agents (703-739-2782, www.astanet.com) provides a list of members, as well as brochures on travel topics (including one on how to choose a travel agent).

By Car

PROS: Road trips are the cheapest way to get from here to there, and they can also be real adventures. In addition, the car is familiar territory for your kids, so they'll feel right at home (for better or worse) during the trip. And, of course, a road trip affords you priceless flexibility.

CONS: You're in for major advance planning, from making sure your car is in good condition to scheduling regular rest stops and having a dependable cache of road snacks, games, and other diversions. Even with those, the hours of close confinement may quickly erode your family's wanderlust.

Get a good map. If you belong to AAA, request a free "TripTik" map. Otherwise, you can map your route and download printed driving directions on Websites like www.map quest.com, www.freetrip.com, and www.mapsonus.com

WHEN YOU BOOK

- Try first for a nonstop flight. If that's not available, fly "direct," which means you'll stop at least once but won't switch planes.
- Book flights that depart early in the day, if possible. If your flight is delayed, you—and the airline—will have time to make other arrangements.
- Specify your ticketing preferences, whether paper or electronic.
- Check to see if a meal will be served in flight. If so, order meals your kids like. Many airlines offer kids' meals or a vegetarian choice that may be pasta. If not, plan accordingly.
- Ask for the seats you'd like, whether they're a window, an aisle, or the bulkhead for legroom.

PACKING TIPS

- Stuff your carry-on for every contingency. Pack all medications, extra clothes for little kids, diapers, baby food, formula, wet wipes, and snacks (they'll also help kids swallow to relieve ear pressure).
- Have each child carry a small backpack with travel toys, a light sweatshirt, and a pair of socks for the flight.

ON THE DAY OF YOUR TRIP

- Call ahead to check for delays.
- Have all photo IDs within easy reach (not necessary for kids under age 18 traveling with their parents on domestic flights; on most international flights, even infants will need a passport).

- If you have heavy bags, check your luggage first and then park.
- If you are early for the flight or run into long delays, don't go straight to the gate. Instead, meander through the airport's diversions: windows onto the runways, children's play areas (many major airports now have these), Web access computers, and, of course, stores where kids can find a treat to tide them over.
- Carry on extra bottled water. It's easy to get dehydrated on a plane, and the drink service may be slow in reaching you.

ON THE PLANE

- Ask if your child can view the cockpit (the best time may be after the flight is over).
- Secure pillows and blankets for family members who may want to nap.
- Take breaks from sitting; occasionally walk the aisles and switch seats.

FLYING FEARS

Most children are fearless fliers—and those who are afraid often can trace their concerns to adults who unintentionally transmit their own fears. If you need help answering your children's questions, you can ask them on-line at www.wic-kid.com

FamilyFun TIP

Bookworms

When you're on the road, there's nothing like a good story to pass the time. For night drives, audio books can be a lifesaver. Try borrowing or renting one from your local library, or visit www.storytapes.com, the Website for Village StoryTapes (800-238-8273). You can either rent or purchase from their excellent selection; three- to four-week tape rentals cost $6 to $17 (for *Harry Potter IV*); to buy, tapes cost $12 to $60.

Be prepared for emergencies, large and small. It goes without saying that your car should be in prime working order before you depart. You should have supplies for road emergencies on board, as well as a good first-aid kit (see page 33 for a list of what to include), and, if you have one, bring a cell phone.

Keep things orderly. We all know what happens to our cars within minutes of the time the kids buckle in; on long road trips, expect the chaos to rise by a factor of ten. In an effort to keep things in check, bring containers to hold trash and toys; pack the children's luggage so it's easiest to reach; divvy up the back-seat space so kids know where their boundaries are; and go over basic behavior rules before you leave.

Drive in time with your family's rhythm. Night driving offers less traffic and a chance that young kids will sleep (you can let them ride in their pj's). Alternatively, an early start may avoid late-afternoon, kid-cranky hours. When possible, go with your family's natural flow.

Help prevent motion sickness. Have frequent, small meals during your trip (symptoms are more likely to occur on an empty stomach). Over-the-counter medications such as Dramamine, as well as ginger ale, ginger tea, or ginger candy also can help, but once symptoms begin, it's usually too late for oral medications. Make sure the car is well ventilated, and have sickness-prone travelers take a window seat, which offers

WEATHER WATCHERS Before you leave, assign forecaster duties to one of your kids. Using the Internet, he or she can research and predict the type of weather you'll encounter (and advise everyone on what to pack). Try www.weather.com

fresh air and a view of the road. If a child feels nauseated, have him look straight in front of the car or focus attention on the horizon. If your child becomes carsick, stop the car to give him a break from the motion; having him lie down with his head perfectly still also may help.

By Train

PROS: First of all, trains are just plain cool, for kids and adults alike. Second, there's room to explore, and everyone can kick back and enjoy the view. And third, if you are headed to a major metropolitan area with a good public transit system, you'll avoid the expenses and hassles of city driving and parking.

CONS: There's only one national passenger rail service, Amtrak, and at press time its future was in question. Also, Amtrak's limited network may not be convenient to your destination (ask about connector trains and rental car agencies when you call). In some regions of the United States, Amtrak's city-to-city service rivals car, bus, and plane travel for efficiency; on cross-country hauls, this is not the case. If you're investing in a long train trip, you're in it more for the experience of train travel.

Inquire about special deals. Children ages 2 to 15 usually ride for half fare when accompanied by an adult who pays full fare. Each adult can bring two children at this discounted rate. Amtrak also offers

A Road Trip Survival Kit

A BAG OF TRICKS
- mini-puzzles with a backboard
- video games, cassette or CD player (with headphones)
- paper, pens, pencils, markers
- travel versions of board games
- stuffed animals
- Etch A Sketch
- colored pipe cleaners
- deck of cards
- cookie sheet (a good lap tray)
- word puzzles
- small action figures or dolls
- stickers
- Trivial Pursuit cards
- cotton string (for cat's cradle games)

A COOLER OF SNACKS
Bring lots of drinks and a cache of snacks like granola bars, trail mix, grapes, carrot sticks, roll-up sandwiches, fruit leather, and popcorn.

Keeping 'Em Busy: 60-Second Solutions

SQUABBLE SOLUTIONS

Give your kids 25 cents in pennies at the start of the trip. Each time they fight or whine, charge them a penny. Offer a reward, such as doubling or tripling their money, if they haven't lost a cent during the ride.

WAGER AND WIN

Kids are natural wagerers—they love to bet how much, how long, how far, how many. If you're in a bind for a moment's entertainment, ask them to guess the number of French fries on your plate or to estimate how many steps it will take to walk to your airport gate. The key here is to be able to verify the guesses—you'll need to wear a watch with a second hand and carry a calculator.

CREATIVE COMPETITION

Kids love challenges. Need to get rid of the trash in the car? See who can smash the trash into the smallest paper ball, then toss it in the wastepaper bag. Want quiet time? Hold a five-minute silence contest. Need to get through errands in a hurry? Challenge your kids to a race against time. You may feel that your motives are transparent, but your kids won't care.

special seasonal rates, other family deals, and Web-only deals.

How to find them. Amtrak's Website, www.amtrak.com, provides information on fares, schedules, reservations, routes and services, station locations, and special offers. You can also call Amtrak at 800-872-7245 for information and reservations. When you book, ask if there is a full-service dining car and ask whether you can reserve a block of seats for your family.

Consider a sleeper car. For overnight trips, sleep-in-your-seat fares are the cheapest, but first-class bedrooms are much more comfortable.

Arrive early. If your train seats are unassigned, get to the station early for the best chance of eveyone's sitting together. You can even have one parent run ahead to grab a group of seats while the other shepherds children and luggage to the platform.

By RV

PROS: It's a home away from home, which means you can eat, sleep, and use the indoor plumbing (as everyone will agree, one of the finest features of RV travel) whenever you want. In an RV, you are free to explore with independence, self-sufficiency, and freedom—three assets that can be priceless when you're traveling with kids.

CONS: It's a home away from home,

Patchwork Pillows

I am 10 years old, and every year my family goes camping. I collect patches from each place we visit, including the Grand Canyon, Yellowstone and Yosemite National Parks; San Francisco; Las Vegas; and, most recently, Santa Fe, New Mexico. I put all the patches I've collected during each year on separate pillows. I keep the pillows on my bed to remind me of our great trips.

Alex Smythe, Tucson, Arizona

which means you face dishes, cooking, and maintenance (generators, water pumps, waste tanks, and the engine, for starters). In addition, RV rentals are not cheap, although they can compare favorably to the cost of a week's lodging, food, and travel (especially for big families).

What they cost. Expect to pay rental fees between $500 and $1,500 per week, depending on location, model, and time of year you'll be traveling, and the luxury factor (RVs can get pretty posh). Gasoline costs will be high, but you'll save considerably on food and accommodations (campground fees average $20 to $40 per night).

How to find them. Rental information is available through auto clubs and through Go RVing (888-GO-RVING, ask for the free video and literature; www.gorving.com). Cruise America (800- 327-7799) offers 150 rental centers across the United States and Canada. The RV America Website (www.rvamerica.

com) has listings of dealers, clubs, and resources.

Be a savvy renter. Choose an RV that's big enough for your family, but know that many campgrounds only permit vehicles less than 30 feet long. Before you rent, ask how many people fit comfortably in the RV, what powers the appliances, how much insurance is required, and whether supplies such as linens and kitchen utensils are included in the rental price. Get a demonstration of how to work everything in the vehicle, read the manual, practice a little ahead of time, and you'll be ready to take the plunge.

By Bus

PROS: The major advantages of bus travel are that it's cheap, that it spares you the stress of driving, and that tickets usually can be purchased on the day of your trip, at the station. **CONS:** Unfortunately, traveling by bus often takes longer than by car. What's more, bus travel offers little opportunity for diversion for your

21

Thinking of Skipping School?

children. And since you're sitting close to other passengers, many lively family games are off-limits (some buses offer a TV movie; ask when you call).

How to find them: Greyhound Lines (800-229-9424) offers service across the United States. In the Northeast, between New Hampshire and Washington, D.C., Peter Pan Bus Lines (800-237-8747) is another option. Both have Websites, www.greyhound.com and www.peterpanbus.com, complete with fare and schedule information. To locate smaller local or regional bus lines, try the local Yellow Pages or the department of travel and tourism in the region you'll be visiting.

By Rental Car

PROS: This isn't exactly a pro, but if you've flown or trained into an area without a safe and dependable public transport system, you'll need a rental to get around. Plus, a rental car is cost-efficient for families (as opposed to solo travelers). Best of all, you won't be putting miles on your own car—and if you rent a minivan, you can have drink-cup slots and elbowroom for every single kid.

CONS: None, really, save the expense and a list of rental and insurance decisions that can be as daunting as a Starbucks menu.

How to find them: Your travel agent can book a car for you, but if you want to do it yourself, you'll find all the major agencies in the 800 directory.

Compare costs. Whether you shop on-line or over the phone, compare costs for as many companies as you can (no one company has the best deals in every city or state). In general, weeklong and weekend rentals are a better deal than per-day rentals. In your research, you may wish to inquire about companies' service records, especially if you're going with a local budget chain.

Ask about discounts. Membership in AAA or other associations, credit cards, entertainment book coupons, and package-deal reservations may net you bargains: ask about potential discounts when you make your reservation.

Ask about services and charges. Rental car companies put a lot of information in fine print. So, before you pay (and before you drive away), ask lots of questions. What are the mileage and one-way drop fees? Is there a fee for early or late car returns? Should you bring the car back with an empty gas tank or a full one to get the best refueling price? Does the company offer 24-hour breakdown service? Do the cars have air-conditioning, a jack, and a spare tire? Is there a fee for extra drivers (married couples are often exempt,

FamilyFun TIP

Compare Quotes

When you book a room at a major hotel chain, call both the hotel's local number as well as the toll-free reservation number; the rates you'll be quoted may differ.

but you should check). Are car seats available at no extra charge? (Even if the answer is yes, your own car seat may be cleaner, and, because it's familiar, more comfortable for your child.)

Pay only for the insurance you need. The car, and any damage to it, will be your responsibility for the duration of your trip. Before you purchase insurance from the rental agency, check to see whether your own auto or liability insurance provides adequate coverage. Some credit card agreements may also include rental protection; call the customer service

FamilyFun READER'S TIP

Tabletop Scrapbook

Here's a fun project my family has long enjoyed while traveling. After we have mapped out our vacation, my kids, and now grandchildren, use a laundry pen to draw our route on a cotton tablecloth. We pack up the cloth along with colored markers, and while on the road, family members take turns marking the name of towns and rivers and noting funny signs. When we stop for picnic lunches, we not only use the cloth but also continue adding drawings of sights we've seen and things we've done. After the trip is over, we have a memory-filled tablecloth to use for years to come.

Janet Askew, Adair, Iowa

number on the back of your card to inquire.

WHERE TO STAY

Where you tuck your kids in at night depends entirely on your family's traveling style and budget—and, of course, on what's available in the area to which you're traveling. There are so many options—hotels, motels, inns, cottages, cabins, condominiums, resorts, time-shares, campgrounds—it can be hard to know where to start.

Lists of local accommodations can be found through tourism boards, the Web, travel books, and the 800 numbers or published directories of major franchises. However, finding the places that really go the extra mile for families isn't easy. This book—and other family travel publications—will be your best bets, as will the time-tested recommendations of friends and acquaintances. Always, always ask your own questions as well: see our checklist on page 25 for some basics.

Hotels, Motels & Lodges

From generic chains, to mom-and-pop operations bursting with character, to ritzy palaces, this category really runs the gamut. If you don't have a dependable recommendation (from a friend, trusted travel agent, or guidebook like this one), you may wish to place your trust in the major chains (budget or no) where you at least know what you're getting.

How to find them: Most major chains can be found in the 800 directory (as well as on the Web) and can provide a list of property locations. Alternatively, you can contact regional travel bureaus or consult a national rating system, such as those in Mobil Travel Guides (available in bookstores or the on-line store at www.mobil.com) or the Automobile Association of America (call your local AAA office to order regional TourBook guides).

PICKY EATERS? If you have picky eaters in the family (or if you suspect a child may not enjoy the food at a certain restaurant), feed them ahead of time—and let them enjoy an appetizer or dessert during your meal.

Inns, B&Bs, and Farm Stays

These have traditionally been the domain of honeymooning couples and retirees. Increasingly, though, they are accommodating a growing family travel market. There are certainly gems out there for your discovery—but do your research rigorously (speak with the owner, if possible) to find out whether kids are *truly* welcome at the destination of your choice. The last thing you want to be doing on vacation is shushing your kids and shooing them away from pricey antiques. Look for inns and B&Bs attached to a working farm—these tend to be more kid-friendly, with animals to watch and feed and plenty of outdoor play space.

How to find them: Try travel magazines, regional chambers of commerce, and two excellent Websites, www.bedandbreakfeast.com and www.bbgetaways.com

Condos and Cottages

These are ideal if your group is staying put for the length of your vacation, since they offer room to spread out and cook your own meals. When you book, ask about amenities: does the condo come with linens, pots and pans, a television, phone, dishwasher, and washer/dryer? Are there extra tax and/or booking fees? If you rent directly from the owner, be even more rigorous in your questioning. Is there

WHAT TO ASK BEFORE YOU BOOK

1 ACCOMMODATIONS: What rooms (or condos or cabins) are available? How many beds are there and what size are they? Are the rooms nonsmoking? What amenities are included (laundry, phone, cable TV, refrigerator, balcony, coffee service, cots, cribs, minibar)? Are the rooms located in the main building? What specific views are available? Is there a charge for kids staying in the same room with parents? Are there family packages? Can guests upgrade rooms upon arrival?

2 DINING: Are there dining facilities on the property? If so, are there restrictions for kids? What are some menu items, and what does the average meal cost? Is there a kids' menu? Is there a complimentary breakfast offered? Are there snack and/or drink machines? If there are no dining facilities on-site, is there a family restaurant nearby?

3 RECREATION: What recreational facilities are available (game rooms, pool, tennis courts, equipment rental, and so on)? At what hours are they available? Are there additional charges for their use? Are there age or time restrictions for any recreation? What recreational options are available in the nearby community (movie theater, minigolf, bowling, and the like)?

a cancellation policy if the place is not up to your standards?

How to find them: The Internet has made it easy to connect potential renters with homeowners and rental brokers. Unfortunately, that means there are literally thousands of sites to sift through. Luckily, most sites offer very detailed information on properties, so you can actually make an informed decision on-line to pursue a place.

For starters, here are the Website addresses for a number of national and international vacation rental clearinghouses: www.eLeisure Link.com (888-801-8808); Barclay

International Group (800-845-6636; www.bar clayweb.com); and 10,000 Vacation Rentals, Inc. (888-369-7245; www. 10kvacationrentals.com).

To rent directly from a property owner, try Vacation Rentals by Owner at www.vrbo.com . You also can locate condos and cottages by inquiring at local tourism bureaus, local realtors (especially for seaside properties), and major resorts, which often keep lists of rentals on property or nearby.

Campgrounds

These range from the extremely rustic—grassy knolls with fabulous views to the luxurious—complexes with video games, sports areas, and fax and modem hookups.

Depending on where and how you prefer to camp, you'll have your pick of sites in state or national parks, national forests, or private campgrounds. (See "Happy Campers," page 38-39.)

When you book a site, inquire: What are the nightly fees? Does the campground accept reservations? If no, how early should you arrive in order to claim a site? Is there a pool or lake? Lifeguards? Equipment rentals? Laundry facilities, rest rooms, and hot showers? A grocery store nearby? Remember that campgrounds near major tourist attractions fill up early, so make reservations in advance (choice spots in some national parks, for example, fill up months ahead).

Family Hostels

A CHEAP SLEEP

If you think hostels are the exclusive domain of students and backpackers, think again: many of the neatest have private family rooms that can be reserved in advance. Some also offer special programs, such as historic walking tours, natural history programs, and sports activities. Hostels in the Hostelling International/ American Youth Hostels system are as varied as their locations and include registered historic buildings, lighthouses, and a former dude ranch. For the latest edition of *Hostelling Experience North America*, call *202-783-6161* or visit www.hiayh.org

How to find them: In addition to the campgrounds recommended in this book, you can find lists of campgrounds on the Internet: check out About.com's camping section at www.camping.about.com, www.camping-usa.com, and the National Association of RV Parks & Campgrounds at www.gocamping america .com. For campgrounds in national parks, visit www.nps.gov and state For a national directory of KOA campgrounds, visit www.koa kamp grounds.com

Resorts

A resort vacation is a big investment, and up-front research is essential to ensure you get your money's worth. When you are making inquiries, don't be shy about taking up the resort staff's time with questions. Be sure to grill them with the entire housing quiz on page 25. Ask, too, about programming for kids and families. If there is a children's pro-

FamilyFun TIP

Walk it through

When you're booking a room or condo over the phone, ask the reservation specialist to "walk" you through the place, virtually, from the front door to the balcony view (if there is one!). They may think you're going overboard — but you'll really know what you're getting.

gram, what days and times does it run? Is it canceled if not enough kids sign up? What is the ratio of counselors to children? What are the age divisions? What activities does the program offer? What are the facilities? What, if any, is the additional cost? Are there games, programs, or organized recreation especially for families? Baby-sitting services? Assistance for kids who get sick? What are the terms for these? If the resort is "all-inclusive," find out

---

FamilyFun **READER'S TIP**

Invent a Travel Kit

When our family flies, I make travel kits for my two sons, Noah, 8, and Paul, 4. I fill old wipes boxes with a variety of treats: chocolate kisses, fruit snacks, a sealed envelope with a love note inside, stickers, and a small wrapped package such as a pencil sharpener, pencils, and a blank book (I staple together scratch paper). I write the boys' names on the front with a permanent marker, and then, in flight, they decorate the boxes with stickers. The trick is not to give them the travel kits until we're on the plane. After they exhaust their supply of goodies inside, they can refill it with things they collect during the trip.

Kathy Detzer, White River Junction, Vermont

Travel Insurance

It's not for everyone, but some travelers like to invest in this just-in-case insurance. Cancellation policies cover losses if you can't make your trip due to illness or a death in the family (you may wish to consider this if you have to put down a hefty deposit or prepay for your vacation in full). Medical policies provide for some emergency procedures. You can buy travel insurance from a specialty broker (see below), from your travel agent, or directly from an insurance company. Do not buy insurance from the tour operator or cruise line you will be traveling with.

Travel Guard International
(800-826-1300; www.travel-guard.com)

CSA Travel Protection
(www.csatravelprotection.com)

Travel Assistance International (800-821-2828; www.travelassistance.com)

Access America (866-807-3982; www.accessamerica.com)

exactly what is covered. If you will be taking advantage of the services included in the price, it may mean a good deal for your family; if not, you might be better off elsewhere.

How to find them: Travel magazines, travel agents, and family travel Websites (see page 34) will all be able to offer recommendations on family resorts. Also, the Globe Pequot Press (www.globepequot. com) has two good resource books: *100 Best Family Resorts in North America* and *100 Best All-Inclusive Resorts of the World.*

SAVING MONEY

A great vacation balances moments of extravagance with activities that are as enjoyable as they are affordable. The key, then, is to find painless ways to cut costs so that you can feel good about indulging. Here's a host of secrets from budget-savvy travelers.

Stock up at home. Specialty items, such as sunscreen, film, batteries, over-the-counter medications, and first-aid supplies can be outrageously expensive in vacation spots. Buy them in bulk at home and bring them with you.

Travel off-peak. Whether it's a ski resort town in the summertime, or Yosemite National Park in the spring, or the Adirondacks in the winter, off-peak travel is one of the best ways to save, as long as you're primed to enjoy the unique flavor of an off-season trip. Rates for travel and lodging are often slashed considerably—and you can enjoy a different perspective (and fewer crowds) at the destination of your choice.

Don't delay. The sooner you begin planning and booking your vacation (six months to a year or more in advance is not too early), the more deals will be available to you.

Shop around. This is the cardinal rule of vacation planning. Take time to compare prices for every service that you'll be buying, from airfares, hotels, and rental cars to tickets for attractions.

Ask for discounts. Don't be shy about asking for discounts. Call ahead to the attractions that you plan to visit and ask where one finds discount coupons. When making

Guided Tours

WHEN DO YOU NEED ONE?

For certain types of specialty travel (technically-challenging outdoor adventures for example), an expert guide is a necessary aid for a safe and enjoyable trip. In addition, using a local guide for day trips (say, fishing or snowmobiling) can be a wonderful way to connect with local lore and culture in the region you're visiting. In general, however, guided tours (especially group tours that include full itineraries and meals) tend to be pricey, tightly scheduled, and lacking the freedom most families value highly.

----

hotel reservations, ask if discounts are available—if not on the room alone, then on a package that may include the room and tickets to a nearby attraction. Coupons are also available on-line: a good place to start is the coupon link at www.about.com

STRAP A SHOE BAG to the back of the front seat and stuff it with your small kid-entertainment supplies: crayons and coloring books; kids' magazines; craft supplies, such as pipe cleaners, markers, glue sticks, and construction paper; songbooks; paper doll kits; a deck of cards; and a cassette player with story tapes. And don't forget a Frisbee, jump rope, and chalk (to draw hopscotch grids) for rest stops.

Make Your Own Postcards

While traveling by car or plane, my kids entertain themselves by creating their own postcards. Before the trip, I buy blank, prestamped postcards from the post office. Once we are under way, the kids draw pictures on the cards — usually of things they have done on vacation or are looking forward to doing. We address the cards to relatives and friends and drop them in the mail, making sure we send a few home for our own travel journal. This activity has been so successful, we now give friends travel kits of the prestamped cards and crayons as a bon voyage gift.

Lynette Smith, Lake Mills, Wisconsin

Look at package deals. At first blush, packages can seem outrageously expensive. But before you pass them up, compare them carefully to what you'd pay if you bought all the pieces of your vacation separately. Rates for airfare, lodging, and car rentals can be substantially lower when purchased together, especially for popular destinations. Contact your travel agent for information or research deals from travel clubs like AAA (call your local chapter or visit www.aaa.com), American Express Travel Services (800-346-3607; www.americanexpress.com), and from tour agencies affiliated with major airlines.

Use member benefits. Membership in an auto club, professional organization, or Entertainment book club may score you discounts on travel bills—ask before you book. Your credit card company, as well, may offer free services, such as collision-damage and travel-accident insurance, if you use the card to pay for travel expenses (call to request a copy of the company's travel benefits policy). If you travel regularly, the savings you'd garner from Web-saver clubs like www.bestfares.com can be well worth the $50 to $70 annual fee.

Tickets to attractions. Buying tickets to attractions in advance through an association or organization or at the hotel desk often will save you money. Equally important, you'll avoid the ticket line itself. On-line, try www.citypass.com for discount tickets in major metropolitan areas.

Keep your distance. Unless on-site housing offers necessary convenience for your family, consider lodging that's outside the major tourist area or city you're visiting. An extra 15 minutes of travel can considerably reduce lodging expenses, especially if you're staying more than a few days.

Check out kids' deals. Look for hotel deals where kids eat and/or stay free with their parents.

Consider cooking. Dining out is certainly part of the vacation experience, but three meals per person, per day add up quickly. Cooking your own meals can save you lots of money, even if you factor in the expense of a room with a kitchenette. In a regular hotel room, you can probably manage breakfast and/or lunch with a well-stocked cooler.

Pack your own minibar. Those high-priced hotel mini-bars are magnets for kids. Make a list of your kids' favorite treats, then purchase them in bulk as individually wrapped items. Pack a selection in a separate box or bag that can double as the designated minibar once you arrive at the hotel.

Let's do lunch. If you have a yen to try a particular fancy restaurant, head there during lunch. The atmosphere will be the same, and the menu will be similar, but smaller lunchtime portions will be accompanied by lower prices.

Revel in free fun. Remember the birthday when your child spent more time playing with the wrapping paper than with the actual toy? Vacations are filled with similar, low-cost but memorable moments, including hours at the beach, hiking trails,

parks, and playgrounds. If you're in a new area, scan the local paper for listings, or call a local travel bureau or chamber of commerce for ideas.

Be savvy about souvenirs. Decide ahead of time how much you're willing to spend on souvenirs. Depending on the age of your kids, give each child his or her own spending money (they'll be stingier with their own funds than they are with yours). As an added incentive, let them keep a portion of any money they don't spend.

Using the Web

With the advent of the World Wide Web, individuals now have access to all the tools that travel agents use (and then some). The trick is to know how to use them well.

PROS: Researching travel ideas on the Web may draw in your kids more readily than a guidebook would.

Packing With—And For—Kids

Like so much of your family vacation, packing is a balancing act—in this case between including everything you need and making sure you can actually lift your bags. No matter where you're headed, this checklist should cover most of the essentials.

Give the kids a role. Every child has favorite outfits as well as clothing that he or she won't wear (and that you shouldn't bother packing). Young children can select the clothes they'd like to bring and set them aside for you. Older kids can do much of their own packing, especially if you help them write up a checklist of their own.

Don't worry about wrinkles. Like aging, this happens even with the best of precautions. Suggest some folding methods, but don't insist on your kids' finessing this. One surprisingly effective technique for kids is simply to roll everything up.

Make each child responsible for his or her own luggage. A backpack and a soft-sided suitcase for each child will do the trick. Let your kids decorate their bags with stencils and stickers — and remember to attach a name tag.

Separate toiletries in sealed, waterproof bags. Lids on toiletries often pop off or open during travel.

Take precautions in case of lost luggage. If you're flying to your vacation destination, pack at least one complete outfit for each family member in each suitcase. That way, if a piece of luggage is lost, everyone still has a change of clothes. Also, pack medications, eyeglasses, and contact lens solution in carry-ons.

Clothing

Include an outfit for each day of the week, plus extra shirts or blouses in case of spills. If your children are younger, encourage them to choose brightly colored outfits that will make them easier to spot in the crowd.

- Comfortable shoes or sneakers
- Socks and undergarments
- Sleepwear
- Light jackets, sweaters, or sweatshirts for cool weather
- Bathing suits
- Sandals or slip-on shoes for the pool
- Hats or sun visors
- Rain gear, including umbrellas

Toiletries

- Toothbrushes, toothpaste, dental floss, and mouthwash
- Deodorant
- Combs, brushes, hair accessories, blow-dryer
- Soap
- Shampoo and conditioner
- Shaving gear
- Feminine-hygiene items

- Lotions
- Cosmetics
- Nail care kit
- Tweezers
- Cotton balls and/or swabs
- Antibacterial gel for hand washing
- Sunscreens and lip balm
- Insect repellent

Miscellaneous "must-haves"
- Essential papers: identification for adults, health insurance cards, tickets, traveler's checks
- Wallet and/or purse, including cash and credit cards
- Car and house keys (with duplicate set packed in a different bag)
- Eyeglasses and/or contact lenses, plus lens cleaner
- Medications
- Watch
- Camera and film (pack film in your carry-on bag)
- Tote bag or book bag for day use
- Books and magazines for kids and adults
- Toys, playing cards, small games
- Flashlight
- Extra batteries
- Large plastic bags for laundry
- Small plastic bags
- Disposable wipes
- First-aid kit
- Travel alarm
- Sewing kit

Keep Your First-Aid Kit Handy

There's no such thing as a vacation from minor injuries and ailments, so a well-stocked first-aid kit is essential to have on hand. You can buy a pre-packaged kit or make your own by packing the following items in an old lunch box:

- Adhesive bandages in various sizes, adhesive tape, and gauze pads
- Antacid
- Antibacterial gel for washing hands without water
- Antibacterial ointment
- Antidiarrheal medicine
- Antihistamine or allergy medicine
- Antiseptic
- Antiseptic soap
- Pain relief medicine—for children and adults
- Cotton balls and/or swabs
- Cough medicine and/or throat lozenges
- Motion sickness medicine
- Fingernail clippers
- First-aid book or manual
- Ipecac
- Moleskin for blisters
- Ointment for insect bites and sunburn
- Premoistened towelettes
- Thermometer
- Tissues
- Tweezers and needle

FamilyFun TIP

The Internet Travel Bible

If you're serious about researching (and especially booking) travel plans yourself, consult *Online Travel* by Ed Perkins (Microsoft Press, $19.95). This paperback tome is an invaluable resource on getting the best deals available and navigating the benefits and pitfalls of today's travel market, both on- and off-line.

Plus, when it comes time to book reservations, the Web can be a treasure trove of bargains—if you know how to hunt for them (see "The Internet Travel Bible" above). Why is that so? In essence, the Internet allows travel service providers to change their bargain pricing structures and unload unsold seats and rooms at a moment's notice. Of course, agents are still out to make as much money as they can—but you often can reap the benefits of their last-minute sales. In fact, many of these sales are available only on-line.

CONS: Keeping tabs on the travel market on-line can be extremely time-consuming if you are determined to find the best deal possible. In addition, since Web search engines can't read your mind and ask you questions, they can't ferret out all your options—just the ones that fall within the parameters you specify. So if you aren't a savvy searcher, you might miss the best deals (or the best destinations) even after hours of research.

Family travel Websites. It's a challenge to locate truly family-friendly sites among the hundreds available. For researching travel ideas and gathering travel tips, here are some of the best sites. Try our own website too—www.familyfun.com—it too has a lot of travel ideas.

♦ www.vacationtogether.com is a searchable database of family vacation ideas, reprinted from various publications (including *FamilyFun* magazine). You'll also find packing checklists and links to reservation sites here.

♦ www.travelwithkids.about.com is a terrific clearinghouse for family vacation ideas, package deals, current bargains, lists of accommodations, packing checklists, travel tips and games, downloadable maps, and more.

♦ www.thefamilytravelfiles.com is a well-organized family travel Website that showcases a range of trip ideas and offers a free travel e-zine.

♦ www.familytravelforum.com is a monthly on-line newsletter specializing in well-screened links to family-friendly accommodations, airfare deals, seasonal events, and more.

General travel sites. In addition to family-specific sites such as the ones listed above, there are literally thousands of useful Websites that can help you plan and book your vacation. They are too numerous to list here! We have included many of our favorites throughout this chapter; in addition to those, here are a few you may find useful.

♦ www.officialtravelinfo.com lists contacts for travel and tourism bureaus worldwide (you can search the United States by state).

♦ www.fodors.com, www.frommers. com, and www.nationalgeographic. com are sites related to travel magazines. Often, they'll post selections from current issues, as well as other travel-related articles.

♦ www.travel-library.com (a wide range of travel topics, travelogues, and destination information) and www. about.com (a general site with good travel links) are sites that can lead you to travel information that you may (or may not!) be looking for.

Book your own airline reservations. Using the same databases as travel agents use, the leading travel sites have made booking your own flight as simple as typing in when you'd like to leave, when you'd like to return, your origin and destination, and airline choice. They kick back a list of flights that most closely match

Broker a Hotel Deal

Great deals at major hotels usually turn up off-season or at the last minute, but here's another tactic families can try: work with a hotel consolidator (also called a hotel broker or discounter).

Consolidators work by securing blocks of hotel rooms at wholesale prices, then reselling them at rates that are—in theory, at least—lower than the published "rack" rate. Some consolidators will only reserve your room; you pay the hotel directly. Others require a prepaid voucher that you present to the hotel upon arrival. Many consolidators claim savings of 10 to 50 percent (some even more), but as with any bargain, it pays to know what you're getting into.

SOME TIPS:
- Ask about service charges. Is there a user fee for the consolidator?
- Are there financial penalties for trip cancellation or rescheduling?
- Compare rates. The consolidator may not beat a hotel's special offers.

With those caveats, try:
Quikbook: Good selection and easy to use, with hotels in 33 cities. Call 800-789-9887 or see www.quikbook.com
Central Reservation Service: Lists hotel deals in ten major cities. Call 800-555-7555 or visit www.roomconnec tion.com

Gumshoe Games

your specifications and then let you choose the flights you want. After confirming your choices, you pay with a credit card, print your itinerary, and either receive your paper tickets in the mail or, more likely, pick up your tickets when you check in at the airport. **NOTE:** Some people prefer paper tickets because if a flight is missed or cancelled an e-ticket may not be exchangeable at a different airline's counter.

Our favorite flight sites are Expedia (www.expedia.com), Travelocity (www.travelocity.com), and Trip. com (www.trip.com). Don't assume that all offer the same flights or the same prices; the important thing is to shop around, even among these sites.

Before you pay for your tickets, you should double-check with two other sources. First, look at your chosen airline's home site to see if they offer extra miles for booking flights on-line, or special, unadvertised Web deals. And call your travel agent, tell her the flight you're interested in, and see if she can beat the price. Lastly, be sure you're aware of the taxes, airport surcharges, and possible site use fees that may be added to your ticket price.

For more information about airlines, airports, and online reservations, go to www.iecc.com/airline/. Also, check out Ed Perkins' *Online Travel* (Microsoft Press, $19.95). To find out more about frequent flier mile programs, visit www.frequent flier.com

Book hotel and rental car reservations. In general, hotel and rental car reservations work the same way that airfare reservations do. The Web is an excellent source of hotel deals (especially for vacation packages, if you're a savvy shopper); rental car companies, on the other hand, generally offer little in the way of discounts above what you can get at the desk.

FREE ATLAS
Best Western offers free road atlases with Best Western sites: call 800-528-1234.

Sign up for e-mail newsletters. If you find a good travel Website that offers a free newsletter, it doesn't hurt to sign up—you may receive timely notice of travel deals that you otherwise would miss. Just be sure that you save any information on how to cancel the subscription in case you want to opt out.

Are Internet travel arrangements foolproof? No, unfortunately. The Internet is prime territory for scams,

although you can guard against most of them with a few protective strategies. First, deal with major sites (like the ones listed in this book) or directly with brand-name company sites (like Avis or Holiday Inn) whenever possible. When you're transmitting your credit card information, make sure your connection is secure (your browser should tell you when one has been established). Also, you should double-check to see that the service provider's Website has a secure server. (Look for a locked padlock in the corner of your browser's window or "https"—the "s" stands for "secure"—in the URL.) If a site doesn't seem completely aboveboard, it may not be. Finally, when in doubt, back out. As long as you don't give a company your credit card number, they can't charge you anything.

FamilyFun **READER'S TIP**

A Colorful Road Game

This homemade road game is a big hit with my 4-year-old son, Tommy. I clip cards out of colored construction paper and print a different letter of the alphabet on each. During a car ride, each of us picks a card and searches for an object or a structure that matches the color and begins with the letter on our card. For example, a player with a *B* on a yellow card might spot a school bus. Since we began playing this game, my son tends to remember many more details about our travels. Instead of hearing, "Are we there yet?" we hear, "Oh no, I haven't found mine yet!"

Susan Robins, Cottage Grove, Oregon

If your family's idea of a vacation involves nightly campfires, sleeping bags, and potential wildlife sightings near (or in!) your living space, check out these great resources for tent and RV camping.

The Trailer Life Directory provides travelers with a list of several thousand campgrounds and RV parks throughout the United States and Canada. Each location is rated on a three-step scale that assesses the park's facilities, cleanliness, and overall appeal; ratings are updated on an annual basis. You can register at www.tl directory.com to search the directory for free or order your own copy for the road on-line or at bookstores.

Woodall's campground directories also rate a large number of parks—more than 14,000 locations throughout the United States and Canada are scored on their facilities and recreation. You can purchase a directory which covers the entire area, or shorter versions of the guide are available for the western and eastern regions. Woodall's also publishes a directory exclusively for tent campers. Again, you can register to access campground listings for free at www. woodalls.com, but the on-line directory does not include Woodall's convenient rating system. The complete directories can be purchased at Woodall's Website or bookstores.

There's no centralized reservation system for every campsite within the **National Park system**, so your best bet is to contact each individual park. Campground reservations here usually must be made several months in advance since the sites are so popular, so don't count on finding a space unless you've planned ahead. Contact information for the National Parks can be found at their Website, www. nps.gov. Policies for state parks also vary from place to place, so you'll have to contact individual campgrounds for camping information.

Veteran car campers recognize **KOA Kampgrounds** by their familiar yellow, red, and black signs. KOAs allow your family to rough it while enjoying many of the amenities of home. Novice campers will be thrilled to have access to hot showers, flush toilets, laundry facilities, and convenience stores. All KOA locations have both tent and RV sites, and some even have cabins that your family can rent. If you plan to stay multiple nights at one or more KOA Kampgrounds, consider purchasing a Value Kard. You'll get a 10 percent discount on your registration fees and a free copy of the KOA directory (you'll still pay for shipping). You can also research KOA locations for free at www.koakamp grounds.com or purchase your own directory on-line or by calling 406-248-7444.

If you're looking for campgrounds where your family can pitch a tent in peace and quiet, check out *The Best in Tent Camping* series (published by Menasha Ridge Press). The books detail the best in scenic, tent-only sites without all of the bells and whistles.

One key to a great camping trip is remembering all of your supplies. If your family is RV or car camping, you can usually purchase any forgotten items on the road. However, if you're traveling far off the beaten path, you'll need to be careful to double-check your belongings.

Here's a checklist of supplies to make your camping experience go smoothly. If you're renting an RV, be aware that you may be able to rent your bedding and cooking supplies for an additional fee and save the trouble of bringing your own.

- Tent(s) and tent stakes
- Plastic ground cloth/tarp
- Sleeping bags (or bedding, for an RV)
- Sleeping pads
- Camp stove (with extra fuel)
- Pots, plastic dishes, mugs, and utensils
- Water bottle or canteen
- Lantern and/or candles
- Bottle and/or can openers
- Sharp knife (parents should hold on to this)
- Plethora of plastic/trash bags

- Dish soap (preferably biodegradable)
- Stocked coolers
- Water (or a portable filter or purifying tablets)
- Waterproof matches or lighter(s)
- Flashlights (and extra batteries)
- Bandanna (for use as a head covering, pot holder, and napkin)
- Trowel
- Folding saw
- First-aid kit, medications
- Sunscreen
- Insect repellent
- Toilet paper
- Day packs
- Child carriers (for little ones)
- Compass and area map
- Clothing (make sure to pack many layers)
- Two pairs of shoes (in case one gets wet)
- A hat
- Sunglasses
- Toiletries (try to take only necessary items)
- Camera
- Binoculars
- Kid supplies (toys, books, favorite stuffed animal)

New York

BEYOND THE BIG APPLE is another New York, one marked by majestic peaks and cavernous gorges, by tranquil lakes and thunderous falls, and by millions of acres of lush forests. From the beginning, these natural wonders have defined the region now known as New York State. Upstate is full of ideal vacation spots for families looking to combine natural adventures with a touch of history and plenty of out-and-out fun. It also boasts its share of *FamilyFun* favorites. Lake Placid is one of our readers' top tourist towns, and Great

Escape in Lake George gets rave reviews. In Cooperstown, the Baseball Hall of Fame earns kudos. The North Country is the Adirondacks Region, home to America's largest state park outside Alaska.

The New York-Canadian border is the Niagara Frontier and spectacular Niagara Falls, which lures 14 million visitors each year. One of the world's top three waterfalls, Niagara Falls is so strongly identified with the Empire State that it shares a place—along with the Manhattan skyline—on New York's recently redesigned license plate. And *FamilyFun* readers consistently rate it a must-see tourist attraction.

ATTRACTIONS
$ under $5
$$ $5 - $10
$$$ $10 - $20
$$$$ $20 and over

HOTELS/MOTELS/CAMPGROUNDS
$ under $125
$$ $125 - $175
$$$ $175 - $250
$$$$ $250 and over

RESTAURANTS
$ under $10
$$ $10 - $15
$$$ $15 - $25
$$$$ $25 and over

***FAMILYFUN* RATED**
★   Fine
★★   Good
★★★   Very Good
★★★★   *FamilyFun*
            Recommended

A ferry trip to the Statue of Liberty and Ellis Island affords terrific views of New York City.

New York City

"The Big Apple," "The City That Never Sleeps," home of the "Great White Way"— what child wouldn't like a city with so many nicknames? Many things to many people, including the more than seven million people who call it home, the towering metropolis of New York is variously known as claustrophobic and airy; overwhelming yet orderly; unfriendly though welcoming; at once both rough and refined. This is fashion's national catwalk and the financial world's capital. Most kids don't care about such things, though. For them, New York is simply a city filled with unforgettable sights and sounds.

New York's fast-paced, often chaotic environment can be exciting, but can intimidate young children. Plan your trip well, though, and this vital city will reward you with

THE **FamilyFun** LIST

MUST-SEE · MUST-SEE

American Museum of Natural History (page 61)

Bronx Zoo/International Wildlife Conservation Park (page 70)

Central Park (page 62)

Children's Museum of Manhattan (page 62)

Empire State Building (page 54)

FAO Schwarz (page 66)

Intrepid Sea-Air-Space Museum (page 53)

Radio City Music Hall (page 55)

Statue of Liberty and Ellis Island (page 48)

United Nations (page 53)

enough family-friendly adventures and memories to last a lifetime. Because you can't see everything on a short visit, try to concentrate on those places that the whole family can enjoy. From all that the city has to offer, the sights and attractions described in this chapter have been specifically selected to help you win points with your offspring. (For example, we figure they're more interested in the dinosaurs at the American Museum of Natural History than the Calder exhibit at the Museum of Modern Art.) We've also highlighted restaurants that welcome young diners and hotels that have family-friendly features, so you can select one with a video library and a game room, rather than one that boasts a jazz lounge and cigar room.

Once in the city, orient yourselves by taking a guided bus tour through the busy streets. For a different vantage point, try a relaxing boat cruise around the island of Manhattan. With a better sense of what's where,

you're ready to hit the pavement—and walking is truly the best way to savor this city. Depending on your mood, start with a stroll through flashy Times Square, historic Greenwich Village, or tree-studded Central Park. **NOTE:** Before you step off a curb, check for speeding taxis, city buses, and bike messengers.

Having read in school about America's beginnings, grade-schoolers will appreciate some of the city's historical sights. From the day Peter Minuet paid Native Americans a mere $24 in beads to purchase Manhattan island (land that the Dutch didn't even own), New York City has been the site of many historical events. George Washington took the oath of office as first president of the United States at the Old City Hall; the United Nations complex opened its doors here half a century ago to promote world peace; and ticker-tape parades along downtown's "Canyon of Champions" have honored Charles Lindbergh, John Glenn,

To the Letter

The next time your family hits the road, invite everyone to put their vocabulary skills to the test with this fun word game. Have one person begin by stating a category and a number of letters and then naming an appropriate item. For example, he might pick the category of animals and the number 3, then say "yak." Players take turns coming up with three-letter animals until everyone is stumped. The player who contributes the last word wins the round and starts the next one.

and many other modern heroes. Several significant spots grace Lower Manhattan and the adjacent harbor where Lady Liberty stands guard, and you'll run into many landmarks scattered throughout the city.

For grandiose excitement and entertainment, New York offers the high-kicking Rockettes, the high-flying balloons of Macy's annual Thanksgiving Day parade, and the high-in-the-sky observation deck on the building once scaled by King Kong. The city is also kind of a living museum of contemporary culture, from Times Square billboards and downtown window displays to familiar television and film locations—such as the 42nd Street Library seen in *Ghostbusters*, the Plaza Hotel from *Home Alone 2*, and Central Park's wolf statue of Balto, based on the eponymous animated film.

We have focused on Manhatan because it would be virtually impossible to see everything the Big Apple has to offer and still visit the other boroughs; we have, however, included some of our favorite "out-of-town" favorites that are well worth crossing a bridge or tunnel for. See "And Worth a Short Ride. . ." on page 70.

Although New York City is not cheap, you can take some cost-cutting measures to make your trip fit more comfortably within your budget. For example, choosing a hotel that offers in-room refrigerators can save you a few pricey breakfasts. In general, dining at restaurants other than the hotel's will cut your tab for lunch and dinner, too. Walking is cheaper, and more enjoyable, than taxi rides. Many hotels and local travel offices (like NYC & Company—The Convention & Visitors Bureau) offer discount packages for sights or events. You can also purchase half-price tickets for Broadway shows and enjoy museums during free evening hours.

So prepare your kids for one of the most exciting cities in the world. Pack comfortable walking shoes and plenty of film for your camera (consider bringing disposable cameras for the kids). From the Bronx Zoo down to the Staten Island ferry, the Big Apple is waiting to delight your whole family with a world of experiences.

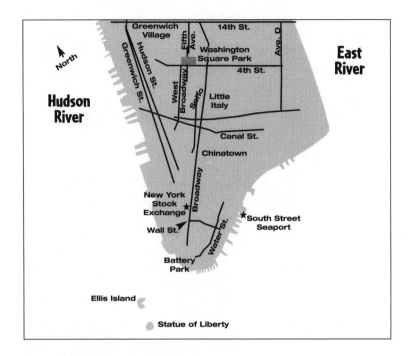

Downtown and Lower Manhattan

The southern tip of Manhattan is both gateway to the city's rich history and home to Wall Street's movers and shakers. You can board the ferry that goes to both the Statue of Liberty and Ellis Island, where your older kids can try to trace their family heritage, if your family arrived as immigrants. A tour of Wall Street's frenzied stock exchange (*212/656-5165*) offers the whole family a glimpse of the financial world in action.

In the 1600s, Lower Manhattan was home to the original Dutch settlement known as Nieuw Amsterdam. Today, well-preserved and refurbished sights—from Castle Clinton in Battery Park to Trinity Church, which anchors Wall Street—reflect the history of old New York. Even if the kids won't quite understand the historical significance of these centuries-old landmarks, the entire family will enjoy South Street Seaport, where you can tour old sailing vessels and explore modern shops.

Just north of the seaport and financial district, bustling Chinatown welcomes families with a taste for Chinese culture and cuisine. Some of the city's best bargains and cheapest eats can be found in this market-filled neighborhood. For kids who prefer pasta and pastry, nearby Little Italy offers a host of *ristorantes* and *caffès*. If you visit during September, your family might catch the annual San Gennaro Festival, a weeklong event famous for eating, drinking, and merrymaking.

A few blocks west is Greenwich Village, New York's hotbed of artistic and cultural innovation for more than a century. Whatever the trend of a generation, the Village has captured it in art, literature, and music—from folk to punk to hip-hop. Younger children may prefer playing in Washington Square Park, but preteens will enjoy cruising nearby shops for the latest in trendy clothes. If the troops get hungry, stop at the Village's cool ice-cream parlors, quirky cafés (where the clientele is often as eclectic as the menu), or popular fast-food outlets.

As a rule, you'll find plenty of buses, subways, and taxis in Manhattan, so avoid driving if you can. This is especially true for Lower Manhattan, where excessive traffic and high-priced garages can make parking a minor nightmare—and it doesn't get much easier as you make your way up to the revamped Union Square, where a popular farmers' market along the park draws locals and visitors weekly. If your kids are seeking souvenirs, check out Toys "R" Us, Barnes & Noble, and the Virgin megastore in this neighborhood.

CULTURAL ADVENTURES

New York City Fire Museum
★★★/$

Tucked away in Lower Manhattan, this novel museum delights youngsters while paying homage to the firefighters' hard work. Toy fire trucks and real vintage fire engines share space with uniforms, hoses, sliding poles, rescue equipment—and a tribute to the Dalmatian; once working dogs, today's Dalmatians act as firehouse mascots.

Older children may find the lifesaving and rescue exhibits fascinating, while younger ones will enjoy talking with New York's bravest, trying on hats, and ogling the collection of toys and fire engines. You can explore the small

The Immigration Center at **Ellis Island** opened its doors on January 1, 1892. A 15-year-old Irish girl named Annie Moore, accompanied by her two brothers, was the first immigrant to be processed at Ellis Island.

47

museum and gift shop in a couple of hours; there's no restaurant. Unlike most museums, this one may be less crowded on weekends, as it's a popular school field trip during the week. Guided tours are available; reservations are required. *278 Spring St., between Hudson and Varick Sts.; (212) 691-1303;* www.nycfiremuseum.org

Statue of Liberty and Ellis Island
★★★/$$$

Half the fun of visiting these two islands is the ferry ride, which gives you breathtaking views of the city and Lady Liberty. On board, a well-stocked souvenir stand carries plastic foam crowns, miniature statues, and other must-have memorabilia.

Post-9/11 security measures have closed the Statue of Liberty, its pedestal, crown, and museum to the public. Visitors may tour the grounds and outdoor exhibits, and free, guided tours of the grounds are given by National Park Service rangers. There's also a gift shop and refreshment stand.

The Statue of Liberty ferry also stops at nearby Ellis Island, where more than 12 million European immigrants first set foot on United States soil. The tiny island is now home to the Museum of Immigration, whose films and exhibits are likely to appeal to kids 10 and over. Do a little advance research on your family tree, and the trip will be even more interesting for the whole family. Ferries to Liberty and Ellis islands run year-round (every 20 minutes in summer, every 45 minutes in winter) *from Castle Clinton in Battery Park; (212) 269-5755;* www.nps.gov/stli

JUST FOR FUN

Chelsea Piers Sports Complex
★★★/$$-$$$

Once the destination port for the ill-fated *Titanic,* Chelsea Piers is now home to this popular indoor/outdoor sports facility along the Hudson River. Here kids and parents can burn off excess energy by in-line skating, ice-skating, basketball, golf, gymnastics, bowling (at $7 per game!), a rock-climbing wall, and more. The massive property also has family dining, a spa for adults, and impressive views of New Jersey across the river; you can get a bit of exercise by simply walking around and exploring. The piers are especially popular

Looking for some interesting facts about the Statue of Liberty? The Statue's crown has seven rays, which represent the seven seas and continents of the world. Also, the tablet in her left hand reads "July 4th, 1776" (in Roman numerals). France gave the Statue to the United States in honor of the nation's centennial.

during winter. Call ahead for a schedule of activities, as venues are sometimes closed for private parties, classes, and sports camps. *Piers 59–62, between W. 17th and W. 23rd Sts.; (212) 336-6666; www.chelseapiers.com*

South Street Seaport ★★★★/$

Cobblestone streets lined with shops, restaurants, and a museum lead to the main attraction at this landmark site: tall sailing ships docked along several piers just below the Brooklyn Bridge. If your kids love boats, they'll make a beeline for these grand old vessels. You can explore the *Wavertree*, built in 1885, and the *Peking* (1911); both are open. On the *Peking*, kids 12 and under can hoist sails, turn the wheel, and generally play sailor.

Looking for a maritime excursion? You can set sail on the *Pioneer* (a 102-foot schooner), board the *W. O. Decker* (a tugboat that seats six), or choose one of the Liberty Cruises sight-seeing boats. For those who prefer terra firma, the eight-block pedestrian enclave—designed to imitate a busy shipping port of past days—gives you a wide range of restaurants, fast-food eateries, a food court, and trendy shops. The whole family will like the Seaport Museum (fee), which has a collection of nearly 10,000 drawings, paintings, model ships, sailors' gear, and shipboard tools that commemorate maritime life over two centuries. During summer and school vacations, the museum's Children's Center offers storytelling, crafts, and fun workshops

(some with animals) relating to the sea. All programs are free with museum admission; call for a schedule. The best months to visit the seaport are between March and October. *Bounded by the East River and Water St., and John and Dover Sts.; Seaport Museum: (212) 748-8600;* Pioneer

Waxing Poetic

Fashioned after London's legendary wax shrine to the royal, presidential, famous, and infamous, the New York version of **Madame Tussaud's Wax Museum** features more than 200 lifelike characters in several themed rooms. There is no chamber of horrors, so the "spooky" factor won't scare the little ones—although the high prices may spook the grown-ups a bit. The galleries might elicit some impromptu history lessons as your kids gaze upon the likes of Albert Einstein, Martin Luther King, Babe Ruth, Charlie Chaplin, and the Beatles. Several floors include a party of celebrities, a room dedicated to reenactments of scenes from the Civil War, and plenty of contemporary faves like Whoopi Goldberg, Regis, and Madonna. Lots of New Yorkers are also immortalized here: Woody Allen, former Mayor Rudolph Giuliani, and the Donald (Trump, that is) take their place onstage. Youngsters also enjoy learning how the wax figures are made. There's a shop on the way out, but be warned: the souvenirs are pricey. *234 W. 42nd St.; (800) 246-8872; www.madametussauds.com*

Public Sails: (212) 732-8257; W. O. Decker: *(212) 732-8257; Seaport Liberty Cruises: (212) 630-8888.*

GOOD EATS

America ★★/$$

The only problem your kids will have at this noisy, cavernous place is deciding what to eat. Listing everything from burgers and fries to pasta and Cajun chicken, the menu is nearly as vast and diverse as its namesake. Bring your appetite—or better yet, share, as portions are huge. The service is somewhat brisk, and the staff can be hard to hail as they hurry past to tend to the crowds. The background music is geared to the teen set. *9 E. 18th St., between Broadway and Fifth Ave.; (212) 505-2110.*

Cowgirl Hall Of Fame ★★/$$

Cowgirl memorabilia and rodeo relics bring the Wild West to the urban jungle at this Tex-Mex eatery. Nachos, chicken-fried steak, and chili (which can be spicy) are among the favorites, but the biggest hit with kids is usually the dessert menu, with its endless list of ice-cream flavors. All dishes are served in Texas-size portions. *519 Hudson St., at W. 10th St.; (212) 633-1133.*

ESPN Zone ★★★/$$$

The ultimate eatery for sports fans of all ages, this place isn't just about food. In fact, though the food is tasty, your crew will want to get the meal over with so they can get down to the real attractions here: sports. But there's plenty to satisfy even the most finicky eaters, chicken wings, cheese fries, burgers, and the always popular all-beef "Hot Dogger." (Grown-ups should save room for some large, and sinfully delicious, desserts—they're designed to serve several, so

---

FamilyFun **READER'S TIP**

Terrific Task Masters

When our family goes on vacation, we assign each of our seven children an important task, one that will make each child an active part of planning. On a trip to Orlando, Florida, these were their assignments.Sylvia, age 15, navigator and accountant, kept track of mileage, maps, and money; TamiSue, 13, photographer, had to use two rolls of film a day; Joshua, 10, auto mechanic, pumped gas and checked oil and tire pressure; Bryan, 7, mailman, got postcards and stamps and mailed the cards kids wrote to themselves each day. Libby, 7, dietitian, made sure the cooler was stocked; Andrew, 6, activities coordinator and music director, was solely in charge of the tape player; and Katie, 5, referee, settled all road disputes.   **Wendy Lira, Alma, Kansas**

get some extra spoons for the kids to dip in.) Before or after you've eaten, indulge in the fun at the arcade games or some of the larger-sized activities, where you can test your skills at hockey, basketball, football, or even virtual boxing. Large screen TVs show the evening's action from various angles; and plenty of special events take place at the Zone itself—so be on the lookout for ex-jocks or even current ones on their night off. *1472 Broadway; (212) 921 ESPN;* www.espn.go.com/espn-inc/zone/newyork.html

Peanut Butter & Company
★★★★/$

The name says it all at this small storefront eatery, where both smooth and crunchy varieties (with and without preservatives) are made fresh daily on the premises. In addition to basic peanut-butter-and-jelly sandwich combinations include the nutty spread with marshmallow, honey, and sliced banana, bacon, or grilled chicken. There's even Ants on a Log—peanut butter on celery sticks with raisins. And for dessert? You guessed it, delicious peanut-butter cookies, cakes, and pies. A milk bar that serves different types of milk—including the ever-popular chocolate and the lesser-known soy—helps you wash it all down. Non-peanut-butter-eaters can order a chicken-or tuna-salad sandwich. *240 Sullivan St., between Bleeker and W. Third Sts.; (212) 677-3995.*

A Travel Scrapbook

This suitcase-style scrapbook is just right for your child to pack with mementos of his vacation adventures—and it's a cinch to make.

Start with two cardboard report covers. Use one for the suitcase itself and one to cut out two U-shaped handles and two 1½- by 18-inch straps.

Attach one handle to the front of the suitcase by gluing the ends to the inside of the upper edge. Match up the second handle with the first one and glue it to the back side. Now close the suitcase and glue on the straps. Position the strap tops on the front of the suitcase one inch down from the upper edge, then wrap the straps around the back of the suitcase. Finally, fold down the strap ends so that they overlap the tops and attach stick-on Velcro-type fasteners.

For a handy photo pocket, glue a large open envelope to the inner cover. Then, fill the suitcase with manila folders for storing ticket stubs, brochures, and other souvenirs.

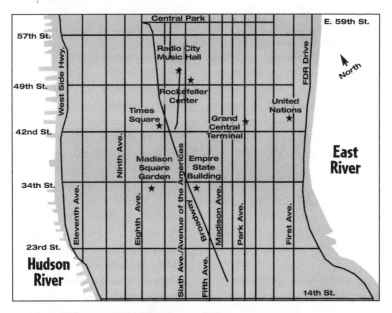

Midtown Manhattan

From east to west, Midtown takes you from the world stage of the United Nations to center stage on Broadway. The area is home to New York City's most seaworthy museum, the *Today* show studios, and many stars of Manhattan's skyline. Your kids will stare in awe at the massive billboards amid the neon lights, towering hotels, revitalized majestic theaters, and high-priced souvenir shops that define Times Square, which is Midtown's leading attraction. The sheer energy of this neighborhood is exciting; the pace, decidedly frantic; the sidewalks, usually packed: hold your children's hands just a little tighter here.

Once a seedy part of town, the theater district and Times Square have been cleaned up and revitalized. The prime attractions here are the Broadway theaters (see "Broadway Bound" on page 54). In planning your visit, read up on the current crop of shows at such Websites as www.theatermania.com and www.broadway.org

Midtown streets are arranged in a grid pattern, so finding your way around is easy. Running north-south, Fifth Avenue divides east cross streets from west. Although this part of town is best navigated on foot because of heavy traffic, plenty of buses traverse the neighborhood (exact change is required for the $1.50 fare; kids under 6 ride free).

Midtown has plenty of places to eat, but many are elegant, high-priced restaurants geared toward business-people with expense accounts. It's best to choose a spot ahead of time (see Good Eats on page 59) or go the fast-food route for lunch.

CULTURAL ADVENTURES

Intrepid Sea-Air-Space Museum
★★★★/$$

All hands on deck! This floating museum honoring American naval history is a marvelous family attraction. Docked on the Hudson River are three retired naval vessels: the USS *Intrepid* aircraft carrier; the USS *Growler* strategic missile submarine; and the USS *Edson*, a Vietnam-era destroyer. Your kids can inspect all thoroughly, as they climb through the narrow, cramped passageways. Perched aboard the *Intrepid* are several American military planes, from World War I models to today's star fighters—the kids can explore these as well. The navy flight simulator, which puts youngsters in the cockpit, is especially popular with would-be pilots. There's also a tribute to the space program, featuring one of the many space capsules retrieved at sea. As it's typically windy on the Hudson

River, bring jackets or sweaters. These ships draw crowds, so be prepared to move along slowly, especially on weekends. The *Intrepid*'s cafeteria is good for light lunches, and a well-stocked gift shop will likely prompt souvenir requests. *Intrepid Square at Pier 86, on the Hudson River near W. 46th St.; (212) 245-0072;* www.intrepidmuseum.org

United Nations
★★★/$-$$ (tours)

Since its headquarters officially opened in 1952, the United Nations has been a favorite class-trip destination for schools throughout the Northeast, especially fifth grade and higher. The UN provides an up-close social studies lesson on an hourlong tour that visits the General Assembly and Security Council meeting chambers, and

FamilyFun TIP

Grand Central Terminal recently underwent a major renovation to return the historic site to its original splendor. One of the major projects was the cleaning of the "Sky Ceiling," which towers over the main concourse; years of smoke and grime had obscured the beautiful depiction of the constellations of the night sky.

Look carefully and you'll be able to see a small section of the ceiling that workers left untouched (it's located in one of the corners).

Broadway Bound

Yes, Broadway shows are expensive, but if your budget allows, two Disney classics—**Beauty and the Beast** and **The Lion King**—are family favorites worth a splurge. No matter how many times your kids have seen the movie versions, nothing is quite like seeing these lavish productions on stage, complete with glorious costumes.

The newer of the two shows, *The Lion King*, with original music by Tim Rice and Elton John, is a tougher ticket to get. Both shows run close to three hours with an intermission, which may be a bit long for the under-5 crowd.

Even if you don't get to see one of these Disney shows, you might look in at the spectacular New Amsterdam Theater (*214 W. 42nd St.*). Disney recently remodeled this grand old structure, which originally opened in 1903, refurbishing elaborate murals, carved stone details, and Art Nouveau design.

Beyond the Disney hits, there are lots of other shows happening here. If you want to avoid surprises, call Ticketmaster or visit www.ticketmaster.com to secure tickets in advance. Otherwise, try the *TKTS booth at 47th Street and Broadway*, where you can buy half-price tickets (cash or traveler's checks only) on the day of the show; Wednesday matinees may be your best bet, but get in line no later than 10 A.M.

explains current exhibits and artwork from member nations along the way. Kids can get a feel for what the United Nations is all about: working toward world peace, providing humanitarian assistance, promoting respect for human rights, and protecting the environment. Flags of the 188 member nations fly high above the complex; ask your kids to point out the ones they recognize. This tract of international land also has a beautiful riverside promenade with sculptures and rose gardens; it's a lovely place for a post-tour stroll. Children must be over 5 to take the tour. *First Ave., between 42nd and 49th Sts.; (212) 963-1234; tours: (212) 963-7713;* www.un.org

JUST FOR FUN

Empire State Building

FamilyFun ★★★★/$-$$

Pick a clear day, head for 34th Street and Fifth Avenue, and tell the kids to look up. For 70 years, the towering structure once scaled by King Kong in the movie of the same name has been a must-see for anyone touring New York City (drawing an estimated four million visitors annually). The view from this historic landmark is spectacular; on a good day you can see for 50 miles. While waiting for an elevator to whoosh you to the top, check out the marvelous 1930s architecture. The views from the observation decks on the 86th and 102nd floors are breathtaking; the lower of the two is outdoors and especially nice in warmer weather. Closer to earth (on the second floor) is Skyride, a seven-minute simulated flight over the Big Apple. **NOTE:** This thrill ride is not advised for kids who get carsick; and kids under 5 or pregnant moms are not allowed. Gift shops in the lobby and on the 86th floor sell an array of Empire State Building models and various hard-to-resist souvenirs. *350 Fifth Ave., between 33rd and 34th Sts.; Observatory: (212) 736-3100;* www.esbnyc.com

The United Nations conducts business in six official languages: Arabic, Chinese, English, French, Russian, and Spanish.

Madame Tussaud's Wax Museum ★★★★/$$$$

Want to shake hands with Elvis? how about one of the Beatles? For more information, see "Waxing Poetic" on page 49.

Madison Square Garden ★★★★/$$$-$$$$

This world-renowned arena hosts exciting events throughout the year. Among the kid-pleasing offerings are dazzling shows—like *The Wizard of Oz* and *Sesame Street on Ice*—and concerts by teenybopper favorites such as Britney Spears and 'N Sync (both of which sell out very quickly). In April, the garden becomes the big top for the spectacular Ringling Bros. and Barnum & Bailey circus. From fall through spring the Knicks and Rangers—New York's hometown basketball and hockey teams, respectively—draw sports fans. Tickets for these games are expensive and very hard to come by, so call well in advance. The New York Liberty, a professional women's basketball team, checks in for a spring/summer season of WNBA basketball; young hoops fan of both sexes will enjoy watching the women players in action. The adjoining theater features such shows as *A Christmas Carol,* performed annually during the holiday season. Behind-the-scenes tours give kids a glimpse at the Knicks and Rangers locker rooms, the Walk of Fame (a hall of fame of sorts), the luxury boxes, and much more. Tours are given Monday through Saturday from 10 A.M. to 3 P.M. , depending on scheduled events; call (212) 465-5800 for tour information. *Seventh Ave., between 30th and 32nd Sts.; Garden box office: (212) 465-6741; Ticketmaster: (212) 307-7171;* www.thegarden.com

Radio City Music Hall
FamilyFun ★★★/$$$

From Barney the Dinosaur to the Backstreet Boys, shows for kids of all ages will hit the landmark Radio City Music Hall. The Christmas Spectacular, presented every year

FamilyFun SNACK

Cranberry-nut Snack Mix

Measure 2 cups raw sunflower seeds; 1 cup pine nuts; 1 cup raw pumpkin seeds; 1 cup sweetened, dried cranberries; and 1 cup raisins into a mixing bowl and stir with a wooden spoon. Makes 6 cups.

from November through January, lives up to its name. The fabulous Rockettes dazzle audiences with their high kicks; kids especially like the March of the Wooden Soldiers. Order tickets for this show as early as August, and well in advance for all others. The music hall, one of the most outstanding theaters in the world, is worth a visit in itself. A recent yearlong multimillion-dollar renovation brought back much of the old charm while adding new technology. Kids used to today's multiplex theaters will stare up in awe at the giant chandeliers hanging from 50-foot ceilings in the magnificent lobby and at the arched, terraced balconies converging on the grand stage. Of interest to the 8-and-over crowd, the Radio City Stage Door Tour (fee) is ideal for any young entertainers in the family, as they can investigate backstage, the dressing rooms, the spotlights, and the famous (massive) Wurlitzer organ, and absorb plenty of great trivia and stories about this former movie house. Not only can they walk onto

the stage, but during rehearsals children might sneak a peek (from stage left) at their favorite performers in action. But you didn't hear it from us. *1260 Sixth Ave., at 50th St.; (212) 247-4777;* www.radiocity.com

Rockefeller Center
★★★/$-$$$

If your kids love to ice-skate, there's no better place to don blades than Rockefeller Center's ice-skating rink (fee)—especially in December, when you can glide beneath the glitter of the world's largest Christmas tree. Skate rentals are available; but for those who opt to stay off the rink, simply watching the skaters and seeing the tree is festive and fun. (But be forewarned: the crowds during the holiday season can be hard to negotiate, particularly when you have little ones in tow.)

Kids 6 and older will be fascinated by the tour of NBC Television Studios at 30 Rockefeller Center (officially the GE Building); departing from the main lobby every 15 minutes, the hourlong tour gives children an inside glimpse at the workings of a real television studio (fee). Across 49th Street is the glass-enclosed studio of the *Today* show; crowds gather on the sidewalk to watch the show being broadcast weekday mornings from seven to ten. Plenty of stores, including some with high-priced souvenirs, and various restaurants balance out Rockefeller Center's attractions. *Between Fifth and Sixth Aves. and 49th and 50th Sts.; (212) 632-3975; tours: (212) 232-7654.*

Toys "R" Us ★★★★/$$
Every toy you ever wanted is on the shelves here. Want to know more? See "Get Your Souvenirs Here!" on page 73.

BUNKING DOWN

Best Western Manhattan ★★★/$$
Near the Empire State Building and just a few blocks from Macy's, this clean, comfortable hotel is a bargain by New York standards. The 175-room property has 25 two-room suites—an ideal choice for families—with on-demand movies, irons, hair dryers, and coffeemakers. Other pluses include continental breakfast and a casual restaurant serving American fare. Kids under 13 stay free in their parents' room. *17 W. 32nd St., between Fifth Ave. and Broadway; (800) 528-1234; (212) 736-1600;* www.bestwestern.com

Doubletree Guest Suites ★★★★/$$$
Ideally located near Rockefeller Center and the theater district, this all-suites hotel is perfect for families. Each unit has two bedrooms with cable television, and a kitchen that includes a microwave and refrigerator. A game area is available for kids. A laundry and a fairly good restaurant, the Center Stage Café, are also on the premises. *1568 Broadway, at W. 47th St., New York; (800) 222-8733; (212) 719-1600;* www.doubletree.com

New York Hilton & Towers ★★★★/$$$$
In the summer, Hilton offers kids a Vacation Station program, which features a toy-lending library and a folder of fun activities to do around the city. Kids under 18 stay free in their parents' room at this massive hotel, which is like a city within a city. There are shops, two restaurants, a café, a barbershop, a health club, laundry

Jeane Dixon Wanna-bes

Think about it: Your kids are always asking you to foretell the future, from what will be at your destination to exactly what time you'll be there. Turn the tables on them this vacation. At the beginning of each day's travels, have everyone fill out a list of predictions.

♦ What time will we arrrive at our destination?

♦ What will the weather be like?

♦ Will there be a pool?

♦ Will the ice machine have ice in cubes or ice in slices?

♦ Will we see any deer along the road?

Vacation Rewards

Set up a Souvenir Budget

FamilyFun readers, the Howells of Morgan Hill, California, aren't the only ones who swear by giving their two kids a set amount of money for vacation souvenirs and letting the kids choose how to spend it. Putting them in charge has not only eliminated those grating requests to Mom and Dad, but has also put the kids in touch with how much things cost. "They're more inclined to pinch pennies," mom Cindy says, "when it's their pennies."

Institute a Good Deed Bank

A trip to see Mickey Mouse inspired the Mohan family of Eden Prairie, Minnesota, to start a Good Deed Bank. "We knew that after paying for the trip we would have little money left for extras at the park," recalls Marci Mohan. So she had her kids decorate a coffee-can bank to look like Mickey Mouse. In the weeks leading up to the trip, whenever Hannah, age 9, or Dylan, 6, got caught doing something helpful, their parents dropped a coin in the bank. The kids' good deeds earned them a chunk of change to spend on vacation. And, says Marci, "We had a more considerate household."

service, and other luxury amenities. FAO Schwarz and Central Park are just a few blocks away. *1335 Avenue of the Americas, between W. 53rd and W. 54th Sts.; (800) HILTONS; (212) 261-5870;* www.hilton.com

Paramount Hotel ★★★★/$$$

Not far from the Intrepid Sea-Air-Space Museum, this property promotes a family-friendly atmosphere and stocks a playroom with games, toys, and fun-house mirrors. Back in the room, the kids can enjoy any one of 1,500 films from the video-on-demand library, while you relax and plan tomorrow's agenda. Although the hotel is on the pricey side (and the rooms are **very** small—except for the suites), in-room refrigerators allow you to stock some staples and save money. *235 W. 46th St., between Broadway and Eighth Ave.; (800) 225-7474; (212) 764-5500;* www.ianschragerhotels.com

Super Eight Hotel
Times Square ★★★/$$

You can get suites and rooms with two double beds at decent prices at this well-situated hotel. Just off Fifth Avenue, it's near shopping, the theaters, and many sights. Well-appointed rooms feature on-demand movies, in-room safes, free local phone calls, laundry service, and other extras. It's a clean, well-managed establishment with good rates. *59 W. 46th St., between Fifth and Sixth Aves.; (800) 567-7720; (212) 719-2300.*

Good Eats

American Festival Café
★★★/$$$

Overlooking Rockefeller Center's skating rink in winter and beautiful garden in summer, this spacious, casual restaurant serves up primarily American fare, including great burgers, steaks, and chicken dishes. **NOTE:** Its convenient Midtown location means that prices are on the high side. *20 W. 50th St.; (212) 332-7620.*

Carnegie Deli
★★★★/$$$

Fabulous franks and homemade knishes for under $10 for the kids, or perhaps one of Carnegie's famous burgers will do the trick. If you dare, order one of the famed gargantuan combos; plan to split it with a youngster (it's worth the $3 sharing charge)—you'll still have food to take back to the hotel room. Save room for the cheesecake. No credit cards taken. *854 Seventh Ave., at 55th St.; (800) 334-5606.*

Mars 2112
★★★/$$$

Looking for a truly out-of-this-world dining experience? This theme eatery, complete with arcade, will wow the kids from the moment they walk in and board a simulated space shuttle that hurls them through the star-studded universe. The wall-to-wall Mars theme is quite striking. A kids' menu, with slightly out-of-this-world prices ($9 for a grilled cheese sandwich or burger?), accompanies a rather eclectic menu for Mom and Dad. While the food is good, the atmosphere is the reason to shell out big bucks. After all, how often do you get to dine on another planet? *1633 Broadway, at 51st St.; (212) 582-2112.*

Virgil's Real BBQ
★★★/$$

Meaty spareribs, tasty burgers, and other barbecue favorites abound at this popular Times Square eatery. Add corn bread, baked beans, and other side dishes and you're all set for a fun family meal in a cheery, upbeat atmosphere. *152 W. 44th St., between Sixth Ave. and Broadway; (212) 921-9494.*

Rain or Shine, It's Playtime!

If it's a rainy day and you're looking for a fun place to take the kids, visit **Playspace** (*212/769-2300*). The indoor playground *on Broadway, near West 92nd Street*, comes complete with a huge sandbox, a tree house, a toddler-size climbing wall, a miniature stage loaded with dress-up clothes, toys, games, and much more for the 6-and-under crowd. The 8,000-square-foot space is safe, clean, well-run, and includes a snack area.

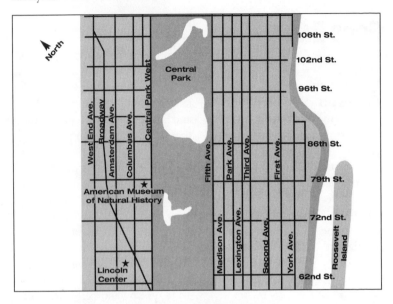

Upper East and Upper West Sides

Manhattan's uptown neighborhoods are separated by Central Park, which extends from 59th Street north to 110th Street, and Fifth Avenue west to Central Park West. Each side of the park has its own character— and residents of each readily proclaim why their side is better.

Amid an architectural array of modern luxury apartment buildings, brownstones, and pre-World War II structures, the Upper East Side boasts what is known as Museum Mile, where you pass the Guggenheim Museum, the Metropolitan Museum

of Art, and other world-class cultural institutions that generally aren't all that much fun for kids (unless they have a real interest in art). What this side does lay claim to is FAO Schwarz (aka kid heaven) and a plethora of family restaurants.

Overall, the West Side has greater kid appeal, largely thanks to the dinosaurs at the American Museum of Natural History, the fun-but-educational activities at the Children's Museum of Manhattan, and plenty of child-friendly shops. (Though diners and fast-food joints dot the area, most West Side eateries are geared to young professionals.)

Lincoln Center—on the West Side—features children's concerts and programs, but it's your call as to how well your kids will receive such a cultural experience (see "Catch a Show at Lincoln Center" below). They're sure to be dazzled by the Big Apple Circus (see "Big Apple Big Top" on page 64), which pitches its giant tent in Lincoln Center's backyard each autumn. Even if you

don't spend much time at the famed cultural complex, the surrounding area has plenty to offer, including Barnes & Noble, a Disney Store, Tower Records, and films on the massive Sony IMAX Theater screen.

As in much of Manhattan, parking is at a premium on both the Upper West and Upper East sides of the city. Walking is the best way to take in the many sights and sounds of these two prime uptown neighborhoods. And don't leave town without spending at least one day exploring the incredible tree-studded, playground-dotted, green expanse that stretches between them.

Catch a Show at Lincoln Center

Lincoln Center *(Amsterdam Ave., from 62nd to 66th Sts.; 212/875-5000)* is among the city's top attractions, but most kids will like only certain aspects of the place. During the summer, you can catch a variety of outdoor concerts and dance events that all ages can enjoy. Particular favorites at other times during the year are the annual Jazz for Young People concert series and the *Nutcracker Suite.* Young ballerinas in the family will be especially excited about the *Nutcracker*— the festive holiday ballet is attended by legions of little girls in velvet dresses (and some brothers in blue blazers). You'll need to get tickets at least two months in advance. A variety of guided tours is also offered. *Call (212) 875-5350 for details.*

CULTURAL ADVENTURES

American Museum of Natural History
★★★★/$$-$$$

Kids and grown-ups alike are wowed by the Dinosaur Hall on the fourth floor, with honest-to-goodness skeletons of T-rex and other stars of the extinct reptile world. But this spacious museum is also home to more than 32,000 artifacts and specimens; exhibits on mammals, reptiles, and amphibians; a re-created rain forest complete with live plants; an IMAX Theater; and a new planetarium. Housed in the new Rose Center for Earth and Space, the Hayden Planetarium's Big Bang

Theater presents a re-creation of the earth's formation. Older kids will especially go for the Earth Event Wall, a massive video screen that uses computer simulation to explain earthquakes, volcanoes, and other natural occurrences. Though films at the IMAX theater are documentary-style, most will keep kids captivated as the giant screen brings to life animals in their natural habitats.

You'll enjoy the museum the most if you keep in mind that you won't get to see everything. Look at the map when you enter and try to devise an itinerary that includes each family member's top choices. Seeing both the planetarium show and an IMAX film in one visit may be too much for younger children; check current programs and choose between the two. **NOTE:** Strategically placed between exhibits are gift shops selling museum toys, games, and books at a premium, so you may want to limit the kids to one shopping stop. The cafeteria is very good here; Mom and Dad can have sushi while the kids munch on dino-shaped chicken nuggets. *Central Park at W. 79th St.; (212) 769-5100.*

⭐ Children's Museum
FamilyFun Of Manhattan
★★★★/$$

Geared for kids ages 5 through 12, this museum makes learning fun, with puppet shows, an arts-and-crafts center, sing-alongs, and other activities. Exhibits cover a variety of child-pleasing subjects, from the stories of

Dr. Seuss to musical instruments from around the world. Your kids can learn how their own bodies work by walking through a replica of the human body, and throughout the year, changing interactive exhibits focus on self-discovery.

The Time Warner Center for the Media, on the second floor, allows children to create and produce their own videos and TV programs (bring your own videotape for them to use, and the center will make you a free copy). Call ahead for schedules of the special events. Though strollers are not allowed inside, special areas are set aside for toddlers to play, learn, and explore. A gift shop stocks educational toys and crafts, but there's no restaurant. The museum is open Wednesday through Sunday, but try to go on a weekday when it's less crowded. *212 W. 83rd St., between Amsterdam Ave. and Broadway; (212) 721-1234; (212) 721-1223; www.cmom.org*

JUST FOR FUN

⭐ Central Park
FamilyFun ★★★★/Free

There are no age limits for having fun in this 843-acre oasis framed by the city's modern skyscrapers. Focal point of the city since the late 1870s, Central Park is the place to escape the city, to play ball, climb rocks, fly a kite, play tennis, roller-skate, Rollerblade, ride a bike or a horse, or do any number of fun outdoor activities. The kids will marvel at how much there is to see in Central Park. As the weather gets warmer, street musicians, magicians, clowns, mimes, jugglers, and puppeteers give impromptu performances (in exchange for tips—toss in some spare change) along the park's pathways. During summer, free concerts and numerous special events take place. Year-round, people-watching is elevated to a world-class sport here.

For many Manhattan residents, Central Park is simply a place to relax, a communal backyard for this city of apartment dwellers. To experience the park like a native, pack a picnic and stake out a patch of grass, or find a comfortable bench and watch your kids play in one of 21 individually designed playgrounds throughout the park. These play spaces offer plenty of monkey bars for climbing, ropes for swinging, and sandboxes for digging and building. Take your kids to the city's largest slide at Billy Jackson's playground near East 67th Street; other playgrounds along the East Side are at 72nd, 77th, 79th, and 91st streets. Near West 81st Street is the Western-themed Diana Ross Playground, which features a running stream; there are also playgrounds at West 93rd and 96th streets.

The park is more than playgrounds and green open spaces, though—Belvedere Castle, the Carousel, Central Park Zoo, the Harlem Meer, Kerbs Conservatory Water, Loeb Boathouse, and Wollman Memorial Skating Rink (*see following entries for details*) are

It's Only a Movie, It's Only a Movie

The **Sony IMAX Theater at Lincoln Square** *(212/336-5000)* dazzles little ones with big action. Once they don the high-tech headsets, kids are transfixed by the eight-story (80 feet by 100 feet) screen from which stampeding buffalo, freighter-size fish, and other larger-than-life creatures seem to be heading straight for them. Instinctively, their hands reach out for the 3-D images. Many of the films shown here are family-friendly—check the local newspaper for current schedules. Those who suffer from motion sickness should stay away. Other theaters at this cavernous, modern multiplex (with a top-notch concession stand) occasionally host major movie premieres—kids might even spot one of their favorite celebrities.

all worth a look. **NOTE:** It's best to avoid deserted areas and roaming around after sundown. Central Park is bounded by 110th Street, Fifth Avenue, Central Park South, and Central Park West. *For information about programs and special events throughout the park, call (212) 360-8236*; www.centralparknyc.org

Belvedere Castle ★★★/$

Perched here since 1872, this scaled-down version of a Scottish stone castle comes complete with fairytale turrets. It overlooks the open-air Delacorte Theater, site of Shakespearean performances in summer, and Turtle Pond, where mornings find rows of turtles sunning themselves along the shore. Inside the castle, the Henry Luce Nature Observatory has microscopes, telescopes, and a fully equipped weather center. It also hosts workshops and programs designed to teach kids about the wonders of nature. Youngsters ages 6 and older can borrow a Discovery Kit—with binoculars, a guidebook, and maps—to use for their day in the park. (Parents must present two pieces of ID, which are held until the kit is returned.) *Central Park, near W. 78th St.; (212) 772-0210*; www.centralparknyc.org

The Carousel ★★/$

Only a lovely 15-minute walk south of the castle, this beautiful carousel has been turning for nearly 100 years. Originally at Coney Island, the ride came to Central Park in the 1950s, and kids and their parents have been stopping here ever since. The hand-painted horses probably impress nostalgic baby-boomer parents more than they do their kids, who simply enjoy the (somewhat speedy) musical ride. *Central Park, near 65th St.; (212) 879-0244*; www.centralparknyc.org

Central Park Zoo/Central Park Wildlife Center ★★★★/$

The best attraction within the park, this five-and-a-half-acre zoo is a fun and inexpensive place to spend an hour or two. Its small size is actu-

BIG APPLE BIG TOP

If it's October, the circus must be in town. **The Big Apple Circus** is a one-ring extravaganza for kids of all ages, as it brings them so close to all the exciting acts. You see clowns, acrobats, jugglers, and lots of other performers from around the world under the big top, along with performing dogs, horses, and other animals that your offspring will love. Look for the big tent in Damrosch Park, behind Lincoln Center, and join the fun. In spring, the Big Apple Circus *(212/268-2500)* visits Cunningham Park in Queens, then travels out to Long Island's C. W. Post Campus.

ally in its favor, especially for families with young children—you don't have much ground to cover, so kids are less likely to get tired and cranky. You can visit the park's resident polar bears and stroll into the Arctic penguin house to watch these tuxedoed waddlers cavort underwater. Kids especially enjoy watching the sea lions at feeding time and the monkeys playing on their giant island anytime. A short walk up a paved walkway is the Tisch Children's Zoo, designed for kids ages 1 through 9. Your kids will have fun feeding and petting the sheep, pigs, and goats. You're likely to find long lines at both zoos on summer weekends, but don't despair—they generally move quickly. A cafeteria and a gift shop are accessible without entering the zoo. *Central Park, near E. 64th St.; (212) 861-6030;* www.centralpark nyc.org

Harlem Meer ★★/$

For the rod-and-reel set, the north end of the park is home to the only place you can fish in Manhattan. Kids can catch and release bass, catfish, shiners, and bluegills in the 11-acre, well-stocked lake; you can use the poles and bait for free. Year-round, the Charles A. Dana Discovery Center hosts kid-friendly exhibits and fun activities, focusing on the environment, science, arts and crafts, and more. *Central Park, 110th St., near Fifth Ave; (212) 860-1370;* www.centralparknyc.org

Loeb Boathouse ★★/$$-$$$

Want to rent a boat and take a ride? Rent one here and row the kids around the Central Park lake. If all have had their fill of water, you can rent bikes here instead and pedal around the park. (Ride only on designated paths, as bikes are prohibited from most walkways.) Hungry? The Boathouse café, snack bar, and ice-cream stand provide treats and more substantial fare. *Central Park, near 72nd St.; (212) 517-2233;* www.centralparknyc.org

Wollman Memorial Skating Rink ★/$$

With the city skyline as its backdrop, this large rink has an overhanging balcony where you and the kids can watch the skaters. Unfortunately, if you don't skate and your children do, they're on their own: nonskaters (including parents of young skaters) are kept at a great distance by an often abrupt staff. If you do skate and plan to accompany your children, try to go on a weekday when the rink is less crowded. In warm weather, the rink is transformed into an in-line skating arena. You can rent skates,

and there's a snack bar on the premises. *Central Park, near W. 64th St., above Sixth Ave.; (212) 439-6900*; www.centralparknyc.org

The Disney Store
★★★★/$-$$$$

When you wish upon a star—all your kids' dreams will come true at this toy/music/memorabilia and more store. For more information, see "Get Your Souvenirs Here!" on page 73.

FAO Schwarz
FamilyFun ★★★★/$-infinity!

Heaven on earth for kids, FAO Schwarz is packed with wall-to-wall toys, games, and dolls—many of which you won't find elsewhere. A glass-enclosed elevator lifts the whole family out of a sea of stuffed animals up to the second floor, while providing a great view of the festivities going on all around. A few toys are set up for hands-on play, Nintendo fans stay entertained at the electronic-game stations—and don't forget the life-size versions of Raggedy Ann, Arthur, and others. Small specialty areas include a candy store and Barbie on Madison, where you'll find every Barbie doll, outfit, and accessory. Although you don't have much chance of leaving FAO Schwarz empty-handed, consider setting a price or size limit, depending on the age of your child. Prices can be on the high side, so try to steer your kids away from the toys you can find elsewhere at lower prices; urge them to look for

something unique. The FAO Schwarz experience (which can easily take several hours) can be delightful for both kids and parents. **NOTE:** During the holiday season, you may have to wait in line just to get in; any time of year, it's best to get here early. *767 Fifth Ave., at 58th St.; (212) 644-9400*; www.fao.com

Frozen Ropes ★★★/$$

How about picking up some sports pointers while you travel? If learning how to play better baseball appeals to your young ballplayers, then this is the place for some fun—and very useful—lessons. Geared to kids ages 5 and older, this place boasts batting cages and instructions on all aspects of the game from highly trained instructors. Grown-ups may want to take a swing or two as well. This location can serve a dual purpose: while some of the family is taking batting practice, the non-baseball lovers in the family can hit the Upper West Side shops in the neighborhood. *W. 74th St. and Broadway at Apple Bank; (212) 362-0344;* www.frozenropesnyc.com

Bunking Down

Beacon Hotel ★★★/$$$

Nothing overly fancy here, but the Beacon is a quality hotel with affordable rates and it sits just a few blocks from Central Park, the Upper West Side museums, and plenty of shopping for all family members. More than half of the 204 rooms have pull-out sofas and kitchenettes. There's also an on-site laundry and a coffee shop. Kids under 12 stay free. *2130 Broadway, at 75th St.; (800) 695-8284;* www.beaconhotel.com

Bentley Hotel ★★★★/$$$

If you want to stay on the fashionable Upper East Side of Manhattan, this hotel overlooks the East River. A nice choice for families, the hotel has several rooms with kitchenettes plus laundry. Easily accessible to many sites such as the United Nations and Bloomingdales department store, you'll also find plenty of family-friendly restaurants, including one on the hotel roof. There's also a pleasant nearby area along the river to take your kids for a relaxing break and watch the boats go by. **NOTE:** The hotel has parking with a preposterous $20 charge every time you use your car. *500 E. 62nd St.; (800) 695-8284;* www.nychotels.com

Lyden Gardens Suites ★★★★/$$$$

Kids can have their own room in these nicely appointed suites featuring kitchens, cable TV, and all the comforts of home. The Upper East Side location puts you out of the tourist traps of Times Square and just five blocks from Central Park. Great shopping, local playgrounds, and plenty of places to eat are also nearby. Prices are reasonable for New York City con-

Megasports

What do you do with a large asphalt facility when you no longer need it to store asphalt? Turn it into a giant indoor/outdoor play space, of course. *On East 90th Street, near the East River,* **Asphalt Green AquaCenter** *(212/369-8890)* has the best (clean, safe, and fun) indoor pools in the city. Older kids can get waterlogged in the 50-meter, Olympic-size pool, while your toddlers can take swimming (splashing) lessons in the smaller (18 feet by 26 feet) heated pool. The 74,000-square-foot facility also houses a kid-size basketball court, a running track, and a great playground (at the York Avenue entrance) with rail-tie climbing structures. Check out the indoor theater that presents puppet shows on weekends.

sidering the size of the accommodations and the neighborhood. There is laundry on-site but hotel parking is at a neighboring garage and can get costly. *215 E. 64th St.; (212) 355-1230.*

The Plaza Hotel ★★★★/$$$$

From the ornate chandeliers to the wide selection of cable TV choices, the kids will say "wow" a lot at this landmark luxury hotel. The Plaza is costly, but for a couple of nights why not enjoy basking in the lap of luxury. The Plaza opened in 1907 and was immediately billed as the most elegant hotel in the world. The Young Plaza Ambassadors Program (YPA), initiated in 2002, offers entertainment and educational opportunities for kids 6 through 16. While they may pass on the etiquette classes offered, they will benefit from reduced rates on a number of the city's popular venues and can enjoy special New York City behind the scenes activities such as a dance class with the Rockettes at Radio City Music Hall, a personal shopping spree at FAO Schwarz, or cooking lessons with the executive chefs at the Plaza. The program is free for a stay of two or more nights. Also in the Plaza you'll find the Palm Court restaurant with various kid-friendly favorites offered like peanut-butter-and-jelly sandwiches, while across the street you'll find the city's favorite place to play, Central Park. In fact, the children's zoo, a short walk from the Plaza, offers special activities for YPA members. *Fifth Ave. & Central Park South; (212) 759-3000.*

The Regency ★★★★/$$$$

This elegant hotel takes part in the Loews Loves Kids program, which entitles all young guests to a welcome kit filled with games, crayons, and coloring books. The 393 luxurious guest rooms, including 87 suites, feature marble baths, goose-down comforters, kitchenettes with microwaves and refrigerators, phones with caller

ID, and televisions in the bedroom and the bath (that should impress the kids!). A family video library is also available. Though the Regency is expensive, a stay here will have your family feeling like royalty. *540 Park Ave., at E. 61st St.; (800) 235-6397; (212) 759-4100.*

GOOD EATS

California Pizza Kitchen
★★★/$$

Kids are given an activity menu and crayons as you're seated at this cheery Upper East Side eatery. The service is quick and attentive, and the atmosphere is much warmer than that of your typical pizzeria. The food will please everyone. Choose from basic to designer toppings (like garlic chicken and white wine-lemon sauce) for an individual pizza, or opt for one of the many pasta dishes. *201 E. 60th St., at Third Ave.; (212) 755-7773.*

Dallas BBQ ★★★★/$$

Kids will enjoy getting messy on big portions of ribs, chicken, or finger foods while Mom and Dad down Texas-size beers or margaritas. The inexpensive and good, if somewhat greasy, fare can be found at six large Manhattan locations. Arrive early for dinner, as these popular rib joints are always jumping. *1365 Third Ave., between 73rd and 74th Sts.; (212) 772-9393. Also at: 27 W. 72nd St.,*

(212) 873-2004; St. Marks Pl. and Second Ave., (212) 777-5574.

Il Vagabondo
★★★★/$$$

There's nothing flashy about this long-standing, family-friendly trattoria, where the fare is mainly Southern Italian. Homemade gnocchi and veal stew are house specialties, but you can order spaghetti with tomato sauce for little diners. Your kids may enjoy watching a bocce game on the city's only indoor court, so ask for a courtside table. And don't worry if they make some noise—the staff takes it all in stride at this good-humored neighborhood spot. *351 E. 62nd St., between First and Second Aves.; (212) 832-9221.*

Pizzeria Uno ★★★★/$$$

Get great deep-dish pizza for the whole family at this very popular chain originated in Chicago, but now found on both the Upper West and Upper East Sides of Manhattan. Choose from daily pizza specials, pasta, steakhouse burgers, and thin-crust pizza, or order smaller portions of pasta, chicken, or pizza from the kids' menu. Be patient—the deep-dish pizza takes some time to cook; we promise you it's well worth the wait. *432 Columbus Ave., between 80th and 81st Sts., (212) 595-4700; and 220 E. 86th St., between Second and Third Aves., (212-472-5656. Other Manhattan locations include: 89 South St., at the Seaport, (212) 791-7999;*

55 Third Ave., in the East Village, (212) 995-9668; and 391 Sixth Ave., in the West Village, (212) 242-5230; www.waiter.com/www.sys/uno

Serendipity 3 ★★★/$$$

Going strong since the 1950s, this quaint storefront eatery will delight kids with frozen hot chocolate and an array of large, decadent desserts. Sweets are the main attraction here, but you can also get foot-long hot dogs, shepherd's pie, and other family fare in big portions—and at relatively big prices. Tiffany lamps hang everywhere, and a novelty boutique is filled with Victorian collectibles, toys, and dolls—some for sale, others for decoration. Seating is limited, so expect a wait. *225 E. 60th St., between Second and Third Aves.; (212) 838-3531.*

Tony's Di Napoli Restaurant ★★★★/$$

This large, festive Upper East Sider serves Italian fare family-style: very large portions for everyone to pass around and share. Bring your appetite for such fresh pasta dishes as ravioli Bolognese and spaghetti with meatballs, as well as veal marsala, chicken parmigiana, and much more. Generally, a couple of appetizers and two or three entrées will be plenty for a family of five. As large as Tony's is, it still packs in quite a crowd, so don't be surprised if you have to wait for a table. *1606 Second Ave., between 83rd and 84th Sts.; (212) 861-8686.*

and Worth a Short Ride . . .

Bronx Zoo/ International Wildlife Conservation Park
★★★★/$-$$

More than 4,000 animals are the stars of this sprawling 265-acre attraction—one of the most celebrated zoos in the world. The resident creatures eat, sleep, and play in well-designed natural habitats that offer maximum viewing opportunities. You'll swear that the apes are posing for photos in the Congo area, and the kids will laugh at the pranks of the Asian gibbons in Jungle World. The Himalayan Highlands section is home to adorable red pandas and sleek snow leopards, and the Bengali Express

monorail takes passengers through Wild Asia, where rare sika deer, zebras, and Bengal tigers roam. Grown-ups may cringe at the World of Darkness, home to bats and other nocturnal creatures, and the Mouse and Reptile houses, but most kids really love them. (Children who fear the dark may need a little extra reassurance in the glass-enclosed World of Darkness, which is pretty dark and filled with scurrying, fluttering things.) Don't miss the sea lion pool, especially fun during feeding time. Youngsters under 7 will also enjoy the Children's Zoo, where they can crawl through kid-size prairie-dog tunnels and inside human-size turtle shells. Try to visit in the mornings, as the animals have just been fed and are in the mood to receive visitors. You'll do a lot of walking here, so wear comfortable shoes. There's a lakeside café and snack stands throughout the park. Open 365 days a year, the zoo closes earlier in the winter months. On Wednesday, admission is free for everyone. *Bounded by Bronx River Pkwy. and Southern Blvd., and Bronx Park South and East Fordham Rd., the Bronx; (718) 367-1010; www.wcs.org*

Coney Island and New York's Aquarium For Wildlife Conservation ★★★/$$

Parents tend to come here for the nostalgia, but kids enjoy Coney Island for its summertime amusement park, and ever-expanding aquarium. Set just off the boardwalk, New York's

Gotham's Gondola Ride

Though the Big Apple is far from any ski slopes, the city boasts its own Swiss-made ski gondola. The **Roosevelt Island tram** is a means of transportation to and from Manhattan for the residents of the tiny island in the middle of the East River. But for kids the tram is a sky-high carnival ride. They love the thrill of being up way above the river, and once the tram reaches its midway peak, you get awesome views of boats plying the waters below and Manhattan's glittering skyline. Once on Roosevelt Island, peek through the window at the tram's Crayola-colored engine room. Your family then can take a stroll around the sleepy island or hop right back on for the return trip. Trams *(212/832-4543)* leave every 15 minutes from *Second Avenue, between 59th and 60th Streets;* round-trip fare is $3.

104-year-old aquarium is the oldest continually operating aquarium in the nation. Recently updated, it is home to sharks, stingrays, beluga whales, and other marine creatures. Bottle-nosed dolphins and barking sea lions put on a show in the 1,600-seat Aquatheater, while playful otters and penguins frolic in the 300-foot

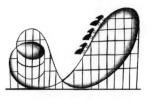

rocky Sea Cliffs exhibit. Kids of all ages will enjoy Discovery Cove, where they can touch live sea stars and horseshoe crabs, compare their body's electrical charges to those of a slithering electric eel, and feel the impact of pounding surf (without getting wet) in Crash Cave. A couple of streets away, Astroland Amusement Park has more than 25 rides, including a dozen kiddie rides. There also are three arcades (which get very crowded during summer months) and two restaurants. Unfortunately, the beach is not highly recommended, as it's not particularly clean. No visit to this playground of the 1920s would be complete without a visit to famous Nathan's hot dog emporium, right on the boardwalk. Open year-round, the aquarium and Coney Island are best visited on summer weekday mornings. Annual events like the Mermaid Parade in late June and the hot dog-eating contest on the Fourth of July are special treats

for older kids. *Aquarium: W. Eighth St. and Surf Ave., Coney Island, Brooklyn; (718) 265-3474.*

Staten Island ★★★/$

A 25-minute ferry ride from Manhattan lands you in the city's quietest borough—Staten Island. The free boat ride alone provides entertainment for kids—it even includes a look at Lady Liberty in the harbor.

Once on the island, two significant attractions are only a short bus ride away (the #40 bus goes to both places). **Snug Harbor Cultural Center** (*1000 Richmond Terrace; 718/448-2500*) features 28 restored 19th-century buildings, including a hands-on children's museum that hosts workshops, storytelling, and free outdoor concerts. Older kids who are studying American history might enjoy a visit to **Historic Richmond Town** (*441 Clarke Ave.; 718/351-1611*). Some of the 27 buildings in the 100-acre village date back 300 years. Demonstrations of baking, carpentry, and other crafts and trades help bring the past to life.

Each of these two journeys into the past can take half a day to thoroughly explore; both in one day may be too much for little legs.

Sheep on the Green

The famed restaurant Tavern on the Green, on the West Side at West 67th Street, was formerly occupied by 200 Central Park sheep. The sheep called the building home from the 1870s to the 1930s until the city parks commissioner decided that the building should be a restaurant.

GET YOUR SOUVENIRS HERE!

NEW YORK is a souvenir hunter's delight. There are countless places to pick up city-themed goodies. The Times Square area is filled with shops selling the obligatory pennants, miniature Statues of Liberty, and a gazillion other items featuring the Big Apple. Be careful: many of these stores are selling inexpensive trinkets with $20 price tags. If you want higher quality mementos, check out the shops in any of the museums.

FAO Schwarz, Toys "R" Us, and **Macy's** and **Bloomingdale's** also sell New York City-related items, and the **Barnes & Noble Superstores** (located throughout the city) have a large selection of books about the city. Sports fans should head for the **Mets Clubhouse Shop** (*E. 54th St., between Lexington and 3rd Aves.*) and the **Yankees Clubhouse Shop** (*E. 59th St., between Park and Lexington Aves.*), baseball memorabilia abound.

In addition to FAO Schwarz (see page 66), your kids will want to make two serious shopping stops:

Toys "R" Us

Just like the giant billboards overhead, in Times Square everything is larger than life, including the massive new Toys "R" Us megastore. Your kids (and you) will stare openmouthed at the 60-foot-high Ferris wheel that greets you upon entering. Kids can climb aboard the seats adorned with *Rugrats, Toy Story,* and others for a ride.

From there it's on to a store that celebrates imagination and the magic of play with a host of theme sections highlighting popular toys, games, action figures, and dolls. Get the camera ready for the animated 20-foot-tall T-rex that stands above the *Jurassic Park* section or stop to admire the giant Lego Lady Liberty before venturing over to the two-story pink Barbie dollhouse. Celebrate *Star Wars* or bask in a land of fuzzy stuffed animals in this three-story complex that's great fun to visit for the grown-ups as well as the kids. Set a spending limit before you enter. *Corner of Broadway and 44th St.; (800) 869-7787.*

The Disney Store

You'll find them on *West 42nd Street, on Fifth Avenue near 55th Street,* and *in Harlem on West 125th.* The Disney Stores (www.disney.com) are entertaining, winning your child's heart with music and imagery, not to mention tons of clothing, toys, posters, jewelry, and other merchandise adorned with the likes of Mickey & Minnie Mouse, Goofy, Snow White, Cinderella, Belle, Simba, Hercules, and Tarzan. The many Disney videos and CDs are here, too. Set a spending limit, or your kids could easily go through their entire vacation allowance here.

Forget traveling in a barrel—boat tours get your family close enough to Niagara Falls to feel the misty spray.

Niagara Falls Region

O NE OF THE WORLD'S natural wonders, Niagara Falls is a favorite of literally millions of tourists worldwide. Over the years, it has also attracted its share of daredevils, from tightrope walkers who crossed above the falls to adventurous souls who plunged into the rapids, protected only by a barrel. For many, it would be their last journey. Others survived, but very much the worse for wear. We, of course, recommend that your family experience the falls from less dangerous, but equally awesome, vantage points: up close and personal on the *Maid of the Mist* boat ride, near the Bridal Veil Falls at Cave of the Winds, or even from above, in a helicopter. You can also enjoy a spectacular vista from the observation tower, and get a different perspective at night, when colored lights illuminate the falls. From mid-May through August, you can catch firework displays on Friday nights, starting at 10 P.M.

Vacationers owe their free, unrestricted views of the falls to landscape architect Frederick Law

THE **FamilyFun** LIST

MUST-SEE · MUST-SEE

Cave of the Winds Tour (page 82)

Maid of the Mist (page 82)

Niagara Falls, Canada
(page 81)

Niagara Reservation State Park
(page 81)

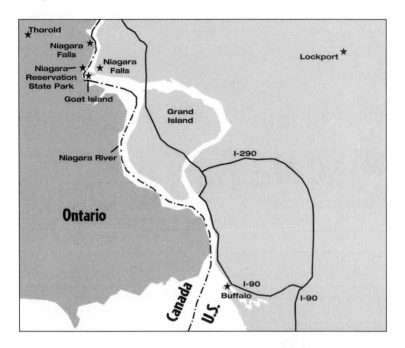

Olmsted, artist Frederick Church, and other members of the "Free Niagara" movement. In the late-19th century, these Americans successfully fought to have New York State purchase the land surrounding the falls from its private owners, remove the buildings on the property, and restore it to its natural state. Before this, anyone who wanted to see the falls had to pay private owners for the right. Even then, they didn't get to see much, only what was visible through holes in a fence.

Today, you and your family can stroll through Niagara Reservation State Park and soak up the sights: the American, or Rainbow, Falls; the Bridal Veil Falls, also in the United States; and the Horseshoe Falls, on the Canadian side.

Canada is just a short walk away, over a bridge, and well worth the trip. In fact, many visitors prefer staying on the Canadian side of the falls. (See "Cross the Border to Fun," on page 79.)

For help planning your trip to the Niagara region, contact the **Niagara Falls Convention & Visitors Bureau** (*310 Fourth St., Niagara Falls, NY 14303; 800/421-5223; 716/285-2400;* www.nfcvb.com). Or get information from the **Niagara County Department of Planning, Development & Tourism** (*139 Niagara St., Lockport, NY 14094-2740; 800/338-7890;* www.niagarausa.com).

CULTURAL ADVENTURES

Albright-Knox Art Gallery
★★★/$

One of the oldest art galleries in the nation, this small, two-story museum is known for its contemporary collection, including pieces by Dali, Gauguin, Matisse, Monet, Picasso, and more modern artists such as Andy Warhol. But for kids, the highlight is the "Mirrored Room," by artist Lucas Samaras. Kids walk into an eight-by-ten-foot room that's completely mirrored—all four walls, ceiling, and floor—and is empty save for a table and chairs. Kids take off their shoes, walk right in, and marvel at the never-ending series of reflections. They'll also go for the Interactive Room, where they can try their hands at some activity related to a current exhibition. Start your visit at the information desk and ask for a Family Guide, which points out those works most enjoyed by children. But be sure the kids see at least some of the permanent collection, which showcases art from 3000 B.C. to the present. The oldest piece is a small (less than eight inches tall) Mesopotamian sculpture. Don't plan on spending more than 30 to 45 minutes here, unless you sign up for a family activity. These are held throughout the year and include performances and hands-on art projects. Call ahead to see what's scheduled during your visit. The on-site Garden Restaurant has a children's menu and serves lunch and snacks. The gift shop features a large selection of children's books and toys for kids of all ages. Open Tuesday through Sunday year-round. *1285 Elmwood Ave., Buffalo; (716) 882-8700;* www.albright knox.org

Play **Mad, Sad, Glad** during dinner to see how everybody's day went. Take turns describing something that made you mad, sad, and glad during the day.

Buffalo & Erie County Naval & Military Park
★/$$

Got military buffs in the family? Then march on over to this park, where you can tour a guided missile cruiser, a destroyer, and a World War II submarine. This attraction is more suited to older kids; younger ones tend to be overwhelmed by the sheer size of the ships. For them, the smaller, more manageable submarine is the best bet. You can also check out an Air Force fighter jet, a tank, and exhibits inside the museum. Open daily, April through October, and on weekends in November. *One Naval Park Cove, Buffalo; (716) 847-1773;* www.buffalo navalpark.org

Buffalo Museum of Science
★★★/$

Kids love mummies, so head directly for Whem Ankh: the Cycle of Life in Ancient Egypt, an exhibit that offers a glimpse of Egyptian family life more than 2,000 years ago. The family is that of Nes-hor, a priest who lived on the east bank of the Nile River in northeastern Africa during the second century B.C. You enter the exhibit through the courtyard of Nes-hor's house and tour parts of the home, the Temple of Min where he served as a priest, and the Hall of Judgment where the Egyptians believed the dead were judged by the gods. Along the way, you'll see more than 250 artifacts, including toys, pottery, and those vital mummies (plus a coffin).

Other permanent, kid-friendly exhibits cover dinosaurs, insects, gems and minerals, and zoology. You'll see specimens from all over the world, although one room in the Hall of Evolution is devoted exclusively to creatures from the Niagara region. Stop by in the evening, when the observatory offers evening star-viewing in winter, spring, and fall, and sun shows during the summer. Check the traveling exhibits, too; the museum has special hands-on kids' programs that relate to them. In a recent exhibit, for example, robotic reptiles and insects were on display. As part of the permanent exhibits, Insects: Magnified and Magnificent features models of insects, enlarged to show details oth-erwise seen only with magnifica-tion. Call to find out what's sched-uled during your visit. There's a gift shop, but no restaurant. Open Tuesday through Sunday year-round. *1020 Humboldt Pkwy., Buffalo; (716) 896-5200;* www.buf falomuseumofscience.org

Niagara Wax Museum of History ★/$

The history of Niagara Falls is told through 46 exhibits, maps, and dis-plays. You'll see life-size wax figures of famous explorers and statesmen, barrels used by the daredevils who flung themselves into the falls, street scenes from the past, and Native American villages. You'll also learn about the falls' important role as a source of hydroelectric power. This place is best for kids 8 and up. They'll flip over the daredevils' barrels. The attached souvenir shop has the usual: postcards, mugs, spoons, T-shirts, and more. Open daily year-round. *303 Prospect St., Niagara Falls; (716) 285-1271.*

JUST FOR FUN

Aquarium of Niagara ★★★/$$

The world's first inland aquarium (founded in 1965) is home to more than 1,500 creatures, including sharks, piranhas, eels, and endan-gered Peruvian penguins. It also boasts the largest collection of fish from the Great Lakes. In the center

CROSS THE BORDER TO FUN

Cross the bridge into Canada, and your Niagara Falls vacation becomes an international adventure. The falls are just as spectacular on the Canadian side, and breathtaking views are available 775 feet up at the **Skylon tower** (*5200 Robinson St., Niagara Falls, Ontario; 905/356-2651*; www.skylon.com). Closer to the Falls, you can ride the *Maid of the Mist* boat ride (*5920 River Rd., Niagara Falls, Ontario; 905/358-5781*) or, at Niagara-on-the-Lake (*17 miles north of Niagara Falls, Ontario*), experience the thrilling **Whirlpool Jet Boat Tours** (*61 Melville St., Niagara-on-the-Lake, Ontario; 905/468-4800; call for reservations*; www.whirlpooljet.com).

Along Clifton Falls, visit **Ripley's Believe It or Not Museum** (*905/356-2238*); **Louis Tussaud's Waxworks** (*905/374-6601*); **Guinness World Records Museum** (*905/356-2299*; www.guinnessniagarafalls.com); **Movieland Museum of Stars** (*905/358-3061*); **The House of Frankenstein** (*905/357-9660*; www.travelinx.com); and **Cinema 180° Adventure Dome, Fun House, and The Haunted House** (*905/357-4330, ext. 6621*; www.falls.com for all three attractions).

One mile from the Falls, you'll find the **Marineland Theme Park** (*7657 Portage Rd., Niagara Falls, Ontario; 905/356-9565*; www.marinelandcanada.com; open May to mid-October), where kids can touch beluga and killer whales, feed fish, feed deer, and see black bears and elk. Marineland also boasts the world's largest steel roller coaster.

If you decide to stay on the Canadian side, you have plenty of choices. Familiar names include **Best Western Fallsview** (*6289 Fallsview Blvd., Niagara Falls, Ontario; 800/263-2580*; www.infoniagara.com/d-best western.html), **Sheraton Fallsview Hotel & Conference Centre** (*6755 Fallsview Blvd., Niagara Falls, Ontario; 800/267-8439; 905/374-1077*; www.fallsview.com), **Niagara Falls Marriott Fallsview** (*6740 Fallsview Blvd., Niagara Falls, Ontario; 888/501-8916*; www.niagarafallsmarriott.com), and **Days Inn** Fallsview District (*6408 Stanley Ave., Niagara Falls, Ontario; 905/356-5877; reservations: 800/263-2522*; www.niagarafallsdaysinn.com). **AN ADDED BONUS:** If the exchange rate is still in your favor, everything will be more affordable here.

For help planning your trip to Niagara Falls, Ontario, contact the **Niagara Economic and Tourism Corporation**, *2201 St. David's Rd., P.O. Box 1042, Thorold, Ontario, Canada L2V 4T7; (800) 263-2988; (905) 984-3626;* www.tourismniagara.com

of the aquarium is a giant circular tank where California sea lions frolic. Upstairs, kids can uncover fascinating fish facts by lifting the flaps at the "Small Fry Fun Stations." Presentations are scheduled throughout the day and include sea lion demonstrations, penguin feedings, shark feedings, and harbor seal sessions. Open daily year-round. The aquarium is just a short walk from Niagara Falls, but free parking is available for those who prefer to drive. *701 Whirlpool St., Niagara Falls; (800) 500-4609; (716) 285-3575;* www.aquariumofniagara.org

Buffalo Zoo ★★★/$$

Officially known as the Buffalo Zoological Gardens, the nation's third-oldest zoo boasts some 1,000 animals on 23^1/$_2$ acres. Expect to spend half a day checking out the Siberian tigers and Asian elephants, king cobras and scheltopusisks (limbless lizards), and much more. Kids can pet Guinea hogs and other critters in the Children's Zoo. On weekends beginning in May, take the kids to the W.I.L.D. (Wildlife in Live Demonstrations) Place, where they can help bathe the elephants, watch birds in flight, have a "cat chat" with an African wildcat known as a serval, and even see an elephant paint with its trunk. The younger kids can imitate animal behavior and try their hands at interactive exhibits in the W.O.W. (World of Wildlife) Discovery Center, and the whole family can get close to giraffes at the Giraffe Feeding Station. Large, colorful birds will perch right by you at one of the new exhibits, Lorikeet Landing. Food is available at the "Beastro," and gifts at the "Zootique." Special events are held periodically; call ahead to find out what's scheduled during your visit. The zoo is open year-round, but

---

Counting the Miles

Last summer, we set out on our first big road trip. To get us through the first long day of driving (500 miles), I strung a long string with a marble-size bead for every 25 miles we would travel. Every fourth bead was a white bead. As we completed each 25 miles, the children moved a bead to the other end of the string. Our children could visualize how far we had to go by how many beads were left. After 100 miles, the white bead was moved, signaling a treat from Mom's Bag. Every day, our kids stayed occupied counting the beads, comparing how far we had come to how far we had to go. Our first grader added the 25's and informed us often of our progress.

Jane Rice, Maple Grove, Minnesota

dress accordingly in cooler months (Buffalo gets pretty nippy). Keep in mind, too, that some animals, such as giraffes, may stay indoors when the weather is bad. Choose a sunny day to see a greater variety of creatures. *300 Parkside Ave., Buffalo; (716) 837-3900;* www.buffalozoo.org

Martin's Fantasy Island
★★★/$$

Just eight miles from Niagara Falls, this amusement park offers more than 100 rides and attractions, most geared to children 11 or younger. The park's latest addition is the Silver Comet roller coaster, billed as Niagara's Newest Fall and modeled after the famous Comet of the former Crystal Beach Amusement Park in Ontario. Although not identical to its predecessor, the Silver Comet has the same look and feel, in part because of its steel construction, wooden track, and 95-foot drop. Other big kid rides include the Wildcat Coaster, the Giant Gondola Wheel, a log flume, and the Up, Up & Away Balloon.

There are kiddie rides, too, plus a wave pool, water slides, a lazy river ride, and a wading pool. Try the puppet show for the little kids; older family members may prefer the Musical Review Extravaganza, with music from the 1950s and 1960s. The whole family will go for the Wild West Shoot-Out. Check on-line for coupons. Open weekends from late May to mid-June; daily from mid-June through Labor Day.

2400 Grand Island Blvd., Grand Island; (716) 773-7591.

Niagara Falls, Canada
FamilyFun ★★★★/Free-$$$

There's lots to see and do north of the border—and visiting another country is just one of them. For more information, see "Cross the Border to Fun" on page 79.

Niagara Reservation State Park
FamilyFun ★★★★/Free

Located on the American side of Niagara Falls, this is the oldest and most visited state park in the United States. Established in 1885, the park covers 435 acres, approximately 300 of which are underwater. Nourished by spray and mist from the falls, the remaining 100-acre preserve includes the Great Lakes Garden, plus miles of trails and picnic areas. The park consists of a mainland area and five islands on the Niagara River. To reach the largest, Goat Island, cross the short bridge either on foot or by car.

Here you'll find the popular Cave of the Winds tour (*see below*) and the Top of the Falls restaurant (see Good Eats). Located between the Canadian and American Falls, Goat Island also has awesome views. In the Prospect Point area of the park, you'll find the Observation Tower (*see below*), the *Maid of the Mist* boat ride (*see below*), and the visitors' center. The center has information and exhibits about the history and geology of the falls, plus material on area attractions. Worth seeing are the 20-minute feature film *Niagara: A History of the Falls* and a virtual-reality helicopter simulator ride. The footage on the latter is a bit dated, but it's still fun.

If your kids are younger and more likely to get tired, pick up the Viewmobile, a tram that takes you on a three-mile guided tour, complete with stops at six scenic spots. Once you buy your ticket, you can get on or off as much as you like throughout the day. Admission to the park is free, but there are fees for the various attractions. Open year-round. *Prospect St., Niagara Falls; (716) 278-1796* or *(716) 278-1770*; http://nys parks.state.ny.us/

Cave of the Winds Tour
FamilyFun ★★★★/$$

Trade in your shoes and socks for slip-proof footwear, don a yellow slicker, and prepare to soak up the falls in the truest sense. Your family will take an elevator down 175 feet into the Niagara Gorge, and follow your guide over a series of wooden decks. The high point of the journey is the Hurricane Deck, beneath the Bridal Veil Falls, where the more daring in your group can stand and get drenched by the cataract. If you'd just as soon skip the soaking, bypass the deck. **NOTE:** The decks can be slippery, so be careful and make sure everyone uses the hand railings. For safety reasons, kids must be at least 42 inches tall to take

the tour. Despite the name, there's no cave here; it collapsed back in 1920. This attraction is seasonal: because they wouldn't survive the harsh Niagara winters, the wooden decks are taken apart in October and reassembled each spring. Call for days and hours, which depend, in part, upon the weather. *On Goat Island, Niagara Reservation State Park; (716) 278-1730.*

Maid of the Mist
FamilyFun ★★★★/$$

One of Niagara Falls' best bets, this boat tour has been attracting visitors since 1846. The adventure begins when you and the kids slip into blue plastic ponchos and climb aboard the *Maid of the Mist*, which will take you almost face-to-face with the rushing waters. You hear the thunder of the falls, feel their mist upon your face and, for the first time, truly appreciate the power of the millions of gallons of water cascading from above. The ride does have its frightening moments, especially as you near the base of the Horseshoe Falls. Even so, all but the very young will love every minute. (All *Maid of the Mist* boats bear the name "Maid of the Mist," followed by a number—which has nothing to do with the number of boats in the fleet. Instead, it reflects the model of the boat. The numbers were added in 1955, when the fifth version of the boat was introduced and called *Maid of the*

Mist I. Maid of the Mist VI was introduced in 1990, and *Maid of the Mist VII* in 1997.) Boats run May through late October, departing every 15 minutes. *Board at the Prospect Point Observation Tower, Niagara Reservation State Park; (716) 284-8897;* www.maidofthemist.com

Prospect Point
Observation Tower ★★★/$
Ride the glass-walled elevator to the tower's observation platform for a spectacular view 100 feet above the gorge. Then, travel 180 feet down to the base of the American Falls, where you can board the *Maid of the Mist* for a boat tour. Open year-round. *In Niagara Reservation State Park.*

Rainbow Air, Inc.
★★★/$$$$
Get a bird's-eye view of Niagara Falls aboard a Rainbow Air helicopter. During the half-hour trip you'll soar from 500 to 2,500 feet and catch sight of all three falls, the control gates, and surrounding attractions. On a clear day you can see as far as Toronto, Canada. Helicopters hold four passengers, plus the pilot. Depending on their size, kids (of all ages) may ride for half price. (This trip, of course, is not a good idea for either kids or parents who get motion sickness or are afraid of heights.) Weather permitting, open daily from May through October; weekends in November. *454 Main St., Niagara Falls; (716) 284-2800.*

BUNKING DOWN

NOTE: For more information about camping in the Niagara Falls Region, see "Calling All Campers" on page 120.

Comfort Inn The Pointe
★★/$–$$$
If your kids can live without a pool or game room, this clean, comfortable inn is a great base of operations. The location is first-rate: within walking distance of Niagara Falls, plus it has kid-friendly restaurants. A small retail complex is right outside the lobby. Other selling points: children under 18 stay free in their parents' room, and continental breakfast is included in the rate. *1 Prospect Pointe, Niagara Falls; (800) 284-6835; (716) 284-6835;* www.comfortinn.com/hotel/ny412

FamilyFun SNACK

Cereal Solution
Before you leave on vacation, empty all your cereal boxes and create this snack mix.

In a large bowl, combine 3 cups of assorted cereals with ⅓ cup each of raisins, peanuts, and pretzels. Melt 4 ounces of white chocolate according to package directions and stir it into the cereal mixture until the bits are well coated. Chill for 20 to 30 minutes. Place in ziplock bags.

Four Points by Sheraton Niagara Falls ★★/$-$$$

A small but accommodating hotel, the Four Points Sheraton has some kid pleasers: an indoor jungle gym with five slides, an indoor heated pool, a game room, and table tennis and pool. Rooms are air-conditioned and outfitted with two double beds and cable TV. *114 Buffalo Ave., Niagara Falls; (800) 325-3535; (716) 285-2521;* www.fourpoints.com/

Holiday Inn Niagara Falls at the Falls ★★/$-$$

Just two blocks from the falls and other major attractions, this Holiday Inn features a large indoor heated pool, a game room, and an outdoor playground with slide and swings. A family of four will fit comfortably in a standard room with two queen-size beds and cable TV. Breakfast, lunch, and dinner are available at the on-site Denny's Restaurant. *231 Third St., Niagara Falls; (800) 955-2211 (reservations only); (716) 282-2211;* www.holiday-inn.com/niagarany

Holiday Inn Select ★★★/$-$$$

You'll find all the creature (and kid) comforts at this six-story hotel: a heated, skylit indoor pool; a game room; a fitness center; a gift shop, newsstand, and post office; pay-per-view movies and Nintendo rentals; plus an on-site restaurant with kid-pleasing fare. The rooms are over-sized, so a standard room with two double beds easily accommodates a family of four—and kids stay free with their parents. For a little more money, you can opt for a suite with separate living and sleeping areas. The kids will like the pool's retractable dome, which makes it sheltered in winter and outdoors in summer. Kids dine free with their parents at Phin's restaurant, and can choose from typical favorites such as grilled cheese, chicken fingers, and pizza. Located in downtown Niagara Falls, the hotel is right next to the aquarium and a five-minute walk from the falls. *300 Third St., Niagara Falls; (800) 95-FALLS (reservations only); (716) 285-3361;* www.bassho tels.com/holiday-inn/

ALTHOUGH IT IS ILLEGAL to go over Niagara Falls (and punishable by a maximum fine of $10,000), 15 people have attempted the stunt. Ten survived the trip, including 7-year-old Roger Woodward, who went over accidentally. The boat he was riding in flipped over in the rapids above the falls. Amazingly, the boy was not injured.

Quality Hotel & Suites at the Falls ★★★/$-$$

The oversized rooms at this refurbished hotel are perfect for families, plus it's only one block from Niagara Falls. Renovated in 2000, all 209 rooms have been updated, and family suites and an indoor children's playland have been added. There's also a heated indoor pool, an arcade, and an on-site restaurant. A family of four can stay comfortably in a standard room with two double beds. If you'd like more space, try the two-bedroom family suite. One side is furnished with a king-size bed; the other has children's decor and two double beds. *240 Rainbow Blvd., Niagara Falls; (716) 282-1212; www.qualityniagarafalls.com*

GOOD EATS

Como Restaurant and Delicatessen ★★★/$$$

The Antonacci family, which has run this restaurant since 1927, insists on making everything from scratch, from the pastas and sauces to the breads and desserts. Even the meat is cut to the chef's specifications in the restaurant's own butcher shop. Italian fare definitely dominates, but the eight-page menu lists plenty of traditional American dishes as well. Adult entrées include tenderloin alla marsala, filet of sole alla francesca, and New York strip steak. The kids' menu features spaghetti and meatballs, cheese ravi-

oli, a hot meatball sandwich, mozzarella sticks, chicken fingers, and more. Brunch is served on Sunday. Reservations are suggested. Takeout food is available in the deli. *2220 Pine Ave., Niagara Falls; (716) 285-9341; www.thecomorestaurant.com or www.fallscasino.com/como*

Goose's Roost Family Restaurant ★★/$$

You'll feel right at home at this casual, affordable restaurant, where you can get everything from salads and cold platters to sandwiches, hamburgers, and Italian dinners—and breakfast. Like the Como Restaurant and Delicatessen, this eatery is owned by the Antonacci family. Kids' choices include spaghetti and meatball, grilled cheese, hamburger, hot dogs, fish sandwiches, and chicken fingers. Two locations: *343 Fourth St., Niagara Falls, (716) 282-6255; and 10158 Niagara Falls Blvd., Niagara Falls; (716) 297-7497; www.fallscasino.com/goose/*

Hard Rock Café ★★★/$$

Your kids will spot the psychedelic Cadillac sticking out of the roof immediately. In typical Hard Rock fashion, the interior walls are adorned with gold records, instruments, clothing, and other memorabilia from rock legends such as John Lennon and Elvis Presley, as well as current groups such as the Goo Goo Dolls. Your kids may be too young to recognize the rock and roll icons, but they'll get a

A Master of a Deal

Families can save on **Niagara Reservation State Park** attractions by purchasing a Master Pass, good for discounts of 25 percent or more on some of the most popular spots. Available for $21 per adult, $16 for children 6 to 12, and free for those 5 and younger, a Master Pass includes admission to the following:

◆ Prospect Point Observation Tower with its awesome Falls view.

◆ Viewmobile transportation and guided tour of the park.

◆ Cave of the Winds adventure.

◆ Festival Theater in the visitors' center, where you'll see the 20-minute film *Niagara: A History of the Falls*.

◆ Schoellkopf Geological Museum, with exhibits on the Falls' history and geological formations.

◆ *Maid of the Mist* boat ride.

◆ Aquarium of Niagara.

For more information on Master Pass, call *(716) 278-1770* or, during your trip, stop by the visitors' center in Niagara Reservation State Park. You can buy your pass at any park attraction.

kick out of the decorations just the same. Adult fare includes "Really Big Sandwiches" plus beef, chicken, seafood, and pasta dishes. The kids' menu offers macaroni and cheese, hamburgers, hot dogs, grilled cheese, and pizza. You can, if you let yourself be talked into it, buy Hard Rock T-shirts (popular with preteens) and other souvenirs at the on-site store. *333 Prospect St., Niagara Falls; (716) 282-0007;* www.hardrock.com

Tommy Ryan's Rock and Roll Diner ★★/$$

The food may be typical diner fare, but the decor definitely is not. The booths with mini jukeboxes are neat, but the real kid pleaser is a train that rides on tracks that are suspended just beneath the ceiling. The glass tabletops display photos of 1950s and 1960s legends, and the walls are chock-full of memorabilia, including wings from a 1950s Chevy. Dine inside or out; choices range from finger food and sandwiches to complete dinners. The kids' menu offers typical favorites. Closed January and February. *1 Prospect Point, Niagara Falls; (716) 282-5025.*

Top of the Falls Restaurant ★★/$-$$

This restaurant serves up views of the falls from every seat. Adults can order everything from hot and cold sandwiches to pasta, steak, chicken, fish, and vegetarian dishes. Young diners can order from the kids' menu, which features all the usual suspects, or select one of the appetizers such as Buffalo wings, mozzarella sticks, or a basket of fries. Consider the Dinner and Dazzle package, complete with dinner here, a night tour of Cave of the Winds, and fireworks-viewing from the base of the gorge, offered Friday night. For information, call *(716) 278-1730.* Top of the Falls Restaurant is open for lunch and dinner from Mother's Day to Labor Day. Reservations are accepted, but not required. **NOTE:** A 15 percent gratuity is added to every check. *At Terrapin Point on Goat Island; (716) 278-0348.*

SOUVENIR HUNTING

Artisans Alley

Whether you want a small treasure to take home or a more expensive collectible, chances are you'll find it here. Artisans Alley specializes in American crafts made from natural materials. Items include jewelry, pottery, stoneware, toys and games, wall hangings, paintings, musical instruments, and holiday ornaments. Open daily year-round. *10 Rainbow Blvd., Niagara Falls; (800) 635-1457; (716) 282-0196.*

Honeymoon Capital Souvenirs

Trendy, custom-designed T-shirts are a big item here, as are books, maps, place mats, and prints of Niagara Falls. You'll find clothing in sizes from infants to XXXL.

Saltwater taffy and maple products are also available. In the summer, you can rent bicycles, strollers, and wagons here. Open daily, year-round. *16 Rainbow Blvd., Niagara Falls; (716) 285-6117.*

Prime Outlets

With 150 outlet shops, this mall (about a 15-minute drive from the falls) has something for everyone. Brand-name clothes outlets include Carter's for Kids, Old Navy, the Gap, Calvin Klein, Guess, and Oshkosh. The kids will want to check out the Kay-Bee Toy outlet; souvenirs of Niagara Falls can be had at CT News and Green Onion. You'll also find a food court and two sit-down chain restaurants: Applebee's and Red Lobster. Open daily year-round. *1900 Military Rd., Niagara Falls; (716) 297-2022;* www.primeoutlets.com

Three Sisters Trading Post

As its name suggests, this shop is owned by three sisters, who stock it with a variety of souvenirs, jewelry and leather items, Native American artwork, and T-shirts and sweatshirts for people of all ages. If you want souvenirs with images of the falls—mugs, magnets, clocks, piggy banks, and candles—you'll find them here. But there's also a nice selection of home decor items, local artwork, and gifts inspired by nature. Open daily Memorial Day to Christmas. *454 Main St., Niagara Falls; (716) 284-3689.*

Lake Placid, famous as the site of two Winter Olympic Games, is also a wilderness of summer hiking and fishing opportunities.

Lake Placid

O NE OF THE NATION's first resort areas, Lake Placid has a stunning natural setting and as much year-round fun as any vacationing family could ask for. The quaint village earned international renown as the host of two Winter Olympic Games (in 1932 and 1980), a distinction shared by only two other communities: Innsbruck, Austria, and St. Moritz, Switzerland. The Olympic venues constructed for those events now double as some of the world's premiere sporting facilities—and some of upstate New York's most fascinating tourist attractions. At the MacKenzie-Intervale Ski Jumping Complex, for example, Nordic skiers practice their jumps atop a 90-meter hill during the summer, landing on a special, plastic-covered hill. (For more information, see "Passport to Fun—And Savings" on page 95). If you and yours want to be participants, not merely observers, make tracks for the only dedicated bobsled run in the United States and rocket down in the company of professional

THE FamilyFun LIST

MUST-SEE MUST-SEE

Cloudsplitter **Scenic Gondola Ride** (page 92)

High Falls Gorge (page 93)

MacKenzie-Intervale Ski Jumping Complex (page 94)

Summer Storm (page 96)

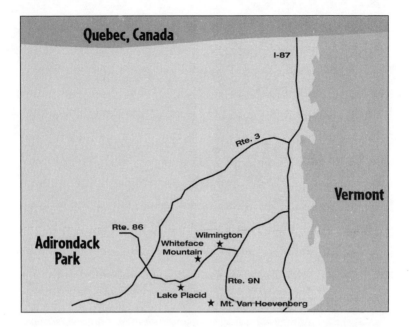

drivers and brakemen. (Your preteen speed demons will always remember this as the highlight of their vacation.)

For a rush of a different sort, head to High Falls Gorge, where even your smallest children will be awestruck as they watch the Ausable River catapult over rocks and cliffs on its journey north to the Atlantic Ocean. Like so many outdoor sights here, the gorge will instill (or reinforce) in your children (and you) both a love of nature and a desire to protect and preserve it for future travelers.

Lake Placid offers simpler pleasures. In winter, you can take to the ice and skate on Mirror Lake or sign on for a dogsled or toboggan ride. If you're downhill and cross-country skiers, you'll find your share of trails here (see "A World-Class Ski (and More!) Destination," page 98), as well as terrain for snowshoeing. For a relaxing walk, try the two-and-seven-tenths-mile path around the lake. When the weather heats up, you and yours can fish, swim, or sail in sight of the Adirondacks. Looking for more civilized diversions? There's always Main Street, home to some 100 shops and boutiques, a movie theater, and your choice of family-friendly restaurants.

With its combination of summer adventures, fall foliage, and winter sports, Lake Placid is a year-round resort. If you're not skiers, your family will probably prefer a summer visit—the season that offers the broadest range of events and activities here. Black-fly season runs from mid-May to mid-July, typically peaking around Memorial Day weekend. Most Lake Placid communities treat the area in the spring, with good results. Still, you may want to pack insect repellent or buy combination sunscreen repellent.

For help with planning your Lake Placid vacation, contact the **Lake Placid/Essex County Convention and Visitors Bureau** (*Olympic Center, 216 Main St., Lake Placid, NY 12946-1592; 800/447-5224;* www.lakeplacid.com).

CULTURAL ADVENTURES

John Brown Farm
State Historic Site ★★★/$
After abolitionist John Brown, of Harper's Ferry fame, was hanged in Virginia on December 2, 1859, his body was sent here to be buried in front of his New York home. Interred along with Brown are ten others who died with him in the struggle to end slavery. Three signs posted on the site describe the graveyard, the Brown family and its history in the home, and changes made to the grounds over the years. The historic wood-sided Adirondack farmhouse is furnished as it would have been in 1859, the year of the raid on Harper's Ferry. Tour guides point out repro-

ductions of period furniture and clothing, including items assembled in preparation for Martha Brewster Brown's first baby. Typically, your kids will be most interested in the schoolbooks and slate used by the young Brown children. You're welcome to take self-guided tours of the 270-acre site, which is dotted with "glacial erratica"—giant round boulders that kids can climb on and slide down. Frogs and ponds are abundant, and nature trail maps can guide you on a ten- to fifteen-minute woodland walk. **NOTE:** Before your visit, tell the kids something—however simple—about John Brown. With even the most basic explanation—that Brown believed everyone deserved respect, and it was wrong to own another person—they'll learn a lot more from their visit. The grounds are open daily year-round; the historic house is open Wednesday through Sunday, May through October. *2 John Brown Rd., Lake Placid; (518) 523-3900;* www.nysparks.com/hist/

1932 and 1980
Lake Placid Olympic Center
and Museum ★★/$
Flags from around the world beckon you to this impressive facility, which is perhaps best known as the site of the 1980 "Miracle on Ice," the U.S. Olympic hockey team's dramatic victory over the Russian team. Just inside the box office entrance to the center is the 1932

and 1980 Lake Placid Winter Olympic Museum, where you'll see photos, videos, and exhibits on the feats of the III and XIII Olympic Games. Lake Placid's own athletes are celebrated in a special gallery of "hometown heroes." In the Olympic center the walls are lined with photos and plaques from past Olympics. Elite figure skaters, hockey players, and speed skaters from around the world practice and compete here year-round, so you may have the chance to watch a future Olympian in action. You can see them anytime, most days as early as 8 A.M. and as late as 10 A.M. Your young skaters can even take to the ice themselves (skate rentals are available; there's a fee; call for the public skating schedule). The center often hosts ice shows and exhibition games on Saturday nights in the summer; call for tickets and information. *Main St., Lake Placid; (800) 462-6236; (518) 523-1655; www.orda.org/olympcenter.html*

Young & Fun, Lake Placid Center for the Arts
★★★/Free

These free, live shows are geared toward children ages 3 to 12, but anyone who's young at heart will enjoy them. The intimate, 355-seat theater is the ideal showcase for the performances, which often feature local performers. Past productions have included the Zucchini Brothers musical trio; the Lake Placid

Sinfonietta performing Peter and the Wolf; Roy Hurd, the best-known singer-songwriter in the Adirondacks; the Red Wing Puppet Theater; and the Rebecca Kelly Ballet. The curtain goes up at 10:30 A.M. on Wednesday and Friday in July and August. The shows are popular, and seating is limited, so it's best to arrive no later than 10:15 A.M. *91 Saranac Ave., Lake Placid; (518) 523-2512; www.lpartscenter.org*

JUST FOR FUN

Cloudsplitter Scenic Gondola Ride
★★★★/$$

Billed as the newest and most scenic gondola in North America, the *Cloudsplitter* will whisk your family from the base lodge to the top of Whiteface's smaller, 3,600-foot peak known as Little Whiteface, in minutes. (The enclosed gondola cars hold eight passengers each and are safe for children of all ages.) Along the way you'll soar over ski trails and woods and enjoy a bird's-eye view of the Adirondack peaks, the Ausable River, the Olympic Jumping Complex, and more. At the summit, you can visit the observation deck, then sit at a picnic table and soak in the view. **NOTE:** There are no rest rooms, just port-a-potties. Open daily, mid-June to early October; call for spring hours. *Rte. 86, Whiteface Mountain; (518) 946-2223.*

High Falls Gorge
FamilyFun ★★★★/$$

More than one billion years in the making, High Falls Gorge is that rarest of attractions, one that's guaranteed to amaze every member of your family, no matter how young or old. Granted, preschoolers may not be interested in the facts. They won't care that you're standing in a "mature climax forest" or that 71 million gallons of water cascade over the falls each day. But they will grasp the immensity of the falls when they witness the Ausable River raging through the ancient granite cliffs. They'll marvel at the enormous anorthosite boulder (more than four feet high and six to seven feet across), and they'll clamor for a second look at the deepest pothole in the Adirondacks (over 35 feet deep and seven feet wide). The self-guided tour offers just the right amount of information through strategically placed signs and listening posts where you can press a button to hear more about the scenery around you. The paths are groomed and separated from the gorge by wire fences and wooden railings that ensure your safety (and that of even the youngest children) without obscuring your view. If you visit at lunchtime, you can eat at the Drumming Partridge Restaurant.

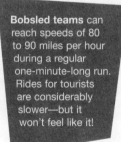

Bobsled teams can reach speeds of 80 to 90 miles per hour during a regular one-minute-long run. Rides for tourists are considerably slower—but it won't feel like it!

Better yet, order a picnic lunch from the restaurant, or bring your own, and enjoy it at one of the riverside picnic tables. **NOTE:** The restaurant is only open seasonally—from Memorial Day through Columbus Day. *Rte. 86, Wilmington, eight miles east of Lake Placid; (518) 946-2278; www.highfallsgorge.com*

Lake Placid Marina Tour Boat Cruises ★★/$$

When everyone's ready to kick back and relax for a while, hop on a turn-of-the-century craft for a tour that takes you around Lake Placid on an hourlong cruise. The wooden boat is enclosed and encircled by windows, so you and your children can admire the view in comfort and safety, rain or shine. Your guide will tell you about the homes that dot the shore, the water itself, the surrounding mountains, and native wildlife during your 16-mile journey— with a few jokes thrown in. Boats typically depart at 10:30 A.M., and 1, 2:30, and 4 P.M. in the summer, less frequently in spring and fall, but call ahead for the schedule just to be sure. Reservations are accepted only for parties of ten or more, so arrive 20 to 30 minutes ahead of time. There's no food service on the boat, but you can bring picnic snacks for the kids. *Mirror Lake Dr., Lake Placid; (518) 523-9704.*

FamilyFun GAME

A Tougher Tic-tac-toe

Make the classic game of tic-tac-toe a little more lively and a bit tougher with this one basic change: with each turn, a player can fill in the empty space of his choice with either an X or an O.

MUST-SEE FamilyFun MacKenzie-Intervale Ski Jumping Complex MUST-SEE ★★★★/$$

The 90- and 120-meter ski jump towers that loom over Lake Placid have become as much a part of the Adirondack landscape as the high peaks themselves. Built for the 1980 winter games, these massive structures stand as monuments to the Olympic spirit. In summer, the 90-meter hill is outfitted with special porcelain and plastic coverings that enable Nordic jump training and competitions to be held all season long. For a skier's view, take the chairlift and elevator to the top of the 26-story, 120-meter jump. After you catch your breath, revel in some of the most spectacular scenery in the Northeast. Beside the towers is the Kodak Sports Park, where freestyle aerial skiers literally make a splash. They can jump on trampolines and launching pads, then flip, twist, and spin in midair before landing in a 750,000-gallon pool. The kids are sure to be wowed. Call ahead for training and exhibition times. The sports park is open daily mid-May through mid-October; the towers are also open daily mid-December through mid-March. *Rte. 73, Lake Placid; (518) 523-2202;* www.orda.org

Mirror Lake ★★/Free

Mom and Dad can enjoy the view of the mountains while the kids play in the sand or cool off in this spring-fed lake in the heart of Lake Placid Village. When the youngsters get restless, talk them into joining you on the 2.7-mile walk around the lake. Or head into the village for a treat at one of the many restaurants and specialty shops. *Off Mirror Lake Dr., Mirror Lake, Lake Placid; (518) 523-2999.*

Santa's Workshop, North Pole, New York ★★/$$$

Your little ones will love America's oldest theme park, where they can visit with Santa and his helpers and watch them at work. Best for kids ages 3 to 10, this attraction combines rides, shows, a petting zoo, and a storybook-style village. Kids can climb aboard the Candy Cane Express train or sit atop reindeer on the carousel. They can feed the Three Little Pigs and Santa's reindeer, and enjoy a Nativity pageant. For an additional fee, youngsters can attend Elfin Training School, where they make a holiday ornament, rehearse and present a Christmas play. Can't get enough of Santa? Head to the park before it opens and join him for breakfast at Mother Hubbard's, the

PASSPORT TO FUN—AND SAVINGS

I F YOU PLAN ON VISITING more than two Olympic venues, an **Olympic Sites Passport** will save you money and give your kids a chance to Go for the Gold. Passports cost $16 apiece (free for children 6 and under) and entitle the bearer to one-time admission to four of the most popular Olympic attractions. Along with the passport, those ages 4 to 14 receive a Go for the Gold game card. Kids who complete it correctly earn a souvenir worth keeping: a gold medal emblazoned with the Lake Placid logo and the Olympic rings.

Your passport provides admission to the following (for descriptions, see pages 91, 92, 94, and 97):

♦ MacKenzie-Intervale Ski Jumping Complex, including the elevator to the 26-story SkyDeck
♦ 1932 and 1980 Lake Placid Olympic Center and Museum
♦ Verizon Sports Complex
♦ Either the *Cloudsplitter* Scenic Gondola Ride or the Whiteface Mountain Veterans Memorial Highway

Each stop also holds the key to three of 15 questions that kids must answer correctly to earn their gold medal. Questions are presented in a multiple-choice format, and some of the proposed answers are bound to produce a chuckle. (For example, the question, "What is the purpose of the summit light at the top of Whiteface?" includes these two answer choices: "to beam in spaceships" and "to keep away bugs.")

Passports and Go for the Gold game cards are available June through October and may be purchased at any Olympic attraction, the Olympic Center Box Office, and many area hotels, motels, and campgrounds. You'll also receive discount coupons to other Olympic attractions. Special events and weather may affect operations, so call ahead: *(800) 462-6236; (518) 523-1655.*

Mom and Dad: since Lake Placid is Olympic central, why not impress your kids with your knowledge of the conversion from meters (used in the Olympics) to feet/inches/yards? Here's the scoop: 90 meters=295.27 feet, or 98.42 yards; 120 meters=393.70 feet, or 131.23 yards.

on-site restaurant. The park also is home to a substation of the Lake Placid Post Office; have the kids mail cards and letters that will arrive with a North Pole postmark. For $2.50, your child will receive a personalized letter from Santa in time for Christmas. Open daily July to Labor Day. Call for spring, fall, and holiday hours. *Whiteface Memorial Hwy., Wilmington; (800) 488-YULE; (518) 946-2211*; www. northpolenewyork.com

Scenic Flights over the Adirondacks
★★★/$$$$

Adirondack Flying Service offers two 20-minute scenic flights that provide dramatic aerial views of the region. The "Whiteface Tour" flies over Lake Placid Village and the lake itself, Whiteface Mountain, and all of the Olympic venues. As its name suggests, the "High Peaks Tour" takes you over New York's highest peaks, plus Lake Tear-of-the Clouds, Lost Pond, Avalanche Pass, Panther Gorge, Ausable Lakes, the Great Range, and more. Flights are in single-engine planes; one holds three passengers; the other, up to five. No age limits; no reservations required.

Open year-round; extended hours in July and August. *Rte. 73, across from the ski jumps, Lake Placid; (518) 523-2473*; www.flyanywhere.com

★ Summer Storm
FamilyFun ★★★★/$$$$

The former Olympic bobsled track is a high-speed thrill ride, which sends you and the kids on an unforgettable race in bobsleds outfitted with wheels. Never fear: along with your trusty helmet, you'll have a professional driver and brakeman to get you through those world-famous spins. There's no age requirement, but kids must be 48 inches tall. Open Wednesday through Sunday mid-June through early October, weather and track conditions permitting. V*erizon Sports Complex, Cascade Rd. (off Rte. 73), Lake Placid; (518) 523-4436*; www.orda.org/verizoncom plex.html

USA Luge-York International Luge Training Complex ★/Free

The only indoor luge start track in North America, this center is the official headquarters of USA Luge, which trains and equips the U.S. National Luge Team for interna-

DID YOU KNOW that the famed "Miracle on Ice" between the United States and Soviet hockey teams was not the gold medal game? Following their historic victory, the U.S. went on to play Finland for the gold; the Americans won, 4-2.

tional and Olympic events. Training is conducted daily, year-round, on three iced ramps, which stand ten feet high and have varying inclines (25, 30, and 35 percent) to simulate the starts used most frequently in international competition. Free guided tours, complete with video shows, are offered weekdays at 2 P.M. *Church St., Lake Placid; (518)523-2071; www.usaluge.org/york_inter national_luge_training.html*

Verizon Sports Complex
★★★/$

If you have a family of mountain bikers, the 45-kilometer cross-country ski trails at the Verizon Sports Complex at Mount Van Hoevenberg are the perfect choice for an outing. Unlike Whiteface Mountain, with its tougher terrain, Mount Van Hoevenberg features trails for all ages and abilities. Trails are clearly marked (on the guide map and in the field), and difficulty levels are indicated, so you can choose the best course for your family. Bigger kids (including parents) can test their skills on the foot-high jumps—younger or less adventuresome riders can simply go around them. You can bring your own bikes or rent them; rental fees are from $10 to $50, depending on what kind of bike you want and how long you are planning to keep it. Helmets are required and may be rented for $3 per day. Open daily in summer; weekends only in fall. *Verizon Sports Complex, Cascade Rd. (off Rte. 73), Lake Placid; (518) 523-4436; www. orda.org/*

Whiteface Mountain Veterans Memorial Highway
★★★/$$

This five-mile paved road leads to the Whiteface summit, the only one of the Adirondack high peaks accessible by car. Your breathtaking journey begins at the tollhouse area, site of an Alpine-style gatehouse (where you buy your ticket) and the small, pristine Lake Stevens. At the information center inside the tollhouse, you can learn about the history of the area and the flora and fauna of the Adirondacks. You also can read the dedication address delivered by President Franklin D. Roosevelt when the highway opened in 1935. If you want to stretch your legs before beginning the climb, take the ten-minute, self-guided walk around the Lake Stevens Tree Trail, on which you'll see all 34 species of trees native to the Adirondacks. Once in your car, you can stop at nine mileage markers, many with picnic areas along with posted information about the mountain surroundings. The road ends at the Whiteface Castle, made from granite that was excavated during highway construction. Here you must decide: do you want to climb to the summit on the steep Stairway Ridge Trail (a fifth of a mile long), or take the elevator that runs through the inside of the mountain? (A good

A WORLD-CLASS SKI (AND MORE!) DESTINATION

Winter sports enthusiasts may be surprised to discover that Lake Placid offers as much for families as it does for world-class athletes. Try your hand (or your legs) at downhill and cross-country skiing, snowboarding, snowshoeing, and ice-skating. If you're more adventurous, head for the luge and bobsled runs. But no matter which outdoor activity you choose, two words of caution: bundle up. The average temperature from November to March is less than 25º — and that's at the foot of the mountain, not the top.

The major attraction for most skiers is **Whiteface Mountain**, which boasts the steepest vertical drop (3,350 feet) east of the Rockies. Don't let that scare you: fully one-third of this mountain's trails are classified as for beginners, and even more for intermediate skiers. (Of course, Whiteface has its share of expert trails, too.) The special Kids Kampus and Family Learning Center was designed with young families in mind. With its separate parking area, base lodge, lifts, and trails, this section is perfect for those who prefer gentler terrain and kid-friendly lifts. Full- and half-day children's programs also give parents time to sample expert slopes, if they're so inclined.

Cross-country skiers can choose from literally hundreds of trails, including those at **Mt. Van Hoevenberg**, built specifically for the 1980 Olympic Winter Games. Here again, you'll find trails for those of every ability level.

Lodging choices run the gamut from economical to elegant; some even have ice-skating or cross-country skiing on the resort property. Many offer "ski and stay" packages. Keep in mind, however, that because Whiteface is part of the Adirondack Park, there are no accommodations on the mountain itself.

For information or help in choosing accommodations, contact the **Lake Placid/Essex County Convention and Visitors Bureau,** *Olympic Center, 216 Main St., Lake Placid, NY 12946-1592; (800) 447-5224;* www.lakeplacid.com

compromise is to ascend by elevator and walk down.) To reach the elevator, you'll walk through a 426-foot-long tunnel that's been bored into Whiteface Mountain. The summit itself is barren of trees, providing a panoramic view of the St. Lawrence Valley and Canada to the north, Lake Champlain and Vermont's Green Mountains to the east, Lake Placid and the Adirondack High Peaks to the south, and the Saranac Lake River Valley to the west. **NOTE:** It gets chilly at 4,867 feet, so bring a jacket or sweater. Open daily in spring, summer, and fall; closed in winter. *Whiteface Mountain, Rte. 86, Wilmington; (800) 462-6236; (518) 523-7175;* www.orda.org/memhighway.html

BUNKING DOWN

NOTE: For more information about camping in Lake Placid, see "Calling All Campers" on page 120.

Art Devlin's Olympic Motor Inn ★★/$-$$

If your family is content with few frills, Art Devlin's is a good choice. The 41-room motor inn is comfortable, affordable, and recently remodeled. The motel was purchased in 1953 by Olympic skier Art Devlin, Sr., whose trophies are on display in the lobby. The current owners are Devlin's son, Art, and his wife, Sue, whose homemade muffins are part of the complimentary continental breakfast. Rooms contain two queen-size beds or two double beds or a king-size bed and a couch. All have cable TV, a refrigerator, and air-conditioning. There's no restaurant or indoor pool, but summer guests can swim in the heated outdoor pool. The adjacent kiddie pool is heated, too. Pets are welcome; in fact, the Devlins' German shepherd, Tara, is a fixture on the property. *348 Main St., Lake Placid; (518) 523-3700;* www.artdevlins.com

Eric Heiden won an unprecedented five gold medals in five speed skating races at the 1980 Olympic Winter Games.

Best Western Golden Arrow Hotel ★★★/$$-$$$

No need to brave the elements at this hotel, which is connected to a mall complete with a minimart, virtual-reality ride, winery, antiques store, gift and specialty shops, and hair salon. If you do head outdoors, you'll also find plenty to do. Summer guests can relax or barbecue on the private, white sandy beach, or venture out on Mirror Lake in paddleboats, canoes, or rowboats, all available free of charge. For duffers, there's a practice putting green. In winter, you need only walk out your door to reach cross-country skiing, ice-skating, tobogganing, and dogsled rides. The kids will go for the

FamilyFun SNACK

Good for You

Make rocket fuel for your kids with a mix of dried apples, pineapples, cranberries, mangoes, cherries, banana chips, and raisins. One cup fulfills two of the recommended five minimum daily servings of fruits and veggies.

kiddie pool. This hotel has both standard rooms (with two double beds) and lakefront rooms (with two double beds in one room, a twin bed in an alcove, and a kitchenette). Two condominium units, located two buildings away from the main hotel, sleep eight guests each. Kids 12 and under stay free, and pets are welcome. The on-site Goldberrie's restaurant serves breakfast, lunch, and dinner and offers kids' fare. *150 Main St., Lake Placid; (800) 582-5540; (518) 523-3353;* www.golden arrow.com

Hilton Lake Placid Resort
★★★/$$-$$$

You're guaranteed a room with a view at this resort, where 30 of the 179 rooms are right on the water and all face Mirror Lake and the Adirondacks. Most have a private balcony or patio. The property is very kid-friendly, too, with two indoor pools and two heated outdoor pools, a game room, 500 feet of lakefront property, and compli-

mentary use of rowboats and paddleboats. It's in the center of Lake Placid Village, near shops and restaurants, and just blocks from the town park. As part of Hilton's Vacation Station program, kids receive a gift at check-in and can sign out age-appropriate toys and games throughout your stay. You'll also receive a Family Fun Kit, complete with discount coupons to local attractions. Kids under 18 stay free in their parents' rooms, and kids' menu meals are free for children accompanied by adults in the Terrace Room, a lake-view dining room serving breakfast, lunch, and dinner. *One Mirror Lake Dr., Lake Placid; (800) 755-5598; (518) 523-4411;* www.lphilton.com

Howard Johnson Resort Inn
★★★/$-$$

Indoors and out, you'll find much to like about this attractive, reasonably priced property. Two of its four buildings front on Lake Placid; all have lake and beach access and offer free use of rowboats, paddleboats, canoes, and a picnic area. There's also a basketball court and a tennis court. Indoors, the main building has a pool and Jacuzzi that are open to all guests. Rooms are air-conditioned, with two double beds, plus color cable TV with free HBO. If you have a larger family, check into the several suites and the efficiency units. Children stay free in their parents' room and get a free fun pack, which includes puzzles, mazes, and a children's magazine. Breakfast, lunch, and dinner, including kid fare, is served in the Howard Johnson restaurant next door. *90 Saranac Ave., Lake Placid; (800) 858-4656; (518) 523-9555;* www.hojo.com

Lake Placid Resort/ Holiday Inn ★★★/$$-$$$

Spread over 1,000 acres, this family-owned resort boasts accommodations of every kind, plus several restaurants, a private beach, 11 tennis courts, 45 holes of golf, and a cross-country ski center. You can choose from among condominiums or chalets (both with full kitchens), or in the hotel itself, an upscale Holiday Inn where children stay free in their parents' rooms and enjoy free kids' meals. The hotel, which has an indoor pool, whirlpool, health club, swings, and a beach, is on one side of Mirror Lake; sports and recreational facilities are on the other side, less than a mile away. Children are welcome in all four restaurants; fam-

ilies of six or more can eat in private rooms in the restaurant, where parents have been known to bring pajama-clad youngsters with them to dinner, so they can have a leisurely meal and return to their rooms with the kids all set for bed. Arturo's and the Veranda are open year-round; the Golf House is open during golf season, and Boat House restaurants are open mid-May to through Labor Day. *One Olympic Dr., Lake Placid; (800) 874-1980; (518) 523-2556;* www.lpresort.com

Mirror Lake Inn Resort and Spa ★★★★/$$$$

This resort is in a class by itself, known for its exceptional service, dining, and luxurious accommodations. It's still kid-friendly, though, with heated indoor and outdoor pools and a game room. In summer, you and the kids can play tennis, relax on the private beach, swim in Mirror Lake, or captain one of the complimentary canoes, paddleboats, or rowboats. In winter, you can go cross-country skiing, snowshoeing,

---

FamilyFun READER'S TIP

Tic-Tac-Tine

While my sister Barb and I and our seven kids were waiting for dinner at a restaurant, my nephew Josh surprised me with a game he invented using dinner utensils and sugar packets. He set up forks, spoons, and knives in the traditional tic-tac-toe grid and gave me the choice of being the X's (regular sugar packets) or O's (artificial sweetener packets).

Theresa Jung, Cincinnati, Ohio

Your Own Olympic Adventure

Give your family a taste of Olympic training at **Gold Medal Adventure day camps**, offered from 10 A.M. to 3 P.M., Tuesday through Friday, from mid-June to mid-September. Sign up for one, two, three, or four days and master new skills such as push-starting a wheeled bobsled, maneuvering a kayak or canoe, even freestyle skiing on a trampoline.

Depending on which day you choose, your coaches could be figure skaters, Nordic ski jumpers, or members of the national luge team. You'll also get to meet world-class athletes and tour the Olympic venues where they train.

Gold Medal Adventure camps are open to children 7 and older. The cost of $55 per person per day (discounts are available for multidays) includes coaching, all equipment, lunch, tours, transportation between venues, and a souvenir. You need reservations for June and September programs, and they are recommended for July and August sessions.

N O T E : Those who opt for a Gold Medal Adventure probably should forgo the Olympic Sites Passport (see "Passport to Fun—and Savings," page 95), since venue tours are included in your camp price. For more information or to make reservations, call *(518) 523-1655, ext. 250.*

and ice-skating on the resort's private, outdoor rink (bring your own skates or rent them, nearby, in town). Families of four are more than comfortable in standard rooms with two queen-size beds. Those who need a little more space can opt for one of the family suites, designed to accommodate five or six. The kids will head for the inn's famous chocolate-chip cookies at the complimentary afternoon tea. An early family dinner hour (usually at 5:30 P.M.; reservations suggested) is perfect if you're traveling with small children. Families who dine at this time receive one free kids' meal (for children up to age 12) for each adult entrée ordered. Equally important, service is unusually quick, geared to young attention spans. Lighter pub fare and a more casual atmosphere are available in the resort's other restaurant, The Cottage, which is just across the street. During the holiday season, the exterior of the Mirror Lake Inn is adorned with more than 90,000 lights. Indoors, you'll find five Christmas trees, each decorated with a different Victorian theme. *5 Mirror Lake Dr., Lake Placid; (518) 523-2544;* www.mirrorlakeinn.com

Ramada Inn ★★★/$$

Families will appreciate the convenient location, accommodating atmosphere, and affordable prices at this 90-room inn. The indoor and outdoor pools have generous shallow areas and are big hits with children.

Nik's Place, the on-site restaurant, serves breakfast, lunch, and dinner, and has something for everyone, kids included. Kids can help themselves to board games, including Chutes and Ladders, backgammon, Monopoly, Trivial Pursuit, and Who Wants to Be a Millionaire. A family of four can stay comfortably in standard rooms outfitted with two double beds and cable TV. There are no suites or efficiencies, but you can rent a refrigerator. Ask about discount tickets for local attractions. *8–12 Saranac Ave., Lake Placid; (800) 741-7841; (518) 523-2587; www.ramadalp.com*

GOOD EATS

Arturo's Ristorante ★★/$-$$$

Kids and parents have plenty of options—including an all-you-can-eat pasta bar—at this family restaurant. Choose from among lots of pastas, sauces, and other ingredients; there's also a selection of appetizers, salads, and entrées of chicken, fish, or steak; the kids' menu features chicken fingers, hot dogs, cheeseburgers, grilled cheese, pizza, and spaghetti. Kids' meals come with fruit, carrot sticks, a drink, and dessert. Because Arturo's is located in the Lake Placid Resort/Holiday Inn, young resort guests eat free with their parents. Open year-round for breakfast, lunch, and dinner. *One Olympic Dr., Lake Placid; (800) 874-1980; (518) 523-2556; www.lpresort.com*

The Cottage ★★/$

Families with a taste for more creative pub fare will appreciate this café on Mirror Lake. Adults can choose among salads and hot and cold sandwiches prepared with a twist. The open roast beef sandwich, for example, is served on toasted French bread with sautéed onion, mushrooms, melted Brie, and horseradish mayonnaise. The kids' menu includes a peanut-butter-and-jelly sandwich, cheese nachos, cheese burrito, hot dog, and focaccia topped with melted Monterey Jack cheese. *At the Mirror Lake Inn Resort and Spa, 5 Mirror Lake Dr., Lake Placid; (518) 523-9845; www.mirrorlake inn.com/thecottage.htm*

Goldberries
★★★/$$-$$$

Owner and grandmother Lynn Kreil knows just what kids like, and she serves it up in abundance. Kids have their own special room, stocked with two toy boxes, where they can play while they wait for dinner. They also can color at the table. On their way out, they get a free toy and a package of graham crackers to go. The kids' menu offers pasta with butter or tomato sauce, macaroni and cheese, chicken fingers, plain or pepperoni pizza, hot dogs, grilled cheese, fried chicken, and a child-size portion of prime rib. There are plenty of choices for adults, too, including three specials each night. Popular menu items include Wiener schnitzel, chicken Oscar, shrimp El Dorado, and five kinds of steak. Open year-round, weekends only the first three weeks of April. *137 Main St., Lake Placid; (518) 523-1799.*

Artificial snow made its Olympic debut at the 1980 Games in Lake Placid.

Jimmy's 21
★★★/$-$$$
Homemade pasta and other Italian fare are the specialties at this casual restaurant. In summer, dine outside and feast on scenes of Mirror Lake and Whiteface Mountain while you enjoy veal, chicken, and seafood dishes. Kids' choices include spaghetti with meatballs, a hamburger or cheeseburger, and fish-and-chips. Coloring will keep them busy until the food arrives. Open daily year-round for lunch and dinner. Reservations accepted for parties of six or more. *21 Main St., Lake Placid; (518) 523-2353.*

Lisa G's ★★★/$$
This affordable restaurant offers everything from pub fare to eight different kinds of salads to specialty entrées, including a fish of

the day. If you're a prime rib fan, order it here. The kids' menu includes hamburgers, hot dogs, chicken fingers, grilled cheese, BLTs, and spaghetti. Buckets of toys, crayons, and coloring books make this a popular choice for the younger set. A planned expansion of the restaurant includes the addition of a place for kids to play if they finish eating before their parents do. Located at the end of Main Street, Lisa G's overlooks Mill Pond Dam. In warmer weather, you can dine on the large, outdoor deck and enjoy the view. Open daily year-round for lunch and dinner. *444 Main St., Lake Placid; (518) 523-2093.*

Nik's Place at the Ramada
★★★/$$-$$$
With 14,000 square feet of glass, this greenhouse-style restaurant serves up great views of Mirror Lake and the Adirondacks. Steak, pasta, chicken dishes, and lighter pub-style fare are available, as are the usual suspects—hamburgers, hot dogs, spaghetti, chicken tenders, pizza—for kids. The kids' menu doubles as a coloring and puzzle sheet. Breakfast, lunch, and dinner are served daily, year-round. *At the Ramada Inn, 8–12 Saranac Ave., Lake Placid; (518) 523-2587;* www.ramadalp.com/niks.html

Souvenir Hunting

When it comes to shopping, Lake Placid's Main Street has something that will appeal to everyone, from brand-name clothing and outlet bargains to unusual gifts, gourmet coffee, toys, and books. The following shops score high in kid appeal. All are open daily year-round.

Candy Man

Chocolate fans will love these Adirondack chocolates, which are made fresh daily. If you get hooked, you can place orders on-line or by telephone after you return home. *61 Main St., Lake Placid; (800) 232-4626; (518) 523-4709; www.candy manonline.com*

Far Mor's Kids

This family-owned specialty store stocks children's sneakers and clothing for newborns to age 14. It also features books, building toys, and creative games and projects. *1 Main St., Lake Placid; (518) 523-3544.*

Imagination Station

As you might expect, items here are designed to spark the imagination. You'll find creative and thinking games for kids, as well as marbles, books, crafts, rubber-band balls, puzzles, and more. *107 Main St., Lake Placid; (518) 523-3971.*

Nature Unlimited

Everything from stuffed animals to science kits are sold here. There's also a selection of T-shirts, sweatshirts, cards, and books about the Adirondacks. *59 Main St., Lake Placid; (518) 523-8733.*

U.S. Olympic Spirit Store

This is the place to buy genuine Olympic souvenirs, which your kids are sure to think are supercool. Better yet, the store is owned and operated by the U.S. Olympic Committee, so your purchases support the U.S. Olympic athletes. *16 Main St., Lake Placid; (518) 523-7207.* There's a second location at *421 Old Military Rd., Lake Placid; (518) 523-8402.*

Clap, Tickle, Tug

It's the sitting—and sitting and sitting—that gets to kids on the road. Get their belted-in bodies moving with this game of competitive copycat. The first player makes an expression or a movement, such as a hand clap; the next player repeats that movement and adds another; and so on. Kids will be pulling on their ears, sticking out their tongues, tipping back their heads, holding their elbows—and smiling! When a player forgets a movement, he's out. When everyone's out, start over.

Lake George offers kids
plenty of water play,
both old-fashioned and
newfangled.

Lake George Region

THE SHOWPIECE of this region is the 32-mile-long Lake George, striking for both its size and its surroundings. Fed by underground springs, the lake covers about 44 square miles, and includes 109 miles of shoreline and some 300 islands. In some places it's as shallow as one foot; in others, as deep as 195 feet. Its width also varies, from one to three miles.

Named for Britain's King George III, the lake has earned the nickname Queen of the American Lakes, in part because of its breathtaking views of the surrounding mountains. None other than Thomas Jefferson called it "without comparison, the most beautiful water I ever saw." Visitors to Lake George typically fall into one of two categories: those who, like Jefferson, want to revel in the natural beauty of the area, and those drawn by the more commercial and ever-hopping Lake George Village.

No matter which camp your family falls into, you'll find plenty

THE **FamilyFun** LIST

MUST-SEE
MUST-SEE

Great Escape & Splashwater Kingdom (page 110)

Lake George Beaches (page 112)

Water Slide World (page 116)

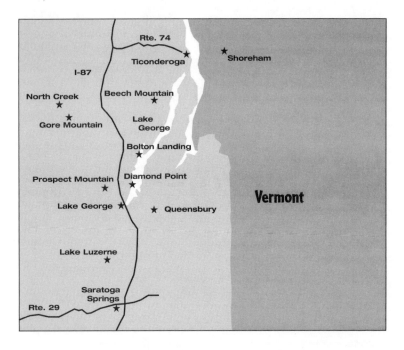

to do here and lots of places to stay. You can relax on the shores of Lake George beaches, rent a boat from one of the local marinas, or take a cruise on a commercial vessel. Hike up Prospect Mountain, go horseback riding, or head "up yonda" to a nature and environmental center. If you're in the mood for action, choose among the many amusement parks, go-cart tracks, water parks, and a Western show. History buffs can tour two forts whose strategic locations earned them prominent roles in the French and Indian War and the American Revolution. Bargain hunters will be in heaven on the "Million Dollar Mile," home to

dozens of outlet shops. You can leave the car behind and take advantage of the trolley service that makes it easy to get around and to avoid the traffic.

Although you can ski at nearby Gore Mountain (see "Go for Gore Mountain" on page 112) or visit in the fall to see the region's stunning foliage, Lake George is primarily a summer destination, with seasonal attractions. Those who do visit off-season will find far more reasonable hotel rates than those listed here. Many of the factory-outlet shops do remain open in winter, as do some of the restaurants. Be prepared, however, for the often harsh Adirondack winters.

CULTURAL ADVENTURES

Fort Ticonderoga ★★★/$$

Forty miles north of Lake George, you and your children can follow in the footsteps of George Washington, Benjamin Franklin, Ethan Allen, and other famous patriots, all of whom logged time at Fort Ticonderoga. Although it's a fascinating attraction, the fort is best for older kids or those with a special interest in military history. Built by the French in 1755 and originally known as Fort Carillon, the star-shaped stronghold was the site of the greatest French victory of the Seven Years' War. It is also where the colonists claimed their first victory in the American Revolution. Costumed interpreters lead 20-minute guided tours throughout the day. If you're interested in one of these historical talks, gather at the flag bastion and wait for the next scheduled tour. Your guide may be outfitted as an 18th-century French soldier, a member of the Revolutionary War army, a Native American ally, or an 18th- or 19th-century woman. At the Fort Ticonderoga museum, you can see displays of colonial artifacts, from muskets, bayonets, and swords to tools of the day to personal items such as the trundle bed that belonged to Benedict Arnold. Also check out the separate room dedicated to the fort's namesake, the aircraft carrier USS *Ticonderoga*, used in World War II and Vietnam. Highlights for kids are the musket and artillery demonstrations, reenactments of wartime skirmishes, and performances (in July and August) by the Fort Ticonderoga Fife & Drum Corps. Breakfast, lunch, snacks, and takeout sandwiches are available at the on-site restaurant. There's a souvenir shop, too. Open early May through late October. *Off Fort Rd. From Lake George, take I-87 north to exit 28. Take Rte. 74 east to Ticonderoga and turn right at Rte. 9N. After about a half mile, turn left at Fort Rd., Ticonderoga; (518) 585-2821; www.fort-ticonderoga.org*

Fort William Henry Museum ★★★/$$

Those who'd prefer a shorter trip for their old-time military adventure will find plenty of excitement at this fort, located in the heart of Lake George Village. In 1757, during the French and Indian War, the fort was captured by the French and destroyed. Although French General Louis Montcalm promised safe passage for those who surrendered, many soldiers, women, and children

---

FamilyFun TIP

Pit Stops

Six top games to beat the fidgets: Leapfrog, Four Square, Spud, Tag, Frisbee, Wheelbarrow Races.

---

were slaughtered in what has come to be known as the massacre at Fort William Henry. The fort was rebuilt for historical purposes in 1953. The highlight of any visit is the tour, led by a guide in 18th-century military garb. You'll learn how musket balls were molded, and watch as a musket is fired and a grenadier bomb is tossed. Tell the kids to plug their ears and warn little ones about the "big boom" before the cannon firing—it's so loud it often triggers the alarms in nearby parked cars. Artifacts from the colonial era are on display, including some unearthed in 1995 and 1997 during archaeological digs at the fort. If you're in town on a Thursday night during the summer, come for the weekly fireworks show. Open mid-May through October. *48 Canada St., Lake George; (800) 234-0265; (518) 668-5471;* www.fortwilliam henry.com/fortmus.htm

JUST FOR FUN

Adventure Racing & Family Fun Center ★★/$$$$

Kids of all ages can find something to do at this action-packed attraction: zip around go-cart tracks (there's even an indoor kiddie track for youngsters ages 4 to 8). Take aim at paintball targets. Play laser tag. Test your skills at video and Skee-Ball games in the arcade. Your kids could probably easily spend half a

day here, but note that you pay per activity, so it can get a little pricey. A snack bar and gift shop are available on-site. Open Memorial Day through Labor Day; call ahead about weekend hours during spring and fall. *Rte. 9, Queensbury; (518) 798-7860;* www.adirondackoutpost. com/adventure

Great Escape & FamilyFun Splashwater Kingdom ★★★★/$$$$

Families *love* this amusement park, located just minutes from Lake George Village. True to its name, Great Escape offers an escape into a world that balances coasters and other thrill rides with a water park that's cool for the whole family. One of the largest amusement centers in New York State and a recent addition to the Six Flags family, this park now covers 140 acres and offers more than 125 rides, shows, and attractions. Great Escape's signature ride is the Comet, widely regarded as the world's number-one wooden roller coaster. Thrill seekers will also want to queue up for three other roller coasters: the Steamin' Demon, Boomerang Coast-to-Coaster, and Nightmare at Crack Axle Canyon. The Desperado Plunge flume ride and the rocketing Alpine Bobsled also rate high on the excitement scale.

For the younger set, there are the usual kiddie rides plus the park's original nursery-rhyme scenes, including Little Bo Peep, Humpty

Dumpty, Jack and Jill, and the cow jumping over the moon. Cinderella fans can meet the lovely princess and ride with her in her pumpkin coach.

If things start to heat up a bit, head over to Splashwater Kingdom, where you'll find three water slides, a lazy river ride, and Lumberjack Splash, a 500,000-gallon wave pool. Time it right at Paul Bunyan's Bucket Brigade and you'll get drenched by the 1,000 gallons of water that come crashing down when the giant bucket tips. Little ones can chill out at Noah's Sprayground, complete with sprinklers, tyke-size slides, and a wave pool. Great Escape admission includes most rides, shows, and Splashwater Kingdom. Go-carts and arcade and carnival games cost extra. For those who can't get enough, multiday passes are available. The park is open daily during the peak summer season; it remains open weekends during the fall and for special events such as Oktoberfest and the Halloween Fright Fest. Call for fall and spring hours. *Rte. 9, Lake George; (518) 792-3500;* www.six flags.com/greatescape

Horseback Riding ★★★/$$$

Giddyup on over to **Bennett's Riding Stable** (*Rte. 9N, Lake Luzerne; 518/696-4444*; www.lakegeorge newyork.com/horses) for guided trail rides through the beautiful Adirondacks. Hourlong rides are available on a first-come, first-serve basis, with one guide for every six guests. Or if your kids are up for it, consider a ride up Beech Mountain. The climb is fairly easy, and the reward is a spectacular view at the top, where you dismount for 15 minutes or so before beginning your descent. The total trip is a little over two hours; reservations are required 24 hours in advance. Depending on their size, children as young as 6 can ride, although those under 8 are usually led from the guide's horse. Riders 14 and under must wear helmets, which are included in the rate; they also are offered, free of charge, to adults. Open daily mid-June through Labor Day. In spring and fall, there's riding on weekends, and on weekdays with reservations. Horseback riding also is available at **Saddle Up Stables** (*3513 Lake*

TAKE A FERRY RIDE across Lake Champlain to Vermont! The Fort Ti ferry has been running from Fort Ticonderoga, New York, to Shoreham, Vermont, since the 1700s. You can take your car for some sight-seeing on the other side or just enjoy a scenic ride on foot. The trip takes only seven minutes.

Shore Dr., Lake George; 518/668-4802; www.ridingstables.com) from mid-May through Labor Day. Call for more information.

House of Frankenstein Wax Museum ★★★/$$

They may be wax, but some of these monsters seem all too real—especially for younger children and those who are afraid of the dark. For kids and adults who enjoy a good fright, however, this place is a scream. The exhibits are as clever as they are gruesome. In the "tourist trap," bodies hang upside down from the ceiling and twitch. Push a button on the wall and watch the werewolf attack, or see Dracula transform from vampire to bat. Beware the mummy's tomb, where jets of air shoot out to shock you. Step carefully on the way out lest the dizzying black hole catch you off balance. *213 Canada St., Lake George; (518) 668-3377;* www.frankensteinwaxmuseum.com

Lake George Beaches
★★★/Free-$

With 109 miles of shoreline, Lake George offers sand and swimming aplenty. The jewel among its public bathing areas is Million Dollar Beach (*Rte. 9/Beach Rd., quarter mile east of Lake George Village; 518/668-3352*), operated by the New York State Department of Environmental Conservation. Reportedly named for its million-dollar price tag when the beach and public facilities

Go for Gore Mountain

One of New York's most affordable skiing options is **Gore Mountain**, located about 45 minutes from Lake George, in the southern portion of the Adirondack Park. With a vertical drop of 2,100 feet, the mountain has 62 trails on 292 skiable acres, and 95 percent snow coverage. Roughly 10 percent of trails are geared to beginners, 60 percent to intermediate skiers, and 30 percent to experts.

An excellent family mountain, Gore offers a variety of programs for children, from Bear Cub Den Day Care to learn-to-ski/snowboard programs for kids ages 4 to 10, and separate programs for those 11 and up. Like Whiteface, Gore has no on-site lodging. However, families can stay in nearby Lake George at year-round hotels and motels, or can choose from inns, condominiums, and bed-and-breakfast options (www.goremountain.com/html/business.asp), some of which offer ski-and-stay packages.

For more information about Gore Mountain, write or call *Gore Mountain, Peaceful Valley Rd., North Creek, NY 12853; (518) 251-2411;* www.goremountain.com

were constructed a half-century ago, the beach stretches some 300 yards. It features five marked-off sections for swimming; at their deepest, the swimming areas reach about six feet. Facilities include rest rooms, showers, lockers, and a concession stand. Admission is free, but you will have to pay to park. Another family favorite is Shepard Park (*Canada St., Lake George*), where kids can jump from a dock into a roped-off swimming area. There's also a playground and picnic area.

Ushers Park (*Rte. 9, Lake George*) provides a place to sun, swim, and picnic on the east side of the lake. Lake Avenue Beach (*Lake Ave., Lake George*) is a small sandy beach with no picnic facilities. Depending on where your family stays, you may also have access to one of the many private beaches that are reserved for hotel and resort guests. Public beaches are typically open on Saturday and Sunday only from Memorial Day weekend until the last weekend in June, and daily until Labor Day. *For details, call the Lake George Regional Chamber of Commerce at (800) 705-0059 or (518) 668–5755.*

Lake George Carriage Rides
★/$$

Tiny tots and sophisticated preteens—and their Moms and Dads— all enjoy a two-mile scenic tour of the Lake George beach area in a traditional horse-drawn carriage. Each carriage can seat up to eight adults

for the 25-minute ride. You don't need reservations—just walk up to the driver, and you'll be helped aboard. Rides are available daily during peak summer season, on weekends in spring and fall. Carriages park in front of the Fort William Henry Museum, in the municipal lot. *Lake George Beach Rd., Lake George; (518) 668-4958;* www.lakege orge-saratoga.com/carriage

Lake George Cruises
★★/$$$

No trip to Lake George is complete without at least one cruise around the Queen of the American Lakes. The area's most famous vessel is the paddle wheeler *Minne-Ha-Ha*, whose whistle is synonymous with summer at Lake George. Operated by the **Lake George Steamboat Company** (*Steel Pier, Beach Rd., Lake George; 800/553-BOAT; 518/668-5777;* www.lakegeorgesteamboat. com), the *Minne-Ha-Ha* departs for hourlong, narrated cruises seven times a day from mid-June through Labor Day and on weekends from mid-May through mid-June. On the top deck is a steam-powered cal-

FamilyFun GAME

Race to Twenty

Two players take turns counting to 20. On each turn, a player can say one or two numbers. (If the first says "One," the second might say "Two, three.") Try to force your opponent to reach 20 first.

liope, which plays throughout your trip. The engine room is enclosed in glass, so kids can watch the engine at work. The Steamboat Company also offers two-hour moonlight cruises and luncheon and dinner cruises aboard the Lac du Saint Sacrement. **Shoreline Cruises** (*2 Kurosaka La., Lake George; 518/ 6684644;* www.lakegeorgeshore line.com) has a one-hour narrated cruise and a two-and-a-half-hour tour around Paradise Bay. Check on-line for coupons.

Lake George Kayak Company
★★★/$$$

If you've ever wanted to take the kids kayaking, this outfitter can get you paddling. Lake George Kayak has launched thousands of kayakers, most of them first-timers. The company rents kayaks and provides lessons and tours. Kids as young as 5 or 6 can go out with a parent on a two-person boat; those ages 8 and up usually can paddle on their own. The rental fee includes basic instruc-

tion and a life jacket. Those who'd like a little more help getting started can take a 90-minute lesson for an additional fee. You also can book half- or full-day kayak tours of Lake George. The company can help you arrange a hike, providing maps, information, and, if you like, a guide. In the winter, the outfitter rents snowshoes and books snowshoe tours. Open year-round, with extended hours from Memorial Day through Labor Day. *Main St., Bolton Landing; (518) 644-9366;* www.lake georgekayak.com

Magic Forest
★★/$$$

Younger kids may be more comfortable at this park than at the larger Great Escape & Splashwater Kingdom (see page 110). Magic Forest features 25 rides, most designed for little ones. You take a tram through the safari area, populated by replicas of dinosaurs, lions, tigers, cowboys, and the like. The kids will also like the live critters— llamas, goats, sheep, and deer—in the animal exhibit area. Youngsters looking for a bit of a thrill can try the Scrambler, Ferris wheel, Paratrooper, or Tilt-A-Whirl. Or check out the three different shows daily: a magic show, a variety show, and a performance by the unusual Rex the Diving Horse. Santa has a summer home on the grounds and is happy to start hearing Christmas wishes. Don't forget to have the kids pose for a picture with the 36-foot tall statue of Uncle Sam. You can buy food in the park or bring lunch to eat in the picnic area. Open weekends beginning Memorial Day; open daily from the end of June through Labor Day. *On Rte. 9, between exits 20 and 21 on Rte. I-87, Lake George; (518) 668-2448;*www.magicforest park.com

Miniature Golf ★★/$

The town has lots of miniature-golf courses, so let the kids decide—do they want to sink putts while traveling around the world, surrounded by fellow "mateys," or in the shadow of a giant "goonysaurus"? At **Around the World in 18 Holes** and **Around the U.S. in 18 Holes** (*Beach Rd., Lake George; 518/668-2531*), the setting calls to mind 18 different countries and the United States, respectively. At **Pirate's Cove Adventure Golf** (*1089 Rte. 9, Lake George; 518/745-1887;* www.pirates cove.net), players putt over bridges, past waterfalls, and even in a cave. The giant, dinosaurlike Sir Goony makes sure that you don't miss **Goony Golf** (*Rtes. 9 and 9N, Lake George; 518/668-2700*), where the theme is nursery rhymes. **Putts 'N Prizes** (*Rte. 9 and Beach Rd., Lake George; 518/668-9500*) is an Adirondack-style course decorated with wooden sculptures. In the arcade, kids can play games like Skee-Ball and accumulate tickets that they can redeem for prizes. All

of the area miniature-golf courses are open daily from Memorial Day through Labor Day, but cut back their hours after peak season. *Call for specific times.*

Prospect Mountain
★★★/$-$$

Leave the crowds in the village below and head up to the 2,030-foot summit of Prospect Mountain. Most of the climb is made by car along a five-and-a-half-mile scenic highway. Stop at the three overlook areas for spectacular views of the Adirondack High Peaks, the Green Mountains of Vermont, and the White Mountains in New Hampshire. You'll also get a bird's-eye perspective of the Queen of the American Lakes. When the road ends (just short of the summit), you can continue the trek on foot or ride in the "Viewmobile" (a minivan). The hike is manageable for all but the youngest vacationers. If you opt for the trail, notice the remnants of what was once the world's largest cable railroad. Built in 1875 to link the summit with Lake George Village, the railway was a financial

failure and ceased operations after only eight years. If you bring along your lunch, you can eat it at the summit's picnic area.

Once you've had your fill of the view, if your family is physically fit (and your children aren't too young), you can venture down one of the well-marked hiking trails. Pay attention to how far you trek and how tired your family feels—at some point, you'll have to turn around and head back to the car. *Veterans Memorial Hwy., half mile south of Lake George Village; (518) 668-5198.*

Minnehaha, the name of one of the steamboats that cruises Lake George, means "laughing waters." It was also the name of the wife of Native American chief Hiawatha.

Up Yonda Farm Environmental Education Center ★★★/$

Hands-on exhibits that let kids make animal tracks in the sand and get a feel for deer antlers, pieces of bark, and other "touchables" are the main attractions for youngsters at this 72-acre nature and trail center.

A working farm for centuries, the site now has a museum and auditorium (both in renovated barns), six walking/hiking trails, a variety of nature programs, and a butterfly garden (summer only). The museum has displays on Adirondack wildlife, including birds and mammals that may be spotted on Up Yonda trails.

Depending on the trail and the season, you may catch sight of deer, fox, and ducks, and tune into the sounds of songbirds and woodpeckers. Highly recommended is the one-and-one-tenth-mile Green Trail-Summit Trail, an easy-to-moderate hike that rewards you with a spectacular view of Lake George. The easy Base Loop Trail leads to the butterfly garden, a 40-foot by 60-foot netted enclosure where your kids can get a close look at the lovely winged creatures. For more formal nature study, sign your family up for an educational program offered by Warren County Parks and Recreation ($2 to $4 per person).

You may learn about wild things (reptiles and amphibians), frequent flyers (birds), Adirondack pests (insects), or wild edibles. You also may try your hand at outdoor cooking, nature drawing, or nature crafts. Open daily year-round. *5239 Lake Shore Dr., Bolton Landing; (518) 644-9767 or (518) 644-3824;* www.up yondafarm.com

Water Slide World
FamilyFun ★★★★/$$$

MUST-SEE This watery playground makes a splash with kids of all ages. There are 12 slides to zip down, from the daring Pirate's Plunge (for those at least 51 inches tall) and Tasmanian

Man Your Battlestations

Fort Ticonderoga hosts two military reenactments each year. The first one, which takes place in late June, is the Grand Encampment of the French and Indian War. A Revolutionary War encampment is re-created in early September. Each event brings out hundreds of avid reenactors.

Twisters (four feet tall and up) to the tamer Lava Flow Mountain and Calypso Cascade. Little ones can cool off in Aruba-Scuba-Duba Bay or in the Pirate Ship Cove and Toddler Lagoon. Kids who like waves will love the Hurricane Harbor pool. For a break from the twists and slides, relax in a tube and float along the Amazon Adventure River. Pack a lunch and eat in the picnic pavilion or dine at Ye Olde Mill Stream, a cafeteria-style restaurant. There's a concession stand and souvenir shop, too. *Open daily from mid-June through Labor Day. Rtes. 9 and 9L; (518) 668-4407;* www.adiron dack.net/tour/waterslideworld

Wild West Ranch & Western Town
★★★/$$-$$$$

Your cowboys and cowgirls can saddle up for a host of activities here. Entry to the town is free, as are the petting corral, hay maze, pig and duck racing in the Little Britches Rodeo, and the roping dummy that kids can try to lasso. And it doesn't cost anything to snap a photo of your young 'uns posed on a bucking bull or in the town jail. Other activities, such as horseback riding

(for guests 8 and up), pony rides (for kids under 8), stagecoach and wagon rides, the Western show, and panning for gold are available for a fee. In winter, sign up for a sleigh ride or ice-skating. The Wild Horse Saloon & Steakhouse serves lunch and dinner. Open year-round, longer hours during peak season. Call for details. *Bloody Pond Rd., Lake George; (518) 668-2121;* www.wild westranch.com

BUNKING DOWN

You'll find plenty of lodging options in Lake George, but it's wise to book well in advance of the peak summer season, especially if you want to stay in one of the more popular places. In addition to the properties listed below, other options include reliable chains such as **Days Inn** (*1454 State Rte. 9, Lake George; 800/DAYS-INN; 518/793-3196;* www.daysinnlakegeorge.com), **Travelodge** (*Rte. 9/Canada St., Lake George; 800/234-0586; 518/668-5421*), and **Quality Inn** (*57 Canada St., Lake George; 800/228-5151; 518/668-3525;* www.qualityinnlake george.com).

Canoe Island Lodge
★★★/$$$-$$$$

Guests return to this retreat year after year for its idyllic setting, comfortable accommodations, and family-friendly atmosphere. The lodge offers a host of water activities on Lake George, hiking on the resort's own mountain, and excursions to its private island. Located three-quarters of a mile across the lake, the five-acre Canoe Island was purchased by the late Bill Busch in 1943 for 124 bushels of buckwheat seed and a promise to pay the balance of the purchase price in cash. These days, the island is the site of a special Tuesday morning breakfast and a Thursday night barbecue. Guests are ferried over via shuttle boats and can telephone for a trip back to the mainland at any time. The island's sandy beach and shallow waters make it a popular spot for families. On the mainland property, you can play tennis, basketball, shuffleboard, go square dancing, fish, sail, windsurf, tube, and water ski. An activities director keeps the kids busy with games, crafts, trips to the island, T-shirt dyeing, cookie baking, and more. Accommodations range from log cabins, redwood cottages, and chalets to rooms in the main lodge. Dinner is included in the rate and is served in three dining rooms in the main lodge. Rates during July and August include breakfast and dinner and most activities. Spring and fall rates include breakfast, lunch, and dinner and all activ-

ities. Previous guests are given preference, so if you're considering staying here in summer, call for reservations by February. Open mid-May to mid-October; a minimum stay of three days is required. *Lake Shore Dr., Diamond Point; (518) 668-5592;* www.canoeislandlodge.com

Dunham's Bay Lodge
★★★/$$$-$$$$

The only facility on the east shore of Lake George, this is a good choice for families that would

Pet Savvy

It's easier than ever to bring your pet along on vacation. A number of hotels now accept pets, and some even offer exercise areas and pet room service. (A few go so far as to bring dog biscuits and bottled water to your room on a silver tray!)

Ready Buddy for travel by making sure his ID tags are complete and by taking him on short trips close to home (so he doesn't think getting in the car means going to the vet). Try calling these hotel and motel chains to find out their pet policies:

Best Western *(800-528-1234);*
Four Seasons *(800-332-3442);*
Holiday Inn *(800-465-4329);*
Loews *(800-235-6397);* and
Motel 6 *(800-466-8356).*

rather not face row upon row of resorts. Lake George Village is just five miles away, so you can always head there for the hustle and bustle. But if you'd prefer to kick back and relax, there's plenty for you and the kids to do right at the lodge. Spend time on the private sandy beach or in the heated indoor/outdoor pool. (There's a wading pool, too.) Play tennis, badminton, shuffleboard, volleyball, or Ping-Pong. Rent canoes, rowboats, paddleboats, or jet skis. Kids will also enjoy fishing and the playground and game room. Guest rooms in the main lodge and motel are air-conditioned and furnished with two double beds. If you can live without air-conditioning, options include connecting rooms with two bedrooms and two full baths, or housekeeping units/suites with one or two bedrooms, a kitchen, and a living room. Housekeeping units are rented weekly, from Saturday to Saturday; all others can be booked either by the day or at a discounted weekly rate. Open primarily for peak season—mid-May through Columbus Day weekend. *2999 State Rte. 9L, Lake George; (800) 79-LODGE; (518) 656-9242;* www.dunhamsbay.com

The Georgian Luxury Resort
★★★/$$-$$$
This 164-room property is a good choice for families who want to be on the lake and in the center of the action. A five-minute walk, or quick trolley ride, from Lake George Village, the Georgian boasts 400 feet of lakefront, a private sandy beach, and an outdoor heated pool. Oversize rooms, outfitted with two double beds, comfortably accommodate a family of four. Prices vary, depending on the view (of the lake, pool, or parking lot). A children's menu is available in the Georgian Supper Club, where dinner is served May through October. Lunch is served on the poolside patio Memorial Day weekend through early September. Open year-round. *384 Canada St., Lake George; (800) 525-3436; (518) 668-5401;* www. georgianresort.com

Holiday Inn Turf at Lake George
★★★/$$-$$$
Fresh from a multimillion-dollar renovation, this family-owned hotel offers a hilltop view of Lake George, a central location, and all the standard amenities. Kids will enjoy the indoor and outdoor pools, arcade games, playground, and, in the summer, the miniature-golf course that's set up in the courtyard. Rooms with two queen-size beds can accommodate a family of four; kids under 12 stay free with their parents. All rooms are air-conditioned and have color TVs; Nintendo and pay-per-view movies are available for an extra charge. The on-site restaurant serves breakfast, lunch, and dinner; children 12

CALLING ALL CAMPERS

With its breathtaking mountain views, countless hiking trails, and thousands of lakes, ponds, and streams, upstate New York is an ideal destination for families who want to camp. In the Adirondacks alone, there are more than 40 public campgrounds. Add private facilities, including KOA locations, and you've got a complete range of choices, from rustic to full-service. Following is a partial list of upstate camp sites to get you started:

Lake Placid Region

Adirondack Loj Wilderness Campground

Adirondack Loj Rd. (off Rte. 73), Lake Placid, NY 12946; *(518) 523-3441*

Lake Placid/Whiteface Mountain KOA

KOA, Fox Farm Rd., Wilmington, NY 12997; *Reservations: (800) KOA-0368; Information: (518) 946-7878*

North Pole Campground and Motor Inn

Rte. 86, Wilmington, NY 12997; *(800) 245-0228; (518) 946-7733;* www.northpoleresorts.com

Whispering Pines Campground

Box 28, Cascade Rd. (Rte. 73), Lake Placid, NY 12946; *(518) 523-9322*

Lake George Region

Adirondack Camping Village

P.O. Box 406, Lake George, NY 12845-0406; *(518) 668-5226*

Hearthstone Point Campsite (NYS EnCon)

Rte. 9N, Lake George, NY 12845; *Reservations: (800) 456-CAMP; Information: (518) 668-5193*

King Phillip's Campsites

P.O. Box 592, Rte. 9 and Bloody Pond Rd., Lake George, NY 12845; *(518) 668-5763*

Lake George Battleground Campground (NYS EnCon)

U.S. Rte. 9, Lake George, NY 12845; *Reservations: (800) 456-CAMP; Information: (518) 668-3348*

Lake George Campsite/Glen Island (NYS EnCon)

Boat access only, Bolton Landing, NY 12814; *(800) 456-CAMP*

Lake George Campsite/Long Island (NYS EnCon)

Boat access only, Bolton Landing, NY 12814; *(800) 456-CAMP*

Lake George Campsite/Narrow Island (NYS EnCon)

Boat access only, Bolton Landing, NY 12814; *(800) 456-CAMP*

Lake George Escape Evergreen Camping Resort

Box 431, 175 E. Schroon River Rd., Lake George, NY 12845; *(800) 327-3188; (518) 623-3207;* www.lakegeorgeescape.com

Lake George RV Park

74 State Rte. 149, Lake George, NY 12845-3501; *(518) 792-3775;* www.lakegeorgervpark.com

Lake George/Saratoga KOA

KOA, P.O. Box 533, Rte. 9N, Lake George, NY 12845; *Reservations: (800) KOA-2618; Information: (518) 696-2615*

Ledgeview Village R.V. Park

321 State Rte. 149, Lake George, NY 12845; *(888) 353-5936; (518)* 798-6621; www.ledgeview.com

Mohawk Camping on Lake George

R.R. 2, Box 2386, Lake George, NY 12845; *(518) 668-2760*

Mount Kenyon

Box 584, Lake George, NY 12845; *(518) 696-2905*

Rainbow View

Rte. 9, Lake George, NY 12845; *(518) 623-3207*

Whippoorwill

R.R. 3, Box 3347, Rte. 9, Lake George, NY 12845; *(518) 668-5565*

Central Leatherstocking Region

Cooperstown Beaver Valley Campground

P.O. Box 704, Cooperstown, NY 13326; *(800) 726-7314*

Cooperstown Famous Family Tent & Trailer Campground

230 Petkewec Rd., Cooperstown, NY 13326; *(800) 959-2267; (607) 293-7766*

Cooperstown North KOA

KOA, P.O. Box 786, Cooperstown, NY 13326; *Reservations: (800) KOA-3402; Information: (315) 858-0236*

(Continued on page 122)

Cooperstown Ringwood Farms
R.D. 2, Box 721, Cooperstown, NY 13326; *(800) 231-9114; (607) 547-2896*

Cooperstown Shadow Brook
R.D. 2, Box 646, Cooperstown, NY 13326; *(607) 264-8431*

Yogi Bear's Jellystone Park at Crystal Lake
111 E. Turtle Lake Rd., Garrattsville, NY 13342; *(800) 231-1907; (607) 965-8265*

Niagara Frontier

Niagara Falls Campground & Lodging
2405 Niagara Falls Blvd., Niagara Falls, NY 14304; *(716) 731-3434*

Niagara Falls KOA
KOA, 2570 Grand Island Blvd., Grand Island, NY 14072; *Reservations: (800) KOA-0787; Information: (716) 773-7583*

Super 8 Niagara Falls
7680 Niagara Falls Blvd., Niagara Falls, NY 14304; *Reservations: (800) 547-8868; Information: (716) 283-3151*

For camping information: *FNYS Department of Environmental Conservation, Summer Recreation, Room 679, 50 Wolf Rd., Albany, NY 12233-5253; (518) 457-2500. Reservations: (800) 456-CAMP.*

and under get free kids' meals when they dine with an adult. You can walk to Lake George Village or, in the summer, stroll down the driveway to the trolley stop. The hotel is close to shopping outlets and Great Escape, too. Open year-round. *Canada St., Lake George; (800) 465-4329; (518) 668-5781;* www.bass hotels.com/holiday-inn

Melody Manor Resort
★★★/$$-$$$
Located on nine and a half acres—including 300 feet along Lake George—Melody Manor is a good option for families who want to bask in the beauty of the Adirondacks and also remain within a ten-minute drive of Lake George Village. After a day in the village, you can return here to rest in Adirondack chairs or enjoy a game of tennis, volleyball, basketball, shuffleboard, pool, or Ping-Pong. Guests can swim in the heated pool or play at the private beach, where the shallow waters are ideal for kids. Paddleboats and rowboats are available, and fishing charters can be arranged. All rooms are air-conditioned and are outfitted with either two double or two queen-size beds and cable TV. For a lakefront room (which cost about $10 more per night), make reservations several months in advance. The resort's Villa Napoli Restaurant serves breakfast and dinner and features a kids' menu (see Good Eats). Open May through October.

4610 Lake Shore Dr., Bolton Landing; (518) 644-9750; www.melody
manor.com

Mohican Resort Motel
★★★/$$-$$$

You'll know you've arrived when you see the giant Mohican standing out front. The story behind this ten-foot-tall sentry speaks volumes about the type of care the Stark family takes, both with their motel and their guests. The Mohican has his roots in a large pine tree that was hit by lightning several years back and had to be cut down. Marilyn Stark is so attached to the trees on the motel grounds that she couldn't bear for even one to be lost. So she hired a carver and found a new way for the tree to grace the property. The whole family can enjoy the full-size basketball court, a playground, a picnic area and gazebo, indoor and outdoor pools, and game room with pool table, air hockey, and video games. You can choose from among standard rooms with two queen-size beds; connecting two-room units that can sleep up to six; efficiencies with two queen-size beds and a kitchenette; condominium units; and town houses. All are air-conditioned and have cable TV. The small on-site coffee shop serves a full breakfast at a reasonable price. Open Memorial Day through Labor Day. *1545 State Rte. 9, Lake George; (518) 792-0474;* www.mohican
motel.com

Roaring Brook Ranch and Tennis Resort
★★★/$$-$$$$

There's so much to do at this resort, your family may see no reason to explore the sights elsewhere. On these 500 acres you'll find two unheated outdoor pools and one indoor pool, five tennis courts, and 30 horses. During July and August, Roaring Brook offers a family program with daily tennis clinics, supervised horseback riding, and a counselor who takes kids on pony rides, to the playground, and to see the ducks and swans at the pond. Families can stay in rooms with two double beds or in suites with two double beds in the bedroom and a pullout sofa bed in the sitting room. Full breakfast and dinner are served in the main lodge. Kids' fare includes hot dogs, hamburgers, and chicken nuggets. Breakfast, dinner, clinics, and children's programs are included in the Modified American Plan; the less expensive European plan covers lodging only. Guests who can't get enough horseback riding can pay a little more to ride every day. Others can choose the non-riding rate and pay per ride. During the summer, dancing and entertainment are scheduled every night. Lake George Village is just two miles away, and it's only five miles to the Great Escape & Splashwater Kingdom. Open mid-May through mid-October. *Rte. 9N S., Lake George; (800) 882-7665;*

123

(518) 668-5767; www.roaringbrook ranch.com

The Sagamore ★★★★/$$$$

For a luxurious, full-service splurge, nothing compares to The Sagamore. Located on picturesque Green Island, this resort has been helping families to vacation in style since 1883. Everywhere you look, choices abound, from accommodations (350 rooms) to dining (six restaurants) to activities. You can opt for a room in the historic main hotel or in one of the lodges, or you can stay in a condominium, a unit in the bi-level Hermitage Executive Retreat, or even in the six-bedroom, four-bath Wapanak Castle. The preferred choice for many families is one of the 120 lodge suites. Decorated in a contem- porary Adirondack style, each suite features a large master bedroom with bay window; an ample parlor with a queen-size pullout sofa bed; and a kitchenette. Special Sagamore touches include a wood-burning fireplace and a balcony that faces Lake George.

The main dining room, not the ultra-formal Trillium, is very family- ly friendly; at breakfast, the kids can head for the children's buffet with an omelette station. The dress code in the main dining room is "resort casu- al," and reservations are required for dinner. The Adirondack camp-style Mr. Brown's Pub, where dress is casu- al, is another good option.

There's a host of Lake George– related activities: relaxing on the private beach, swimming, boating, and, at the nearby marina, water-

DAY TRIP
Saratoga Springs

About 30 miles south of Lake George is Saratoga Springs, the commu- nity that bills itself as "the summer place to be." For five weeks, from the end of July through Labor Day, Saratoga is synonymous with horse racing. Visitors from around the globe are drawn to **Saratoga Race Course** (*Union Ave., Saratoga Springs; 518/584-6200*), the nation's oldest—and perhaps most elegant— thoroughbred racetrack. Families can pack a lunch and set up camp in the picnic area; visit the **Discovery Paddock**, a hands-on exhibit where kids can learn how horses and jock- eys prepare for racing, and enjoy special activities such as Juggling for Kids. Those who are happy to see the horses (minus the racing) may prefer to come for the buffet breakfast, served from 7 to 9:30 A.M. **NOTE:** The track is closed Tuesday.

If you're planning to see more than the racetrack, include a stop at the **Saratoga Springs Urban Cultural Park Visitor Center** (*297 Broadway, Saratoga Springs; opposite Congress Park; 518/587-3241*) for maps and

skiing, parasailing, and charter fishing. But you can also enjoy the indoor pool, walking and jogging trails, indoor and outdoor tennis and racquetball courts, horse-and-buggy rides around the property, and a Project Adventure–style challenge course. Golfers can practice at the driving range, then tee up at the 18-hole championship Donald Ross course, used for regional PGA and amateur championship matches. In winter, you can go hiking and snowshoeing, plus skiing at nearby Gore Mountain. Families also are invited to participate in organized activities such as miniature-golf tournaments, *Family Feud* games, and ice-cream socials. For an additional fee, kids ages 4 to 12 can sign up for the Teepee Club, where they'll

enjoy arts and crafts, swimming, scavenger hunts, sand sculpting, face painting, puppet theater, miniature golf, pirate picnics, and more. **NOTE:** For a peak-season summer vacation, make reservations from six months to a year in advance. Open year round. *On Lake George at Bolton Landing; (800) 358-3585 (reservations); (518) 644-9400;* www.thesagamore.com

---

information on self-guided walking tours of the city. Save time, too, to stroll along Broadway, where many of the shops are one of a kind.

Museum aficionados can visit the **National Museum of Dance** (*99 S. Broadway, Saratoga Springs; 518/584-2225*), **National Museum of Racing & Hall of Fame** (*191 Union Ave., Saratoga Springs; 518/584-0400*), and **The Children's Museum** (*69 Caroline St., Saratoga Springs; 518/584-5540*). History buffs will want to take a detour to **Saratoga National Historical Park** in nearby Stillwater (*15 miles southeast of Saratoga Springs off Rtes. 4 and 32; 518/664-9821, ext. 224*), the site of one of the most decisive battles of the Revolutionary War. For outdoor fun, visit **Saratoga Spa State Park** (*Rte. 9, Saratoga Springs; 518/584-2535*). The 2,200-acre park is a great spot for picnicking, biking, and walking along nature trails. The kids will also like the two pools, including the Olympic-size Peerless Pool, complete with a double slide.

For more information, contact the **Saratoga County Chamber of Commerce—Tourism**, *28 Clinton St., Saratoga Springs, NY 12866; (800) 526-8970;* www.saratoga.org

GOOD EATS

Finding a restaurant in Lake George Village is as easy as strolling down Canada Street, where kids will spot all of their fast-food favorites and then some. For sit-down fare, try some of these eateries.

Adirondack Coach House
★★★/$$-$$$$

There's something for everyone at this restaurant, which resembles an old Adirondack log home (albeit one with an enclosed glass terrace out front). Lunch choices range from soups and a salad bar to burgers, wraps, and sandwiches, including a good grilled salmon BLT. For dinner, try the charbroiled steaks and chops and a wide selection of veal, chicken, and seafood dishes. Scouts and Sprouts can have chicken fin-

gers, grilled chop steak, spaghetti with meatballs, roasted turkey, or the child's sirloin. The salad bar is included in the kids' meal. Crayons and coloring sheets keep little fingers busy until the food arrives. Open year-round. *Rte. 9, Lake George; (518) 743-1575;* www.menumart. com/adirondackcoachhouse

The Boardwalk Restaurant and Marina ★★/$$-$$$

The closest restaurant to the lake, the Boardwalk offers spectacular views, a varied menu, and some all-you-can-eat options, such as a crab-leg buffet. Lunch choices include salads, burgers, seafood, steak, and barbecue. For dinner, adults can order food From the Farm (beef, chicken, and ribs) or From the Waters. The Sunday breakfast buffet is an excellent value. Kids can choose from the children's menu or the list of appetizers: nachos

---

FamilyFun **READER'S TIP**

Taste-testers

While traveling, my husband and I grew tired of our children's requests to visit the same old fast-food places for the latest kids'-meal prize. So we instituted the no-fast-food rule: when our family hits the road on vacation, we only stop at restaurants we can't visit back home. In other words, no nationally franchised restaurants or fast-food joints. The idea is to find some regional flavor. As it gets closer to lunch or dinner, we look for one-of-a-kind diners, rib joints, custard shops, and the like. Thanks to this rule, we have eaten Indian fry bread in the Badlands, great sloppy ribs in Tennessee, sensational seafood in South Carolina, and more. Dylan, age 7, and Ryan, 10, enjoy being on the lookout for the quirkiest place and don't even miss the "prize inside" scene.

Lisa Tepp, Milwaukee, Wisconsin

with cheese, chicken wings, mozzarella sticks, chicken fingers. Dine inside or out. Open April through September. *Lower Amherst St., Lake George; (518) 668-5324;* www.the lakegeorgeboardwalk.com

Capri Pizzeria & Restaurant
★★/$-$$

Open around the clock during peak season, Capri has an extensive menu of appetizers, pizzas, calzones, hot and cold sandwiches, and Italian specialties. The children's menu offers spaghetti, ziti, ravioli, and chicken fingers, or kids can munch on popular appetizers such as cheese sticks and chicken wings. Adults can try mussels marinara, gnocchi, stuffed shells, and veal, chicken, or eggplant parmigiana. Delivery is available within seven miles, including to area hotels. Open year-round; 24 hours a day Memorial Day through Labor Day. *221 Canada St., Lake George; (518) 668-5027;* www. lakegeorgeny.com/capripizza/

East Cove Restaurant
★★★/$-$$$

Located on the east side of Lake George, this log cabin offers an extensive menu (for both kids and adults) in a family-friendly atmosphere. Adult entrées include steak and pork chops from the grill, surf and turf, cracked-pepper salmon and other seafood choices, plus Wiener schnitzel, veal and artichokes, and chicken Victoria. The kids' menu offers the typical hamburgers, cheese-

burgers, and chicken fingers, but there are also child-size portions of prime rib, chicken Parmesan, and fried fish with French fries. Sunday brunch is also served. Kids get crayons and a place mat to color while they wait for the food to arrive. Reservations are a good idea during peak season. Visit the restaurant's Website for coupons. Open daily May through October; closed Mondays and Tuesdays November through April. *3873 Rte. 9L, Lake George; (518) 668-5265;* www.eastcove.com

The Log Jam Restaurant
★★★/$$$-$$$$

After a shopping excursion along the "Million Dollar Mile," sit back and enjoy casual Adirondack dining at the Log Jam. For adults, lunch choices include soup; a salad bar; sirloin burgers; creative sandwiches such as a pork melt, Hawaiian chicken wrap, and lobster salad croissant; and entrées such as crabmeat-stuffed shrimp, the catch of the day, and chicken feta. The kids' lunch menu has a salad bar, a grilled cheese sandwich, a hamburger or cheeseburger, and chicken tenders. The dinner menu is as complete as they come, with a wide variety of appetizers, meat dishes (steak, ribs, lamb), and seafood options, including Maine lobsters. Kids fare just as well as adults: fried chicken tenders, a small steak, barbecued baby-back ribs, the catch of the day, a child's prime rib, bow-tie pasta, and grilled

cheese sticks. Open year-round for lunch and dinner. Reservations are recommended, especially in the peak summer season. *Rtes. 9 and 149, Lake George; (518) 798-1155;* www.log jamrestaurant.com

Villa Napoli ★★★/$$-$$$

For a dinner of classic Northern Italian cuisine, visit this former estate turned restaurant. The menu features Tuscan specialties, including veal, chicken, swordfish, and seafood combinations in flavorful sauces. Kids can choose from spaghetti and a meatball, fresh ravioli in tomato sauce, baked ziti with meat sauce, baked lasagna, chicken nuggets and French fries, and grilled breast of chicken. Manager and mother Rose Alessi designed the children's menu with a choice of soup or salad, so kids have something to eat while parents enjoy an appetizer. Dress is casual; reservations are suggested. Open May through October. *At the Melody Manor Resort, 4610 Lake Shore Dr., Bolton Landing: (518) 644-9750;* www.melodymanor.com

SOUVENIR HUNTING

Lake George Village is as commercial as it gets. Walk down Canada Street, and you're visually bombarded with possible souvenirs, including $2 T-shirts and homemade candy. Since those stores are easy to find on your own, we've highlighted the more unusual places to shop. Those who like to shop will also want to check out the factory outlets along the "Million Dollar Mile."

Gift Cottage

This country store stocks good-quality souvenir T-shirts and caps, plus an assortment of gifts: Will Moses prints, tapestries, candles, stuffed animals, and dolls, dolls, dolls. Open April through December. *197 Canada St., Lake George; (518) 668-2234.*

Factory Outlets of Lake George

The area boasts four outlet malls—Factory Stores of America, Lake George Plaza Outlet Center, French Mountain Commons Outlet Center, and Adirondack Outlet Mall—all along Route 9. You'll find discount prices on everything from shoes and designer clothing to cosmetics, luggage, and home furnishings. Stores include Polo/Ralph Lauren, Tommy Hilfiger, Gap Outlet, Levi Strauss, Lancôme, Pfaltzgraff, Coach, Samsonite, and more. For the kids, there's a Book Warehouse, Toy Liquidators, and Carter's Childrens' wear. *Hours vary seasonally; call (518) 743-9021 for more information;* www.factoryoutletsoflakegeorge.com

The Secret Garden

Owners Frank and Rita Chiaravalle Imbimbo designed this shop as a sanctuary that emphasizes the positive side of life. Along with garden accents and statues, you'll find fresh ivory topiaries, wall hangings, lotions, incense, candles, jewelry, and a selection of higher-end gifts for young children, including the Beatrix Potter figurines collection. Items are also available on-line. Call for off-season hours. *139 Canada St., Lake George; (877) 314-2513; (518) 668-4210;* www.shopthesecret garden.com

Sutton's Marketplace

You'll find a collection of charming shops at this family-owned marketplace. Kids will want to check out the Toy Cottage, which stocks classic toys, craft kits, books, and collectible dolls. Mom may want to browse through the Clothing Boutique, which has casual and dress clothing for women in natural fabrics, plus accessories. Stop in at the Country Café for breakfast or lunch, and pick up gourmet items and other treats in the bakery. There's also a gift shop and a furniture store. Open daily, year-round. Call for specific store hours. *Rte. 9, Queensbury; (518) 798-1188;* www. suttonsmarketplace.com

BACKSEAT GAMES

In the privacy of your own car, you can laugh as loud as you want or shout out the answers to questions. So don't hold back when you play these games —laugh, yell, or sing your heart out. The ideas are well suited to driving, as they don't involve writing.

THE CAR NEXT DOOR

Invent stories about people in the car next to yours. What do you think they do for work? What's their favorite food? Where do they go on vacation? Get into lots of details, such as whether they snore loudly or are afraid of spiders. Give them names, hobbies, pets, and so on.

BUZZ

This is a team effort to try to reach 100 without making a mistake. Take turns counting, beginning with one. Every time you get to a number that's divisible by seven (7, 14, 21, . . .) or has a seven in it (17), say "Buzz" instead of the number. If one person forgets to say "Buzz," everyone has to start over. If this is too hard, say "Buzz" for every number divisible by 5. If you want a real challenge, try Fuzz Buzz. Say "Fuzz" for every number with a three in it or that's divisible by three, and "Buzz" for every number with a seven in it or that's divisible by seven.

Tyrus Raymond
Ty Cobb won more batting championships (12) and compiled a higher lifetime average (.367) than any player in the game's history.

Check out America's national pastime through the stats and stuff of legends like Gehrig, Ruth, and Cobb at the National Baseball Hall of Fame and Museum.

Cooperstown

ACH YEAR, this village of about 2,400 residents hosts some 400,000 guests, most of whom come to pay homage to the heroes in the National Baseball Hall of Fame and Museum. Baseball, it's fair to say, is why most families come here. Dads, Moms, and kids of all ages immerse themselves in the national pastime, reveling in a community where establishments bear names such as "National Pastime" and "Third Base." Children even have their own field of dreams here. Tournaments begin each June at Cooperstown Dreams Park, where young athletes from around the world vie against their peers. Eventually, however, even the biggest fan looks around and realizes that, although Cooperstown is rightfully equated with baseball, it also offers much more.

Located at the southern tip of Otsego Lake and the start of the 444-mile Susquehanna River, Cooperstown was founded in 1876 by William Cooper. His son, James Fenimore Cooper, would grow up to be one of our nation's first great novelists and the creator, in Natty Bumppo (alias the Deerslayer), of an American

THE **FamilyFun** LIST

MUST-SEE · MUST-SEE

Howe Caverns (page 137)

National Baseball Hall of Fame and Museum (page 138)

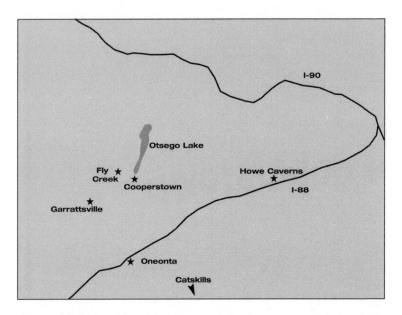

archetype, the "Western hero." James Fenimore Cooper also would immortalize some of the landmarks in his hometown, including the Indian meeting place of Council Rock and his "Glimmer-glass," Otsego Lake.

Much of what draws visitors to Cooperstown today can be traced to the Clark family, which settled in the village just before the Civil War. The Clarks built Cooperstown's famed resort hotel, the Otesaga, and they were instrumental in the establishment of the National Baseball Hall of Fame and Museum and the construction of the buildings that would eventually house the Fenimore Art Museum and the Farmers' Museum. Your family will enjoy these local treasures, but be sure to sample the town's natural

pleasures as well. Take a boat ride on Otsego Lake, hike and swim in Glimmerglass State Park, and stroll along quaint, unspoiled Main Street.

If you still have time after Cooperstown proper, you may want to branch out a little bit. It's just a short drive to neighboring Oneonta and the National Soccer Hall of Fame. Farther away, but still within easy driving distance (about 45 minutes), are Howe Caverns and the Iroquois Indian Museum.

The residents of Cooperstown cherish what they call their "Main Street way of life." They take pride in their historic architecture, their one traffic light, and the absence of national chains and franchises within their village borders. Although some establishments are open year-round, for the most part the towns-folk have Cooperstown to themselves in the winter. Peak season is May through October, when parking can be in short supply. In Cooperstown fashion, the village has provided a solution: three lots on the perimeter of town, where parking is free and trolley service is frequent. You can buy a one-day trolley pass, good for unlimited rides, for a nominal fee.

The busiest time of all is Hall of Fame Induction Weekend, typically held in July or August. Fans arrive in droves to applaud the new inductees, catch a glimpse of those previously enshrined, witness the Hall of Fame Game and Home Run Derby, and, of course, get autographs. **NOTE:** If you are true fans and want to hit this weekend, be aware that hotels are booked as early as a year in advance, so make reservations well ahead of time.

For help planning your trip, contact the **Cooperstown Chamber of Commerce** (*31 Chestnut St., Cooperstown, NY 13326; 607/547-9983;* www.cooperstownchamber.org) or **Cooperstown GetAway** (*888/875-2969;* www.cooperstowngetaway.org). Additional information is available at www.cooperstown.net. During your visit to the Baseball Hall of Fame, the Fenimore Art Museum, and the Farmers' Museum, ask about discount, combination tickets to these attractions. Also nearby are the Catskills, rich in all-season fun for the entire family. For more informa-

tion, see "Skiers, Consider the Catskills" on page 142 and "The Catskills" on page 148.

CULTURAL ADVENTURES

Farmers' Museum ★★★/$-$$

Things are still done the old-fashioned way at this historic village and working 19th-century farm. A day here is fun for kids of all ages—tiny tots like the animals, while older kids enjoy learning about life in the "olden days." You enter through the Main Barn, which serves as the exhibition center and is the site of spinning, weaving, and broom-making demonstrations, along with artifacts of rural upstate life. The village is composed of nearly 20 buildings, relocated from small towns across central New York State. Together, they form a rural hamlet typical of 1845. Many are staffed by trades-people engaged in period activities, from printing to blacksmithing to making wallpaper with an 1837 block press. Alongside the buildings are

gardens in which the appropriate crops are grown; medicinal herbs, for example, grow outside Dr. Thrall's Pharmacy. At one end of the village is Lippitt Farmstead, which includes a barn, animal sheds, a smokehouse, and a family farm. Here, oxen plow the fields, and farmers use hand tools from the 1840s to harvest the crops. Cows' milk is used to make butter, and apples are pressed for cider— your kids can help with this task if you visit in the fall. Heritage breeds of chickens and ducks supply eggs. Grazing in the nearby hillside pasture are Devon cattle, a breed that's rare today but was popular 150 years ago. On the outskirts of the hamlet is an Iroquois log cabin, built around 150 years ago. A traditional herb garden is planted in the surrounding woods.

On your way back to the Main Barn, stop at the exhibition tent to see the Cardiff Giant, known as "America's Greatest Hoax." Commissioned by Binghamton, New York, resident George Hull in 1968, the giant was carved from a five-ton block of gypsum, buried, "rediscovered" a year later and—until the hoax was exposed—passed off as the petrified remains of a large, ancient man. (Preteens get a kick out of this.) Also near the main entrance are the museum shop and the Herder's Cottage restaurant, which offers family-friendly fare. Throughout the year, the Farmers' Museum hosts a variety of programs; call ahead to find out what's scheduled during

your visit. Open April through November. During peak season, June through September, the museum is open daily; it's closed Mondays in April, May, October, and November. *Lake Rd., Cooperstown; (888) 547-1450; recorded information, (607) 547-1500;* www.farmersmuseum.org

Fenimore Art Museum
★★★/$$

Along with a critically acclaimed American Indian Wing and an impressive collection of fine and folk art, this museum has an education room for kids, away from the galleries. Your kids can use the puzzles, books, architectural building blocks, and drawing materials to explore art on their own. Ask at the desk about interactive programs for families, provided by museum educators (included in the price of admission), June through December. Presentations are geared to your children's ages and interests. Examples include treasure hunts and games that relate to the museum's exhibits. Also, periodically throughout the summer, you can take the "Feathered Friends at Fenimore Art Museum" mystery tour, during which families scour all three floors of the museum in search of bird motifs in art. Summer art classes (fee) also are scheduled from 1 to 3 P.M. on Wednesdays for kids ages 6 through 14. Registration is accepted, but not required.

Outside, kids can visit the bark house, a reproduction of a Mohawk dwelling from the 1750s. In addition to the kid-themed activities, be sure to make time to see some of the works for which the museum is best known: paintings depicting American history and landscapes, American folk art, memorabilia of James Fenimore Cooper and his family, and, perhaps most interesting to kids, American folk art and the Eugene and Clare Thaw Collection of American Indian Art. Temporary exhibits typically involve an interactive component for kids. The museum is operated by the New York State Historical Association, whose headquarters are in the museum building, a 1930s Neo-Georgian mansion overlooking Otsego Lake. Open April through December. From June through September, the museum is open daily; it's closed Mondays in April, May, October, November, and December. *Lake Rd., Cooperstown; (888) 547-1450; recorded information, (607) 547-1500;* www.nysha.org

Iroquois Indian Museum
★★★/$

Let the kids spend a couple of hours exploring the world of the Iroquois at this hands-on attraction. Since its founding two decades ago, the museum has sought not only to teach visitors about Iroquois history, but also to make it clear that Iroquois culture is very much alive today. The museum is home to the world's largest collection of contemporary Iroquois art, and the building itself is a modern interpretation of a longhouse, the traditional Iroquois dwelling. The kids will have the most fun downstairs in the Children's Iroquois Museum, where they can handle furs, traditional clothing, and Iroquois game pieces. They also can pound corn into meal, using a wooden mortar and pestle and learn about stone tools by playing an archaeology game. An exhibit on storytelling introduces youngsters to legendary Iroquois characters. Upstairs, on the

---

FamilyFun READER'S TIP -----------------------------------

It's in the Cards

My family loves to travel, and I have found a wonderful way to preserve our vacation memories. First, we buy postcards at all the different locations we visit. On the backs, I jot down the highlights of the trip or funny things that happened while we were there. After we have returned home, I laminate all the postcards, punch holes in the top left corners, and put them all on a ring clip. It's exciting to see all of the places we have been, and the cards are inexpensive souvenirs of our travels.

Stefanie Wirths, Camdenton, Missouri

main floor, you can view exhibits of Iroquois art and artifacts. For a change of pace after a few hours in the museum, head for the nature trails in the 45-acre park. Call ahead for information on special events, including festivals on Labor Day and Memorial Day weekends, and demonstrations by artists on weekends in July and August. Present a ticket stub from Howe Caverns (just up the road) and receive $1 off the price of admission. Open April through December. *Caverns Rd., Howes Cave; (518) 296-8949;* www. iroquoismuseum.org

JUST FOR FUN

Cooperstown Fun Park
★★/$$$

When you've seen enough and relaxed sufficiently, pick up the pace a bit at this family entertainment center. The kids will have a blast racing in the go-carts and jostling each other on the bumper boats. (Children must be taller than 45 inches to ride without an adult; life jackets are required and provided for those ages 12 and under.) Sandlot sluggers will want to test their swinging skills at softball and baseball batting cages, where speeds range from slow to medium to fast and very fast. Have a family golf tournament at Puttin' Around Miniature Golf, an 18-hole course that's not quite as simple as it looks. Inside, you'll find

an arcade with some 20 games, plus the inevitable baseball souvenirs and a snack bar. If your family wants more than ice cream, however, you'll do better to head next door to Clete Boyer's Hamburger Hall of Fame (see Good Eats). Discount coupons are available on-line. Open 9 A.M. to 11 P.M. daily in the summer; call for spring and fall hours. *4850 State Rte. 28, Cooperstown; (607) 547-2767;* www.cooperstownfunpark.com

Fly Creek Cider Mill and Orchard
★★/Free

If you're in Cooperstown between mid-August and late November, head over to Fly Creek and watch the Michaels family make apple cider the old-fashioned way. When the presses are running, the building literally shakes, thanks to the 1924 gas engine that powers the apple grinder. The cider press dates back to 1889 and is powered by water from Fly Creek. An 1872 turbine waterwheel turns the pulleys and belts that set the press in motion. During peak season, the Michaels press 300 gallons a day during the week and 800 gallons a day on weekends.

Your older kids, especially any budding engineers, will be fascinated to see the turn-of-the-century equipment at work; younger children will enjoy Tractor Land, where they can ride Little Tikes toys; and kids of all ages will want to feed the ducks and chickens. There's also a "snack shack" and gift shop. Special events, including an antique-engine show, an applefest, and a cider festival, are held during cider season; call for details. **NOTE:** The rest rooms are the portable kind, located out back. *288 Goose St., Fly Creek; (607) 547-9692;* www.flycreekcider mill.com

Glimmerglass State Park
★★/$$

For a break from sight-seeing, set aside half a day or more at this 600-acre recreation spot. Eight miles outside the village of Cooperstown, Glimmerglass State Park offers biking, camping, fishing, hiking along the Beaver Pond trail, swimming in Otsego Lake, a concession stand, a playground, picnic tables, and even a covered bridge. Lifeguards are on duty during the summer months. Although there's no boat launch, you can bring canoes, kayaks, and Windsurfers—any craft that you can carry to the water. In the winter, you can go tubing, snowshoeing, snowmobiling, ice fishing, ice-skating, and cross-country skiing. **NOTE:** You're not allowed to go skateboarding, in-line skating, or scooter riding, so leave those wheels at home. If you think your older kids would enjoy seeing the restoration of a historic house in progress, buy a ticket to tour **Hyde Hall** (*607/547-5098;* www.hydehall.org). Located next to the park, the historic country mansion boasts 50 rooms and impressive family collections.

Batters Up

Cooperstown plays host to one major league game each year. Doubleday Field hosts the contest, which takes place during the Hall of Fame weekend in July. For more information on this year's game, go to the Baseball Hall of Fame Website at www.baseballhalloffame.org or phone *888-HALL-OF-FAME.*

The tour lasts 75 minutes; this may be a good time for one parent to skip the tour and play in the park with the younger kids. Hyde Hall is open May through October. *1527 County Hwy. 31, Cooperstown; (607) 547-8662;* www.nysparks.state.ny.us

Howe Caverns
FamilyFun ★★★★/$$$

Forty-five minutes from Cooperstown and 156 feet beneath the earth is a natural attraction that's "cool" in every sense of the word. Millions of years in the making, these caverns were discovered in 1842 by a farmer, Lester Howe, who graciously gave credit to his cow, Millicent. Howe had noticed that on hot days his herd always headed for the same spot. He went to investigate and felt cool air coming from some nearby bushes. Howe moved the branches, saw an opening, and returned with rope and lanterns to begin exploring the caves that now lure 200,000 visitors each year.

Howe's first public tours were rugged adventures. For 50 cents, visitors were outfitted with suitable clothing for an eight- to ten-hour journey through mud, clay, and 42° water. Today's tours last 80 minutes and begin with an elevator ride down to the caverns. Bring a light jacket or sweater, as the temperature down below is a constant 52°. Led by a tour guide, you walk along illuminated brick pathways and, midway through, take a quarter-mile boat ride on the underground Lake of Venus; it's an easy walk, good for kids of all ages. Throughout the tour, the guide points out fascinating stalactite, stalagmite, and flowstone formations. Some of the chattier guides also regale visitors with amusing tall tales.

Back aboveground, for an additional fee, kids can pan for gemstones and choose a geode for cutting. A snack bar is open year-round, and a full-service restaurant, complete with kids' menu, serves breakfast, lunch, and dinner mid-April through Columbus Day. If you prefer, pack a lunch and eat in the picnic area. Accommodations are available on-site at the 21-room Howe Caverns Motel (*518/296-8950*), also open mid-April through Columbus Day. The caverns are open year-round except Thanksgiving, Christmas, and New Year's Day. *Off Rte. 7. From Cooperstown, take Rte. 28 South to I-88 East. Get off at exit 22 and follow the signs. Howes Cave; (518) 296-8900;* www. howecaverns.com

National Baseball Hall of Fame and Museum
★★★★/$$

The repository of our national pastime, this hall may be the world's best-known sports shrine. Since its opening in 1939, more than 11 million fans have come to see, among other artifacts, the original baseball fashioned at Abner Doubleday's request, Joe DiMaggio's locker, and the glove that Willie Mays used for his famous over-the-shoulder catch in the 1954 World Series. The centerpiece of the three-story museum is the Hall of Fame Gallery, where the oak walls are lined with bronze plaques featuring likenesses of all who've earned baseball's greatest honor. In the front section of the gallery, a display pays tribute to the most recent inductees. On the second floor, the exhibit The Game: the General History of Baseball covers the sport from pre-1900 to the present. Here you'll find the equipment, uniforms, and other possessions of legends Babe Ruth, Jackie Robinson, Hank Aaron, and other baseball greats. The Major League Locker Room exhibit gives you and the kids a close-up look at the uniforms of today's teams. Pride and Passion: the African-American Baseball Experience traces the role of African Americans in baseball, from the 19th century to the Negro Leagues to the majors.

Don't miss The Baseball Experience, a multimedia presentation in the Grandstand Theater; it's a heartwarming look at baseball from the hometown fields to the professional stadiums. Third-floor exhibits recall the great ballparks of yesteryear, trace the evolution of baseball uniforms and equipment, and highlight postseason play, the role of women in baseball, and youth and minor leagues.

You also can check out the baseball cards of generations past. The museum also hosts changing exhibits. Recent offerings have included the Great American Home Run Chase, which featured famous sluggers from Babe Ruth and Roger Maris to Mark McGwire and Sammy Sosa, and You're in the Hall of Fame, Charlie Brown! showcasing some of Charles Schultz's memorable baseball-related cartoons. Call ahead to find out what temporary exhibits they'll have going during your stay. **CURATOR'S TIP:** Start your visit on the second floor. From there, head up to the third floor and finish on the first floor. Open year-round except Thanksgiving, Christmas, and New Year's Day. *25 Main St., Cooperstown; (607) 547-7200; www.baseballhalloffame.org*

National Soccer Hall of Fame
★★★/$

Soccer fans will get a kick out of this lesser-known hall of fame, only 22 miles from Cooperstown. The kids can test their soccer knowledge and skills, learn about the history of U.S. soccer from the Civil War to the present, and watch real-life games (matches are held here every weekend from June to December; players can be as young as 9 to men and women over 40; college and major league teams play here as well).

One of the most popular features

MORE THAN 480 WEDDINGS have been performed at the Bridal Altar in Howe Caverns. Couples recite their vows while standing on a heart-shaped piece of calcite that is embedded in the floor.

is the $2.50 game card that lets kids try their hands—and heads and feet—at game stations throughout the museum. They're challenged by such things as a computerized trivia test, a header cage, a chip-shot game, and a dribbling contest. At each station, kids swipe the card and get two to four tries to beat the clock. Once you've completed the contests, you can get a printout of your scores. The card can also double as a souvenir, with your picture and name inscribed on it. The more-than-20,000-square-foot museum houses the U.S. soccer archive, whose 80,000 items make it one of the world's largest collections of soccer records and artifacts; it boasts the world's oldest soccer ball.

Videos depict each era of soccer and tell the story of the World Cup from 1930 to the present. In the rotunda is the Hall of Fame, where visitors can learn about more than 200 legends of the game. Athletes young and old travel from across the country to play on the regulation fields. The museum complex currently is in the midst of an expansion that will add a stadium, indoor soccer arena, and four more world-class fields, for a total of nine outdoor and two indoor playing areas. You can buy souvenirs and soccer equipment in the Kick's Hall of Fame Store. *18 Stadium Cir., Oneonta; (607) 432-3351;* www.soc cerhall.org

BUNKING DOWN

The bed-and-breakfast experience is very much a part of a visit to Cooperstown. For information on bed-and-breakfast accommodations, contact the **Cooperstown Chamber of Commerce** (*607/547-9983;* www.cooperstownchamber. org/stay/bandbs). For camping information, see "Calling All Campers" on page 120.

Bay Side Inn & Marina
★★/$$-$$$$
You have a choice of accommodations on this four-acre site, seven miles north of Cooperstown. The main inn has six rooms, the newer motel 20 more. Or opt for one of the ten one-, two-, and three-bedroom cottages. All are air-conditioned, and offer partial views of Lake Otsego—as well as cable TV with HBO. You can use the inn's private beach, free paddleboats, and canoes; the kids can hit the children's play area and a game room, and there's a picnic area with a grill. You can fish, but you'll need to bring your own poles. Open May through October. *7090 State Hwy. 80, Cooperstown; (607) 547-2371;* www.cooperstown.net/bayside/

Best Western Inn & Suites at the Commons ★★/$$-$$$
The kids will love what's next to this hotel—a McDonald's and a Pizza Hut. The setting isn't bucolic—it's

in a shopping plaza three and a half miles outside the village of Cooperstown—but this 98-room Best Western also features a heated indoor pool, a game room, and a fitness center and spa. A family of four can fit comfortably in a standard room with two queen-size beds. For just a little bit more, you can get a suite with two queen-size beds; a kitchenette with a microwave, refrigerator, and cabinets; and a sleep sofa. Children under 12 stay free with an adult; the rate includes free continental breakfast. *Rte. 28, 50 Commons Dr., Cooperstown; (607) 547-9439;* www.bwcooperstown.com

The Cooper Inn
★★★/$$$-$$$$

This Federal-style manor house has been a Cooperstown landmark since 1813, when it was built as the residence of Henry Phinney, son of printing pioneer Elihu Phinney, Sr. Today you can choose among 20 renovated guest rooms and suites. The inn's atmosphere is a little formal for most children, but if yours are older, sophisticated travelers, it might be fine. Rooms are decorated in the style of the early 1800s; each is equipped with a telephone, cable TV, air-conditioning, and a private bath. Families would be most comfort-

able in a two-room suite. Through an affiliation with Cooperstown's famous Otesaga Resort (just one block away), the Cooper Inn offers guests access to the facilities at that luxury property and a 50 percent discount in greens fees at the Otesaga's Leatherstocking Golf Course. *Main and Chestnut Sts., Cooperstown; (800) 348-6222; (607) 547-2567;* www.cooperinn.com

Hickory Grove Motor Inn
★★/$$

Owners Heidi and Henry Stucky have gone to great lengths so that your family will feel at home in this 12-room hotel on Otsego Lake. Each room has at least a partial view of the lake. You can choose from among three kinds of lodging: a room with two double beds, a room with a queen-size bed and a pullout sofa bed, or a room with a queen-size bed plus rollaways. Just down the hill in the beach area, you can sunbathe, or be more active—swim, or venture out in paddleboats. Kids are welcome to fish off the dock. Picnic out back, behind the motel, or head into Cooperstown for a bite to eat. Hickory Grove is just six miles north of the village and ten minutes from a free public parking area, where you can pick up the trolley and avoid the hassle of finding a space in town. Open mid-April

Cooperstown's **Otesaga Resort** gets its name from an Iroquois phrase that means "the meeting place."

SKIERS, CONSIDER THE CATSKILLS

I F SKIING IS your idea of winter fun, a vacation in New York's Catskill Mountains may be just the ticket. Hit the slopes at family-friendly Ski Windham, Belayre, or at the larger Hunter Mountain. Since they're just ten miles apart, you can always try all three.

BELAYRE (*P.O. Box 313, Highmount, NY 12441; 845/254-5600*) features, along with programs for adult skiers, the ski-wee program. Vertical drop is 1,404 feet and has 41 lifts, which accommodate all levels of skiers. For accommodations information, contact (800) 431-4555; ski conditions, call (800) 942-6904.

HUNTER MOUNTAIN (*P.O. Box 295, Hunter, NY 12442; 518/263-4223*; www.huntermtn.com) boasts a vertical drop of 1,600 feet, 53 trails over 230 acres, and 100 percent snowmaking coverage. Fully 30 percent of trails are for beginners and another 30 percent for intermediate skiers.

In addition to child care, Hunter offers a ski-wee program for kids ages 4 to 6, Hunter Mountaineers for those ages 7 to 12, MINIrider snowboarding program for kids ages 6 to 12, and Learn with Me Family Lessons, where you and your kids can learn to ski together. A broad range of accommodations is available via central reservations at *(800) 775-4641*.

SKI WINDHAM (*P.O. Box 459, Windham, NY 12496; 800/754-9463; 518/734-4300*) has a vertical drop of 1,600 feet, and a total of 36 trails, ranging in length from 300 feet to 12,500 feet long. Ten of the trails are considered "easiest" for beginners; snowmaking machines blanket 97 percent of trails. Kids' programs are offered in the Children's Learning Center and include activities for non-skiing young guests, the Mini-Mogul program for 4- to 7-year-old skiers, and Mogul Masters for skiers ages 8 to 12. Snow tubing also is available. Accommodations range from slope-side condominiums to local bed-and-breakfasts and can be booked through central reservations at *(800) 754-9463*. One nice option for families is the **Windham Arms Hotel** (*P.O. Box 459, Windham NY 12496; 800/754-9463; 518/734-3000*; www.windhamarmshotel.com), which features free shuttle service to Ski Windham.

through October; peak season is mid-June through Labor Day. *6854 State Hwy. 80, Cooperstown; (607) 547-9874; reservations (877) 547-8567;* www.cooperstown.net/hickorygrove

Lake 'N Pines Motel
★★★/$-$$$

The only area motel with heated indoor *and* outdoor pools, the Lake 'N Pines is both affordable and loaded with kid appeal. Its sandy, lakefront beach and free paddleboats are big hits with children, as is the game room. The fishermen in your group may use the motel's rowboats, a boat ramp, and dock space. Families can stay in rooms furnished with two queen-size or two double beds, or in one of four cottages. Each of the air-conditioned cottages faces the lake and has two or three bedrooms (with linens), a living room with cable TV, and a full-size kitchen equipped with dishes and pots and pans. There's no restaurant, but guests can help themselves to doughnuts, coffee, hot chocolate, and hot tea in the lobby in the morning. Open from late March through November. *7102 State Hwy. 80, Cooperstown; (800) 615-5253 (reservations); (607) 547-2790;* www.cooperstown.net/lake-n-pines

Lake View Motel and Cottages
★★/$-$$$

Just six miles north of Cooperstown, this clean, lakefront property has 20 rooms and seven cottages, all with access to Otsego Lake and the motel's private beach. You can swim, fish, and have free use of paddleboats and rowboats. Rooms and cottages are individually furnished, air-conditioned, and have cable TV with HBO. Open from April through October. *6805 State Hwy. 80; (888) 452-5384; (607) 547-9740;* www.cooperstownvacations.com

Otesaga Resort Hotel
★★★★/$$$$

The grande dame of upstate resorts, the Otesaga is Cooperstown's most elegant accommodation. With 700 feet of property along Otsego Lake, the five-story, Federal-style hotel boasts one of the best locations in town, plus a heated lakeside pool and the top-ranked Leatherstocking Golf Course. You can also swim in the lake, take advantage of free canoes and rafts, and fish off the dock with poles and bait supplied by the resort. There are outdoor tennis courts and a game room, too. The full-time concierge is more than happy to help arrange outings, from sailing, skeet shooting, and fly-fishing to trips to area attractions. The 136 guest rooms are as impressive as the location; recently renovated, they retain the 1909 hotel's period details. No two rooms are alike; all are large and now have, as part of the renovation, windows that open to take advantage of lakeside breezes. A family of four can choose a standard room, two bedrooms with a shared bath, or a suite. The kids will go for the sumptuous breakfast, with waffle and pancake stations, served in the dining room, and lunch is available both in the dining room and on the terrace overlooking the lake. Dinner in the dining room is a formal affair, with jackets required for gentlemen and boys ages 12 and older; no shorts, jeans, or sneakers are allowed. For those who prefer a more relaxed atmosphere, there's the Hawkeye Grill (reservations recommended), where you can arrive in resort casual dress, and children's meals are available. Open mid-April until November. Rates include breakfast and dinner in the dining room or Hawkeye Grill. *60 Lake St., Cooperstown; (800) 348-6222 (reservations); (607) 547-9931; www. otesaga.com*

Tunnicliff Inn
★★★/$$$-$$$$

If your family enjoys staying at small country lodgings, consider Cooperstown's oldest historic inn. One of the village's few year-round properties, the Tunnicliff has been a Cooperstown landmark since 1802. The hotel is centrally located—only a half block from the National Baseball Hall of Fame and Museum—and each of its 17 air-conditioned rooms is outfitted with period furnishings, a private bath, a telephone, and cable TV. A family of four can fit comfortably in a single room with

a king-size bed and two rollaways. A more expensive alternative is adjoining rooms: one with a king-size bed, the other with two singles. Families can eat dinner downstairs in the Tap Room and Restaurant, a tavern-style eatery that locals affectionately refer to as the Pit. Dinner also is served in the James Fenimore Cooper Room, which probably is too formal for most families. *34–36 Pioneer St., Cooperstown; (607) 547-9611; www.cooperstowncham ber.org/tunnicliff/*

GOOD EATS

Cider Mill Snack Bar & Donut Shop ★/$

Surprise—this outdoor eatery offers plenty of apple- and cider-related treats: apple pies, dumplings, and muffins, candy apples, cider mill doughnuts, cider floats, and cider slush. But you can also get soup and chili, hot pulled-pork sandwiches, hot dogs, sweet sausages, nachos, popcorn, hot pretzels, and ice-cream cones, cups, and sundaes. Open Memorial Day through the third week of December. Hours may vary, so it's best to call ahead. *288 Goose St., Fly Creek; (607) 547-9692; www. flycreekcidermill.com*

Clete Boyer's Hamburger Hall of Fame ★★/$

New York Yankee fans will feel right at home in this restaurant, where even the curtains pay tribute to the Bronx Bombers. Pictures of ballplayers adorn the walls, almost all of them current or former Yankees. During peak season (May through Labor Day), owner and former Yankee third baseman Clete Boyer is a regular here. The restaurant serves breakfast, lunch, and dinner.

Although there's no children's menu per se, you'll find lots of kid-pleasing choices, including mozzarella sticks, chicken nuggets, and peanut-butter-and-jelly sandwiches. Hamburger lovers have 11 half-pound options, including the Mickey Mantle Cheeseburger Deluxe, the Whitey Ford Blue Cheese Burger, the Andy Pettitte Pizza Burger, and the Jeter Burger Supreme. Baseball memorabilia also is sold here. The restaurant is open daily during peak season (May through Labor Day), when diners can eat inside or out. Open Wednesday though Sunday the rest of the year, except January, when the restaurant is closed. *4874 State Hwy. 28, Cooperstown; (607) 544-1112.*

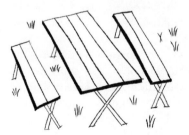

Cooperstown Pepper Mill Family Restaurant
★★★/$-$$

Its central location, plentiful parking, and affordable prices make this restaurant a good pick for families. Adults can choose among steaks, chicken, pasta, seafood, and hamburgers; there's also a light menu featuring half-size servings that cost one-third the price of a full dish. Kids can order hot dogs, hamburgers, cheeseburgers, mozzarella sticks, or chicken wings. Open for dinner only; closed January through March. *5418 State Hwy. 28, Cooperstown; (607) 547-8550.*

Doubleday Café
★★/$-$$

The casual atmosphere and familiar fare make this a comfortable spot for families. Choices range from full-course dinner and Mexican selections to pasta specials, quiche, burgers, and homemade soups. Although there's no kids' menu, there's lots to please younger palates: hot dogs, chicken tenders, grilled cheese, and more. The interior is what you'd expect in the Village of Cooperstown: brick walls and baseball memorabilia. The place serves breakfast, lunch, and dinner; everything can also be ordered to go. Opening and closing hours vary with the season; call ahead. *93 Main St., Cooperstown; (607) 547-5468.*

Hawkeye Bar & Grill
★★★/$-$$$

This surprisingly low-key, Early American–style grill is in the lower lobby of Cooperstown's grand resort, the Otesaga. Unlike the hotel, the Hawkeye is open year-round, serving lunch Tuesday through Friday and dinner Tuesday through Saturday. Adults can get soup, hot and cold sandwiches, pasta of the day, risotto, or turkey stew with puff pastry for lunch. Dinner offerings range from lamb, veal, salmon, and duck dishes to pub fare. Kids can choose from hot dogs, hamburgers, grilled cheese, chicken fingers, popcorn shrimp, and spaghetti and meatballs. Kids' sandwiches come with fries, and all children's meals include ice cream for dessert. All menu items are available for takeout, too. *60 Lake St., Cooperstown; (607) 547-9931.*

The Home Plate T.J.'s Place
★★/$-$$

The menu at this eatery is chock-full of baseball-themed choices, from "omelettes and extra innings" at breakfast to "openers" (appetizers) and "home plates" (entrées) at dinner. It also doubles as a newspaper and souvenir that families are welcome to take home. Breakfast fare includes pancakes, waffles, eggs, biscuits, omelettes, and "sliders" (side orders). For lunch, there's soup, hot and cold sandwiches, baskets of clams or shrimp, and more.

Dinner choices run the gamut from Italian platters to burgers, steak, chicken, and fried fish—expect large portions. The kids' menu offers several choices each for breakfast, lunch, and dinner. T.J.'s is popular with Hall of Fame inductees, so if you're in town for Hall of Fame Weekend, keep your eyes and autograph books open. *124 Main St., Cooperstown; (607) 547-4040.*

SOUVENIR HUNTING

Cider Mill Gift Shop

Country crafts abound in what was once the Fly Creek Cider Mill's grist room. Choose from harvest-themed decorations and potpourris to Yankee candles and garden gifts that can take root once you return home. There also are wooden puzzles and T-shirts for kids. Downstairs, take your pick of apples, aged cheeses, specialty crackers, and fudge. You'll also find gourmet dips, cooking mixes, and, of course, plenty of cider. Open early July to mid-December. *288 Goose St., Fly Creek; (607) 547-9692;* www.flycreekcider mill.com

Cooperstown Bat Company

Sluggers of all ages come here to buy official Major League Baseball bats or custom ones, made of ash. Kids just love to have their name or signature engraved on "the sweet spot." During the summer (June through August), you can take factory tours; they're free, and no reservations are necessary. Open May through October. Off-season, bats are sold at the Cooperstown Bat Company factory on Route 28N in nearby Fly Creek. *118 Main St., Cooperstown; (888) 547-2415; (607) 547-2415;* www.cooperstown bat.com

Metro Fashion

Stop in at this boutique for custom-designed T-shirts, most with Cooperstown themes. The T-shirts also can be viewed and ordered on-line. The shop also sells women's clothing, handbags, and jewelry. Call for hours. *147 Main St., Cooperstown; (607) 547-2749;* www.coopers towntshirts.com; www.baseball tshirts.com

National Pastime

Browsers are welcome in this establishment, which seems as much museum as store. Among the antiques and memorabilia are old baseball bats and gloves and original baseball pins, prints, posters, and pennants. Items are also sold on-line. *81 Main St., Cooperstown; (607) 547-2524.*

Third Base

You'll find cap upon cap at this store, which stocks literally thousands of team-logo baseball caps for kids and adults. You can also buy team jerseys, jackets, and T-shirts. The whole family can leave here clad in team attire—there's even a section of baseball outfits for infants and toddlers. *83 Main St., Cooperstown; (888) 318-CAPS; (607) 547-8802.*

Tin Bin Alley Country Store

Step into a simpler time at this country store, where you'll find home-made fudge, preserves, and other sweets. The kids will love choosing their favorites from the barrels of penny candy (parents take note—nothing costs a penny anymore). There's also a selection of folk art, pottery, and collectibles, plus the Cooperstown Commemorative Afghan, featuring the National Baseball Hall of Fame, Doubleday Field, and other Cooperstown sights. *114 Main St., Cooperstown; (607) 547-5565;* www.cooperstowncham ber.org/tinbin/

THE CATSKILLS

WITHOUT A DOUBT, nature is the single greatest attraction in this region, dubbed "America's First Wilderness," because the environmental conservation movement had its roots here. Officially, the Catskills span six counties and more than 6,000 square miles between New York City and Albany. Most vacationers, however, are drawn to the four "forest preserve" counties: Ulster, Greene, Delaware, and Sullivan counties. Here, public and private lands combine in the 98-peak **Catskill Park** to create a four-season destination for those who seek their fun outdoors.

The **Catskill Forest Preserve** refers to the state-owned land that comprises roughly 40 percent of the Catskill Park. The preserve was created in 1885 and, since then, has grown from 34,000 to 300,000 acres of forests and meadows, mountains, streams, lakes, and waterfalls. Under an 1894 amendment to the New York State constitution, this entire area will remain "forever wild." Another 400,000 acres nearby are privately held, home to approximately 50,000 year-round residents and some of New York's most popular recreation resorts.

In the winter, families hit the slopes at **Hunter Mountain and Ski Windham** (See "Skiers, Consider the Catskills," page 142). Spring and fall are peak seasons for trout anglers, who long to cast their lines in the birthplace of American fly-fishing. Nature enthusiasts come all year long to hike, camp, or simply enjoy the view. For them, the least popular season tends to be summer, when the Catskills can be hot, humid, and even buggy. But that's peak time for more commercial venues, such as the Catskill Game Farm and Zoom Flume, two kid favorites in Greene County.

For more information on planning your Catskill excursion, contact CATS, the **Catskill Association for Tourism Services**, *P.O. Box 449, Catskill; (800) NYS-CATS (697-2287)*; www.catskillgetaways.com Information also is available from the following county organizations: **Delaware County Chamber of Commerce**, *114 Main Street, Delhi; (800) 642-4443;* www.delawarecounty.org **Greene County Promotion**, *Route 23B, Catskill; (800) 355-2287,* www.greene-ny.com and **Sullivan County Visitors Association**, *100 North Street, Government Center, Monticello; (800) 882-CATS (882-2287);* www.scva.net

Catskill Fish Hatchery ★★/Free

Your kids may be surprised to learn that many of the fish caught in New York waters are born and bred not in the wild, but in hatcheries like this one. The state Department of

Environmental Conservation (DEC) operates 12 hatcheries that, combined, stock more than 1,200 public bodies of water with several million fish each year. The Catskill hatchery is home exclusively to brown trout. Although there are no official tours, visitors are welcome. If your kids are interested in fishing, combine a stop here with a visit to the Catskill Fly Fishing Center and Museum. Then head a mile up the road to the Willowemoc Wild Forest (in the southwest portion of the Catskill Park) for some hiking or fishing. Open year-round, weekdays from 8:30 A.M. to 4 P.M.; holidays and weekends, 8:30 A.M. to noon. *402 Mongaup Road, Livingston Manor; (845) 439-4328;* www.dec.state.ny.us/website/dfwmr/fish

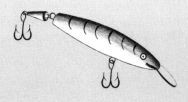

Catskill Fly Fishing Center and Museum ★★/Free

Located on 53 acres along a mile of prime "no kill" trout water, this attraction caters to the true fly-fishing fan. Exhibits tell the story of trout and this time-honored sport, and feature vintage rods and reels. Overnight environmental education programs are offered on summer weekends for children ages 8 to 11 and 12 to 14. Rod makers, environmentalists, and naturalists also present weekend programs. If you're new to fly-fishing, you can watch instructional videos. If you're an old hand, bring your rod and reel, and catch and release trout in

Willowemoc Creek. There's also a picnic area and small nature trail. Although admission is free, a nominal donation is suggested. April through October, open daily, 10 A.M. to 4 P.M.; November through March, open Tuesday through Friday, 10 A.M. to 1 P.M., Saturday, 10 A.M. to 4 P.M. *1031 Old Route 17, Livingston Manor, NY 12758-1295; (845) 439-4810;* www.cffcm.org

Catskill Forest Preserve
★★★★/Free

Families that appreciate the outdoors can spend their entire Catskill vacation enjoying the activities available here: camping, hiking, mountain biking, horseback riding, fishing, swimming, boating, tubing, and, in winter, snowshoeing, snowmobiling, and cross-country skiing. The preserve has 300 miles of trails, some as short as a half-mile. Older kids will enjoy the Kaaterskill Falls Trail, which ends at the base of the 260-foot Kaaterskill Falls, the highest in New York State. The falls consist of two tiers: an upper level that drops 175 feet, and a lower level that falls 85 feet into a rocky basin. Your best bet for information on family-friendly

activities is to request the free brochure, *The Catskill Adventure: Day Hikes and Paddles for Families*, from the state Department of Environmental Conservation (DEC), *21 South Putt Corners Road, New Paltz; (845) 256-3082 or 3083; www.dec.state.ny.us* DEC also offers free trail maps, as well as brochures on horseback riding, cross-country skiing, and snowmobiling. Although entry to the preserve is free, you will pay a fee to park at campgrounds and day-use areas. Open daily, year-round. *(888) HUNTER-MTN*

Catskill Game Farm
★★★★/$$$$

This attraction has been entertaining kids since 1933. You'll find some 2,000 animals representing more than 150 species, from farm critters to lions and giraffes. Highlights include a petting zoo, complete with a nursery, where children can bottle-feed baby pigs, goats, and sheep. A three-act animal show, scheduled three times a day, features dogs, horses, and ele-phants showing off their tricks. If the weather is warm, kids can run through the sprinklers and water jets in the Splashpad area, so pack a bathing suit. Kiddie amusement rides are available for an extra fee. You can buy lunch in the game farm or bring food to enjoy in the picnic area. Open daily, July through Labor Day, 9 A.M. to 6 P.M.; May, June, and October, 9 A.M. to 5 P.M. *Off Route 32, Catskill; (518) 678-9595;* www.catskillgame farm.com

Hunter Mountain Skyride
★★★★/$$

For a different perspective on the Catskills, climb aboard the Hunter Mountain Skyride and travel 5,500 feet to an elevation of 3,200 feet above sea level. The longest and highest chairlift in the Catskills, the skyride takes you from base to summit in 11 minutes. At the top, you can see the Berkshire Mountains in Massachusetts, the Green Mountains in Vermont and, of course, the Catskills. Families sit in chairlifts that accommodate four passengers. You can choose to ride round-trip or, if your family is more adventurous, take a guided tour down via mountain bike. (The bikes are strapped on the outside of the lift, much as skis are during the winter.) Bikes, helmets, and lessons are available at the mountain for an additional fee. Families can ride without a guide on scenic trails at the summit and easy, wooded trails at the bottom. Weekends only, July through September, 10 A.M. to 5 P.M., weather permitting. *P.O. Box 295, Hunter; (888) HUNTER-MTN (486-8376);* www. huntermtn.com

Kaleidoworld
★★/$-$$

The world's largest kaleidoscope (recognized by *The Guinness Book of Records*) is housed in a restored 19th-century barn, in a 65-foot-tall silo. Known as the Kaatskill Kaleidoscope, it projects amazing images of more than 50 feet in diameter during a stirring 10-minute show, *America, the House We Live In.* Visitors step into the kaleidoscope, lean back against supports with headrests, and cast their eyes overhead. Chairs are also available, or you can lie down on the floor if you find that more comfortable. A second, shorter show, *Starworks*—in the world's second-largest kaleidoscope—focuses on outer space and the Big Bang the-

ory. Kaleidoworld is located in Catskill Corners, including a collection of shops, a lodge, and restaurants. If you decide to stay for lunch, most kids will probably choose the Spotted Dog Firehouse Restaurant with its firefighter motif. Open Wednesday through Sunday, 10 A.M. to 5 P.M. and until 7 P.M. Friday and Saturday; closed Tuesday. *Route 28, Mt. Tremper; (888)303-3936, ext.15.*

Zoom Flume
★★★★/$$$$

On a hot day, no place is more refreshing than the Catskills' largest water park. Kids can easily spend a full day zipping down body slides, enjoying tube rides, and splashing one another in the activity pool. Tackle the Wild River with its 10,000-gallon-a-minute "rapids." For a more relaxing ride, float down the lazy river. Little ones can get a taste of the action in Pelican Pond. Dine in the restaurant or in the snack bar area, or pack a picnic lunch. If Mom or Dad has no intention of getting wet, save money by opting for a spectator pass, which includes access to the park, sundecks and picnic areas, but not use of rides and pools. Coupons are available on-line. Open from the end of June through Labor Day, Monday through Friday, 10 A.M. to 6 P.M.; Weekends, 10 A.M. to 7 P.M. *Shady Glen Road, East Durham; (800)888-3586;* www.zoomflume.com

New Jersey

F ROM SCHUSSING down snowy slopes to careening around high-speed roller coasters, family excitement abounds in the Garden State. Your children can build sand castles along miles of beautiful shoreline and explore bucolic parks that offer hiking, bird-watching, and an endless supply of picnic spots. On sun-shy days, little ones will squeal with delight as they watch their favorite fairy tales come to life at Fairy Tale Forest, while older kids can hop a stagecoach ride through the Wild West or a virtual ride through outer space at

Around
the
State

The Jersey Shore

Wild West City. No matter how old your children are, New Jersey will take your family on a journey full of adventure and discovery.

Thanks to the state's location, both skiing (to the north) and seaside frolicking (to the south) are within an easy drive of several major cities. New Jersey is not large, and an abundance of connecting turnpikes and parkways makes it possible to get just about anywhere in the state within a few hours (that's entirely depending on traffic, of course). Although shore retreats and mountain resorts are worth a longer visit, they're also convenient day trips from New York, Philadelphia, and Washington, D.C.

ATTRACTIONS
$	under $5
$$	$5 - $10
$$$	$10 - $20
$$$$	$20 and over

HOTELS/MOTELS/CAMPGROUNDS
$	under $100
$$	$100 - $150
$$$	$150 - $200
$$$$	$200 and over

RESTAURANTS
$	under $10
$$	$10 - $15
$$$	$15 - $25
$$$$	$25 and over

***FAMILYFUN* RATED**
★	Fine
★★	Good
★★★	Very Good
★★★★	*FamilyFun* Recommended

Surrey rides offer a unique way for your kids to take in the smells of homemade candy and sounds of rolling waves off Ocean City's famous boardwalk.

OCEAN CITY BIKES.
8th & Atlantic

RENT ME
$10.00

The Jersey Shore

THE 127-MILE STRETCH of coastline known as the Jersey Shore is the state's most popular vacation area. The buff-colored ribbons that stretch from Sandy Hook down to Cape May are edged by bustling boardwalks, family eateries (some with great seafood), and reasonably priced lodgings. With the exception of the lavish resort/casinos in Atlantic City, most hotels are on the simple side, providing basic accommodations that fit family budgets. At the shore, you're typically paying for access to fun in the sun, not luxurious amenities. The high season runs from May through September, with discounts offered between Labor Day and Memorial Day. But keep in mind that lower prices mean lower water temperatures: in late September the ocean

is usually still warm enough for full body plunges, but early spring means very chilly surf and toe-dipping at best.

THE **FamilyFun** LIST

MUST-SEE
MUST-SEE

Cape May County Park and Zoo
(page 167)

Historic Cold Spring Village
(page 167)

Island Beach State Park
(page 157)

Jenkinson's Beach, Boardwalk, and Aquarium (page 157)

Lucy the Elephant (page 161)

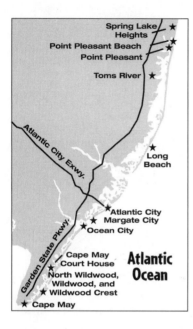

Where you should stay along the Jersey Shore largely depends on your children's ages and whether you prefer bumper-car entertainment or relative peace and quiet. Point Pleasant Beach has boardwalk arcades and rides that please everyone from the stroller crowd on up to teens. The tame kiddie rides in Ocean City will appeal to tiny tots and their parents, while families with older kids might prefer Seaside Heights and Wildwood, where amusement parks thrill with daredevil rides. Long Beach Island tends to be more popular with preppies of all ages (restaurants, shops, nightspots); Atlantic City has plenty of casino action, but very little to amuse the kids. And if arcades and carny rides leave you yearning for earplugs, smaller, quieter Cape May might be just the place for you and yours.

Point Pleasant

About a quarter of the way down the New Jersey coast is Barnegat Peninsula (actually an island), where Point Pleasant and Point Pleasant Beach offer plenty of fun-filled parks and sandy stretches for soaking up the sun and sea air. All summer long, laser shows, nightly fireworks displays, and free concerts—pop, jazz, and country—add welcome variety to a seaside stay. You can also stroll the busy boardwalk, where arcades and food concessions dominate. If you visit in late September—when the water is still warm enough for swimming—you may hit the annual Sea Weekend, which features a street fair, bountiful seafood, tube races, and a parade.

Point Pleasant has ample accommodations, but they're all pretty much the same. Most are small motels, similar in price and overall appearance. "Upscale" here means closer to the beach, boardwalk, and amusement parks; a large room or a large pool is a bonus. Many hotels include beach passes in the room rate; if yours doesn't, you can buy day or season passes along the boardwalk. Dining options range from pizza joints to somewhat pricey seafood establishments, but you'll find lots of family-friendly eateries that serve hearty, inexpensive fare. Most hotels and restaurants are near the boardwalk, so you won't have to go far for sun and surf or food and fun.

JUST FOR FUN

⭐MUST-SEE⭐ Island Beach
FamilyFun State Park
⭐MUST-SEE⭐ ★★★★/$$

Point Pleasant is at the top of the Barnegat Peninsula, and this state park anchors the southern half of the 20-mile-long island. The park itself is 10 miles long and lined with beautiful beaches on both the bay and ocean sides, making it perfect for swimming, surfing, and scuba diving. Canoe tours are offered. Near the entrance, a welcome center displays exhibits about the park's wildlife, much of which can be spotted along lovely nature trails. Picnicking and barbecuing are allowed on the beach, making this a perfect spot for dining alfresco. *Off Rte. 35, Point Pleasant; (732) 793-0506;* www.state.nj.us/dep/forestry/parks/island.htm

⭐MUST-SEE⭐ Jenkinson's
FamilyFun Beach, Boardwalk,
⭐MUST-SEE⭐ and Aquarium
★★★/$-$$

Cornering the Point Pleasant market on games and activities, this amusement park captivates kids with rides, miniature golf, and batting cages. Add the beach and a couple of family eateries, and your day is complete. Perhaps the biggest draw, however, is a first-rate aquarium—home to sharks, alligators, seals, penguins, and exotic birds. Allow about 90 minutes for a visit—ample time for oohing and aahing over the many sea creatures, including those in the touch tank. *Boardwalk and Parkway, Point Pleasant Beach. Aquarium: (732) 899-1212; Arcade: (732) 295-4334;* www.jenkinsons.com

Playgrounds Galore

They're elaborate and filled with structures to climb on, tunnel through, and cross over: Ocean City–area playgrounds are among the best you'll find anywhere. Several have baseball and soccer fields and basketball and tennis courts; one even has a running track and four volleyball courts. When the kids hit the hyper mode, head to any of the following locations: *North Point Beach, North Street, Haven Avenue, or 6th, 8th, 15th, 29th, 34th, or 52nd Streets.*

BUNKING DOWN

Amethysts' Beach Motel
★★/$$

Large guest rooms with king-size beds, as well as several suites and a few apartments, draw families to this 40-room property. Each room is well appointed with modern furnishings and a refrigerator, and you can get a microwave at no charge. Other pluses include complimentary breakfast, a heated pool, and picnic grounds. Jenkinson's Pier and several eateries are just a short stroll away. *202 Arnold Ave., Point Pleasant Beach; (732) 899-7000.*

Dunes Motel
★★/$$

The main attraction at this small, no-frills motel is an outdoor pool larger than those at other motels. Free beach passes and easy access to the nearby beach and boardwalk also make it a good choice. *1601 Ocean Ave., Point Pleasant Beach; (732) 899-1143.*

Ramada Inn & Suites-Toms River/Lakewood ★★/$$

This 154-room inn offers some 40 suites, each with a full kitchen, living room, and separate bedroom. There's also a large outdoor pool and a family restaurant with a children's menu. The hotel is almost a 20-minute drive from Point Pleasant Beach, but the Ramada provides roomier accommodations than many of the Point Pleasant motels. *2373 Rte. 9, Toms River; (800) 2-RAMADA; (732) 905-2626;* www.ramada.com

GOOD EATS

The Beanery ★★★/$$

Furnished with fine antiques, this eatery offers healthy vegetarian fare at attractive prices. Also on the menu are turkey sandwiches, tuna fish, and other alternatives to fried and fast food for kids. (Lunch items are a reasonable $5 to $8.) *Bay Ave., Point Pleasant Beach; (732) 295-9669.*

I Scream, You Scream, We All Scream for Ice Cream!

Having steadily gained a reputation up and down the coast since it opened back in 1955, **Hoffman's** is widely held to have the best homemade ice cream in Point Pleasant Beach. Local dairy king Bob Hoffman serves up 52 delicious flavors to his faithful following—who are willing to wait in line for up to 30 minutes to get their licks.

When your kids start screaming for ice cream, head for one of the two Hoffman's branches: *on Route 35 South in Point Pleasant Beach or on Route 71 in Spring Lake Heights (732/892-0270).*

Captain Ed's ★★★/$$$

The giant aquarium in front of this popular restaurant provides endless predinner entertainment for your youngsters. Later, if you order "Steak on a Stone," the kids can watch the chef prepare a savory cut right at your table. Other reasons to stop in: excellent steaks and seafood and friendly service. *1001 Arnold Ave., Point Pleasant Beach; (732) 892-4121.*

Duffy's ★★★/$$

Diner food, including plenty of kid favorites, dominates the menu at this popular spot. *Arnold Ave. and Rte. 35, Point Pleasant Beach; (732) 899-6553.*

Luigi's Famous Pizza & Trattoria ★★★★/$-$$

This pizza joint serves up excellent thin-crust pies that you can enjoy here or take out. The adjoining trattoria has plenty of excellent kid-friendly pasta dishes, plus seafood for Mom and Dad. *Rte. 35, Point Pleasant Beach; (732) 899-4848.*

The Southern House ★★★/$$$

This family favorite serves sizable portions of ribs and chicken with all the trimmings. It's perfect fare for kids who get a charge out of eating with their hands. *Rte. 35 North, Point Pleasant Beach; (732) 899-7427.*

Tesauro's ★★★/$$$

A longtime family-owned *ristorante*, Tesauro's is known for its friendly service and tasty Italian dishes. Families appreciate the pleasant, casual atmosphere and kid-pleasing menu. *401 Broadway, Point Pleasant Beach; (732) 892-2090.*

Ocean City

Touting itself as America's greatest family resort, this oceanside community packs in loads of fun in the sun during the summer months. Thanks to offshore sandbars, some eight miles of pristine, well-maintained beaches deliver mild, rolling waves, perfect for small children.

The boardwalk is ideal for renting bicycles, enjoying a surrey ride, or simply strolling. Miniature golf, arcades, family restaurants, and a couple of first-rate amusement parks sit just off the boardwalk. Trust your kids to track down the shops selling homemade fudge and candy, including that shore specialty, saltwater taffy. Free summer activities include sand-sculpting contests, hermit-crab races, outdoor concerts, and an antique-car show. **NOTE:** The town is dry—meaning no bars, no alcohol—so nightlife is centered mainly at the amusement parks and on the boardwalk.

Advance planning is the secret to a successful Ocean City vacation, so

reserve early (*call 800/BEACH-NJ; the number is for Ocean City only, not all New Jersey beaches*). Unlike the massive hotels of nearby Atlantic City, the town has smaller, cozier accommodations, and they tend to fill up quickly. Several family-friendly motels lie within a block or two of the boardwalk, although the rates may seem a bit high, given the no-frills, often rather small, rooms. If your budget allows, consider paying a few dollars more for roomier accommodations at an all-suite hotel; enjoying a few meals in your room might ultimately save money. **AN O.C. BONUS:** most hotels include beach access in the price of your room.

Come See "O.C."

Each beach community has its share of fun, but **Ocean City** offers a long and hard-to-beat list of annual attractions and free family events. Among the midsummer highlights are a wacky hermit-crab beauty contest, crab races, and a board-walk art show. Also in July and/or August is the Baby Parade. For this event, which has been toddling strong since the early 1900s, babies and young children are dressed up and paraded down the boardwalk in decorated strollers, on bicycles, or on foot. The Night In Venice boat parade has Ocean Beach residents setting sail around the bay as partying crowds cheer them on from shore. September means the Kayak Festival, followed by October's sand-sculpting contest and Pumpkin Halloween Festival and Parade. Off-season, festive annual holiday events reward those willing to brave the December cold.

JUST FOR FUN

Gillian's Island Water Theme Park & Adventure Golf
★★★/$$$

A short stroll down the boardwalk from Wonderland Pier, this water park thrills kids with speedy Serpentine Slides and the popular Skypond Journey Tube Slides—which curve into a 15-foot-high elevated pool for splashing and swimming. Daredevils will love sliding down Shotgun Falls, a chute with a six-foot drop into a large pool. For younger children, a 19,000-square-foot spray park has plenty of plastic turtles and other fun structures to climb, while a light spray keeps 'em cool. Along with water fun, this well-kept

Music by the Sea

From June through September, Ocean City's Music Pier hosts a full schedule of free concerts. Several performances by the **Ocean City Pops Orchestra** (http://www.oceancitypops.org/orchestra/htm) are designed to delight the whole family, and strains of jazz, gospel, and folk music draw a solid mix of loyal fans. An annual draw for beauty-queens-in-the-making (and their ogling brothers) is the **Miss New Jersey Pageant**, also held at the 72-year-old pier.

facility also features a cleverly laid out miniature-golf course. *Plymouth Pl., on the boardwalk, Ocean City; (609) 399-0483;* www.gillians.com

Gillian's Wonderland Pier
★★★/Free–$$

This marvelous amusement park has rides for children of all ages. Older kids will like the Ferris wheel, which offers spectacular views from the top. The City Jet Coaster is a magnet for those who crave twists and turns, and on warm days the Canyon Falls Log Flume may "wet" everyone's appetite for fun. *6th St., on the boardwalk, Ocean City; (609) 399-7082;* www.gillians.com

Lucy the Elephant
FamilyFun ★★★/$

Just 20 minutes north of Ocean City, near Atlantic City, this 65-foot-high wooden pachyderm has been wowing kids (and parents) for more than a century. Originally built as a hotel in the 1880s, the historic elephant has been refurbished and is now a popular landmark. On Saturday and Sunday, kids can go inside and climb up to the top for

only $1 ($3 for adults). *9200 Atlantic Ave., Margate City; (609) 823-6473.*

BUNKING DOWN

Biscayne Suites ★★★/$$$

Large two-room suites with kitchen facilities and easy access to all Ocean City activities are the highlights of this contemporary 64-room hotel. Kids will go for the heated rooftop pool, and complimentary beach passes are included. On-line weekly special rates are offered on the Website (www.biscaynesuites.com). *820 Ocean Ave., Ocean City; (609) 391-8800.*

The Flanders Hotel
★★★★/$$$$

This classic hotel on the boardwalk offers some choice perks for kids, like their own arcade and easy access to the beach and nearby amusement parks. All of the 90 guest rooms are suites with full kitchens and bedrooms that can sleep six comfortably. Other amenities include an outdoor heated pool and a grill restaurant that serves family favorites and Sunday brunch with reduced rates

Candyland

As you stroll along the **Ocean City boardwalk**, don't be surprised if your kids are drawn down Ninth Street by the smell of something sweet. For more than 100 years, Shrivers has been making fresh candy here: saltwater taffy (17 flavors), mouthwatering mint rolls, and other treats your kids can't live without. Chocolate lovers will delight in watching the fudge being made.

for kids. This gracious property commands slightly higher rates than many of the area motels, but the roomy accommodations and upscale service make it worth every penny. *719 E. 11th St., Ocean City; (888) 39-SHORE; (609) 399-1000.*

Watson's Regency Suites ★★★/$$$

Sister hotel to the Flanders, this newer all-suite hotel also has spacious guest rooms with sleep sofas and full kitchens. All rooms have balconies, many boasting ocean views, and you have easy access to all boardwalk activities. Watson's indoor pool makes it an excellent choice for spring and fall. *901 Ocean Ave., Ocean City; (609) 398-4300; (609) 398-3500.*

GOOD EATS

Cousins ★★★★/$$$

One of the most popular eateries in the area has a children's menu offering lasagna, linguini, chicken tenders, and pizza, and tasty veal, pasta, and seafood dishes for adults. Between 4 and 5:30 P.M., the early-bird dinner specials make your wallet happy, too. *104 Asbury Ave., Ocean City; (609) 399-9462.*

Culinary Garden ★★★★/$$$

Another local favorite, this spot serves superb continental fare. Stop by for a first-rate breakfast, lunch, or dinner. *841 Central Ave., Ocean City; (609) 399-3713.*

The Wildwoods

Flanked by the dry town of Ocean City to the north and quaint Victorian Cape May to the south, the Wildwoods seem something like a flashy middle child, rebelling with neon lights and wild rides. Since the late 1800s, droves of vaca- tioners have come to these three shore towns—North Wildwood, Wildwood, and Wildwood Crest— for sun and invigorating summer fun. The Wildwoods are home to five miles of wide, free, white-sand beaches; awesome amusement parks; and a boardwalk packed with beachgoers and lined with arcades and eateries serving pizza, hot dogs, and other fast-food favorites. Thanks to nearby Atlantic City, musicians and other performers often put on free outdoor shows here. Affectionately dubbed Childwood, Wildwood is also a magnet for teenagers—which means your pre- and early teens will consider this a cool place to be, even if Mom and Dad have to tag along.

While nightclubs lend Wildwood a touch of Atlantic City/Vegas glitz (without the gambling), you'll still find plenty of family fun at the beach, boardwalk, and amusement parks. Your clan can lose their marbles at the National Marbles Hall of Fame, then try bicycling, boating, miniature golf, or a whale-watching cruise. Check local newspapers (the *Wildwood Leader* and *Wildwood Herald*) for a schedule of events; annual offerings include a clown convention, stunt kite-flying championship, model aircraft-flying demonstration, baby parade, rodeo on the beach, and monster truck competition. Though much of the activity is in the town of Wildwood, families will find quieter Wildwood Crest a better choice for lodging, with several first-rate hotels featuring resort amenities.

> New Jersey is home to nearly 600 **diners**, more than you'll find in any other state. Only about 3,000 diners still operate in the United States.

JUST FOR FUN

The Piers—
Splash Zone Waterpark
★★★★/Free-$$$$

Exciting rides and water slides of all stripes (fees) fill several piers off the boardwalk. The new **Splash Zone Waterpark** (*E. Schellenger Ave. at Boardwalk*), is an interactive, activity-themed water park. **Morey's Pier** (*26th Ave.; free*) features two great roller coasters—the Nor' Easter and the new RC48—whose exceptionally steep turns will have older kids begging for return trips. **Mariner's Landing** (*E. Schellenger Ave.*) offers 38 rides, including the lion's share of kiddie rides in town, plus one of the highest Ferris wheels in the U.S. Both Morey's and Mariner's have water parks called Raging Waters; both have water slides, raft rides, play areas for little ones and more. In 1987, Morey's rebuilt an old amusement park on Spencer Avenue and named it **Wild Wheels Raceway & Adventure Pier**. One of the highlights there is an old-fashioned wooden roller coaster called the Great White. *Splash Zone: (609) 729-5600; Morey's Pier & Raging Waters Park, Mariner's Landing & Raging Waters Park, and Wild Wheels Raceway & Adventure Pier: (609) 522-3900.*

BUNKING DOWN

Crusader Oceanfront Resort
★★★/$$$

This pleasant 60-room hotel offers families relaxing ambience, modern suites with efficiency kitchens, a family restaurant, an Olympic-size pool, a heated children's pool, a game room, and baby-sitting services. The three-story property is a short walk from both the ocean and the gentle waves on the bay side. *Cardinal Rd. and Ocean Ave., Wildwood Crest; (800) 462-3260; (609) 522-6991;* www.jerseyshoreonline.com/crusader

El Coronado ★★★★/$$$

This six-story mini-resort has eight two-bedroom suites, plus many one-

---

Heart of the Shore

The Wildwoods boast a convenient central location on the Jersey Shore. Distances and driving times from here:

♦ **Atlantic City—44 miles (under an hour)**

♦ **Baltimore—144 miles (2$^{1}/_{4}$ hours)**

♦ **Cape May—8 miles (10 minutes)**

♦ **Ocean City—29 miles (35 minutes)**

♦ **Philadelphia—87 miles (1$^{1}/_{2}$ hours)**

♦ **Washington, D.C.—182 miles (3 hours)**

---

and two-room efficiencies; kids under 12 stay free. A heated pool, a kiddie pool, a game room, a barbecue grill, in-room movies, and a social director make families feel especially welcome. Older kids will lunge for beach volleyball—and maybe even let Mom and Dad play. *8501 Ocean Ave., Wildwood Crest; (800) 227-5302; (609) 729-1000;* www.elcoronado.com

Grand Hotel of Wildwood Crest ★★★/$$$

An expansive outdoor pool, an indoor pool, and two kiddie pools highlight this oceanfront hotel. All 195 rooms (including a few suites) are large, with modern furnishings. Among the other highlights are free activities for all ages in summer, year-round special weekends (like an Elvis weekend and festive holiday weekends), and a trolley ride to and from the nearby Wildwood boardwalk. The hotel's casual restaurant has a children's menu; meals are free for little ones under 3. *9601 Atlantic Ave., Wildwood Crest; (609) 729-6000.*

Oceanview Motel ★★★/$$$

A pleasant little family resort, Oceanview has supervised (and free) daily activities for children, miniature golf, plus a game room, a playground, and a large heated pool with a separate kids' area. Guest rooms are spacious, with simple furnishings, efficiency kitchens (refrigerator, stove, sink, coffeemaker), and, true to the motel's name, great ocean views. *7201*

Ocean Ave., Wildwood Crest; (800) 647-6656; (609) 522-6656.

Port Royal Hotel ★★★/$$$

Right on the beach, this six-story hotel offers plenty of first-rate family amenities—including a heated pool, kiddie pool, and game room. A social director leads kid activities during the summer. Each of the 100 guest rooms has a refrigerator; half are one- or two-room efficiency units. There's also a casual restaurant and a pool-side patio for snacks. *Palm Rd., Wildwood Crest; (609) 729-2000.*

GOOD EATS

Groff's ★★★/$$$

This Wildwood landmark (1925) serves large portions of Pennsylvania Dutch–style dishes, including freshly baked breads, homemade glazed-fruit or apple pies, baked ham,

and turkey with stuffing and mashed potatoes the way Grandma made 'em. A very family-friendly restaurant, Groff's has comfort food for kids and parents alike. Bring your appetite. *423 E. Magnolia Ave., near the boardwalk, Wildwood; (609) 522-5474.*

Papa Joe's Bayside Pizza Pasta House ★★★/$$

Nothing fancy at this joint, but excellent hoagies (or subs, depending on where you're from) and pizza and pasta dishes will have you coming back for more. Top it all off with an ice-cream sundae or shake. Good service and low prices make this a solid value for families. *6710 New Jersey Ave., Wildwood Crest; (609) 729-3236.*

Cape May

At the southernmost tip of New Jersey is Cape May County, which embraces the communities of Cape May, Cape May Point, and Cape May Court House (a town, not a municipal building). Although the names are easily confused with one another, it hardly matters; the entire area has a small-town charm that makes it a great place to enjoy good old-fashioned (low-tech) family fun.

Founded in the early 1600s, Cape May was originally a whaling town, but by the early 1800s the oceanside community had become the place for Philadelphians to spend their summers. Hotels sprang up, many with what has become the Cape's trademark Victorian architecture.

Today the town of Cape May boasts some 600 Victorian-style buildings preserved in a two-square-mile historic area. Cape May Point (http://www.capemaypoint.com), founded in 1875, is home to a massive state park that's ideal for outdoor adventures. At the lighthouse, which preceded the founding of the town (1859), your family can tackle the 199-step climb to the top for spectacular views. A nearby bird observatory gives bird-watchers plenty to chirp about. Cape May Court House, 11 miles north of the town of Cape May, is home to a wonderful zoo and park.

With only a few arcades and no big amusement parks, Cape May moves at a happily slower pace than Wildwood. Bike and surrey are two of the more popular methods of transportation (both can be rented). Instead of a boardwalk, the

FamilyFun TIP

Calling All Campers

In Cape May, Seashore Campsites let you pitch a tent and be lulled to sleep by the sounds of the surf for about $25 a night (609-884-4010).

Washington Street pedestrian mall is the place for strolling; there you'll find free outdoor concerts and busy ice-cream parlors that dish out the latest scoops. Before or after swimming, your family can mine Sunset Beach for Cape May "diamonds" (actually sparkling quartz stones), take a ferry ride or whale-watching cruise, or tour by horse and buggy. A children's theater (*Cape May Kids' Playhouse; Convention Center, Beach Dr.; 609/884-5404*; http://www.cape may.to/) presents shows all summer, and in June the Emlen Physick Estate

FamilyFun READER'S TIP

Time in a Bottle

Our kids (Kiersten, 12, Nicolai, 10, Jarin, 4, and Micah, 1) love to collect rocks, so whenever we go someplace special, we choose one to mark the trip. We write on them—where we went, the date, the initials of those who were there, and other notes, if there is room—and save them in glass jars. We love looking at the rocks and remembering the places we've been and the people who were with us. For instance, one rock says "Horseback Riding, September 27, 1997" and includes the names of family members and the horses we rode (and some we will never try to ride again, like the one that loved to try to buck us off!). Memories of Sunday drives, camping trips, fairs, birthday parties, and family vacations are all recorded and "bottled."

Ron and Marci Clawson, Sandy, Utah

hosts its annual Victorian Fair, featuring period children's games such as hoop rolling and beanbag tosses.

CULTURAL ADVENTURES

★ Historic Cold
FamilyFun Spring Village
★★★★/$-$$

Plan on spending a good four to five hours at this outdoor, 20-acre museum, which re-creates a 19th-century New Jersey village. Featured are 25 restored buildings, including an old wooden schoolhouse, jail, and country store. Just ten minutes from the heart of Cape May, this place will especially impress school-age children by bringing the past to life. Costumed crafters—including blacksmiths, printers, bookbinders, basket weavers, and broom makers—teach kids (and grown-ups) how things were done more than 150 years ago.

Call ahead for a schedule of the numerous special events that are scheduled throughout spring and summer, including an arts-and-crafts show, antique car show, Harvest Fest, and Civil War weekend. Free Saturday night concerts are held throughout July and August. To top off your day, have dinner at the Old Grange restaurant, which serves family fare and ice-cream desserts. *720 Rte. 9, Cape May; (609) 898-2300; www.hcsv.org*

JUST FOR FUN

★ Cape May County
FamilyFun Park and Zoo
★★★/$

If you're looking for a day away from the beach, this terrific park will please children of all ages. You'll find plenty of places to picnic, ride bikes, and play ball, and there's even a pond for fishing. But the real highlight is the well-kept zoo, where more than 300 species of mammals, reptiles, and birds roam. A 35-acre African savanna is home to giraffes, zebras, lions, and other fierce creatures kids will recognize from *The Lion King*. Especially popular with children are the reptile house, full of snakes and creepy crawlers, and the aviary, which shelters a bevy of beautiful birds. Also on-site are a souvenir shop and the Safari Café. *Rte. 9, at Pine La., Cape May Court House; (609) 465-5271; www.capemay countyzoo.com*

BUNKING DOWN

Atlas Inn and Island
Beach Resort ★★★/$$$

Amid the area's many quaint bed-and-breakfast inns, this large hotel stands tall, offering families spacious deluxe rooms, some of which sleep six comfortably. All rooms feature mini-refrigerators; efficiency suites also have microwaves. Over-

A SLOW BOAT TO DELAWARE

Lewes, Delaware, is a lovely historic village near nice beaches and Rehoboth's shopping outlets. But for children, the best reason to visit is the journey itself. Hop aboard the **Cape May-Lewes Ferry,** and they'll spend much of the 75-minute trip exploring the boat's narrow stairways, from the car hold on up to the open-air top deck. Kids love the idea of taking the car on the boat, which can accommodate 100 cars and 800 people. For more information, call (609) 889-7200; http://www.capemay.to/ for the departure schedule, www.lewesde.com

looking the ocean, the property sports a sundeck, pool, and children's pool, and serves up complimentary breakfast. Summer Sunday brings music and barbecue parties, and Yesterday's Heroes restaurant scores big with young sports fans, who love to ogle the Babe Ruth memorabilia. *1035 Beach Dr., Cape May; (888) 285-2746; (609) 884-7000.*

Chalfonte Hotel
★★★/$$$

This 125-year-old granddaddy of the Cape May hotels is a historical landmark and a step back in time. For generations, families have come here to enjoy the simpler pleasures in life. But can your family handle serenity, conversation, and bonding? The Chalfonte has no televisions or telephones in the rooms (only in a public area), and the place is cooled with ceiling fans and ocean breezes, not air-conditioning. During the summer months, a separate children's dining room lets the under-6 crowd play and make

friends while eating (often wearing) dinner. For many families, this can be a marvelously relaxing retreat; but for couch-potato clans, a stay here could turn into a *Survivor* episode. Among several packages is a midweek family special, which includes breakfast, dinner, arcade tokens, and passes to Cape May Miniature Golf. *301 Howard St., Cape May; (609) 884-8409;* www.chalfonte.com

Montreal Inn
★★★/$$$

Families particularly appreciate the spacious rooms with two double beds and efficiency kitchens at this 70-room oceanfront hotel. A game room, Ping-Pong table, shuffleboard court, miniature-golf course, pool, and wading pool provide plenty of on-site family entertainment, while discounts are offered for such outside activities as A.C. Surf baseball games. *1028 Beach Ave., Cape May; (800) 525-7011; (609) 884-7011;* www.capemayfun.com/mi.htm

Good Eats

Dry Dock Ice Cream Bar & Grille
★★★/$$$

After a day at the beach, come here for a quick fix of fun food. Burgers, milk shakes, and a dozen flavors of fresh ice cream are just some of the favorites served up at this popular eatery. *Texas Ave., Cape May; (609) 884-3434.*

The Mad Batter
★★★★/$$$$

A delightful atmosphere and good fare make this Victorian-style spot one of the Cape's most highly acclaimed eateries. If you don't want to splurge on dinner, enjoy breakfast, lunch, or pastries and coffee on the terrace. Dress is casual, and a children's menu offers pasta dishes, hamburgers, pancakes, a fruit bowl, and other tasty treats. *19 Jackson St., Cape May; (609) 884-5970.*

Mangia Mangia
★★★★/$$$

Families just love this Italian restaurant for its large portions, reasonable prices, and solid kids' menu. The friendly staff only adds to its appeal. Consider sharing one of the hefty main courses with the little ones, or just getting them side-order-size portions. *Broadway and Sunset, W. Cape May; (609) 884-2429.*

FOOTPRINTS IN THE SAND

On beach vacations, sand seems to end up everywhere, especially between the toes. The simple plaster-casting project lets your child capture that sandy barefoot feeling—and a record of his feet.

MATERIALS
- Plaster of paris
- Small bucket
- Freshwater
- 4-inch lengths of string or wire (for hangers, if desired)

Choose a site to cast your molds—the moist, hard-packed sand near (but not too near!) the water's edge works best. Have your child firmly press both feet into the sand. The prints should be about $1^1/2$ to 2 inches deep. If your child can't press down that hard, he can use his finger to dig down into the print, following its shape. Mix up the plaster, according to the directions on the package, so that it has a thick, creamy consistency. Pour the wet plaster gently into the footprints.

If you want to make hangers, tie a knot about a half inch from each end of your pieces of string or wire. As the plaster begins to harden, push the knotted ends into the plaster and let dry. After 20 to 25 minutes, gently dig the footprints out of the molds and brush away any excess sand. Set sole-side up in the sun (away from the rising tide) for about an hour to let harden.

Families traveling in the mountains of northern New Jersey can find adventure year-round, from splashing through a water park, to snowboarding down powdered hills, to picking a bushel of apples.

Around the State

Whether you're looking for an escape from a cloudy day at the shore, a day off from Vernon's ski slopes, or just a fun diversion as you pass through New Jersey en route to somewhere else, you'll find a number of great family attractions scattered throughout the Garden State. Your family can uncover the mysteries of the universe at Liberty Science Center, then go from lasers to lances with dinner and a show at the nearby Medieval Castle. Farms and orchards around Northern New Jersey's mountain ranges attract families for apple, pumpkin, and strawberry picking in spring and fall; in summer, Mountain Creek Water Park is a swimmers' (or splashers') paradise; and winter here affords skiers of all levels superior slopes. Along the Pennsylvania border, little ones can have fun at the

THE **FamilyFun** LIST

MUST-SEE MUST-SEE

Garden State Discovery Museum
(page 172)

Hidden Valley Resort (page 173)

Hot Diggity's at Fairy Tale Forest
(page 173)

Liberty Science Center
(page 172)

Mountain Creek at Vernon Valley
(page 174)

New Jersey Aquarium
(page 173)

Northlandz (page 175)

Six Flags Great Adventure
(page 175)

Wheaton Village (page 176)

Wild West City (page 176)

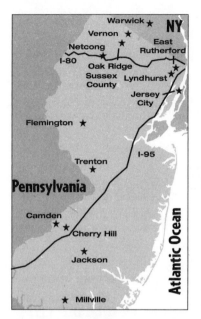

Garden State Discovery Museum and sharks to touch at the New Jersey State Aquarium. Nearer the Jersey Shore (just over an hour from both New York and Philadelphia), Six Flags Great Adventure will have your kids riding, sliding, splashing—and begging for more.

CULTURAL ADVENTURES

★★★/$$ Garden State Discovery Museum ★★★/$$

Another learning-made-fun site, this museum includes more than a dozen hands-on exhibits for kids ages 2 through 10. Among the favorite play areas are a multilevel tree house with animal puppets, a faux farm produce stand, the "Discovery Diner," a rock-climbing wall, a children's theater, and a play veterinarian's office. Kids can also make music, create art, build boats, and enjoy plenty of other activities. Special events at the museum include craft-making demonstrations and storytelling (call for schedule). *2040 Springdale Rd., Cherry Hill; (856) 424-1233;* www.discoverymuseum.com

★★★/$$-$$$ Liberty Science Center ★★★/$$-$$$

If your kids like to make things happen by pressing buttons, turning knobs, and pulling levers, this massive hands-on facility is going to make them very happy. Kids have fun learning about everything from television's blue-screen technology to weightlessness in outer space; they can peer through giant telescopes, touch sea creatures, and meander through a perception maze featuring optical illusions.

Interactive exhibits on several floors explore everything from microbiology and health to inventions and quantum physics in such intriguing ways that your kids will forget they're learning (sshh!). For a virtual thrill ride, visit the world's largest IMAX domed theater (recent films here included *Africa: The Serengeti*, and *Journey Into Amazing Caves*); don't be intimidated by the long line to get in—you can see the massive screen from any seat. **NOTE:** On weekends, the science center gets extremely crowded, often making hands-on more like hands-near; you're better off going early on a weekday. *Liberty State Park, at exit 14C off the New Jersey Turnpike extension, Jersey City; (201) 200-1000;* www.lsc.org

JUST FOR FUN

⭐ Hidden Valley Resort
FamilyFun ★★★/$$$$

Not a resort in the usual sense—no lodging is offered—this is a prime location for teaching children to ski or snowboard. There are 12 trails and three lifts. For half- and full-day programs (lunch included), you'll need to sign up at least 24 hours in advance. The SKIwee program teaches 4- to 12-year-olds how to master the slopes, and MINIriders gets 7- to 12-year-olds carving it up on snowboards. Though the resort has an upscale restaurant, the cafeteria is much more suitable for kids and serves the usual burgers and hot dogs. *44 Breakneck Rd., Vernon; (973) 764-4200.*

⭐ Hot Diggity's at Fairy
FamilyFun Tale Forest ★★★/$$

Designed for the under-6 crowd, this unique little theme park features 20 carefully designed, hand-crafted cottages that are home to Cinderella, Hansel and Gretel, the Three Bears, and other favorite nursery-rhyme or fairy-tale characters. In full swing from Memorial Day through Labor Day, the park captivates young imaginations with storytelling, music, dance, and special shows; a carousel and fire engine ride let them experience life in the fast lane. Off-season events include a Fall Pumpkin Patch, a Halloween-costume contest, and a Christmas Wonderland. There's also a well-stocked gift shop and a grill restaurant. *140 Oak Ridge Rd., Oak Ridge; (973) 697-5656;* http://www.fairytaleforest.com/

⭐ Mountain Creek
FamilyFun at Vernon Valley
★★★/$$$$

In winter, this ski area sparkles under a blanket of white (sometimes machine-made) snow. About an hour northwest of Manhattan, it has nearly 50 trails for all levels of skiers; the whole family can improve their technique with individual or group lessons. There are 11 lifts, and equipment

---

FamilyFun TIP

Tour Guides on Tape

Ride With Me tapes *(800-752-3195)* are cassettes keyed to common roadways. Put in a tape at the prescribed mile marker, and it's like having a guide versed in history, geography, and trivia along as you drive through a state. (But you won't have to give up an extra seat or share your lunch.)

The Sporting Life

If your kids love spectator sports, New Jersey has plenty of action.

Two pro teams, the NHL's **New Jersey Devils** (http://www.new jerseydevils.com/) and the NBA's **New Jersey Nets** (http://www.nj.com/nets/), play at the Continental Airlines Arena in East Rutherford *(New Jersey Turnpike, Western Spur Exit 16W— Sports Complex; 201/935-3900)*. Trenton is home to the Eastern Hockey League's **Trenton Titans** (http://www.trentontitans.com/) and to the **Trenton Thunder** (http://www.trentonthunder.com/), an AA minor-league baseball team. The Titans chase the puck at the 7,800-seat Sovereign Bank Arena *(S. Broad St. and Hamilton Ave.; 609/656-3200);* the Thunder, a Boston Red Sox affiliate, takes to the field at Mercer County Waterfront Park *(609/394-TEAM)*. More baseball action can be seen at Skylands Stadium in Sussex County *(Rtes. 15 and 206)*, where the **New Jersey Cardinals** *(888/NJ-CARDS;* http://www.njcards.com/), a St. Louis Cardinal's Class A club, plays. And as gridiron fans know, both New York football teams actually play in New Jersey, at Giants Stadium in East Rutherford *(New Jersey Turnpike, Western Spur Exit 16W— Sports Complex; 201/935-3900)*, just 20 minutes from New York City. But Jets and Giants game are sold out well in advance—you need to know someone to get tickets.

rental is available. In summer, a water park is the big attraction here; the kids will go for the numerous rides, slides, and pools. There's also a massive two-mile maze that parents explore along with their children, and in-line skaters and skateboarders can take advantage of the well-designed skate park on the premises. Kid Kamps, for ages 4 through 12, offer swimming, hiking, wilderness exploration, tubing, canoeing, wall climbing, and other activities. You need to sign up in advance (by late May) for one-day or multiday sessions. For affordable fare at the park, both the Hawk's Nest and the Mountain Express restaurant serve burgers and sandwiches; Wave Pizza and a Rib Shack have outdoor picnic tables. *200 Rte. 94, Vernon; (973) 827-2000.*

New Jersey State Aquarium

MUST-SEE
FamilyFun
MUST-SEE

★★★★/$$$

Two of the more impressive exhibits at this extraordinary aquarium are the multimedia Ocean Base Atlantic and the Shark Zone, complete with touch tank. Not only can kids view some 4,000 fish and sea creatures in more than 80 exhibits, they can also explore a sunken sea vessel, a sea turtle's nest, and a Caribbean pier. Fifty feet under water, the Sea Lab research station reveals deep-sea life through portholes and bubble windows; a diver exhibition uses scuba phones to let divers talk to visitors. Budding ecologists in the family will

enjoy S.E.A. TV, a small television studio where kids can record their own ideas about taking care of our planet. Everyone will enjoy the seal shows, especially at feeding time. **NOTE:** The shark exhibits might frighten children under 5. *1 Riverside Dr., Camden; (800) 616-JAWS; (856) 365-3300;* www.njaquarium.org

MUST-SEE FamilyFun MUST-SEE Northlandz ★★★/$$$

"Wow!" doesn't begin to describe this must-see locomotive fantasyland. Your kids (and you) are likely to stare openmouthed as your family enters this remarkable miniature world. Some 125 model trains ride on eight miles of track through an amazing hand-designed layout complete with mountains, valleys, 40-foot-long bridges, and literally thousands of hand-carved buildings. Doll lovers in the family are treated to a 94-room dollhouse and a museum that features more than 100 dolls collected from around the world. The Club Car Café serves Nathan's hot dogs, pretzels, ice cream, and other kid favorites. *95 Rte. 202, Flemington; (908) 782-4022.*

MUST-SEE FamilyFun MUST-SEE Six Flags Great Adventure ★★★/$$$$

Over the years, this popular amusement park has grown faster than your kids, adding new rides and attractions for visitors of all ages. Until recently, the emphasis was on thrill rides for teens and adults who refused to grow up. Now, if you prefer not to be turned upside down at 60 mph, you can choose from a greater variety of less stomach-churning activities. Whimsical new Looney Toons Seaport sports 15 attractions, and Bugs Bunny and his pals stroll around to meet younger kids. Some 40 family rides in all have been added for kids under 54 inches tall, with most designed so that grown-ups can join their children. Especially popular with younger kids are the safari and water park.

The Wild Safari—home to 1,200 elephants, lions, giraffes, monkeys, and other African creatures—is best driven through early in the day, when the animals are bright-eyed and bushy-tailed. (The sight of energetic monkeys pulling at your windshield wipers may not thrill you, but it sure will amuse your kids!)

The new 45-acre Hurricane Harbor Water Park refreshes in hot weather with a huge wave pool, a relaxing tube ride, and a family-activity lagoon with slippery slides, tipping buckets, and fun water sprays for the littlest ones.

Six Flags can be overwhelming,

so try to plan ahead and select rides and activities according to your children's ages and interests. **NOTE:** Metal detectors at the gates are now part of the park's standard security measures; keep a close watch on your kids and belongings amid the crowds. Call or visit the park Website (www. sixflags.com) for a variety of ticket plans, plus admissions to adjoining attractions, including Safari and Hurricane Harbor. *Rte. 537, Jackson; (732) 928-1821;* www.sixflags.com

Wheaton Village
FamilyFun ★★★/$$

Each year, some 15,000 school-children troop through the T. C. Wheaton Glass Factory—and leave quite enthralled with the art of glass-blowing. If your kids have never seen glass being fired, twirled, and shaped into figurines, bowls, and vases, take them to this modern version of the original 1888 factory. Then board the C. P. Huntington train, which departs regularly from the restored 1880 station, for a fun family ride around the grounds. The village also offers demonstrations of other crafts—including woodworking, tinsmithing,

and ceramics—as well as special programs and an impressive scale-model train display in an 1876 schoolhouse. The village is a great change of pace from the beaches, and you can see it all in only three or four hours, including a picnic or lunch at the casual on-site restaurant. *1501 Glasstown Rd., Millville; (800) 998-4552; (856) 825-6800.*

Wild West City ★★/$$
FamilyFun Wyatt Earp–wanna-bes can go back in time and enjoy a day of roping and riding, stagecoach holdups, and other Wild West reenactments—many of which have parts for kids to play. Your family can also take a ride on a pony, a miniature train, or a stagecoach, and visit the petting zoo. In addition to picnic grounds, you'll find several restaurants, including Frank's pizzeria (okay, so it's not an Old West classic). **NOTE:** While the Western shows are fun to watch, be forewarned: the gift shop has numerous toy guns, darts, and other toy weapons you might not want your kids to own. *Lackawanna Dr., off Rte. 206, Netcong; (973) 347-8901.*

ATLANTIC CITY is the basis of the popular board game Monopoly. Although the game was created in 1935, you can still find several of the streets that are a part of the classic game, including Atlantic Avenue, Ventnor Avenue, Park Place, and Marvin Gardens.

Bunking Down

Crystal Springs Golf & Spa Resort ★★★★/$$$$

If you want to go all out, this resort, formerly Great Gorge, offers large, hillside, duplex-style accommodations with one or two bedrooms. Each unit is spacious and comfortable, with a kitchen, cable TV, and private decks. The children will appreciate the resort's several pools (some with caves), kiddie pools, volleyball and tennis courts, softball field, and children's spray park. Parents may want to check out the spa, fitness center, and/or five golf courses. If you don't feel like cooking, head to neighboring Mountain Creek, site of several good family eateries. *Rte. 94 N., Sussex County; (973) 827-2222.*

Tip Tam Camping Resort ★★/$$

Something a little different: if you want your own great adventure while visiting Great Adventure, spend the night roughing it at this camping resort. Rent a tent, trailer, or cabin, or park your own RV. All sites include 30-amp hookup and water. Nothing fancy, mind you, just a safe, fun camping experience between the whirling and twirling of the rides and wild animal perusing at Six Flags, which is just minutes away. Reservations with deposit and ten-day cancellation notice are required. *301 Brewers Bridge Rd., Jackson; (877) TIP-TAM-1; (732) 363-4036.*

Warwick Motel ★★★/$

Five minutes from Mountain Creek, over the state line in New York, stands this quaint 17-room hotel run by a staff that cares. Guest rooms are comfortable and feature full- or king-size beds; family-friendly amenities include an outdoor heated swimming pool, complimentary breakfast, and ski packages. Another plus for families: kids under 12 stay free. Book well in advance for this popular, small property. *Rte. 17A, Warwick, New York; (888) 892-7942; (914) 988-9544.*

Good Eats

Medieval Times ★★★/$$$$

Utensils are discouraged during the four-course feast at this dinner theater (kids love it that they're *supposed* to eat with their hands). And as if the castle setting weren't exciting enough, your kids will be mesmerized by the nearly two-hour spectacle of damsels in distress, knights jousting atop stallions, and general courtly mayhem. **NOTE:** Children under 5 may be frightened by the characters and the mock conflict. *149 Polito Ave., Lyndhurst; (201) 933-3352.*

Pennsylvania

AN IDEAL family destination, Pennsylvania has more fun activities than your littlest ones can count. Whether you're looking for history, culture, hands-on activities, zoos, or amusement parks, you'll find them all here.

History buffs will revel in the options: Pennsylvania was the birthplace of our nation (Philadelphia was the first capital of the United States), the place where the tide turned during the Civil War (in Gettysburg), the setting for great Revolutionary War battles (outside Philadelphia), and the development of the

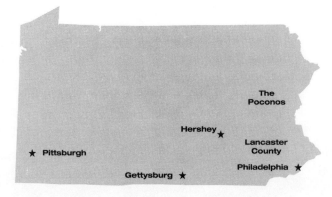

American coal, steel, and railroad industries (Pittsburgh). Pennsylvania Dutch culture (in Lancaster) shows how the past remains alive in the present.

Folks young and old who enjoy dropping from great heights, hurtling through space at great speeds, and generally being twisted and turned about will be pleased to learn that they can ride four of the world's top ten coasters without leaving the state.

For pure relaxation, families will find camping in gorgeous settings throughout the Poconos, with hiking trails, great water slides, and go-carts.

Pick your favorite pursuits—they're all here.

ATTRACTIONS

$	under $8
$$	$8 - $10
$$$	$10 - $15
$$$$	$15 and over

HOTELS/MOTELS/CAMPGROUNDS

$	under $65
$$	$65 - $85
$$$	$85 - $120
$$$$	$120 and over

RESTAURANTS

$	under $20
$$	$20 - $40
$$$	$40 - $60
$$$$	$60 and over

***FAMILYFUN* RATED**

★	Fine
★★	Good
★★★	Very Good
★★★★	*FamilyFun* Recommended

For a unique tour of the Steel City, wind your way through Pittsburgh's rivers on a Gateway Clipper boat.

Pittsburgh

PITTSBURGH is a study in contradictions. Still trying to replace its big-steel image with a high-tech facade, it offers an incredibly eclectic collection of neighborhoods. It's a place where Chinese markets, vegetarian curries, and kosher food shops stand side by side—a cultural melting pot that makes for great restaurants and some interesting shopping districts in the downtown areas. Funky stores like the Cuckoo's Nest Magic Store and the Groovy Pop Culture Emporium on Carson Street add to the experience.

The city's museums are as eclectic as its neighborhoods, and you could easily spend weeks touring through them all. In warmer months, you can supplement those visits with outdoor adventures. There are great roller coasters,

THE FamilyFun LIST

Carnegie Museum of Natural History
(page 183)

Carnegie Science Center
(page 184)

Kennywood Amusement Park
(page 186)

OMNIMAX Theatre (page 184)

Pittsburgh Children's Museum
(page 185)

Pittsburgh Zoo and Aquarium
(page 187)

Senator John Heinz Pittsburgh Regional History Center
(page 185)

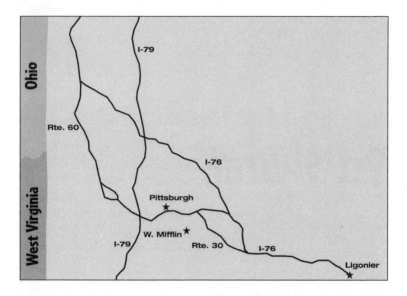

unique river tours, and water parks nearby. In the winter, your kids might enjoy outdoor ice skating at Schenley Park.

The trick to exploring Pittsburgh with kids is not trying to do it all. You may want to focus your attention on a specific area like the North Side or Oakland. Or pick a theme for your visit—a "Pittsburgh Safari," com- plete with trips to the Pittsburgh Zoo and Aquarium, the Carnegie Museum of Natural History, and the National Aviary, is sure to be a hit with a family of animal lovers.

CULTURAL ADVENTURES

Andy Warhol Museum ★★/$$
Pick up a Hanging Out With Andy kid's activity sheet in the elevator. The family tour starts on the fifth floor, where Silver Clouds gallery is an absolute must-see. Art lovers of all ages are encouraged to gently push the huge cloud-shaped helium-filled Mylar balloons into the breezes cre- ated by the installed fans. The rows of Elvis Presley images and the walls

---

FamilyFun GAME

Geography

Start with anyplace in the world: Kansas, say. The next person has to think of a place that begins with the last letter of Kansas, such as South Africa. Whoever goes next needs a place that starts with A. It has to be a real place—and no using a map!

---

papered with hot pink cows are other works that the kids will love. **NOTE:** Steer clear of the sixth and seventh floors, which are definitely not rated G (Andy's life wasn't, either). There are also a few smaller prints on the fourth floor that more conservative parents might find offensive and/or inappropriate for their children; you may want to skip this floor, too. *117 Sandusky St., Pittsburgh; (412) 237-8300;* www.warhol.org

Carnegie Museum of Art ★★/$$

This great collection of Impressionist and contemporary works is included in your admission to the Carnegie Museum of Natural History (*at right*). The excellent collection of classical paintings will entertain visitors of all ages. But if you have a toddler in tow, beware of the chairs. Chairs of various periods and styles are displayed nearly everywhere; some were obviously chosen for their artistry, but others really look as if they're provided for visitors to sit on. Don't! As you might expect, this place doesn't rate nearly as high on the kid WOW scale as the Museum of Natural History. But it's in the same building, sandwiched between the popular Ancient Egypt exhibit (third floor) and even more popular Hall of Dinosaurs (first floor). Since you really shouldn't miss those exhibits, you might as well expose the kids to a few works of art in between. You may be pleasantly surprised: children are often particularly taken with the lovely swirls and bright colors of the Postimpressionist collection. *4400 Forbes Ave., Pittsburgh; (412) 622-3131;* www.carnegiemuseums.org

Proving that talent runs in the family, **Andy Warhol**'s mother often did the lettering of his artwork.

Carnegie Museum of Natural History ★★★★/$

MUST-SEE **FamilyFun** **MUST-SEE**

This place houses one of the best dinosaur collections in the country, which will place it at the top of most kids' Pittsburgh itinerary. Be sure to catch the laser-and-sound show held hourly in the Hall of Dinosaurs. The kids will also like the Hillman Hall of Minerals, with its huge geodes and gorgeous rock crystals set amidst a unique display of mirrors. The best exhibit, however, is one you could easily miss. In a back corner of the Egyptian room is what appears to be simply a hole in the wall. Your children and you (if you aren't too large) can crawl through a long series of twisting passages to arrive at a child-size reproduction of an ancient Egyptian tomb, complete with wall paintings and a pint-size sarcophagus. Be prepared: your kids will want to make more than one visit here. *4400 Forbes Ave., Pittsburgh; (412) 622-3131;* www.carnegiemuseums.org

Carnegie Science Center ★★★★/$$

MUST-SEE **FamilyFun** **MUST-SEE**

Another of Pittsburgh's claims to fame, this is one of the country's top science centers. Plan on spending at least four hours here. The Works, a spectacular exhibit on electricity and machinery, is one of the most intense—and loudest—around. In fact, it may be too intense for preschoolers. Another 250 exhibits cover virtually every scientific topic imaginable, so your kids are sure to find something of interest.

A special section exclusively for the under-6 crowd (no older kids allowed) features live animals and a popular water-play area. That latter is a large table with running water, building materials that allow children to reroute the water, tons of floating Ping-Pong balls, and various plastic toys. The museum provides waterproof aprons, but dream on—kids always seem to get wet anyway. **NOTE:** Try to avoid the Science Center on days when the Pittsburgh Steelers are playing at home. To avoid a whopping $20 parking fee at the stadium, savvy locals park across the street at—you guessed it—the Science Center. Traffic is awful on game days, too. *One Allegheny Ave., Pittsburgh; (412) 237-3400*; www. carnegiemuseums.org

OMNIMAX Theatre ★★★★/$$

MUST-SEE **FamilyFun** **MUST-SEE**

If your most intense movie experience to date has been IMAX, prepare to be blown away. The Science Center's four-story OMNIMAX Theatre (additional fee) has a domed ceiling, stadium seating, and a sound system that could flatten all of Pittsburgh. See something here—anything! **NOTE:** The all-encompassing sounds and images may be too much for preschoolers. *One Allegheny Ave., Pittsburgh; (412) 237-3400*; www. carnegiemuseums.org

USS *Requin* Submarine ★★/$$

This 300-foot World War I submarine, parked directly in front of the

---

FamilyFun **READER'S TIP** -

A Travel Craft

I love to do crafts with my kids, Jimmy, 9, and Amy, 6, but the materials often disappear even before the projects start. To avoid this, I make a kit that includes all the materials. I put all the items needed for each project in a clear plastic bag. I then label the bag with a number, the name of the project, and any other necessary tools or supplies. Then, when the kids want to do a craft, they pick a number, find the corresponding kit, and we're all set!

Yolanda Pate, Hayward, California

Science Center, is a great treat for little boat fans. Skip it if you're claustrophobic. No children under 3 are permitted. *One Allegheny Ave., Pittsburgh; (412) 237-3400*; www.carnegiemuseums.org

Cathedral of Learning ★★★/$

This building is so dark and Gothic, it's like being inside a Batman movie. At 42 stories, it was the world's tallest schoolhouse when completed in 1937. The best time to visit is in December, when the various "Nationality" rooms are decked out in everything from traditional Old World Christmas trimmings to contemporary Kwanzaa decorations. Admission to the building is free, but there's a nominal charge for a one-hour guided tour that gets you into the decorated rooms.

If you're visiting with daughters, be sure to point out the fresco of Elena Piscopia in the Italian Room: she was the first woman ever to earn a doctorate degree—in 1678! Also ask the tour guide to point out the engraved name of Mulan in the Chinese Room. Yes, there really was a Mulan! Children love such interesting tidbits—and the Christmas trees—but they don't always appreciate the "sitting still" parts of the guided tour. If your kids are under 5, you may want to skip the tour and wander the dark stone Gothic hallways on your own. *Fifth Ave. and Bigelow Blvd., Pittsburgh; (412) 624-6000.*

Pittsburgh Children's Museum

★★★★/$$

FamilyFun

This fantastic children's museum caters to all ages with activities that range from puppet shows to silkscreening. Dads especially love the pulley system that lets you design and fly your own planes. The place is incredibly well staffed and supervised. If you leave here in under three hours, it will be amidst some serious tears. *10 Children's Way, Allegheny Sq., North Side, Pittsburgh; (412) 322-5058.*

Senator John Heinz Pittsburgh Regional History Center

★★★★/$$

FamilyFun

Completely child-friendly, with five floors of engaging exhibits, this center makes learning a pleasure. The third floor is almost completely hands-on. One area lets kids learn about the lives of children in Pittsburgh over several centuries. Kids can stuff toy pickles into jars in much the same way that young pickle-bottler Lillian Weizman did in 1902. Or they can use an (unheated) old-fashioned iron like Mary Todd, an 8-year-old indentured servant, did in 1841. The personal details really make history come alive. Younger visitors who need to work off some steam can romp through an indoor playground. But even there, kids are encouraged to use their imaginations. One sign reads

PRETEND YOU ARE A PIECE OF IRON AND CLIMB THE STAIRS TO THE BESSEMER FURNACE. *1212 Smallman St., Pittsburgh; (412) 454-6000.*

JUST FOR FUN

Gateway Clipper Fleet ★★★/$$

To really get a feel for Pittsburgh, take an excursion on its rivers. The Gateway Clipper Fleet offers several family-oriented cruises. The Lock 'N' Dam Adventure Cruise will give you and the kids details on pioneer activities; the Family Fun Cruise features mascots River Rover, Deckster Duck, and Penelope the Pittsburgh Pooch; and Lolli the Clown is on hand during the classic *Goodship Lollipop* Cruise. *9 Station Square Dock, Pittsburgh; (412) 355-7980;* www.gatewayclipper.com

Just Ducky Tours ★★★★/$$$

Can't decide between a land and water tour? Why not do both in the same vehicle? Just Ducky Tours loads your family into an old military-style amphibious truck for a city tour, then drives right into the

Allegheny River for a short river cruise past the Carnegie Science Center. The duck theme is applied liberally; kids especially enjoy all the quacking at passersby. *Station Square Dock, Pittsburgh; (412) 402-DUCK.*

★ Kennywood FamilyFun Amusement Park ★★★★/$$$$

MUST-SEE / MUST-SEE

Trite though it may sound, this park really does have "something for everyone." Absolutely don't leave Pittsburgh without first riding the Thunderbolt, an intense wooden coaster that is consistently voted the world's best. It offers great "air time," fantastic turns, and an overall wonderful ride. Unlike the steel rail "hypercoasters," this is also a fun rather than frightening ride and appropriate for most kids over 8. You can follow that up with rides on the Jackrabbit, the Racer, or the Exterminator—all first-rate coasters in their own right. Kennywood's Kiddyland is one of the oldest in the country and still one of the best. You'll find pint-size versions of 14 rides, including the Lil' Phantom coaster. Another plus is that the park is well shaded, with lots of comfortable benches scattered throughout, giving parents a much-needed rest between rides. Unlike most amusement parks, where the food is barely tolerable, Kennywood has won awards for its eateries; be sure to sample the award-winning fries at the Potato Patch. **NOTE:** Don't be put off by the metal detectors at the gate; the neighborhood is definitely not that bad. *4800 Kennywood Blvd., W. Mifflin; (412) 461-0500;* www.kennywood.com

Monongahela Incline ★★★/$

It's just a 20-minute diversion, but a really cool one nonetheless. Almost a cross between a cable car and a train, this incline is the country's oldest (since 1854) and steepest. You can take a one-way ride on the incline, but do try a round-trip. It's a really long way down! *Directly across from Station Square, Pittsburgh.*

National Aviary ★★★/$$

Really and truly for the birds, this place is home to a wide variety of exotic feathered friends. Ask the keeper about the "Time Out" cage. (Kids will be amused to learn that "time outs" are used as punishment for the smart birds that have figured out how to open the doors using the handicapped-access buttons.) The birds fly free through most of the area, so everyone should wear a hat. Also, call ahead to ask about temporary exhibits. The aviary often hosts art exhibits of objects that may be a bit too tempting—and too breakable—for little hands. *Allegheny Commons West, Pittsburgh; (412) 323-7235;* www.aviary.org

★MUST-SEE★ Pittsburgh Zoo and FamilyFun Aquarium ★★★★/$$

★MUST-SEE★ This award-winning children's zoo is one of the more engaging ones you'll find, and the

A Trip to Idlewild Park

Still haven't had your fill of amusement parks? Just outside of Ligonier, Pennsylvania (50 miles east of Pittsburgh), **Idlewild Park** makes for a nice one- or two-day excursion from the big city. Amusing local families since 1931, the park really focuses on rides that all family members can enjoy together.

If there are preschoolers in the family, start with a trip through Idlewild's Storybook Forest. Little ones absolutely love seeing the Old Woman in the Shoe, walking through the Crooked House, and playing in life-size recreations of all their favorite nursery rhymes. From there, head to Raccoon Lagoon and ride Mister Rogers's trolley to meet up with King Friday XIII, X the Owl, Henrietta Pussycat, and all the other TV show neighbors you've come to know and love. Then it's on to the Hootin' Holler Jumpin' Jungle and Olde Idlewild for great rides and family fun. (There's even a ball pit that's big enough for Mom and Dad to play in, too!) The most recent addition to the park, Dr. Hydro's Soak Zone, adds kid-friendly water slides and a wonderful activity pool. Picnic areas are scattered throughout the park, and the concessions are wonderfully affordable. Located *on Route 30, two miles west of Ligonier*, Idlewild *(724/238-3666)* is open late May to early September.

aquarium is impressive, too. Among the special features here are "Zoo Keys": insert the key at most exhibits to hear educational songs about the animals on display.

Also a big hit with young visitors are the various "in-cage" experiences: kids can climb underneath the stingray tank in the aquarium for an underside view or crawl beneath the meerkat display and pop up inside a plastic bubble to greet the meerkats eye to eye. Playground equipment that mimics the animal's environments is scattered throughout. Kids can clamber up the spider climbs or scamper through a kid-size "habitrail" that's just like the little ones for small rodents. Don't miss the great tree slides inside the Discovery Pavilion. An added plus is that the animals' habitats are very well done. Those fancy peacocks actually don't belong here—it says a lot when animals migrate into a zoo on their own! *One Wild Place, Pittsburgh; (800) 474-4966; (412) 665-3639;* www.pittsburghzoo.com

Sandcastle Water Park
★★★/$$$$

Ask the kids: "What would you do with an old steel mill?" Bet turning it into a water park isn't the first thing you think of. But for the ingenious folks who own Kennywood Amusement Park, it was, and they've filled this old mill site with water rides and games. Budding daredevils will be in heaven here. For older kids, the water slides are beyond intense. These are among the fastest and most twisty water rides we've seen. The Lightning Express actually features a 60-foot near-vertical drop to a "braking" lane in four inches of water. Believe it or not, this is a "body" slide—be prepared to travel 30 mph without being strapped into anything.

For younger kids (and the more faint of heart), Sandcastle provides four full-size activity pools geared to specific age groups. Wet Willie's Waterworks is basically a water playground, and limited to children under 54 inches tall. The Tad Pool focuses on toddlers, while the Sandbar Pool is designed for all ages and includes a lovely waterfall. The real draw, however, is the wave pool, Mon Tsunami. For the calmer crowd (and those still recovering from the Lightning Express), the lazy river ride extends nearly a quarter mile for a wonderfully smooth and relaxing ride. *1000 Sandcastle Dr., Pittsburgh; (412) 462-6666;* www. sandcastlewaterpark.com

How did the **Pittsburgh Penguins** get their name? The winner of a 1967 naming contest suggested the penguin because the team would be playing in the Pittsburgh Civic Arena, a building nicknamed "the Igloo."

BUNKING DOWN

Best Western University Center
★★★/$$$

Close to museums, cruises, and downtown, this member of the chain caters to kids with cookies and juice in the rooms. *3401 Blvd. of the Allies, Pittsburgh; (800) 245-4444; (412) 683-6100*; www.bestwestern.com

Ramada Plaza Suites
★★★/$$$$

Boasting a convenient downtown location, this all-suite hotel also has a kid-pleasing indoor pool. An added plus: kitchens include microwave ovens. *One Bigelow Sq., Pittsburgh; (800) 225-5858; (412) 281-5800;* www.ramada.com

Sheraton Station Square
★★★/$$$$

Great views and a perfect location are the highlights here. It's within walking distance of boat cruises and the Monongahela Incline. *7 Station Square Dr., Pittsburgh; (800) 255-7488; (412) 261-2000;* www.sheraton.com

Victoria House Bed and Breakfast ★★★/$$$$

This restored mansion in the historic district is within walking distance of the Carnegie Science Center, the Warhol Museum, and the National Aviary. Not recommended for preschoolers. *939 Western Ave., Pittsburgh; (412) 231-4948.*

GOOD EATS

Buon Giorno Café on the Strip
★★★★/$$$

Definitely worth the splurge, this place offers simply incredible nouveau Italian food, like feta and roast tomato pasta. Phenomenal pizza and good vegetarian options are available, too. Servings are big, but the place itself is small, with very cramped tables; if you're traveling with a stroller you may want to choose a roomier dining spot. *1814 Penn Ave., Pittsburgh; (412) 288-9895.*

Gullifty's
★★★/$$$

Good meals and award-winning desserts—need we say more? Kids also get a kick out of the house specialty sandwiches. It's not that the sandwiches are particularly unusual, but their name, "wedgies," inspires plenty of giggles. *1922 Murray Ave., Squirrel Hill, Pittsburgh; (412) 521-8222.*

Poli's ★★★/$$$

Don't let the valet parking scare you. Despite its upscale decor, this place is incredibly reasonable. Here's your chance to treat the kids to fancy dining at plain prices. Dinners include soup or salad and dessert, and early-bird prices are especially good. The food rates three stars, but the atmosphere deserves four. *2607 Murray Ave., Pittsburgh; (412) 521-1222.*

Help your children become
Civil War buffs through the Junior
Ranger Program at Gettysburg
National Military Park.

Gettysburg

THE CIVIL WAR battlefield both surrounds and anchors Gettysburg, but don't overlook the lesser known attractions with lots of kid appeal. With its nearby apple orchards, stunning in spring, the town is a nice alternative to overbuilt and heavily commercialized vacation spots.

You can start your day with a ride through the town on a trolley very similar to Mr. Rogers's favorite toy. The battlefield (or at least part of it—it's huge) is a must-see: be sure to take in one of the many living history presentations offered free by the National Park Service. For indoor fun, stop at Explore 'N' More, a hands-on children's museum with a wide range of educational exhibits. Kids will even learn a bit about local history as they try on Civil War costumes and play house in a canvas rebel field tent.

The horse lovers in your family will get a kick out of touring the town in a horse-drawn carriage, watching the miniature steeds perform at the Land of Little Horses, or

THE **FamilyFun** LIST

MUST-SEE · MUST-SEE

Devil's Den and Big Round Top (page 194)

Explore 'N' More Hands-on Children's Museum (page 195)

Gettysburg National Cemetery (page 193)

Gettysburg National Military Park (page 193)

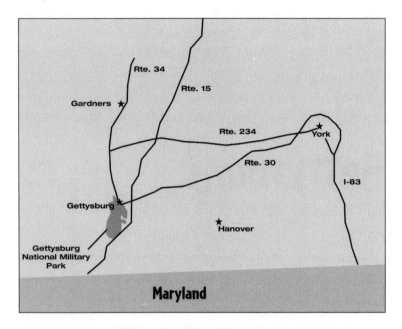

Rte. 34

Rte. 15

Gardners ★

Rte. 234

York ★

Rte. 30

I-83

Gettysburg ★

★ Hanover

Gettysburg
National Military
Park

Maryland

spending a day horseback riding through the battlefields. If you'd rather tour on wheels, stop by **Gettysburg Bicycle and Fitness** (*307 York St.; 717/334-7791*) to rent bicycles. You can also rent baby seats, kids' trailers, onboard computers, and route maps.

Serious Civil War buffs should check the calendar for events related to the battle (July 1–3, 1863). The most dramatic is the annual reenactment of some part of the battle (it's different every year), with upwards of 17,000 reenactors in full period costume. Many of them remain steadfastly in character and will tell your kids about life as a soldier. (Also see "Seasonal Attractions," page 201.)

CULTURAL ADVENTURES

Eisenhower National Historic Site
★★★/$

When your kids begin to tire of the Civil War, take a side trip to the 1960s. At this living history museum, in summer, guides outfitted as FBI agents or some other period characters lead tours of the only home ever owned by Dwight and Mamie Eisenhower. The 231-acre farm, including the house and cattle barns, is set up exactly as it was when Ike and Mamie retired here. Ask about the

Junior Secret Service Agent activity program. The site is accessible only by buses that leave from the Gettysburg National Military Park visitors' center, and there is a fee. *Gettysburg; (877) 438-8929; (717) 334-1124, ext. 439.*

Gettysburg National Cemetery
★★★/Free

Here, Abraham Lincoln delivered what is now known as the Gettysburg Address. Part of Gettysburg National Military Park and directly across from the national park's visitors' center, the cemetery is open year-round. You can attend free programs provided by the National Park Service, some of which involve reenactors; one tour guide plays the part of a local civilian from the 1860s.

For your 12-and-up crowd, there's also a more academic program on Lincoln's speech. Your older kids may also be interested in the grave of Jenny Wade, the only civilian killed during the Battle of Gettysburg. The grave is marked by a perpetual flame and flag; it required an act of Congress to keep

The average age of a **Civil War soldier** was roughly 21 years.

the flag flying day and night (national park flags generally must come down at sunset). *Baltimore Pike, SR 134, Gettysburg; (717) 334-1124;* www.nps.gov/getc

Gettysburg National Military Park
★★★/Free

The park is huge and does not have one single entrance; you'll pass part of it regardless of the direction from which you enter town. The visitors' center (*717/334-1124*) should be the first stop on your battlefield tour: for an overview of the park and the battle, check out the electric map, a 30-minute audio-visual presentation (fee). Your kids will also like the great collections of Civil War uniforms, firearms, and cannons. Be sure to pick up the calendar of free events; the evening campfire programs are especially interesting.

Children are also intrigued by the "living history" presentations that feature reenactors playing the roles of historical figures. Ask about the Flying Nun program, in which a park ranger dressed as an 1860s Daughter of Charity

DWIGHT D. EISENHOWER was the first president to score a hole in one. He accomplished this feat during a 1968 golf game in Palm Springs, California.

discusses nursing battlefield victims. If your kids are younger, skip the programs on battlefield medicine— some of the details are much too graphic. A Junior Park Ranger activity booklet is available at the information desk. The Cyclorama, adjacent to the visitors' center, has exhibits, paintings, and a huge 360-degree painting of the battle.

From the visitors' center, your family can set out on a driving tour of the park's 26 miles of paved roads. Follow the self-guided tour outlined in the Park Service brochure; you can also buy audiotape tours, or take a double-decker bus tour with taped commentary (*717/334-6296*). If your family includes some true history buffs, you can arrange for a licensed guide (battlefield guides at Gettysburg must pass an extremely rigorous test before they are authorized to offer tours, and their rates are strictly controlled. They'll ride in your car with you and give you a customized tour—the highlights of

what Maine regiments did, for example, if you're from Maine. (You can be very sure they know what they're talking about.) Guides are available at the visitors' center, or at *1 West End Guide Station, US Rte. 30.*

The best time to view the battlefield is in late fall or early winter, when the trees have dropped their leaves. But come in summer if you want to see what the soldiers saw during the battle. **NOTE:** Despite its historical value, the battlefield has a big downside for families with preschoolers—it is definitely not stroller accessible. *SR 134, Baltimore Pike, across from the National Cemetery, Gettysburg; (717) 334-1124;* www.nps.gov/gett

Devil's Den and Big Round Top ★★★/Free Head to one of these two national park sites when your offspring need to work off some excess energy. Devil's Den is a group of HUGE boulders that Confederate

---

Fledgling Photographers

Last summer, I put an extra flash in our vacation. Instead of having grown-ups be the only photographers, I bought each of our five children, whose ages range from 7 to 19, a 24-exposure disposable camera and let them snap their own pictures. The kids loved it, and we were able to see our vacation through their eyes. Plus, since they were inexpensive cameras, I didn't worry about them being dropped or lost. For very little money, these simple cameras brought our family a lot of smiles.

Kathi Kanuk, Chardon, Ohio

sharpshooters hid behind during the battle. Today young tourists can spend hours climbing up, down, and around the big rocks. **NOTE:** Some of the boulders are a bit high, so keep toddlers in check; this place is really best for kids over 6. The younger kids can work off steam a bit more safely on the hill at nearby Big Round Top. Several short trails wind through the woods, with monuments to different regiments, states, or other units scattered around. **ANOTHER NOTE:** These are also among the most crowded sites. During high season, you may want to ask a park ranger to point you to some interesting but more obscure spots. *On the battlefield, Gettysburg National Military Park; (717) 334-1124.*

Explore 'N' More Hands-on Children's Museum ★★★★/$

If your family needs a break from history, spend a few fun-filled hours here. Three blocks from the town square, directly behind the public library, this unassuming little house holds the county's only hands-on children's museum. Exhibits include an 1860s-era playhouse where kids can don vintage clothes; a Civil War soldier's tent; a construction zone complete with hard hats; and a fantastic art area where kids can create flowerpots, masks, paintings, ceramic-tile items, and much more. Though the museum is aimed at 3-

Joining Up

If you plan to do a lot of traveling in Pennsylvania, here are three memberships to look into:

Pennsylvania Heritage Society (PHS)

A $50 family membership buys you free admission to state-run museums and historical sites for one year. *(800) 747-7790.*

Association of Science/ Technology Centers (ASTC)

If your kids like science centers and hands-on museums, a family membership at an ASTC institution can save you big money. Membership cards gain you free admission to more than 200 science centers around the world. Museums within 60 miles of one another aren't required to offer reciprocal memberships, so your best bet is to get a family membership at an ASTC institution in your home state; the usual fee is between $50 and $65 a year. Out-of-state ASTC cards earn admittance to science museums across Pennsylvania. www.astc.org

American Zoo and Aquarium Association (AZA)

Being an AZA member of a zoo in any state guarantees you free admission to the National Aviary in Pittsburgh, the Philadelphia Zoo, the Pittsburgh Zoo and Aquarium, and ZooAmerica North American Wildlife Park in Hershey. www.aza.org

to 8-year-olds, your older kids will stay occupied with the art activities for hours. Drop-off child care is offered, but it comes at a price—about $10 an hour per child. *20 E. High St., Gettysburg; (717) 337-9151.*

Jenny Wade House and Olde Town ★★/$

The Olde Town display of period shops staffed with wax figures is a bit kitschy, but kids don't seem to notice. They're more interested in the story of Jenny Wade. Hit by a stray bullet while baking bread, Jenny was the only civilian killed during the Battle of Gettysburg. You can also visit Jenny's grave at the National Cemetery. The house and Olde Town are closed in winter. *547 Baltimore St., Gettysburg; (717) 334-4100.*

National Civil War Wax Museum ★★/$

Like most wax museums, this one falls somewhere along the spectrum from a little tacky to thoroughly tasteless. Nevertheless, your kids will likely be fascinated by it. More than 200 wax figures appear in scenes

---

that tell the story of the Civil War. **NOTE:** The Battle Room at the end of the exhibit is definitely too intense for preschoolers and may frighten some older kids, too. *297 Steinwehr Ave., Gettysburg; (717) 334-6245.*

JUST FOR FUN

Ghosts of Gettysburg Walking Tours ★★★/$$

These candlelit tours around town follow the tales in Mark Nesbitt's Ghosts of Gettysburg book series. Although some of the historical details are good, the narratives are heavy on the supernatural and more than a bit over the top. (Many of the ghost tales seem to involve college students out in the wee hours.)

The guides manage to keep wonderfully straight faces, but the stories are tongue-in-cheek enough to keep most school-age kids from being genuinely frightened. At a few points along some tours, actors play the parts of the described ghosts. The friendly and extremely knowledgeable guides dress in period garb. **NOTE:** The scare factor here is on par with Nickelodeon's *Who's Afraid of the Dark?* Kids over 7 should be fine, but younger children might find the tours a little too spooky; the tours run after dark, so tiny tots may also be a bit tired. Reservations are recommended. *271 Baltimore St., Gettysburg; (717) 337-0445;* www. ghostsofgettysburg.com

---

FamilyFun GAME

Word Stretch

Give your child a word challenge by asking her to make as many words as she can from the letters in a phrase such as "Are we there yet?" or "When will we be at the zoo?"

Land of Little Horses
★★★/$$

Little kids who love horses will adore this place. The main attraction is a herd of performing miniature Falabella horses, which are about half the size of standard horses. For a small additional fee, you can also take wagon rides, horseback rides (small children only—these are really tiny horses), and ride a carousel with live horses. The petting zoo has llamas, pygmy goats, and deer. Bring along some quarters for the deer-food vending machines. Closed in winter, except for the Christmas holiday season, when there's a light-show extravaganza. *Three miles west of Gettysburg; take Rte. 30 or Rte. 116 and follow the signs to 125 Glenwood Dr.; (717) 334-7259; www.landoflittlehorses.com*

A typical **Falabella horse** is between 28 and 30 inches tall, half the size of a standard horse.

BUNKING DOWN

Baltimore Street Bed and Breakfast ★★★★/$$$$

This three-story, nine-room Gothic–Revival Victorian dwelling is incredibly classy (but still kid-friendly)—and right in the heart of town. The Courtyard and Winebrenner suites offer such family-friendly features as full kitchens and washer/dryers. Full breakfast is included in the rate. *449 Baltimore St., Gettysburg; (888) 667-8266; (717) 334-2454.*

Days Inn Gettysburg
★★★/$$$

There's nothing new or unusual here at this 112-room chain motel, but the digs are comfortable. An outdoor, heated pool and free continental breakfast make it even more appealing to families. *865 York Rd. (U.S. Rte. 30), Gettysburg; (800) 544-8313; (717) 334-0030; www.daysinn.com*

Drummer Boy Camping Resort
★★★★/$

This great family campground is convenient to town. The 300 sites and family-size cottages come with lots of extras: children's programs, a heated pool, a whirlpool, a rec room, volleyball and basketball courts, a miniature-golf course, a playground, and bicycle rentals. *1300 Hanover Rd. (S.R. 116), Gettysburg; (800) 293-2808; (717) 334-3277.*

Econo Lodge
★★★/$$

Convenient and reasonably priced, this 42-room place offers free continental breakfast and an outdoor pool. *945 Baltimore Pike (S.R. 97), Gettysburg; (717) 334-6715.*

Gettysburg Hotel
★★★★/$$$$

It's a bit pricey, but the advantage of this 83-room Best Western hotel is that it's right on the town square.

Rooms are modern with period decor. Families may want to opt for one of the efficiency apartments or one of the 22 suites (some with fireplace and Jacuzzi). The pool is another nice plus. *One Lincoln Sq., Gettysburg; (800) 937-8376; (717) 337-2000.*

Who Lives There?

Travel exposes your family to new places and different styles of living. As you pass a lime-green house with a yard full of plastic pink flamingos and a working waterwheel, it's hard not to wonder what type of family lives there. Why not run with that? Suggest that your kids speculate on who lives inside the houses you pass and what they might be doing at that moment. Perhaps the people in the green house invented mint chocolate-chip ice cream. Perhaps they have seven children and three pets—a Lhasa apso, an iguana, and a Persian cat wearing a pink leather collar. If it's dinnertime, perhaps they're gathered around the kitchen table enjoying tuna casserole topped with potato chips that will be followed by a dessert of cherries flambé. They'll be playing a game of Pictionary after dinner and . . . well, you get the idea.

Gettysburg KOA Kampground
★★★★/$$

This KOA campground is a wonderful exception to the chain's habit of locating in awful spots. The facility also offers easy access to both the battlefield and Washington, D.C., tour buses, plus a heated pool, a nice playground, and special nature and children's programs. Choose from the 99 sites and seven cabins. *20 Knox Rd., Gettysburg; (800) 562-1869; (717) 642-5713;* www.koa.com

Hampton Inn ★★★/$$

This is a great family hotel, but it's right on the strip of fast-food restaurants, Wal-Mart, and the like, so don't expect small-town ambience. Families appreciate the suites and the complimentary breakfast. *1280 York Rd., Gettysburg; (717) 338-9121.*

Mountain Creek Campground ★★★★/$

The 200 sites at this family campground accommodate tents, 45-foot RVs, and everything in between. You can also rent cabins. The kids will like the heated pool, hot tub, and kiddie pool, and on weekends you can try bingo and free hayrides. The Appalachian Trail is just across from the camp store. This is also the start of the Cumberland County Hiker-Biker Trail, which runs five miles from the campground to the Pine Grove Furnace Recreational Area. *349 Pine Grove Rd., Gardners; (717) 486-7681.*

Quality Inn Larson's
★★★/$$$

Young history buffs will like the idea of sleeping in a historic war hospital. Right on the land that was the scene of part of the battle (but isn't part of the military park), this hotel is in an 1830s stone structure that was used as a field hospital during the battle. There are 41 rooms and two suites; free breakfast and an outdoor pool complete the picture. *401 Buford Ave., Gettysburg; (717) 334-3141.*

GOOD EATS

Dobbin House ★★★★/$$$$

Known to local kids as the Goblin House, this period eatery is in an authentic Civil War home. Try to be seated at the Canopy Bed (converted into a table). There's a kids' menu featuring all the usual suspects. It's a tough choice between the yam fritters and mashed, spiced sweet potatoes. After dinner, have a look at the hidden rooms once used to hide runaway slaves on the Underground Railroad. Reservations are recommended. *89 Steinwehr Ave., Gettysburg; (717) 334-2100;* www.hamptoninn.com

Ernie's Texas Lunch
★★★★/$

If you want a quick bite, join the locals at this place. It's also something of a kids' paradise: Ernie— and there is an Ernie, he's owner and cook—serves every variety of hot dog you can think of—with or without bun, with or without skin, with cheese, with chili. The food—including breakfast—is great and very reasonably priced. Ernie's is small and very popular, so try to arrive before or after standard lunch hours to avoid a wait. **NOTE:** This is a smoking facility; there is no non-smoking section. It's also a cash-only business; credit cards are not accepted. Closed Sunday. *58 Chambersburg St., Gettysburg; (717) 334-1970.*

Farnsworth House
★★★★/$$$

Another period restaurant, this one focuses on authentic Civil War cuisine. Don't miss the goober (peanut) soup or pickled watermelon rinds. Waiters and waitresses in period costume add to the quaint atmosphere. Some summer evenings a hoopskirted "widow" tells ghost stories in the basement.

Reservations are recommended. *401 Baltimore St., Gettysburg; (717) 334-8838.*

Lincoln Diner ★★★★/$$$

The diner food here is just that: diner food. But the desserts are to die for. An on-site pastry chef keeps the place stocked with 12 to 15 different—and sumptuous—layer cakes, cheesecakes, tortes, and pies. If the main ingredient is sugar, you'll find it here. They've got excellent ice-cream dishes as well, and most are large enough to share. Order one big dessert—and a few extra spoons. **NOTE:** No credit cards; cash or traveler's checks only. *32 Carlisle St., Gettysburg; (717) 334-3900.*

Lupita's Mexican Restaurant ★★★/$$

Lupita's offers a great selection of authentic Mexican food. Rice and beans aren't standard with the kids' meals, so be sure to order enough sides. Also, skip the Mexican sodas (much too sweet and pricey) and go American on the drinks. *51 West St., Gettysburg; (717) 337-9575.*

Thistlefield's Tea Room ★★★/$$$

If you have a girl with a capital G, don't miss this Victorian-style teahouse (skip it if your troops are exclusively male). The elegant decor will remind your young lady of a dollhouse. The food is a bit preten-tious ("tea" sandwiches and the like), but just right for the dainty setting. This is the perfect place for a special mother-daughter lunch. *29 Chambersburg St., Gettysburg; (717) 338-9131.*

Tommy's Pizza ★★★★/$$

Absolutely the best pizza in Adams County can be found right here, close to several major motels. Great toppings, fantastic sauce, and good service make this a worthy choice when everyone wants pizza. *105 Steinwehr Ave., Gettysburg; (717) 334-4721; (717) 334-8966.*

Souvenir Hunting

Abe's Antiques

The real attraction here is the proprietor—a dead ringer for Abe Lincoln. Kids get a real kick out of him. *238 Baltimore St., Gettysburg; (717) 337-2122.*

Olde Country Confections Chocolate Factory

Candy lovers will enjoy watching chocolates and other confections being made on-site from 100-year-old German recipes. The big draw? Free samples! *51 Chambersburg St., Gettysburg; (717) 337-9971.*

SEASONAL ATTRACTIONS

L IKE MOST TOURIST AREAS where history is the lure, happenings in Gettysburg tend to revolve around certain dates. In this town, the times to keep in mind are the anniversary of the Battle of Gettysburg (July 1–3) and the anniversary of Lincoln's Gettysburg Address (November 19), known locally as Remembrance Day. The following are the town's top annual events.

Battle of Gettysburg Reenactment (JULY 1–3).

Tens of thousands of reenactors dressed in full period attire and armed with muskets and cannons re-create different parts of the famous battle on land near, but not on, the military park. This is a commercial event that's unconnected with the National Park Service. History buffs shouldn't miss it; non-history buffs will be bored after about five minutes. You sit on the ground most years; shade is very scarce. If it is very hot or very muddy, any parts scheduled to include horses (a major draw for kids) won't happen because of dangers to the animals.

National Apple Harvest Festival (OCTOBER)

If you can make it with apples, you'll find it here: crafts, food, and fun.

Halloween Parade (OCTOBER)

This is the big parade of the year! Nearly everyone in town who isn't in it will be watching it. There are six large sections of entrants, with prizes for best floats and costumes.

Anniversary of Lincoln's Gettysburg Address (NOVEMBER)

An often quite moving ceremony featuring local Lincoln impersonator James Getty (who delivers the Address) is held at the national cemetery. A parade of reenactors precedes the speech.

Remembrance Day Celebration (NOVEMBER)

This parade of Civil War troops boasts the country's largest gathering of Civil War reenactors.

For dates and details on these and other seasonal events, contact the **Gettysburg Convention and Visitor's Bureau**, *35 Carlisle St., Gettysburg; (717) 334-6274;* www.gettys burgcvb.org

You can find chocolate almost anywhere in Hershey, from the streetlights shaped like Kisses to the aroma of cocoa-bean mulch wafting through town.

Hershey

KNOWN AS The Sweetest Town on Earth, Hershey is a chocolate lover's delight. Nestled in gentle farmlands (which ensure a good supply of milk for the chocolate), Hershey is home to the candy company that shares its name, and the entire town is practically dipped in its most famous product. Where else would you find Chocolate World and Chocolate Street? And don't forget those famous Hershey Kiss–shaped streetlights. The tranquil landscape is liberally strewn with tons of ground-cocoa-bean mulch, which is what gives the town its luscious signature scent. (Expect your kids to be hungry for the duration of your stay!) But beyond chocolate, Hershey offers something with perhaps even more kid appeal—a big, bright, exciting amusement park.

CULTURAL ADVENTURES

Hershey Museum
★★★/$

This medium-size museum has something for the entire family. Adults and older kids will be interested in the exhibits on Milton Hershey, founder of this town and

THE FamilyFun LIST
MUST-SEE MUST-SEE

Chocolate World (page 204)

Hershey Park (page 205)

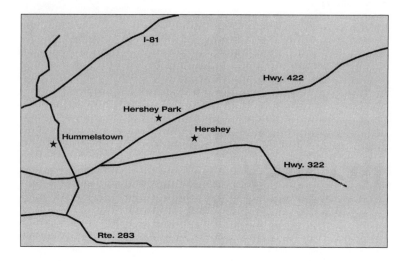

a chocolate empire; and the German-American heritage of the region. Younger kids go for the Native American artifacts and the hands-on Discovery Room, where they can grind corn in a Hopi pueblo or pretend they're living in an Eastern Woodland Indian wigwam. *170 W. Hershey Park Dr., Hershey; (717) 534-3439;* www.hersheymuseum.org

JUST FOR FUN

Chocolate World
FamilyFun ★★★★/Free

Stop here first when you hit town. If you took the Hershey chocolate factory tour as a kid, you'll find this attraction much changed. The walking tour through the actual factory has been replaced with an automated theme-park ride that whisks you through the history of Hershey and the process of making chocolate candy. The tracks wind through life-size reproductions of the equipment used to produce your favorite candies, with film displays and animations scattered throughout. The 12-minute ride is a multi-sensory experience: you'll travel through a very hot tunnel (illustrating the almond-roasting process) and be enveloped in the almost painfully heavy scents of chocolate, vanilla, and nuts throughout. The lines can be pretty long in high season, so try to get here very early or late in the day. The entrance to Chocolate World is immediately in front of the gates to Hershey Park, but don't think hitting the free chocolate ride first will convince your kids to skip the theme park. *100 W. Hershey Park Dr., Hershey; (800) HERSHEY; (717) 534-4900.*

Hershey Park
FamilyFun ★★★★/$$$$

The chocolate may be tasty, but here's the real reason kids want to come to Hershey. This first-rate amusement park features more than 55 rides, including eight roller coasters, six water rides, and 20-plus kiddie rides. The impressive Lightning Racer wooden roller coaster is sure to please coaster aficionados, but those who prefer less spine-tingling adventures will find plenty to do, too. In keeping with the chocolate theme, height restrictions for rides are given in terms of candy: Hershey Kisses designate the Kiddyland rides, Reese's Peanut Butter Cups the next step up (42 inches to 47 inches), and so on. The park also hosts musical acts (country and rock and roll), Broadway-caliber song-and-dance reviews, strolling performers—even a dolphin and sea lion show. The park is open late April to New Year's Day, with restricted hours outside the standard amusement park season. From late November to New Year's Day, the Christmas Candylane show features holiday light displays and some children's rides. *100 W. Hershey Park Dr., Hershey; (800) HERSHEY; (717) 534-3900; www.hersheys.com*

Indian Echo Caverns ★★/$$

These caverns have a fascinating history, which guides relate during the 45-minute-long tour. Kids will be spellbound by stories (more hokey than scary) about the "Mummy," the "Giant," and the "Pennsylvania Hermit," who lived inside the caverns for 19 years. Tours are suitable for all ages, but are not stroller accessible. After the tour, youngsters can search for fool's gold as well as chunks of amethyst, jasper, agate, and other minerals at Gem Mill Junction (there's a fee). The caverns are open year-round; Gem Mill Junction is open only during the summer tourist season. *368 Middletown Rd., Hummelstown; (717) 566-8131.*

ZooAmerica North American Wildlife Park ★★★/$$

The zoo is actually part of Hershey Park, but you can also visit it separately and in the off-season when the park itself is closed. To help the kids to really enjoy this one, explain in advance that only North American creatures live here—mountain lions, yes, but no lions of the Serengeti. Highlights include an excellent collection of nocturnal animals and birds, especially owls, and a nice play-

ALTHOUGH NO ONE KNOWS how Hershey's Kisses received their name, there is a popular notion that the moniker came from the sound or action of the chocolate dropping onto the conveyor belt during production.

ground slide above the otters' "home." Well-insulated buildings provide enough warming breaks to make this a doable excursion in midwinter. But some of the more interesting animals hibernate when it's cold. *100 W. Hershey Park Dr., Hershey; (800) HERSHEY; (717) 534-3860; www.her sheypa.com/attractions/zooamerica*

BUNKING DOWN

Addey's Inn of Hershey ★★★/$$

Small but sweet, this is an interesting cross between a country inn and a roadside motel. The 12-room property's Homestead Suite takes up the entire second floor of a 1920s brick farmhouse and can accommodate up to eight people; it also has an eat-in kitchen. *150 E. Governor Rd., Hershey; (717) 533-2591.*

Hershey Highmeadow Campground ★★★/$

This place charges more than your average campground, but it's incredibly convenient to all the local attractions—there's even free shuttle service to Hershey Park. The property features 300 tent/RV sites and ten cabins, plus two pools, a wading pool, a game room, playgrounds, and basketball and volleyball courts. Organized activities (no charge) such as campfire sing-alongs and arts-and-crafts workshops add to the fun. *1200 Matlack Rd. (P.O. Box 866), Hummelstown; (800) 437-7439.*

Hotel Hershey ★★★★/$$$$

Pricey, but incredibly family-oriented, this 235-room, four-suite hotel is a good place to splurge. The wide range of resort facilities means that everyone will be happily

MAJOR LEAGUE FUN

FOR MINOR LEAGUE MONEY

G OT FANS in the family? While you're traveling through Pennsylvania, take the opportunity to introduce your kids to the excitement of the minor league sports. Unlike the majors, minor league teams offer great family fun—at very reasonable prices. For example, a day at the ballpark with the Harrisburg

Senators is only $5 a person (the hot dogs are inexpensive, too). Here are Pennsylvania's minor league teams and the places they play. Who knows? The minor leaguer you see today could be a major league star tomorrow. But even if not, it's a good way to show the kids that baseball was not always about multimillion-dollar contracts.

engaged during the day: indoor and outdoor pools; basketball, tennis, volleyball, and bocce courts; horse-shoe pits; and nature trails. In winter you can go cross-country skiing or tobogganing (for a small fee); the rest of the year you can play football, fly kites, catch butterflies (nets provided), take a carriage ride, or rent bikes. There's also a game room, and the Cocoa Kids Club offers a schedule of organized activities. Baby-sitting is available. *Hotel Rd., Hershey; (800) 533-3131; (717) 533-2171.*

GOOD EATS

For a tourist town that attracts approximately two million visitors annually, Hershey has few restaurants—mostly lounge or restaurant/bar combos that cater to business folks. The assumption here is that you'll spend your mealtimes within the park as well.

Hershey's Chocolate Town Café ★★★/$$

Right next to Chocolate World, this chocolate-themed restaurant offers great desserts and okay lunches and dinners. Hershey characters (those talking M&M's and Reese's candies, for example) often stop by the children's play area. The overall experience—the atmosphere, the characters—more than make up for the fairly ordinary fare. *800 Park Blvd., Hershey; (717) 533-2917.*

Mr. Sorrento's Pizza ★★★/$

A great pizza and pasta joint with excellent specials, this place is ideal for families—and easy on the budget to boot. You can easily feed a family of five here for under $20. *10 W. Chocolate Ave., Hershey; (717) 534-1660.*

BASEBALL
- Altoona Curve—Blair County Ballpark, Altoona; *(814) 943-5400*
- Erie Sea Wolves—Jerry Uht Park, Erie; *(814) 456-1300*
- Harrisburg Senators—Riverside Stadium, City Island, Harrisburg; *(717) 231-4444*
- Reading Phillies—GPU Stadium, Reading; *(610) 375-8469*
- Scranton/Wilkes-Barre Red Barons—Lackawanna County Stadium, Moosic; *(570) 969-BALL*

HOCKEY
- Hershey Bears—Hershey Park Arena, Hershey; *(717) 534-3911*

SOCCER
- Harrisburg Heat—Farm Show Arena, Harrisburg; *(717) 625-HEAT*
- Philadelphia Kixx— Spectrum, Philadelphia; *(888) 888-KIXX*

When you tour Lancaster County with Abe's Buggy Rides, your driver is likely to be a member of the local Amish, Mennonite, or Brethren community.

Lancaster County

A VISIT TO Lancaster County is a wonderful opportunity to teach your children that some people have lifestyles and beliefs different from their own—and that they should respect those lifestyles and beliefs no matter how outlandish they seem. A few days here may also foster a renewed appreciation of the various modern appliances that kids tend to take for granted ("They have no TV sets?").

Lancaster County is home to large Amish, Mennonite, and Brethren communities. The strict religious sects require their members to live simply and, in varying degrees, avoid modern conveniences. The members of these communities are known collectively as the "plain people." (All other Americans are known in Lancaster as simply the "English.")

The Amish are the most conservative faction of the Anabaptist movement, which also produced the Mennonites and the Brethren. Forefathers of these groups primarily came from Switzerland and Germany

THE **FamilyFun** LIST

MUST-SEE

MUST-SEE

Abe's Buggy Rides (page 214)

Amish Experience Theatre (page 212)

Amish Farm and House (page 212)

Dutch Wonderland (page 214)

Hands-On House Children's Museum (page 213)

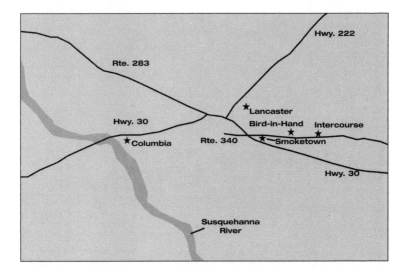

(which is why they are also known here as the "Pennsylvania Dutch"—actually a corruption of Pennsylvania Deutsch, or German). Driven from their homelands by religious persecution, they emigrated to the United States over about 125 years, starting around 1720. Some quite substantial differences in both theology and lifestyle exist among the various sects of plain people, but in general, all believe that the Bible teaches a life of simplicity and the separation of church and state, so they shun technology—no phones, no cars, no Nintendo. Dress is also very plain—no visible buttons—and in many orders, the women wear small net caps called "coverings."

> Instead of the traditional white dresses that most Americans associate with weddings, **Amish brides** typically wear shades of blue or purple.

The heart of what is known as Pennsylvania Dutch Country spreads throughout Lancaster County. As you're driving through the area, you'll see horse-drawn buggies along the roads and families in their traditional garb working their fields. Have the children keep a lookout for the plain people and their farms. Bear in mind that a lack of power lines doesn't necessarily mean an Amish farm. The farms of many "English" residents (as the plain people call their nonplain neighbors) now have buried power cables. Better clues include hanging laundry (Amish clothing, of course), a buggy inside the garage, and windows with green blinds and no drapes. (If you saw what Amish women use for ironing, you'd understand their reluctance to hang curtains!)

Older kids might be interested in learning about the different traditions of the various sects. For example, if you see a completely black buggy driven by a man with no beard, he is an Old Order Mennonite, not Amish. The Amish buggies are all gray with black trim, and all married Amish men sport a beard.

Although their plain dress and conveyances are picturesque, don't start snapping photos—most Amish and Mennonite people prefer not to be photographed. And while many plain people have become accustomed to the attention of tourists (some feel that their lives can serve as a good example to others), remind your children to be polite and not to intrude on the privacy of these families.

Lancaster County, though, is more than Pennsylvania Dutch territory. Some of the other diversions include several kid-friendly museums and a top-notch amusement park. Spring is a great time to visit here; you can expect virtually no lines to any attractions, excellent

weather, and your pick of first-rate accommodations. However, if you opt for a springtime visit, do remember that all those surrounding Amish farms use "organic" fertilizer.

In spite of the scent, the local landscape, with its rolling hills and green fields, is lovely and serene. In many ways, the land itself is as plain and simple as the people it nurtures. On the other hand, many of the place names, like Bird-in-Hand and Paradise, are quite fanciful. And preteens are bound to get the giggles when they hear mention of the town called Intercourse.

Cultural Adventures

American Music Theatre
★★★★/$$$

This local theater stages original musicals that are appropriate for the whole family. Last year's production, *Hitwave*, featured a full band, tap dancers, and a lighting scheme reminiscent of *Fantasia*. At various points in the production, confetti dropped from the ceiling, whistles sounded, puppets appeared, and disco balls flashed. The midsize venue is large enough to feel professional but small enough so that small children won't be intimidated; it's an excellent choice for your youngsters' first theater experience. Dress is casual but neat: you won't need a

jacket or floor-length dress, but you would feel out of place in cutoffs and a T-shirt. Open year-round; special family rates on Friday nights. *2425 Lincoln Hwy. E. (Rte. 30E), Lancaster; (800) 648-4102; (717) 397-7700; www.americanmusictheatre.com or www.amtshows.com*

Americana Museum of Bird-in-Hand ★★/$

It's essentially an indoor "town," including re-created stores from the Gay '90s through the Roaring '20s. The 12 shops include a milliner, a barber, a blacksmith, a general store, and an apothecary. Pick up the children's activity sheet (sort of a scavenger hunt) that lists unique items for kids to find during the guided tour. The displays are wonderful, but a few of the untouchables might be too tempting for children under 5. *2709 Old Philadelphia Pike, Bird-in-Hand; (717) 391-9780.*

MUST-SEE FamilyFun Amish Experience Theatre ★★/$$

Part of the Plain & Fancy Farm complex, the theater is a novel blend of old values and new technologies. It presents *Jacob's Choice*, a multimedia production that chronicles the thoughts and experiences of a young Amish man who is deciding whether to remain part of the Amish community. The production includes a film projected across a re-created barn, almost holographic-style appearances of historical characters, and wonderful special effects. Though the sound effects might be a bit too intense for tiny tots, the show will definitely hold the attention of their older siblings. *Rte. 340, between Bird-in-Hand and Intercourse; (717) 768-3600.*

MUST-SEE FamilyFun Amish Farm and House ★★★/$

Mom and Dad will probably appreciate the house most, but

Scenic Views

As a mother of two preschoolers, I am always trying to make car travel more fun for them and easier on me. One idea that has worked very well is a picture scavenger hunt. I cut pictures out of old picture books, magazines, and catalogs and paste them on a piece of poster board. Then I punch holes in the two top corners of the poster, tie a piece of elastic between them, and hang it from the back of a front seat. Each time they see one of the items—an airplane, tractor, bicycle, flag, cow, or horse, for example—they place a dot sticker on that picture. My kids love this game so much that it entertained them throughout a recent 13-hour trip from our home in Texas to Arkansas.

Lisa Reynolds, San Antonio, Texas

kids will be delighted by the farm. The playground area includes an Amish-made wooden tractor and barn with a slide, all surrounded by corrals of small farm animals. (Remember to bring quarters to buy feed for the pygmy goats.) This is a working farm, so there's a wide range of livestock to see. You can take buggy rides for an additional fee. *2395 Lincoln Hwy./Rte. 30 E., Bird-in-Hand; (717) 394-6185;* www. amishfarmandhouse.com

Discover Lancaster County History Museum
★★★/$$

Formerly called the Wax Museum of Lancaster, this is still basically a wax museum, with 32 scenes that contain more than 172 life-size figures. Unlike most wax museums though, this one intersperses hands-on exhibits amidst the figures so your kids will have plenty of things to actually touch and do. The best part of the museum is a dress-up area complete with the clothing of early Colonists, Native Americans, and plain people. (Okay, a real Amish woman wouldn't have Velcro up the back of her dress, but kids get the idea.) A few of the costumes are even large enough for Mom and Dad. Bring a camera. **NOTE:** At the last display, the Amish barn-raising, the exit doors go one way only, so make sure that you're really ready to leave. *2249 Lincoln Hwy./Rte. 30 E., directly beside Dutch Wonderland, Lancaster; (717) 393-3679.*

FamilyFun TIP

Cool It

Whether you use a cooler, an insulated bag or box, or Tupperware, here are some ways to keep snacks cool without messy, melting ice: add frozen juice boxes; make sandwiches on frozen bread; pack some frozen grapes; include a smoothie frozen in a tightly sealed container.

MUST-SEE FamilyFun Hands-On House Children's Museum
★★★/$$

No need to say, "don't touch," at this wonderful museum for children ages 2 to 10 and their parents. Exhibits cover food and farming (E-I-E-I Know), color and creativity (Rainbow's End), how things work (Marty's Machine Shop), and the world beyond (Space Voyage Checkpoint). Plan on making a day of it. *721 Landis Valley Rd., Lancaster; (717) 569-KIDS.*

National Watch and Clock Museum ★★/$

A little bit out of the way, this fascinating collection of timepieces is worth the slight detour. (If you're heading from Lancaster to Gettysburg, it'll be right on your way.) On display here are more than 12,000 timepieces ranging from sundials to the elaborate Engle Clock, an 1877 creation that measures 11 feet high and 8 feet wide and has 48

213

High-Flying Games

Games that use a pen or pencil are perfect to play on airplanes, since you can lean on the tray top. The following ideas are especially enjoyed by players who are sitting in a row. Unlike backseat games, which can get fairly boisterous, these airplane pastimes are a bit quieter, so you won't make enemies of your fellow fliers.

CRAZY CREATURES

Create strange-looking people, beasts, or any combination of both by folding a piece of paper into three equal sections. One person draws the face in the top section, then folds down the paper so the next person can't see it. That person then draws the midsection of the body, folds down the paper, and passes it to the third person, who sketches the legs in the bottom section. Finally, unfold the paper and name your creature.

TOUCHY TELEPHONE

This is a good game for people sitting in a row. Player 1, on one end, thinks of a word. Player 2, next to 1, closes his or her eyes and holds out an arm. Using a finger, Player 1 "writes" the word on Player 2's arm. The word gets passed down the row—and maybe across the aisle—until it reaches the last person in your party. That person says the word he thinks was written on his arm out loud, and Player 1 says the original word. Let Player 2 start the next round, and so on.

performing animated pieces. A procession of some type occurs at the top of each hour, but to see the most elaborate animation, try for the 11:45 A.M. showing. The Learning Center provides additional hands-on exhibits. Family rate includes two adults and all kids under 18. Closed Monday. *514 Poplar St., Columbia; (717) 684-8261.*

JUST FOR FUN

Abe's Buggy Rides
FamilyFun ★★★/$$

Don't leave Lancaster without taking a buggy ride. Believe it or not, you can actually fit a family of six into one vehicle. This excellent two-mile tour through Amish farmlands comes complete with fascinating running commentary. Most of the drivers are "plain," either Amish, Mennonite, or Brethren; the few who aren't have relatives who are and are knowledgeable. Expect wonderful details on the way of life and history of the Amish. Closed Sunday. *Rte. 340, a half mile from Bird-in-Hand; (717) 392-1794;* www.800pa dutch.com/abes.html

Dutch Wonderland
FamilyFun ★★★★/$$$$

You won't find hyper-coasters or rides that hit "zero G" at this first-rate amusement park, which is geared toward families with small children. You also won't find herds of rowdy teenagers, overpriced concessions, or long lines. In fact, about the only lines you will find are for the water rides—and the turnpike ride. There are currently 28 rides, with another 20 attractions—everything from playground equipment and storybook buildings to live farm animals—scattered throughout. Among the rides are a nice wooden rail coaster, the Sky Princess; a smaller steel rail "family coaster" called the Joust; several virtual-reality rides; and a fantastic tube water coaster called the Pipeline Plunge. (When it says you will get wet, it really means you will get drenched!) Several arcades are scattered throughout the park—pack a few rolls of quarters. The gondola ride takes you on a cute little "world tour"; you'll pass pint-size reproductions of Big Ben, a Japanese pagoda, a Swiss chalet, and the Eiffel Tower. Kids will also like the boat ride, and parents will enjoy the botanical displays along the way.

Two shows provide breaks from the rides: the Acapulco Cliff Divers put on an astounding diving show, and the amphitheater features changing shows (musicians, magicians, etc.) with audience interaction. Both venues have limited seating, so get your seats a few minutes in advance. The park has many picnic areas, but if you choose to buy your lunch or dinner here, you'll find the prices refreshingly affordable: many kid-favorite foods (like

hot dogs) are under $2, and children's drinks are under $1. The park admission itself is among the more reasonable ones around. *2249 Lincoln Hwy./Rte. 30 E., Lancaster; (717) 291-1888;* www.dutchwonderland.com

BUNKING DOWN

Lancaster Host Resort and Conference Center ★★★★/$$$
Amenities at this excellent family resort include indoor and outdoor pools, tennis courts, bicycle rentals, a game room, basketball and volleyball courts, and Ping-Pong and pool tables. Family vacation package deals are available. *2300 Lincoln Hwy./Rte. 30 E., Lancaster; (800) 233-0121; (717) 299-5500.*

Old Mill Stream Camping Manor ★★★/$
These campgrounds make a wonderful base from which to tour Amish country. Nice features for families include modern rest rooms, two Laundromats, a game room, a very nice playground, and access to paddleboats and fishing. Another plus: the sites are shady (shade is hard to come by in an area best known for its farmland). *2249 Lincoln Hwy./Rte. 30 E., Lancaster; (717) 299-2314.*

Willow Valley Resort & Conference Center ★★★★/$$$
Another excellent family resort, this one has three swimming pools (two

215

outdoor, one indoor), free bus tours of Amish country, an Amish wagon tour, a seasonal corn maze, an animal petting barn, tennis courts, a basketball court, a playground, and various game rooms. There's an on-site family restaurant, too. *2416 Willow St. Pike, Lancaster; (800) 444-1714; (717) 464-2711.*

GOOD EATS

It might not compare to French nouvelle or Northern Italian, but Pennsylvania Dutch is most definitely a distinctive cuisine. Nearly every meal is based on meat—homemade sausage, pork roast, pork chops, meat loaf, scrapple (fried ground meat and corn meal),

etc., etc. Vegetarians in the family could starve here. Or they could survive on dessert—count on a good selection of pies, including the local favorite, shoofly pie, a concoction that has molasses on the bottom, cake in the middle, and sweet crumbs on top. Spaetzle, a kind of noodle, is a regular, as is chicken-corn soup. Family-style restaurants are popular: expect to be seated at long tables alongside other guests, with large platters of food being passed around. Here are some of our favorites.

The Amish Barn
★★★/$$
The draws here are the huge portions and excellent service. The ham and pork dishes, made according to

FINS, FEATHER, FUR, AND FUN!

I**N ADDITION** to several zoos and aquariums, Pennsylvania plays host to a number of rather odd animal attractions:

Claws 'N' Paws
Animal Park
★★★/$$
Children can get up close and personal with the residents of this private zoo. Hourly activities include a lory parrot feeding, reptile show, dino dig, and giraffe feeding. Kids are wowed by the size of the giraffe

as they hand-feed him carrots.

Feeding the parrots is another experience not to be missed. You enter an enclosure and hold out bits of fruit that the birds take right out of your hands. Your big and small bird lovers will delight in this experience. The on-site snack bar is limited to chili, hot dogs, and—surprise!— chili dogs, but they're tasty and reasonably priced. *Rte. 590, four miles east of Hamlin, in the Pocono Mountains; Lake Ariel; (570) 698-6154.*

traditional recipes, are especially good, as is the potpie. The children's menu is good, and all kids' meals include pudding. The desserts are very reasonably priced—you can get a slice of great shoofly pie for under $2. A petting zoo next door makes a fun after-meal diversion. *Rte. 340, between Bird-in-Hand and Intercourse; (717) 768-8886.*

Good 'N' Plenty Restaurant
★★★★/$$$

Boasting what is likely the largest menu for family-style dining in Lancaster, this excellent eatery offers roast beef, baked ham, fried chicken, pork and sauerkraut, chow-chow (a mix of pickled vegetables), pepper cabbage, shoofly pie, and more. The dishes just keep coming

and coming. Closed Sunday. *Rte. 896, Smoketown; (717) 394-7111.*

Lapp's Family Restaurant
★★/$$

The lunch and dinner selections are quite good. But skip the breakfast buffet—it's a bit overpriced for morning eats in the area. *2270 Lincoln Hwy./Rte. 30 E., Lancaster; (717) 394-1606.*

Plain & Fancy Farm Restaurant
★★★★/$$$

Enjoy family-style dining that includes all the Pennsylvania Dutch classics—potpie, baked sausage, sweet and sour relishes, shoofly pie, and much more. Arrive hungry and expect to leave stuffed. *Rte. 340, Lancaster; (717) 768-4400.*

Clyde Peeling's Reptiland ★★/$$

This specialty zoo focuses on critters that slither, slide, and hop. The large collection of reptiles and amphibians includes turtles, tortoises, lizards, frogs, alligators, and snakes of all

styles and sizes. There are live shows daily. *On U.S. Rte. 15, ten miles south of Williamsport, Allenwood; (570) 538-1869.*

Mister Ed's Elephant Museum ★★★★/Free

No live elephants live here, but this combination elephant museum/candy store has a great kitschy collection of elephant memorabilia. Kids love the elephant-shaped potty chair and selection of stuffed elephants. The candy is pretty good, too. *Twelve miles west of Gettysburg on Rte. 30 in Orrtanna; (717) 352-3792.*

Although the Liberty Bell no longer rings with its clapper, kids are sometimes treated to its music when it is tapped for special occasions.

Philadelphia

WHAT BETTER PLACE to take your young siblings than the City of Brotherly Love? Even if it fails to reduce brotherly (or sisterly) squabbling, a visit to Philadelphia is a great way for your family to learn about American history, brush up on some science, and just generally have a blast. Philadelphia really does have it all—historical sites, cultural events, and some of the best art and science museums in the country.

Even better, the city's wide range of attractions is concentrated within a fairly small area—many are within walking distance of Center City accommodations. (Given how difficult and expensive downtown parking is, this is a really good thing.)

Visitors who plan to see everything might consider getting a City Pass. This gains you admission to

THE **FamilyFun** LIST

MUST-SEE ★ MUST-SEE

Academy of Natural Sciences
(page 220)

**American Helicopter Museum &
Education Center** (page 221)

Franklin Institute Science Museum
(page 221)

**Independence National Historic
Park** (page 222)

Independence Seaport Museum
(page 223)

Philadelphia Zoo (page 225)

Please Touch Museum
(page 225)

Sesame Place (page 225)

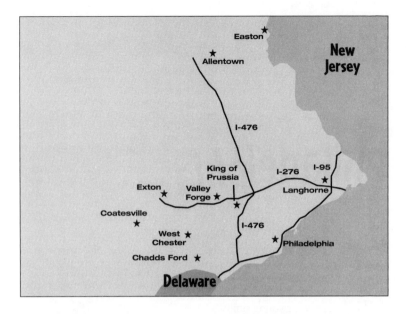

Easton ★
★ Allentown
New Jersey
I-476
King of Prussia
I-276 I-95
Exton ★ Valley Forge ★
Langhorne ★
Coatesville ★
I-476
West ★ Chester
★ Philadelphia
Chadds Ford ★
Delaware

the Academy of Natural Sciences, the Franklin Institute, the Independence Seaport Museum, the Philadelphia Museum of Art, the Philadelphia Zoo, and the nearby New Jersey State Aquarium, all for about half the price of the individual admission fees. You can buy a City Pass at any of the participating attractions; call *(707) 256-0490* for more information.

Whatever you do or see, make sure you eat one of the famous Philly cheese-steak sandwiches (available almost anywhere) and the hot dogs and hot pretzels sold by street vendors. A cheese-steak sandwich or a hot dog and pretzel can make a wonderful lunch or dinner—or (if you're really in the Philadelphia spirit) breakfast.

CULTURAL ADVENTURES

Academy of Natural Sciences ★★★★/$$
Don't miss this great natural history museum with its wonderful display of dinosaurs. To record the experience, have your child pick up a Passport to Adventure on your way in; they can get it stamped at each exhibit. If you're traveling with younger kids, be sure to visit the third floor, with the combination indoor playground/discovery room called Outside-In. It's an ideal place for toddlers—or even older children—to work off excess energy.

They can crawl through a log, dig in a sandbox, play with microscopes, and examine small animals. As you work your way down through the floors, the animals get larger and the exhibits more intense. Pint-size paleontologists love The Big Dig, an interactive exhibit where kids actually don protective goggles, then use chisels and brushes to uncover casts of dinosaur fossils buried within simulated rock. The Butterfly Garden is also great. Butterflies live here all year long, but peak in numbers and varieties in the summer. *1900 Benjamin Franklin Pkwy., Philadelphia; (215) 299-1000;* http://sapphire.acnatsci.org

★★★★/$$ American FamilyFun Helicopter Museum & Education Center

Ever wondered what it would be like to sit in the flying machines displayed at the Smithsonian Air and Space Museum and play with all the buttons? Come here and find out. Almost half of the displayed helicopters are open to exploring hands: youngsters can sit in the cockpits, flip the rotors, and hit all of the buttons again and again (and again). The Vertical Flight Theatre provides an overview of the history of helicopter development, with examples of how they've been used in rescue and military situations. Unfortunately, the format is pretty dry, and the film goes on a bit longer than it should. If your offspring are under 9, you'll probably want to skip it and go straight to the helicopters. *About a half hour from Center City Philadelphia. 1220 American Blvd., Brandywine Airport, W. Chester; (610) 436-9600.*

Betsy Ross House ★★★/$

The woman who sewed the first American flag wasn't the owner of this house, but a boarder, who rented a room and worked here from 1773 to 1786. But it was in this house that she sewed the first American flag. Although she was an upholsterer by trade, Betsy Ross got the chance to stitch the original Stars and Stripes (and thus earn a place in American history) not because of her outstanding sewing skills but because she sat next to George Washington at church. This is one of Philadelphia's most popular attractions; only the Liberty Bell and Independence Hall draw more visitors. *239 Arch St., Philadelphia; (215) 686-1252.*

Franklin Institute FamilyFun Science Museum ★★★★/$$

Unique displays let your kids walk through a giant human heart, create their own Web pages at the Cyber-Zone, and in other ways celebrate

A Star in a Snip!

George Washington's original sketch of the American flag called for 6-pointed stars, but Betsy Ross demonstrated that she could easily cut 5-pointed stars with a single snip. Try this fun trick yourself!

Fold an 8¹/₂ x 10 inch piece of paper in half so it becomes 8¹/₂ x 5 inches.

Write the letters A, B, C, and M on it as shown. (Fold it in quarters to find the center.)

Fold corner A to just short of B. Mark the newly formed corner D.

Fold corner C over the paper edge running from B to D (along dotted line of diagram below).

Make another fold along the dotted line from C to D, making sure your edges line up. Cut the paper on an angle as shown below. Open a perfect star!

Ben Franklin's scientific legacy. True to that legacy, there are plenty of electricity-related exhibits. The "hairball" static electricity generator is especially popular. The complex also includes the Fels Planetarium, which offers wonderful kid-oriented star shows like *Where in the Universe is Carmen San Diego?*, and the Tuttleman Omniverse Theater, which shows fantastic films on a four-story domed screen, with sound pouring from 56 speakers. Separate fees are charged for the star shows and the films; to get even more bang for your buck, come for a Friday or Saturday night double feature at the Omniverse Theater. Three on-site eateries provide a nice range of dining options, and there are two areas for brown baggers. Currently, the institute has closed some areas for renovation; if there's something you really want to see, check to make sure it's open. *222 N. 20th St., Philadelphia. Museum information: (215) 448-1200; movie schedule: (215) 448-1200; theater tickets: (215) 448-1111;* www.fi.edu

Independence National Historic Park
★★★★/Free

This park covers a good bit of downtown Philadelphia and much of our country's early history. Pick up your maps and program schedule (Park Service programs are free) at the visitors' center (*Third and Chestnut Sts.*). Next, move on to the **Franklin Court**

Museum (*Market St. between Third and Fourth Sts.*). This free attraction is cool on several levels. First of all, Franklin Court itself is a ghost structure—just a steel outline of a house that isn't there anymore. Second, the museum part is completely underground. Finally, many of the exhibits are hands-on, fairly unusual for a history museum. You enter through a mirror-lined room bordered by alternating neon signs chronicling all of Franklin's various roles: statesman, inventor, scientist, publisher, and so on. Then you find yourself in a room full of telephones with a neon directory on the wall listing numbers your kids can call to hear quotes about Franklin from dozens of historical figures. Be sure to catch the ranger playing the glass armonica; your kids will definitely want to try it out. Advance next to **Independence Hall** (*Chestnut St. between Fifth and Sixth Sts.*) for an excellent 30-minute tour and presentation by the National Park Service. And of course, you won't want to miss the **Liberty Bell Pavilion** (*Market St. between 5th and 6th Sts*). The building around the bell is ugly (and scheduled to be replaced), but the ten-minute guided tour is great for even the youngest family members; *(215) 597-8974; www.nps.gov/inde*

★ MUST-SEE ★ FamilyFun Independence Seaport Museum
★★★★/$$

Even though it's 90 miles from the ocean, Philadelphia is considered a seaport (it has rivers that have access to the ocean). And if you and the kids want to learn about seaports (or just play on some ships) this is certainly the place to do it. Scattered throughout the museum are lots of buttons to push, fishing reels to wind, and hands-on activities to keep little hands busy. Kids can climb aboard a "shipboard" bunk to get a feel for traveling in steerage, as immigrants did; play the crane game, loading and unloading ships at port; or conduct their own races using rowing machines linked to video screens. D-Bay is especially fun, allowing children to play at welding or riveting in dry dock.

Throughout the museum, you and your kids can also listen to recorded messages from people who played a

NO ONE KNOWS WHY the Liberty Bell has such a large crack in it. The fissure became visible in 1846 and began to alter the sound of the bell. It was repaired and the bell rang again to honor Washington's birthday. Unfortunately, a new crack appeared during the celebration, so the Liberty Bell is no longer rung with its clapper.

223

role in the area's maritime history. Docked outside the museum are the USS *Olympia* and the USS *Becuna*, a World War II Balao class submarine. Children of all ages are welcome on the ships, although you can't get strollers or wheelchairs on either one. You can get combination tickets that include admission to the nearby New Jersey State Aquarium (see page 173) and the ferry ride across the Delaware River. *Penn's Landing Waterfront, 211 S. Columbus Blvd., at Walnut St., Philadelphia; (215) 925-5439;* www.phillyseaport.org

Mummers Museum ★★★/$

The Mummers are best known for their annual New Year's Day Parade, an extravaganza around City Hall that lasts upwards of 14 hours and features more than 25,000 marchers in truly outrageous feathered and beaded costumes. If you can't make the annual New Year's Day parade, this museum is the next best thing. And if you've never seen a Mummer

Mint Condition

Take a close look at your pocket change. Every coin minted in the United States has one of four letters on it: D, P, S, or W. The letter tells where the coin was produced (either in Denver, Philadelphia, San Francisco, or West Point, New York).

(and have no idea what one is), imagine a Las Vegas showgirl wearing considerably more clothes and about 150 pounds of beads and feathers. Based on an old Swedish practice, the parade has its roots in local traditions extending back to the early 1800s. The costumes displayed here are the best of past parade winners. Fans of the Broadway show *The Lion King* will particularly appreciate the Spirit of Africa costume. Mirrored displays let kids picture themselves in various costumes. (Alas, the museum lacks a real dress-up area; most youngsters would love to get into the glittery getups.) On Tuesday night from May through September, the museum holds free outdoor string concerts complete with dancers who teach the signature "Mummer's Strut." *1100 S. Second St., Philadelphia; (215) 336-3050.*

Philadelphia Museum of Art ★★★/$$

For an art museum, this place is incredibly family-friendly. The costume collection is especially interesting, and if you have budding artists in your family, the early works of Picasso and Matisse are must-sees, too. Check out the special family workshops that are offered each Sunday. Parents and kids can try their hands at creating painted bottles, frescoes, Japanese paper cases, and other works of art. *Benjamin Franklin Pkwy. and 26th St., Philadelphia; (215) 763-8100; family programs information: (215) 684-7605.*

MUST-SEE **Please Touch Museum**
FamilyFun ★★★★/$$
MUST-SEE For the under-8 crowd, this is the fun (and educational) place to be in Philadelphia. As a result, the three-story, 30,000-square-foot building is usually packed. Kids get to play on a full-size trolley or shop in a huge and well-stocked play supermarket. The Growing Up section includes dolls from all cultures; little mommies and daddies can cuddle a "baby" in an African sling or tie one into a Native American papoose. Kids love the many opportunities for dress-up play throughout the building. **NOTE:** This is definitely one of the best kid's museums in the country, also one of the priciest. At press time, the admission fee for adults and children (over one year) was $8.95. *210 N. 21st St., Philadelphia; (215) 963-0667;* www.pleasetouchmuseum.org

JUST FOR FUN

MUST-SEE **Philadelphia Zoo**
FamilyFun ★★★/$$
MUST-SEE Opened to the public in 1874, this was the first zoo in America—and it's still a great one, with a population of more than 1,700 animals. The PECO Primate Reserve is especially impressive. Designed to look like an abandoned timber mill, the two-and-a-half-acre facility holds 11 primate species—everything from Sumatran orangutans to pygmy marmosets. Be sure to stop by the Children's Zoo for a camel or elephant ride. *3400 W. Girard Ave., Philadelphia; (215) 243-1100.*

MUST-SEE **Sesame Place**
FamilyFun ★★★★/$$$$
MUST-SEE The name alone carries a guarantee of family fun. Your little guys will enjoy strolling down Sesame Neighborhood and stopping at Ernie and Bert's house, Oscar's garbage can, and all their other favorite places on *Sesame Street.* The older kids can drench themselves on the Sky Splash ride or fly the Vapor Trail steel rail coaster. (Only at Sesame Place would you find a roller coaster created by Fisher Price!) The water rides are especially fun: try Little Bird's Birdbath and Amazing Mumford's Water Maze. For added excitement, call ahead to reserve Breakfast with Big Bird & Company. Open May through October. During October, be sure to check out The Count's Halloween Spooktacular. **NOTE:** You definitely don't want to miss this fantastic park, but it is very expensive. All visitors age 2 and older must pay the same $30-plus admission fee. *About a half hour from Philadelphia. 100 Sesame Rd., Langhorne; (215) 752-7070.*

BUNKING DOWN

Clarion Suites
Convention Center ★★★/$$$
An excellent location, close to Independence National Historical

Park and museums, is just one of the attractions here. The 96 large suites have charming features: exposed-brick walls and beamed cathedral ceilings, and—most important for a family—a kitchen. There's also a free continental breakfast buffet. *1010 Race St., Philadelphia; (800) CLARION; (215) 922-1730.*

Embassy Suites Philadelphia Airport ★★★★/$$$$

Special weekend rates are geared to families, as are "Honest-to-Goodness Two-Room Suites" that let your kids have a room of their own. Children stay free, and the whole family gets a complimentary cooked-to-order breakfast that includes bacon and eggs. Another selling point: the recreational facilities include an indoor swimming pool, basketball hoop, and an electronic games room. *9000 Bartram Ave., Philadelphia; (800) EMBASSY (362-2779); (215) 365-4500;* www.embassysuites.com

Philadelphia/West Chester KOA ★★★/$$

Riverside tenting may make some Moms nervous, but you can opt for a cabin or rental trailer instead. The property also has a pool, fishing, and easy access to guided tours of Philadelphia, Valley Forge, and the Amish Country. *About a half hour from Philadelphia. 1659 Embreeville Rd., Coatesville; (800) 562-1726; (610) 486-0447;* www.koa.com

Wyndham Franklin Plaza Hotel ★★★★/$$$$

Within walking distance of Independence Hall and the Franklin Institute, this pricey but oh-so-family-friendly member of the Wyndham chain has an indoor pool; racquetball, handball, tennis, and basketball courts; and a play area. Parents like it that children stay and eat for free and that baby-sitting can be arranged. *17th and Race Sts., Philadelphia; (877) 999-3223; (215) 448-2000.*

GOOD EATS

Bugaboo Creek Steakhouse ★★★★/$$$

Named after the Bugaboo Glacier region of British Columbia, Canada, this theme eatery combines a rustic hunting-lodge setting with Walt Disney World–style animation. Your kids will love the talking animatronics animals as well as Timber the Talking Tree. Bill the buffalo, woodpeckers, an owl, various decoy-style geese, and a raccoon all compete for their attention. The children's menu is fairly predictable (grilled cheese, hot dogs, etc.) but reasonably priced. But the kids won't care about the food—the entertaining setting is the point. The downside is that this very popular place doesn't take reservations. To avoid a wait, come on a weekday or a bit before or after traditional mealtimes. *601 Franklin Mills Cir., Philadelphia; (215) 281-3700.*

FamilyFun GAME

Car Scavenger Hunt

Hand your kids a pack of index cards and ask them to write or draw pictures of 50 things they might see on a trip. Keep the cards for scavenger hunts when players vie to match the cards with what they see.

City Tavern ★★★/$$$$

Actually a part of Independence National Historical Park, this is a reconstruction of the tavern where our nation's founders dined during the First and Second Continental Congresses. The historically accurate menu and atmosphere give you the experience of dining in the 18th century. Even the kids' menu has colonial touches: there's turkey potpie, cornmeal-crusted chicken tenders, and meat and cheese pie. Older children will be intrigued by the waiters' and waitresses' period costumes. But if your kids are under 7, you may want to wait a few years before trying this one. Preschoolers don't appreciate the period food and formal ambience. *138 S. Second St., at Walnut St., Philadelphia; (215) 413-1443.*

Eastside Mario's
★★★★/$$

While you're in Philly, why not give your kids a taste of the Big Apple? Eastside Mario's has a New York City theme: walk in past the Statue of Liberty, and then dine under a re-creation of the Brooklyn Bridge. The walls are designed as storefront facades, with such unexpected details as hanging laundry lines strung above the tables. Huge servings and kid-friendly offerings like Bambino Pizza complete the experience. Unlike in the real New York, the prices here are very family-friendly. Kids' meals are all $4. *Thirty minutes from Philadelphia. 180 Old Lincoln Hwy., Exton; (610) 363-0444.*

Rainforest Café
★★★★/$$$

Yes, it's a nationwide chain, but it's also a nationwide favorite among the grade-school set. Imagine having your lunch at the Tikki Room at Walt Disney World. Now, imagine that you walk through an aquarium, past a small zoo with real talking birds, and around an arboretum just to get there. The dinner show here includes displays of animatronics animals and a light and sound thunderstorm. Kids get generous portions, cute cups, and a plastic frog with each meal. The gift shop is an irresistible lure for little folk, but fear not—the T-shirts are reasonably priced, and on the kid-cool scale, Rainforest Café T-shirts rank just above Hard Rock Café T-shirts and just below T-shirts from Planet Hollywood. **NOTE:** You'll surely have to wait for a table. *In the Franklin Mills Mall, 1133 Franklin Mills Cir., Philadelphia; (215) 224-5449; www.rainforestcafe.com*

FUN EXCURSIONS FROM PHILLY

A FTER YOU'VE SEEN the sights of Philadelphia, you may want to take a day trip or two to some other area attractions. The following destinations are all within a day trip's distance from central Philadelphia.

Brandywine Battlefield
★★/Free

Best for older children with an interest in history, this park was the site of the largest single engagement in the Revolutionary War. Park buildings include Washington's Headquarters, Lafayette's Quarters, and the Brandywine Battlefield Museum. *One mile east of Hwy. 100 on the north side of Hwy. 1 (roughly 30 miles from Philadelphia), Chadds Ford; (610) 459-3342.*

Crayola Factory
★★★★/$$

It's arguably the best factory tour in the country, although, in truth, the tour no longer goes through the actual factory. But kids do get to see how crayons and markers are made—and to play with all the great toys Crayola makes. On your way in, make sure everyone picks up an activity bag to hold his or her artwork. Various activity stations include a Chalk Walk for sidewalk chalk drawing; an area called Inside Out where budding artists are encouraged to write on the clear walls; and the Easton Press & Bindery, where kids can do screen printing and bind "books" to take home. They can also sculpt with Model Magic, have a hand in the Silly Putty demos, and literally dance their way through the Light and Sculpture exhibit. Add to this a color garden area for preschoolers, and the most massive—perhaps the only—crayon carousel you'll ever see (with more than 100 colors to create with), and you've got the makings for some pretty happy kids.

The Crayola Factory fee includes admission to the **National Canal Museum** (*610/559-6613*) and **National Heritage Corridor Visitor Center** (*610/515-8000*), both in the same building. The Canal Museum has great hands-on displays, including dress-up opportunities for kids. Allow at least four hours just for the Crayola Factory, more if you plan to

visit the Canal Museum, too—and expect to leave without having done everything. **NOTE:** The Crayola Factory is probably the most popular attraction in the region. Do the Model Magic activity early; it's always the most crowded. And don't even think about coming on a rainy day. *Two Rivers Landing, 30 Centre Sq., Easton; (800) 515-8000; (610) 559-6607;* www.crayola.com

Dorney Park
★★★★/$$$$
Your family can easily spend two busy days here—and they'll still want to do more. Amusement park rides run the gamut from family standbys to one of the world's best hypercoasters, the Steel Force, and envelope-pushing thrill rides like Dominator.

Camp Snoopy is hands-down the best little kids' amusement park in Pennsylvania. It offers mini-versions of all the top rides, including a pint-size version of the Dominator called Woodstock's Airmail. If your kids are 7 or under, don't miss it.

The water park is also first rate and HUGE. The only negative thing about Dorney Park is that it uses an insane number of height levels to restrict the rides—eight separate levels for the water and land parks. To make things even more complicated, children are measured with shoes in the amusement park and without shoes in the water park. A kid who clears the four-foot barrier in one area may not in the other. It's hard to remember which kids can ride where. **NOTE:** This is a great place to stop if you're leaving Philadelphia on your way to New York or New Jersey—it's right by Route 78, which goes into Manhattan. *3830 Dorney Park Rd., Allentown; (610) 395-3724.*

Valley Forge National Park
★★★/Free
Come to this lovely park for a day of history and simple relaxation. Begin with the film at the visitors' center and then strike out on the self-guided walking tour (maps are free, or you can rent a tape for a small fee). There are miles of great hiking trails, and picnic areas with barbecues dot the park. The Park Service holds historical programs in December, February, May, and June. The park is also the site of the World of Scouting Museum, which chronicles the Girl Scout and Boy Scout movements worldwide. The Valley Forge Visitor's Bureau offers a free book of 13 family-friendly driving tours called *Fun Field Trips;* call *(610) 834-1550.* For a free visitors guide to Valley Forge, call *(888) VISIT-VF. Eighteen miles west of Philadelphia, two miles from King of Prussia on Rtes. 202 and 422, Valley Forge; Washington's Headquarters information: (610) 783-1077; Scout Museum information: (610) 783-5311.*

If your kids want an alternative to the ski trails in the Poconos, consider going sledding or tubing down the slopes.

The Poconos

The Pocono Mountains are best known as a honeymoon destination. But what many people don't realize is that a surprising number of those newlyweds return years later, kids in tow. Encompassing a large part of eastern Pennsylvania, the Poconos are, in fact, a great year-round family vacation spot. Cold-weather activities include downhill and cross-country skiing and snow tubing. When the weather gets warmer, you and the kids can go camping and hiking, frolic in area water parks, visit a great amusement park, see spectacular waterfalls, and enjoy a host of other activities. NASCAR fans will find the Pocono Raceway a must-see; others will want to check the NASCAR schedules to avoid the Poconos during major races. In addition to the attractions listed here, be sure to stop by Claws 'N' Paws Animal Park in nearby Hamlin (see "Fins, Feathers, Fur, and Fun!" page 216).

The Poconos are also fairly well known for many outlet malls. Though they're very popular with

THE FamilyFun LIST

MUST-SEE
MUST-SEE

Bushkill Falls (page 233)

Camelback Ski Area and Camelbeach Water Park (page 233)

Carousel Water & Fun Park (page 234)

Knoebels: Pennsylvania's Hometown Park (page 234)

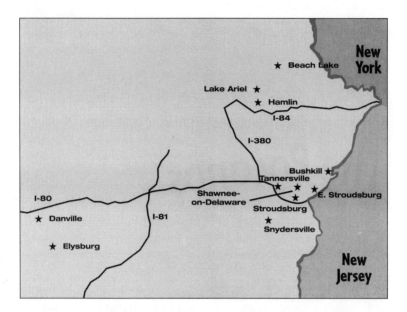

visiting New Yorkers (who are used to higher prices), the goods aren't all that cheap for the area. We'd skip the shopping and focus on having fun!

CULTURAL ADVENTURES

Pocono Indian Museum
★★–★★★★/$

It's a cute little museum surrounded by a wonderful gift shop. (We've given the museum two stars; the shop, four.) The museum collection focuses on the Lenape (Delaware) Indians of the Pocono region. The tour is "semi" self-guided; you get a tape recorder with prerecorded commentary at the entrance. The gift shop is truly a clas-

sic. Remember the little Indian dolls and Daniel Boone coonskin hats you had as a kid? They're sold here, along with wonderful contemporary Native American artwork and a fantastic selection of books covering Native American culture and herbal medicine. *Rte. 209, Bushkill; (570) 588-9338.*

Quiet Valley Living Historical Farm ★★★/$$

After a day on the water slides or the amusement park rides, Quiet Valley is a relaxing change of pace. The approach at this working farm and restored house is distinctive. Unlike most other living-history museums, which focus on a single historical era, this place covers life on this particular farm from the late 1700s to the early 1900s. Each of the guides plays the role of one of the actual residents of the homestead between 1780 and 1913. As at Colonial Williamsburg, the guides wear period costumes and stay steadfastly in character, adding to the fun. Hands-on displays let kids churn butter and learn how to separate wheat from chaff. *1000 Turkey Hill Rd., Stroudsburg; (570) 992-6161.*

JUST FOR FUN

Bushkill Falls
FamilyFun ★★★★/$$

The so-called Niagara of Pennsylvania is actually a series of eight waterfalls, some truly spectacular, surrounded by pristine woods filled with wonderful hiking trails. The trails are varied enough to meet the needs of any family; hiking times range from 15 minutes to two and a half hours. If you opt for

the more vigorous Bridal Veil Falls Trail, be sure to take bottled water and wear sturdy walking shoes. Because the trails are "naturally" cut into the surrounding mountainside, most are not stroller accessible. For really tiny tots, this is backpack or Snugli territory. Back at the entrance, you'll find miniature golf, paddleboats, and various arcade activities for the kids. There's also a nice museum on the Lenape Indians, native to this region, and an exhibit on Pennsylvania wildlife. The concessions serve a good variety of food—don't miss the Creamsicle fudge or Moose Tracks ice cream. Closed November through March. *Rte. 209, Bushkill; (570) 588-6682.*

Camelback Ski Area
FamilyFun and Camelbeach
Water Park
★★★★/$$$$

Camelback is a great place for a family skiing/snowboarding vacation. With 33 well-groomed trails and 13 lifts, it is the largest ski area in the Poconos. The mountain offers plenty of novice and intermediate trails for the kids, and even a few black diamond runs for the experts in the family. (They aren't long—the mountain only has a vertical drop of 800 feet—but they are steep.) There's night skiing seven days a week, snowmaking on all trails, equipment rental, and lessons for all ages and abilities. And there's a day-care center for kids still too little to hit the

FamilyFun TIP

Bread & Butter

After a trip to Quiet Valley Farm, try making your own butter another way. Pour a carton of heavy cream into a tightly sealed mason jar and shake. The cream will come together to form solid butter! Keep shaking until most of the liquid is gone. Add some salt to make it taste like the stuff from the store.

slopes. For those who prefer not to slide down snowy mountainsides with long boards strapped to their feet, there's a snow tubing park. There, kids of all ages (Mom and Dad, too) can slide down snowy mountainsides in big inflated inner tubes. No skill is needed, and individual and family tubes are available. NOTE: The ski area can be terribly crowded on weekends.

In summer, the slopes are given over to a fantastic array of water rides for the whole family. The Titan lets you load a family of five into a single raft for a wild ride nearly 900 feet long. The interactive activity pool has mini slides, water mushrooms, and a giant tipping bucket, and is centrally located so parents can splash with their tiny tots while still watching bigger kids circling in the Blue Nile Lazy River ride. Older kids will also love the bumper boats, positioned in the winter snowmaking reservoirs. The total tally of summer attractions includes eight water slides, a 3,000-foot Alpine slide, and two pools. Safety is obviously a major concern at the water park. The number of lifeguards is impressive—there are more than 60 on staff—and adults unaccompanied by a child are not allowed in the family pool area. Summer visitors can also take a ski lift to the peak and enjoy a snack at the mountaintop restaurant. *Take exit 45 off I-80 and follow the signs. Tannersville; (570) 629-1661; www.skicamelback.com*

MUST-SEE FamilyFun MUST-SEE Carousel Water & Fun Park
★★★/$$$

Very few "wet and dry" parks appeal to both toddler girls and teenage boys—but this is one of them. The activity pool holds frog- and boot-shaped toddler slides at the wading end, while a wicked tube slide and deceptively fast speed slide feed into the deeper end. On the dry side, the go-carts are the biggest draws. Budding NASCAR fans ages 8 and up can drive themselves; 3- to 7-year-olds are welcome to ride with Mom or Dad. For visitors under 8 who really want to put themselves behind the wheel, a Power Wheels grid runs behind the go-cart track. Bumper boats, 18 holes of miniature golf, and batting cages round out the list of attractions. You can pay by the ride or purchase an all-day wristband. *Rte. 652, Beach Lake; (570) 729-7532;* www.carouselpark.com

MUST-SEE FamilyFun MUST-SEE Knoebels: Pennsylvania's Hometown Park
★★★★/$$$

A slight detour from most of the Poconos attractions, this park is really, really worth the drive. Recently voted the Best Amusement Park for Families by the National Amusement Park Historical Association, Knoebels offers more than 40 rides and a great old-fashioned, money-saving feature—no overall admission fee. It is one of the few parks left in the country where you can buy your ride tickets $10 at a time. At press time, the cost of kiddie rides ranged from 50 to 80 cents, and even a ride on the Phoenix, considered the world's second-best wooden roller coaster, was only $1.50. One-price, all-you-can-ride admission fees are offered during the week, but not on weekends—company president Dick Knoebel felt that families couldn't get their money's worth on weekends because of the lines for rides. (But on a recent July weekend, lines were almost nonexistent. The longest wait—20 minutes—was for the new, world-class Twister coaster.) Knoebels offers excellent rides for kids (and parents) of all ages and an especially neat Haunted Mansion. Picnic facilities are scattered throughout the park, and you can even rent a grill if you want to barbecue. The concession food is excellent and dirt cheap. With pierogis at 50 cents apiece and fried potato cakes (called Tri-Tators) at three for $1, the prices seem to come from the same bygone era as the classic carousel. If your crew is loathe to leave, you can even pitch a tent in the shadow of the coasters. The on-site campground can accommodate nearly 2,000 campers in more than 500 sites; even so, be sure to reserve ahead for campsites. *Rte. 487, Elysburg; (570) 672-2572; www.knoebels.com*

Shawnee Mountain Ski Area and Shawnee Place Play and Water Park ★★★/$$$

A great place for skiing, snowboarding, and snow tubing in the winter becomes a lovely water playground come summer. The ski area has 23 slopes, nine chairlifts, and a 700-foot vertical drop. There's a half-pipe area and snowboard park for the riders in

---

FamilyFun READER'S TIP

The Gasoline Log

It's a rare child who isn't motivated by the jingling of change. In our family, my 12-year-old son Joshua has a chance to earn some extra money once a month, but only if he does his math. Josh is in charge of the gas log. Every time I get gasoline, I make sure he is in the car. He has to record the mileage, gas price, gallons added, price paid, and miles the car got per gallon. At the end of the month, when we figure out the totals, Joshua pockets any money left over in our monthly gas budget. Understandably, he's become an expert on math, budgeting, town gas prices, and local shortcuts. I end up spending the same amount of money on gas each month. Josh just helps to figure out how much he gets to keep.

Melissa McComas, Reisterstown, Maryland

the family, and a snow-tubing park offers additional cold-weather fun. Other pluses include night skiing, snowmaking on all trails, equipment rental, and a ski school offering a wide range of lessons.

In summer, the mountain becomes a dream of a playground for the under-8 set. Two large water slides surround a smaller activity pool with a "water mushroom" and lemon-drop water fountain. There are even plastic canoes for kids who'd rather ride than slide. "Dry" activities include two bouncing castles, a sand pit, two large ball pits, and a central playground filled with nearly every climb-on toy ever made by Little Tykes. An overhanging net climb, tube slide, and water glide complete the setup. Scheduled activities include juggling lessons and water-balloon-catching contests. Parents are encouraged to play along and are welcome on the slides and in the ball pits, though many prefer to view their children's antics from centrally placed lounge chairs.

Considerably smaller than other water parks, Shawnee Place is also refreshingly uncrowded. There are weekly family specials; Dads are admitted free on Sunday, and grandparents get in free every Thursday. The on-site snack bar is a bit pricey; budget-conscious families may want to use the picnic area. *Take I-80 to exit 309, follow the signs. Shawnee-on-Delaware; (570) 421-7231;* www. shawneemt.com

BUNKING DOWN

Comfort Inn, Hamlin ★★/$$

In addition to 124 clean, comfortable rooms at good prices, this place offers a deluxe complimentary continental breakfast. Cereal, oatmeal, fresh fruit, muffins, and even Poptarts are served. *Take exit 17 off I-84 to Rte. 191 North, Lake Ariel; (800) 228-5150; (570) 689-4148;* www.com fortinn.com

Days Inn (Danville) ★★★/$$

Amenities here include a wonderful indoor courtyard pool, a miniature putting green, and a good continental breakfast. *50 Sheraton Rd., Danville; (800) 544-8313; (570) 275-5510;* www.daysinn.com

Hampton Inn in the Pocono Mountains ★★★★/$$

Pristine rooms, a heated indoor pool, and good service earn this member of the nationwide chain a high rating in our book. Even the complimentary breakfast is first-rate—toaster waffles, four kinds of cereal, muffins, bagels and cream cheese, doughnuts, fresh fruit, fruit juice, milk, and coffee. *114 S. Eighth St., Stroudsburg; (800) HAMPTON; (570) 424-0400;* www.hamptoninn.com

Knoebels ★★★★/$

If you would like to play and rest all in one place, this is the spot. For more information, see page 234.

Otter Lake Camp Resort
★★★★/$

It's pricey for a campground—but what a campground! Amenities include an outdoor pool, wading pool, indoor pool, two hot tubs, a sauna, four tennis courts, five playgrounds, a softball field, two racquetball courts, horseshoe pits, a lake with a sandy beach and swimming, catch-and-release fishing, and fire truck rides. You can also rent paddleboats.

If you plan to just kick back at your campsite and stay put, this is definitely where you want to stay. The campsites are smallish (fairly typical at private campgrounds), but local wildlife is abundantly evident here. Be sure to hide the Cheerios from the chipmunks and remind younger kids not to pet the black-and-white-"striped kitties."

NOTE: Tent campers should be aware that the gravel spread reduces puddles but also wreaks havoc with tent stakes—bring at least a few spares.

Reservations are highly recommended. A three-night minimum stay is sometimes required in late summer. *Located in Marshalls Creek, just ten miles from the Delaware Water Gap off exit 309 of I-80 in Stroudsburg; (570) 223-0123.*

GOOD EATS

Dansbury Depot ★★★/$$
A converted railroad station and freight house, the depot now serves as a very large restaurant. The menu includes American standards, seafood, and Italian fare. Unlimited house salad and scrumptious bread accompany each meal. There's a children's menu, too. *50 Crystal St., E. Stroudsburg; (570) 476-0500.*

John's Italian Restaurant
★★★/$$

Good pizza and great pasta are served. The extensive children's menu includes ziti, lasagna, and even veal parmigiana. **NOTE:** The standard dressings here are fat free—fairly atrocious if you're used to the high-octane version. You may want to ask for "non-fat-free" dressing. *Rte. 590, Hamlin; (570) 689-2659.*

Snydersville Diner ★★★/$
Skip dinner and go straight to the pies. The varieties available every day are blueberry, cherry, raisin, apricot, peach, apple crumb, coconut—too many to list. And they can be had for less than $2 a slice. Enjoy. *Business Rte. 209, Snydersville; (570) 992-4003.*

Yankee Doodle Diner
★★/$$

Kids love the miniature jukeboxes at the tables at this 1950s-style diner. There's good food, with some unusual Greek offerings in addition to traditional American fare. The kids' menu offers the usual suspects. *5000 Milford Rd., E. Stroudsburg; (570) 223-7272.*

Delaware

EASILY ACCESSIBLE from Washington, D.C., Baltimore, New York, and Philadelphia, Delaware is the perfect choice for a family weekend getaway. The tiny L-shaped state, which you can drive top to bottom in two hours, has within it a range of attractions way out of proportion to its small size.

If you tell the kids you're going to Delaware, and they respond with a blank stare, begin by telling them it holds a special place in history as the first state to ratify our Constitution (hence the nickname "First State"). If that

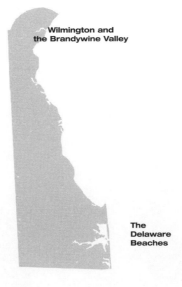

Wilmington and
the Brandywine Valley

The
Delaware
Beaches

doesn't dazzle 'em—which it probably won't—point out that Delaware also has some fun beaches that dolphins visit often. Don't forget to add that the state insect is the ladybug (that ought to do it).

Unless your family is on a mission to visit every state capital, you should probably skip Dover in favor of Wilmington, just across the state line from Philadelphia. A little farther south, beach lovers surely will find a Delaware town—be it sleepy Lewes or vibrant Rehoboth—to match their taste, as well as clean stretches of sand that are ideal for shell seeking, castle building, sunning, splashing, strolling, and more.

ATTRACTIONS

$	under $5
$$	$5 - $10
$$$	$10 - $20
$$$$	$20 and over

HOTELS/MOTELS/CAMPGROUNDS

$	under $100
$$	$100 - $150
$$$	$150 - $200
$$$$	$200 and over

RESTAURANTS

$	under $5
$$	$10 - $15
$$$	$15 - $25
$$$$	$25 and over

FAMILYFUN RATED

★	Fine
★★	Good
★★★	Very Good
★★★★	FamilyFun Recommended

Lead your family through Wilmington and explore
the original capital of America's first state.

Wilmington and the Brandywine Valley

HISTORY IS the big attraction here. In the 1700s, a busy port called Willingtown grew up by the Brandywine River and became a commercial mill center where farmers came to grind corn, wheat, and barley. The town's name was changed to Wilmington in 1739; several years later it became Delaware's state capital. Although the capital was moved to Dover in 1781, Wilmington has remained Delaware's largest and most important city. Home to the influential and wealthy du Pont family and the DuPont Company, the port near the Brandywine Valley also played an important role in the American Revolution. George Washington was outmaneuvered by General William Howe at the Battle of the Brandywine, delivering Wilmington into British hands. Today, like many East Coast cities, Wilmington is making a comeback, and its many interesting museums make it a great place to bring inquisitive children. But, as in most cities, it's still wise to use caution when walking in downtown areas at night.

THE **FamilyFun** LIST

MUST-SEE
MUST-SEE

Hagley Museum
(page 243)

Winterthur (page 243)

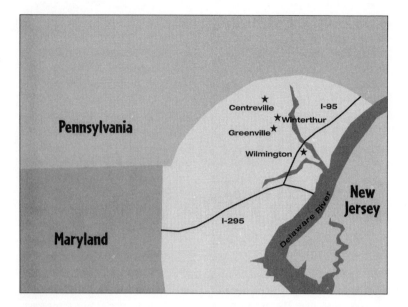

CULTURAL ADVENTURES

Delaware Art Museum
★★★★/$

Your kids might not go wild over the impressive collection of 19th- and 20th-century American art, including works by Winslow Homer, Thomas Eakins, and Edward Hopper. But they'll love the Children's Gallery, which encourages budding artists to create huge mosaics using foam blocks and Velcro. Overall, the museum does an excellent job of entertaining (and educating) young visitors. Among the regularly held special children's festivities are an Arts and Crabs Party and Howard Pyle's Pirate Birthday Party (reservations required; there's a fee). *2301 Kentmere Pkwy., Wilmington; (302) 571-9590;* www.delart.mus.de.us

Delaware Museum of Natural History ★★/$

Exhibits here cover everything from the flora and fauna of Delaware to the ecology of Africa. Your kids can take off for the interactive Discovery Room to conduct their own experiments or join one of the special children's programs led by naturalists (registration is required; there's a fee). Each week, "Monday Fundays" feature a special activity for families; call for details. *Rte. 52, between Greenville and Centreville; (302) 658-9111;* www.delmnh.org

Hagley Museum
FamilyFun ★★★★/$

In the early 1800s, French immigrant Eleuthère Irénée du Pont built a powder mill in Wilmington that would become the genesis of the du Pont fortune. This museum preserves the factory and the house that was home to five generations of du Ponts. Weekends and during the summer there are such kid-friendly events as the Hagley Storybook Garden Party, where kids can dress up in 19th-century duds. Also here is the partially restored workers' community known as Blacksmith Hill; your older children may be struck by the contrast between the workers' homes and the du Pont mansion. Call ahead to see if you can catch any demonstrations on quilting, canning, or gardening. In fall, a crafts fair showcases the wares of 40 artisans. *Rte. 141, Greenville; (302) 658-2400;* http://hagley.lib.de.us

Winterthur
FamilyFun ★★★★/$$

The former country home of Henry Francis du Pont, who purchased the estate in the early 19th century, is now a museum of American decorative arts surrounded by an extensive 60-acre garden. This is not just a collection of antiques, but entire rooms that Henry du Pont bought intact throughout Europe and America and had transported and reassembled back home. The lovely gardens are especially breathtaking in spring when the Azalea Woods are at their peak.

Winterthur makes a special effort to entertain young visitors with family programs and hands-on activities that let children experience life before modern conveniences: they can churn butter, make nature crafts

---

DAY TRIP
A Visit with the du Ponts

9:30 A.M. Arrive at the **Hagley Museum**, the first home of the du Pont family (see this page).

Noon Have lunch at the museum's **Belin House Coffee Shop**. After lunch, drive to Winterthur, a short distance away.

1 P.M. Arrive at **Winterthur** (this page) and ride the tram around the gardens. Spend the rest of the day here.

6 P.M. Eat dinner at **The Charcoal Pit** (see page 244).

in the garden, or weave on a floor loom. For information on children's programs, call *(302) 888-4907.* Admission includes a 30-minute narrated tram ride through the gardens, also fun for little ones. Don't miss the gift shop, which has a fine collection of such children's items as books, puzzles, toys, and stuffed animals. *Rte. 52, six miles northwest of Wilmington, Winterthur; (302) 888-4600;* www.winterthur.org

Bunking Down

Doubletree Wilmington
★★★/$$
Kids will be especially happy about the Nintendo video games. Parents will love the fact that children under 12 stay free. *Rte. 202 (Concord Pike), Wilmington; (302) 478-6000;* www. doubletree.com

Hotel du Pont ★★★★/$$$$
In 1913, French and Italian craftsmen constructed this ornate Italianate hotel. The luxurious du Pont has suites with separate sitting areas and opulent bathrooms. **NOTE:** This place is very fancy; best for older kids—or especially well-behaved younger ones. *11th and Market Sts., Wilmington; (800) 441-9019; (302) 594-3100.*

Good Eats

Many fast-food and chain restaurants line Rte. 202 (Concord Pike), including The Olive Garden and TGI Fridays.

The Charcoal Pit ★★★★/$$
This Wilmington institution is justifiably proud of its Philly cheese steaks. It's the perfect place to intro-

From Gunpowder to Teflon:
AN AMERICAN SUCCESS STORY

Your children may not have heard of **the DuPont Corporation**, but they use some of its products daily: Lycra spandex clothes, Stainmaster stain-resistant carpet, and Teflon pans, to name just a few. So kids may be interested to learn that the story of the duPonts, descendants of the French du Pont de Nemours family

and founders of the DuPont company, is intricately woven into the history of Delaware.

In the early 19th century, Eleuthère Irénée du Pont founded the gunpowder works (now part of the Hagley Museum) that grew into the present-day DuPont Company. During the Civil War, his son Samuel served as a rear admiral in the Union

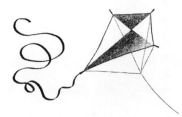

duce your kids to this regional specialty. Two locations: *2600 Concord Pike, Wilmington (302/478-2165); and 5200 Pike Creek Center Blvd., Wilmington (302/999-7483).*

Hotel du Pont
★★★★/$$$$

If you want to treat your family to a fancy (and expensive) meal, go to the Green Room or the Brandywine-Christina Room at this hotel. The golden chandeliers, ornate walnut paneling, and elegant menu may awe the children into silence. The Brandywine-Christina Room is less formal (although there's no kids' menu), but it's only open Sunday through Thursday; we recommend this place for older kids only. *11th and Market Sts., Wilmington; (800) 441-9019; (302) 594-3100.*

SOUVENIR HUNTING

Delaware Art Museum
The gift shop here carries excellent puppets, dolls, games, plastic building blocks, and books for children. *2301 Kentmere Pkwy., Wilmington; (302) 371-9590;* www.delart.mus.de.us

Zany Brainy
Arts-and-crafts demonstrations are given every day in this store, part of the chain that specializes in creative, educational toys. *3632 Concord Pike, Wilmington; (302) 477-1790.*

Navy and led an unsuccessful attack on Charleston, South Carolina. Henry, grandson of Eleuthère, built Winterthur (see page 243) and became a U.S. senator from Delaware.

By the 20th century, the family had expanded its fortune and consolidated it under the DuPont company name. Heirs became increasingly involved in charities and began donating millions to schools, hospitals, and other public institutions, a practice that they continue to this day. A modern-day du Pont, Pierre, continued the family's political tradition by serving as governor of Delaware in the 1970s and 1980s.

By the beginning of the 21st century, DuPont was the 42nd-largest U.S. industrial/service corporation, with about 94,000 employees and about 135 manufacturing and processing facilities throughout the world. Perhaps the story about the du Pont family will inspire one of your family's young entrepreneurs.

Each beach on the Delaware coast has its own personality; Bethany, for instance, enjoys a laid-back, quieter reputation than nearby Rehoboth, known for its carnival-like boardwalk.

The Delaware Beaches

F OR MANY FAMILIES in the mid-Atlantic region, the Delaware shore is the place for an annual reunion. Year after year, from generation to generation, they return for their week-long stay at a seaside cottage, be it a tiny turn-of-the-century house or a sprawling mansion.

Only a few hours' drive from both Philadelphia and Washington, D.C., Delaware's beaches also are close enough for a weekend trip. But for families, the best vacation strategy is to rent a house for a week (usually Saturday to Saturday), rather than staying in one of the area hotels, which are often populated by noisy college students or empty nesters. Many good rentals are snapped up by February, so it's best to plan early. Properties right on the beach are pricey, with better deals found on

the bay or in town. Each community has its own character (see "Seaside Siblings" on page 254), so do your research before booking a week: what activities does your family enjoy? Do you like the honky-tonk of a

THE **FamilyFun** LIST

MUST-SEE MUST-SEE

The Beach (page 248)

The Boardwalks of Bethany and Rehoboth (page 249)

Cape Henlopen Seaside Nature Center (page 249)

Cape May-Lewes Ferry (page 250)

Funland (page 250)

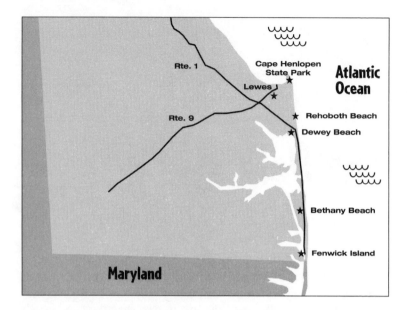

boardwalk or do you prefer to simply sit and watch the waves roll in? Are good restaurants important, or is a backyard barbecue your idea of living large? Wherever you build your castles in the sand, you're bound to have a memorable vacation. And you just might want to return next year for your own family reunion.

JUST FOR FUN

The Beach
FamilyFun ★★★★/Free

The undisputed main attraction, Delaware's white-sand beaches, are places where families can have good, clean fun in the sun. Dolphins are frequent visitors to the Delaware shore, and they enter-

tain by leaping in the air just beyond where the waves break. Each beach reflects its town's personality, but there's a great, statewide family-friendly ban: alcohol is prohibited on the beach. Although lifeguards are vigilant, parents should be aware of the riptide that may carry a child down the beach, far from the family blanket; swim only in the daytime, when lifeguards are present. You can rent strong umbrellas (a must for babies) and boogie boards (a must for older kids) by the day or by the week at spots set up on the beach. After 6 P.M. and before 9 A.M. you can bring dogs and kites on the beach. *For further information on Bethany/Fenwick, call (800) 962-7873; for Rehoboth/Dewey, call (800) 441-1329.*

⭐ The Boardwalks of
FamilyFun Bethany and Rehoboth
★★★★/Free

Like the towns themselves, the board-walks of Bethany and Rehoboth satisfy different tastes. But each is worth an evening's stroll. A bandstand at the center of Bethany's four-block boardwalk hosts nightly shows (7:30 P.M.) that might feature Elvis impersonators, classic rock or bluegrass bands, children's theater, or magicians. Families crowd the band shell, ice-cream cones in hand, or visit the shops along Garfield Street, perpendicular to the shore. Evenings on Bethany beach find children flying kites, and dogs (normally banned on the sand) romping in the surf.

In contrast, an evening on Rehoboth's ten-block-long boardwalk jumps like a carnival. Entertainment is provided by dollar stores, T-shirt shops, arcades, and a small amusement park, and dinner here tends to be an indulgent blur of French fries, ice cream, funnel cakes, and saltwater taffy. It's good carny fun, and preteens and teenagers may find it more stimulating than the laid-back boardwalk in Bethany.

⭐ Cape Henlopen
FamilyFun Seaside Nature Center
★★★/Free

At Cape Henlopen State Park—home to one of Delaware's better family beaches—the Seaside Nature Center gives your kids a chance to study the

The Beach on Independence Day

Something about the Fourth of July and fireworks makes families flock to the beach—and the Delaware shore draws more than its share of folks for the entire holiday week.

Bethany, for example, swells from its wintertime population of around 400 to its annual peak population of more than 20,000. Lines form outside even mediocre restaurants and beachgoers vie for spots on the sand.

If you don't mind the crowds, all of the fun holiday festivities make for a truly memorable weekend. Bethany holds a parade at noon on the Fourth, inviting anyone and everyone to march, ride, or Rollerblade. Entire families in matching T-shirts join the parade, kids decorate their bikes with crepe paper, the VFW and barbershop quartets march. In **Lewes**, downtown hops with children's activities, and the harbor hosts a parade of boats. Both Bethany and Rehoboth present fireworks on the beach—and these are no penny-ante displays. The impressive shows set the shore aglitter, delighting spectators picnicking on the sand or watching from boats moored nearby. *Chamber of Commerce: (302) 539-2100 or* www.the quietresorts.com

When a Day at the Beach is No Day at the Beach

Beach vacations mean fun in the sun, but over the course of a week or two, clouds are likely to bring a little liquid sunshine (aka rain) now and then. Here are a few suggestions for enjoying those bad beach days as much as the good.

♦ See a movie. Most local theaters run **Bad Beach Day Matinees**. Movie theaters can be found on Route 1 north of Rehoboth and five miles south of Fenwick Island in Ocean City, Maryland.

♦ Try out all the kiddie rides at **Funland**, a covered amusement park in Rehoboth.

♦ Play a couple of rounds of **miniature** golf. Unless it's raining cats and dogs, this is a good bet. Bethany has an old-fashioned course just right for the under-6 set. More sophisticated players might prefer the theme courses on Rehoboth's boardwalk and on Route 1 south of Fenwick Island.

♦ Hunt for inexpensive treats at **Rhodes 5 & 10** in downtown Bethany. Simply visiting this old-fashioned shop is fun.

♦ Make a pottery souvenir at **Kil N' Time**. (Parents can belly up to the cappuccino bar.)

♦ Spend an afternoon at the **outlets** north of Rehoboth.

sea through a touch tank, an aquarium, and special outings. They can join beach hikes at night, go crabbing, and watch for dolphins—all great alternatives to television after a full day at the beach. *Rte. 9, Lewes; (302) 645-6852;* www.beach-net.com/

Cape May-Lewes Ferry
FamilyFun ★★★/$$

MUST-SEE From June through October, ferries run from Lewes, Delaware, to the Victorian seaside town of Cape May, New Jersey. The 17-mile ride takes two hours, and you can have dinner on board from late June through September. Shoreside transportation takes you into Cape May, which makes a great day trip. (For details on Cape May, see page 165.) The $15.50 ticket includes a book of coupons that you can use in Cape May shops. *For departure times, call (302) 426-1155; for reservations, call (800) 64-FERRY;* www.beach-net.com/

Funland ★★★★/$
FamilyFun This child-size amusement park is great for parents, too. It's enclosed—making it a perfect destination on a rainy day—and cheap. Most rides cost a dollar (individual tickets are 25 cents), with plenty of old-fashioned choices like toy boats and fire engines for the under-5 crowd. Older children will enjoy bumper cars, the Haunted House, and Chaos—which uses centrifugal force to plaster 'em to

the sides of a spinning tube. Give the games a try: unlike at most amusement parks, it's not hard to win huge stuffed animals at the frog bog, the horse race, or the ring toss here. Put a dollar's worth of dimes in your kids' pockets and let them play ten games of Skee-Ball. It's possible for a family of four to leave Funland and still have change from a twenty. *On the Rehoboth Beach Boardwalk, at Delaware Ave. No phone.*

Jungle Jim's Sports Complex ★★★/$$

Are the older kids getting bored at the beach? Let them try the water slides, rock climb, challenging go-cart course, batting cage, and bumper boats here. The complex is not cheap, so give kids a budget and a two-hour time limit—then let them have at it. *Rte. 1, just north of Rehoboth; (302) 227-8444.*

Rehoboth Summer Children's Theatre ★★★/$

For nearly 20 years, this theater has been delighting young audiences with shows like *Peter Pan*, *Robin Hood*, and *Pinocchio*. Productions run through the month of August, with most performances starting at 7:30 P.M.; an 11 A.M. matinee is presented on Tuesdays (and is especially welcome on a bad beach day). Tickets are under $5. Performances at two locations: *Cape Henlopen High School, 1250 Kings Hwy., Lewes,*

DAY TRIP
The Bethany Beat

8 A.M. Have an early breakfast, then head into town. Rent bikes or a surrey, which accommodates two side-by-side peddlers, and take a ride through the still-sleepy town. Bicycle rentals are available at Bethany and Resort Rental Service *(201 Central Blvd.; 302/539-6244).*

10 A.M. Go to the beach—lifeguards are on duty at 10—and stay until lunch. Don't forget sunscreen and bottled water. You can rent sturdy umbrellas at beach kiosks, but you will need to leave a driver's license.

Noon Have lunch in town at Patsy's Gourmet (see page 254) and spend several hours (the hottest part of the day) painting pottery and sipping lattés at Kil N' Time (see page 254).

2:30 P.M. Return to the beach for a couple of hours.

6 P.M. Order pizza from Grotto's (see page 253)—they deliver.

7:30 P.M. Go into town for a concert at the bandstand, then arm the family with ice-cream cones and stroll the boardwalk.

and Epworth United Methodist Church, 20 Baltimore Ave., downtown Rehoboth; (302) 227-6766.

BUNKING DOWN

Families who want the convenience and comfort of renting a house for their beach vacation should contact one of the many companies that handle rentals along the Delaware Shore. They include: *Long and Foster (1150 Coastal Hwy., Bethany; 800/228-8833; 302/539-9040); Hickman (300 Ocean View Pkwy. and Rte. 1, Bethany; 800/HICKMAN; 302/539-4086); and Lewes Realty (418 East Savannah Rd., Lewes; 800/705-7590; 302/645-1955).*

Addy Sea ★★/$$
This Victorian bed-and-breakfast inn has 13 oceanfront guest rooms with faded, but clean, seaside charm—and, some say, a few ghosts. Haunted or not, your kids might like the intriguing thought. *99 Ocean View Pkwy. and Atlantic Ave., Bethany; (302) 539-3707;* www. addysea.com

The Bethany Arms ★★/$$
The main draw of this, one of the few motels in Bethany, is its prime location, both on the shore and in the center of town. *Atlantic Ave. at Hollywood St., Bethany Beach; (302) 539-9603;* www.beach-net.com/beth anyarms.html

Sun, Surf, and Safety

A beach vacation offers many pleasures, but some perils. Fight overexposure to the sun with a strong sunblock—reapplied after each swim—and by limiting the amount of time spent under the rays. Fair-skinned children should have no more than 15 minutes of direct sun on the first day out. A hat, T-shirt, and sunblock (SPF 25 or higher) are musts.

Also keep in mind that a waterfront beach house presents some built-in hazards to young children. Steep steps and the lure of the beach can prove to be dangerous. The best choice for families with young children may be a cottage that's within easy walking distance of, but not right on, the beach.

The Hampton Inn
★★★★/$$$

Near the outlets and about a ten-minute drive from the beach, this 85-room inn has a heated indoor pool, exercise facility, and game room. In the morning, load up a tray at the free breakfast bar and bring it back to your oversized room. *4529 Rte. 1, Rehoboth; (800) HAMPTON; (302) 645-8003; www.hamptoninn.com*

Henlopen Hotel ★★★/$$$

This centrally located, oceanfront hotel has 93 guest rooms, all with balconies and ocean views; many family suites and deluxe rooms have handy refrigerators and microwaves. A restaurant is also on the premises. *511 N. Boardwalk, Rehoboth; (302) 227-2551; (800) 441-8450; www.henlopenhotel.com*

GOOD EATS

Grotto Pizza
★★★/$

This casual chain, with branches all along the Delaware shore, serves good pizza. No beach vacation is complete without a slice. Two central locations: *Read St. and Hwy. 1, Rehoboth Beach (302/227-3407); and 10 South Boardwalk, Rehoboth Beach (302/227-3601).*

Mango's at Bethany Beach
★★★/$$$

This new, Caribbean-theme restaurant overlooks the ocean and serves up sophisticated seafood—but offers enough on the menu to please young

---

FamilyFun TIP

Eco Etiquette

When snacking on the beach, make sure you throw away plastic bags and garbage, which can easily drift into the water. Eating garbage is one of the leading causes of death in aquatic animals. Turtles, ocean sunfish, and other animals often mistake plastic bags for jellyfish.

---

diners as well. *Garfield Pkwy. and the Boardwalk, Bethany; (302) 537-6621.*

McCabe's Gourmet Market
★★★★/$$$$

When you don't feel like cooking, stop here to pick up great takeout food. McCabe's also packs gourmet picnics with wonderful salads like tortellini or chunky chicken, the freshest cold cuts on the beach, and overstuffed sandwiches made to order. *York Beach Mall, S. Bethany; (302) 539-8550.*

Patsy's Gourmet
★★★★/$$$$

Eat in or take out superb American fare. You can choose from among whole rotisserie chicken, stuffed salmon, vegetable-tomato penne, orzo with mushroom and sun-dried tomatoes, and oven-roasted potatoes and more. The dishes are tasty and well-prepared but not exotic, so finicky eaters have nothing to fear. *121 Campbell Pl., Bethany; (302) 537-CHEF.*

SOUVENIR HUNTING

Chesapeake Kite and Flag

This place stocks a large supply of gifts, mobiles, kites, yo-yos, and toys. *122 Rehoboth Ave., Rehoboth; (302) 226-2193.*

Kil N' Time

The combination of a make-your-own-pottery shop and coffee bar adds up to the perfect place for both

SEASIDE SIBLINGS

THE DELAWARE SHORE has five main communities, each with its own distinct personality and attractions. In order, from north to south, they are:

Lewes

The quietest of the beachside communities, Lewes is a cozy town that attracts many artists. Its charming main street is dotted with inns, good restaurants, and antiques shops. Founded 300 years ago, Lewes has several historic sites and a public beach within walking distance of the town, but no boardwalk. The ferry to Cape May, New Jersey, leaves from Lewes.

Rehoboth

The shore's busiest and most populated area is popular with families and gay vacationers. The bustling boardwalk is home to Funland, a quaint amusement park with kiddie rides and carny games, and Rehoboth's wide main street features excellent shops and restau-

you and your kids to spend a rainy day. *111 Garfield Pkwy., Bethany; (302) 541-4544.*

Rehoboth Outlets

Between Lewes and Rehoboth are several outlet centers housing 150 brand-name outlet stores, including Gap, Oshkosh B'Gosh, and Lillian Vernon. A bonus: shopping in Delaware is tax free. *Rte. 1, Rehoboth.*

Rhodes 5 & 10

A Bethany institution, this old-fashioned five-and-dime has a seashore theme. Give your children their age in dollars ($6 for 6-year-olds, etc.) and let them buy souvenirs. *Garfield Pkwy., downtown Bethany; (302) 539-9191.*

Shorty's Shop

Don't miss this amazing shop, where Charlie Slagle (aka Shorty) makes handcrafted toys, whirligigs, detailed miniature carousel horses, and wooden puzzles of astonishing intricacy. His elaborate electrified marble roller takes up most of the shop's ceiling and mesmerizes small shoppers. *Pennsylvania Ave. at Rte. 1, Bethany; (800) 635-7322.*

rants. If you enjoy boisterous, diverse crowds, book here.

Dewey Beach

This town's main street is filled with bars—earning it a reputation for the liveliest nightlife of any town on the shore. A magnet for college students, Dewey is probably not a good choice for young families.

Bethany

Founded as a religious community, Bethany has remained the most family-oriented place on the beach. Quieter than Rehoboth, Bethany has a low-key boardwalk and a charming town center. Don't miss the town's Fourth of July parade and spectacular fireworks display. There are only two motels in the town, so renting a house is a must.

Fenwick Island

This pretty community has a collection of charming clapboard homes but no real town center. To get to the beach, you may have to cross a busy road and clamber up the dunes—but the reward is some of the most pristine stretches of sand and sea in Delaware.

Maryland

EVERY VACATIONER, young or old, will find something to enjoy in Maryland. This small state is the United States in miniature; you can see every type of landscape—mountains and beaches, cities and farms, towns and suburbs. Shaped a bit like one of its famous crabs, it is at most only a two-hour drive from north to south, but from east to west it stretches 300 miles from West Virginia to the Atlantic.

Your family has a lot of choice in the pace and rhythm of a Maryland vacation. The big rhythms of Baltimore are

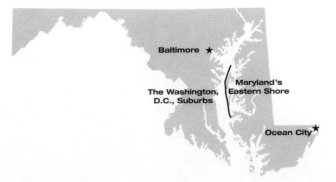

Baltimore ★

The Washington, D.C., Suburbs

Maryland's Eastern Shore

Ocean City ★

fun, but so are the gentle lapping waves of the Eastern shore and the quiet of the rural west. Situated right in the middle of the Eastern seaboard, Maryland enjoys four distinct seasons: a brisk fall with spectacular foliage, warm summers perfect for the beach, winters cold enough to ski, and a spring adorned with lavish floral displays.

Your kids might like riding the waves at the beach or soaking up art in a museum, hiking along a mountain ravine, or sailing in the Chesapeake—it's all here. Maryland is both manageable and affordable: you can spend a few days in each region without exhausting your children—or your bank account.

ATTRACTIONS
$	under $5
$$	$5 - $10
$$$	$10 - $20
$$$$	$20 and over

HOTELS/MOTELS/CAMPGROUNDS
$	under $100
$$	$100 - $150
$$$	$150 - $200
$$$$	$200 and over

RESTAURANTS
$	under $5
$$	$10 - $15
$$$	$15 - $25
$$$$	$25 and over

***FAMILYFUN* RATED**
★	Fine
★★	Good
★★★	Very Good
★★★★	*FamilyFun* Recommended

Within a half an hour of the nation's capital, your family can ride a trolley, pick fruit at an orchard, and view hundreds of vintage aircraft.

The Washington, D.C., Suburbs

THE WASHINGTON, D.C., suburbs in Maryland make for some interesting excursions for families visiting the nation's capital. Extending roughly 20 miles north of D.C., these are some of the wealthiest communities in America and offer many child-centered activities geared toward both tourists and residents. Many of the towns in southern Maryland predate the Revolution—and Washington, D.C. Although the growth of the capital has brought more urban sprawl, many retain some of their original character, at least in sections. Most of the attractions listed below are within a 20-minute drive of the Capitol building—when there's no traffic, which is almost never. **NOTE:** Be warned that Washington's traffic, especially during rush hour, can be fearsome, and its drivers, particularly on the notorious Beltway around the city, are some of the most aggressive around. None of the sites recommended here are accessible by Metro, the rail system that extends into many Maryland suburbs.

THE FamilyFun LIST

MUST-SEE · MUST-SEE

C&O Canal Historical Park/Great Falls (page 263)

Glen Echo Park (page 260)

NASA/Goddard Space Flight Center (page 261)

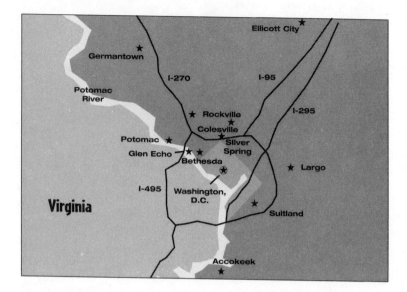

CULTURAL ADVENTURES

B&O Railroad Station Museum ★★/$

At one time Ellicott City was an important railroad town, the first passenger terminus of the B&O railroad. Now its 19th-century stone buildings house antiques shops and restaurants. Set in the old railroad station, the museum features a working scale model of the original 13 miles of the first railroad in America, from Ellicott City to Baltimore. Serious train buffs of all ages will want to make the trip here. *Maryland Ave. and Main St., Ellicott City (near Camden Yards in Downtown Baltimore); (410) 752-2490.*

★MUST-SEE★ FamilyFun ★MUST-SEE★ Glen Echo Park/ Discovery Creek Children's Museum/ Adventure Theater ★★★★/$$

Just outside of the city, on the way to the C&O Canal Historical Park/Great Falls (see page 263), Glen Echo is a former amusement park. Closed in the 1960s and then taken over by the National Park Service, it still boasts a renowned ornate carousel with hand-carved horses and has a magnificent Wurlitzer band organ. Be sure to take the kids on this extra-special merry-go-round: rides are only 50 cents, and it operates in all weather (but not every day, so call ahead for the schedule). The carousel is a fine reason to go to Glen Echo, but the park also features the Discovery Creek

Children's Museum and Adventure Theatre, both housed in buildings of the former amusement park.

Discovery Creek offers well-run science, art, and history programs geared to kids ages 5 to 10. (*There's a branch in Washington, D.C., at 5125 MacArthur Blvd. N.W.*).

Your younger children will enjoy the inventive productions of Adventure Theatre, housed in the old penny arcade. These professional plays are usually clever twists on familiar fairy tales—and kids love collecting the cast's autographs at the end. Performances are Saturday and Sunday, 1:30 and 3:30; admission is $5 per person. *7300 MacArthur Blvd., Glen Echo; (301) 492-6282; Adventure Theatre: (301) 320-5331; Discovery Creek: (202) 364-3111;* www.nps.gov/glec

NASA/Goddard Space Flight Center ★★★/Free

Tell the kids up front—no rockets are launched from this site. This is the "brains" of NASA, where space flights are tracked. But your 9-and-older astronauts will enjoy the one-hour guided tour of NASCOM (the communications unit) and the films, hands-on exhibits, and interactive computer programs that explain NASA's mission. Kids can "build" their own rockets using computer technology, track weather systems, and "dock" a satellite using a simulator. On the first and third Sundays of each month, Goddard launches model rockets that have been built by local rocket clubs. If your child is interested in space exploration, this is a must-see. *Take Rte. 495 (the Beltway) to the Baltimore-Washington Parkway; go north and follow signs to NASA; (301) 286-8981;* http://pao.gsfc.nasa.gov

National Capital Trolley Museum ★★★/$

Before the Metro in Washington (the first lines opened in the late 1970s), there were trolleys. This museum gives children a glimpse into the days before gasoline-powered buses and the universal dependence on the car. You can see memorabilia from European trolley lines as well as Washington's, all housed in a replica of a terminal. But the highlight is a one-and-a-half-mile trip through the park grounds that surround the museum. That, and the nifty gift shop. *1313 Bonifant Rd., Colesville; (301) 384-6088;* www.dctrolley.org

FamilyFun SNACK

Bag o' Bugs

Place a few graham crackers in a plastic bag, seal it shut, and crush the crackers into a fine sand using a large spoon. Add a few raisins and let your kids dig for bugs in the sand. Experiment with other tasty critters: dried cranberry ladybugs, chocolate- or carob-chip ants, even gummy worms.

National Colonial Farm ★★★/$

What was it like to live on a farm before the American Revolution? Your kids can find out at this working Colonial farm, just across from George Washington's Mount Vernon, on the Maryland side of the Potomac. Operated by the National Park Service, this is a real tobacco plantation, and real farmwork is done every day to maintain it. Cows are milked and fields are plowed, while wide-eyed children look on. Historical interpreters offer commentary on life on a farm in the mid-18th century. Group tours (by reservation) are offered Tuesday through Sunday. Special Children's Days are held in the fall and spring, and the Potomac River Heritage Festival is held in late September. Closed Monday. *3400 Bryan Point Rd., Accokeek; (301) 283-2115.*

Smithsonian National Air and Space Museum Paul E. Garber Facility ★★★/Free

If your young aviators did not get their fill of historic planes at the Smithsonian's Air and Space Museum in Washington, take them to the museum's suburban facility, where vintage planes are restored and preserved. During the three-hour tour, you'll get to see more than 100 planes, including a few one-of-a-kind models, in varying stages of repair. Call two weeks in advance for reservations for the free tour. **NOTE:** The large hangars are unheated, and there are no rest room facilities during the tour. Dress warmly and wear comfortable shoes. *3904 Old Silver Hill Rd., Suitland; (202) 357-2700;* http://www.nasm.si.edu/

DAY TRIP
The Canal and the River

9 A.M. From Washington, drive 20 minutes out MacArthur Boulevard to Potomac, Maryland, and the C&O Canal Historical Park/Great Falls (see page 263). Have a picnic breakfast near the falls before hiking the Billy Goat Trail near the canal. After the hike, take the one-hour barge ride on the C&O Canal. Drive back toward Washington.

Noon Stop for lunch on the terrace of **Old Angler's Inn** (see page 265).

1:30 P.M. Continue on MacArthur Boulevard toward Washington. Stop at the **Glen Echo Park** (see page 260). If it's the weekend, buy tickets for Adventure Theatre (there's a 3:30 performance). Take several turns on the Glen Echo Carousel (at 50 cents a ride, it's a cheap thrill), and visit the **Discovery Creek Children's Museum.**

3:30 P.M. See the one-hour performance at the **Adventure Theatre** and then head back to the hotel. Rest.

Just for Fun

Butler's Orchard ★★★/Free

Picking fruit is a novelty to most city kids and those 6 and under will especially enjoy a trip to this 300-acre farm, one of a dwindling number of family farms in suburban Maryland. The Butlers grow apples, strawberries, and many other fruits and vegetables, but the best time to go is in the fall (aka pumpkin season). During the Pumpkin Festival, you can take hayrides and see fancifully dressed pumpkins, as well as pick your own pumpkin. The pumpkins and other produce are sold by the pound. Open May through Christmas. *22200 Davis Mill Rd., Germantown; (301) 972-3299.*

License Plate Bingo: See how many different states you can spot on your trip.

MUST-SEE FamilyFun MUST-SEE C&O Canal Historical Park/Great Falls
★★★★/$

It's hard to believe that spectacular waterfalls and relatively unspoiled natural beauty could exist so close to Washington (in Georgetown, at Jefferson Street). Accessible by a scenic road that winds its way out of the capital, Great Falls and the C&O Canal Historical Park are an ideal combination of nature and history. If you can take only one excursion outside of the city limits, this should be it. The falls themselves are formed by the Potomac as it runs over spectacular rock formations. The river drops more than 70 feet, forming rapids, with little islands in midstream. Hiking along the river is popular, and the well-marked, three-mile Billy Goat Trail is a good bet for less experienced hikers and families with small children. **NOTE:** Keep a close watch on your kids; the rapids are dangerous, and every year several people are swept into the river.

Parallel to the river is the C&O Canal, a man-made 19th-century engineering miracle that connected Georgetown to Cumberland, Maryland, 128 miles away. Your children will especially enjoy a ride on the *Canal Clipper,* a mule-drawn barge operated by interpreters in period costumes who lead passengers in song. The boat ride (fee) lasts an hour and includes a demonstration of a working canal lock. *11710 MacArthur Blvd., Potomac; (301) 299-3613;* www.nps.gov/choh

Six Flags America ★★★★/$$$

Just a 30-minute drive from D.C. (if you get lucky on traffic), this sprawling amusement park is a great change of pace from the monuments and museums of the typical capital city tour. Formerly known as Wild World, the park has expanded beyond water rides by adding several high-speed roller coasters—including Superman Ride of Steel,

Planes and Trains

Try this itinerary if you're traveling with older kids who are transportation aficionados; it's too much for very young children.

9 A.M. Start the day with the tour of the Smithsonian's **Paul E. Garber Facility** (see page 262).

Noon Pick up a picnic lunch at the **Parkway Deli** (see page 265) before driving to the National Capital Trolley Museum in nearby Wheaton. Enjoy your picnic on the grounds of the museum.

2 P.M. Tour the **National Capital Trolley Museum** (see page 261) and then take a one-and-a-half-mile ride on a trolley.

5 P.M. Go to Bethesda for an early dinner at the **Tastee Diner** (see page 265). The diner was in business when trolleys ran on Washington's streets, and the 1950s decor and menu complete your trip back in time.

which plunges more than 200 feet at 70 mph. Roller-coaster aficionados who cherish wooden coasters will enjoy The Wild One's 98-foot uphill lift—and its five-second drop.

You can keep your preschoolers amused at Looney Tunes Movie Town, with low-key rides (including a pint-size roller coaster), and the Looney Tunes Prop Warehouse, an interactive soft-play area. Six Flags has about six live shows (including the Batman Stunt Spectacular), and enough rides and activities to keep everybody happy for an entire day. Admission includes all shows and rides (games are extra); children 3 and under enter free. The park is open daily Memorial Day through Labor Day; weekends in April, May, September, and October. *Largo, Maryland, five miles from the Beltway; (301) 249-1500;* www.sixflags.com

BUNKING DOWN

Hyatt Regency Bethesda
★★★★/$$$

This 381-plus-room hotel has the requisite indoor pool. In the winter months, the kids can go for a spin on the adjacent skating rink. It is conveniently located right above a Metro stop, offering easy access to the city and attractions in the Washington suburbs. Children under 18 stay free. *1 Bethesda Metro Center, Bethesda; (800) 233-1234; (301) 657-1234;* www.hyatt.com

PERSONAL ADVENTURES

Take turns sharing the memorable events of your lives. What was the scariest thing that ever happened to you? The funniest? The best? The worst? The most embarrassing? What have you done that you are most proud of?

Marriott Bethesda ★★★★/$$$

In addition to the usual Marriott accommodations, this 407-room hotel has indoor and outdoor pools, lighted tennis courts, and an exercise room. Children under 17 stay free. *5151 Pooks Hill Rd., Rockville; (800) 228-9290; (301) 897-9400; www.marriott.com*

Park Inn International and Suites ★★★/$$

This reasonably priced motel on busy Rockville Pike is nine miles from the District line. Children stay free (up to four people in a room), and there is an outdoor pool. *11410 Rockville Pike, Rockville; (800)752-3800; (301) 881-5200.*

GOOD EATS

Old Angler's Inn ★★★★/$$$$

This charming 19th-century tavern is pricey; but if you're ready to splurge, nothing tastes better after a hike along the Potomac or the C&O Canal than a light lunch on the outdoor terrace here. *10801 MacArthur Blvd., Potomac; (301) 365-2425.*

Parkway Deli and Restaurant ★★★/$

The Washington area is short on delis, so this one would be especially welcome even if it didn't serve great, kid-friendly food. It offers up big portions of matzo-ball soup, huge sandwiches, and, of course, bagels. *8317 Grubb Rd., Silver Spring; (301) 587-1427.*

Tastee Diner ★★★/$

This is the real thing, not a re-creation. All menu items are classic diner favorites at 1950s prices. It's the Plain American Food that most kids prefer. *7731 Woodmont Ave., Bethesda; (301) 652-3970.*

SOUVENIR HUNTING

Zany Brainy

This toy and children's bookstore is an inviting, playful place to visit. The kids will go for the regular craft demonstrations and storytelling. *1631 Rockville Pike, Rockville; (301) 984-0112.*

Check out the moon, planets, and stars for free on Thursday nights at the Maryland Science Center's Crosby Ramsey Memorial Observatory.

Baltimore

OFTEN OVERSHADOWED by New York and Philadelphia to the north and Washington to the south, Baltimore is a family-friendly city in its own right. More ethnically diverse than Washington (only 40 miles away) and not as big or as bustling as New York, Baltimore has a unique character. It is a place of neighborhoods, row houses, and famously scrubbed marble front steps. A night out here often means grandparents, aunts and uncles, parents and kids all pounding hard-shells at one of Baltimore's famous crab houses. In the 1970s, the city's famous Inner Harbor was decaying. Though the scent of spices imported by McCormick's still wafted in the air, much of the area had become seedy and somewhat dangerous. Eventually, a festival marketplace of

THE FamilyFun LIST

MUST-SEE
MUST-SEE

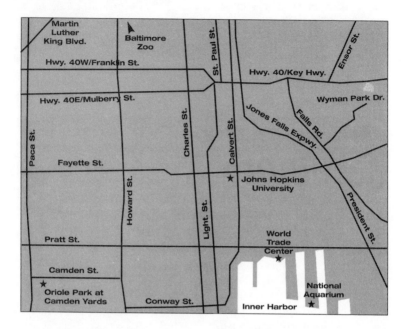

shops and restaurants—dubbed Harborplace—was built here, drawing businesses and residents back to the city. Other attractions soon followed: a nationally acclaimed aquarium, baseball and football stadiums, and cutting-edge museums. Today, Baltimore fuses new spirit with old charm.

Getting around Baltimore is part of the fun of touring the city, using a system of water taxis to zip across the harbor. Baltimore has a subway and an easy-to-use trolley and light-rail system. Best of all, this is a great walking city; much of urban life is lived in the parks. After a visit to Baltimore, your children will have had a good taste of a world-class, working-class city.

CULTURAL ADVENTURES

American Visionary Art Museum ★★★★/$

What appeals to kids at this place? Believe it or not, it's the art. Works here have a refreshing immediacy, much like a child's own imaginative creations. Founded in 1995, this inspiring museum is dedicated to the display of "outsider art"—sculpture, paintings, signs—by people who ordinarily are not represented in conventional museums. You'll see works by people who are homeless, mentally ill, and illiterate. Almost all are amateurs, and many use found objects like matchsticks, lumber, and twine to construct their art. The museum's unconventional home is a historic industrial building containing six galleries and a barn with 45-foot ceilings that accommodates huge sculptural works. **NOTE:** Whether this spot is appropriate for your family depends largely on the theme of each year-long exhibit. For example, the recent Love: Error and Eros exhibit might have appealed to older children and intellectually adventurous families, but certain sexually explicit portions required parents to edit the viewing for young children. Check before you visit. An excellent restaurant on the top floor offers stunning views of Baltimore Harbor, and a truly unique gift shop has outsider art for sale. *800 Key Hwy., Baltimore; (410) 244-1900;* www.avam.org

Baltimore Museum of Art (BMA) ★★★★/$
Part of BMA's mission is to make all exhibitions family-friendly, partly through fun youth programs. Frequent hands-on workshops bring the principles of art down to kid level by teaching them (and their parents) how to draw and paint portraits, make topographical maps, experiment with light and color techniques, and so much more. One program, inspired by Alberto Giacometti's bronze sculpture Man Pointing, had kids using wire, twigs, and bamboo skewers to create their own sculptures. For children as young as 3, the museum sponsors Tours for Tots. Programs are on a drop-in basis, but call the Education Department *(410/396-6320)* to see what's scheduled. Even if your visit doesn't coincide with a workshop,

Stick It!

Home of the **Lacrosse Hall of Fame**, Baltimore is crazy about the fast-paced game. Young Baltimoreans learn to play almost from the time they can walk, and local Johns Hopkins University boasts a championship team. In parks throughout the city, you can see youngsters practicing skills they've learned at one of the many lacrosse camps in the area.

So what is this strange game? Sharing soccer's back-and-forth field action, lacrosse requires players to use a long stick with a basketlike net at one end to catch, cradle, and throw a hard rubber ball (slightly smaller than a tennis ball) down the field for a goal. Lacrosse originated as baggataway, a form of sacred mock combat played by Native Americans, often with teams of several hundred players. Native Americans first played the game in the 15th century; nearly four centuries later, French Canadian settlers adapted it and called it "la crosse," because the stick resembled a bishop's crosier.

the kids will enjoy the extensive collection of works by pop artist Andy Warhol (including his Brillo boxes). Youngsters also like the sculpture garden, which has pieces by Alexander Calder and Auguste Rodin, and the extensive collection of miniature furniture set in intricate rooms that tell much about life in Colonial America. Mom and Dad: BMA is best known for the Cone Collection, donated 50 years ago by two Baltimore sisters; it includes paintings by Gauguin, Matisse, Van Gogh, and Renoir. The museum is free for those under 16 and for everyone on Thursday. *Art Museum Dr., between Wyman Park Dr. and N. Charles St., Baltimore; (410) 396-7100;* www.artbma.org

Baltimore Museum of Industry ★★★/$

After a visit here, your kids just might thank you for their weekly chores. Honoring Baltimore's role in the Industrial Revolution—as a gritty city whose factories churned out goods during the 19th and 20th centuries—this museum revisits life

before the existence of child-labor laws. The sights and sounds of a machine shop, a garment loft, a print shop, and a steam tugboat are re-created in an 1870 oyster cannery. Children will love trying their hands at shucking oysters, making labels for cans, and producing small cardboard cars on an assembly line (but ask them what they'd think of doing it for pennies a day, 12 hours at a time). *1415 Key Hwy., Baltimore; (410) 727-4808;* www.thebmi.org

Baltimore Streetcar Museum ★★★/$

Once the most popular form of transportation in American cities, streetcars have all but vanished (except in rare examples like San Francisco) in favor of subways and buses. This museum celebrates more than 100 years of Baltimore's streetcars, both horse-drawn and electric, and entertains the entire family with unlimited rides (included in admission) on the vintage trolleys. **NOTE:** The museum is open only on weekends in summer and on Sunday in winter. *1901 Falls Rd., Baltimore; (410) 547-0264;* www.baltimoremd. com/streetcar/

B&O Railroad Museum ★★★★/$

If Thomas the Tank Engine—or anything else—has turned your child into a train buff, this museum is a must. Not only are there models, exhibits, archives, and a theater that illustrate the history of the mighty B&O Railroad, but the whole thing is housed in a magnificent railroad structure, an 1884 passenger roundhouse. Tracks in the roundhouse hold some of the rarest locomotives in the country—11 in all—including an 1836 John Hancock, an 1848 Mennon, and an 1856 William Mason. Many other engines and cars are crammed into the museum yards for viewing and exploring. Enthusiastic volunteers provide mountains of information when asked and are full of details about the B&O. Train rides, given several times a day on weekends, are very popular with kids young and old. *901 W. Pratt St., about ten blocks from the Inner Harbor, Baltimore; (410) 752-2490;* www.borail.org

Fort McHenry National Monument and Historic Shrine
★★★/$

In 1814, after the Battle of Baltimore, the tattered American flag flying over Fort McHenry inspired Francis Scott Key to write "The Star-Spangled Banner." In 1933, two years after Key's poem became the national anthem, Fort McHenry became part of the National Park system. Your grade-schoolers who have studied American history will enjoy the restored barracks and military memorabilia that bring the fort's past to life (it was used variously as a prison, a hospital, and a Coast Guard training facility). Younger kids will probably like the cannons the most. If you're visiting the whole region, try to stop to see the original Star-Spangled Banner

---

DAY TRIP
Experience the Inner Harbor

9 A.M. After breakfast, head for the Inner Harbor. If you haven't gotten tickets for the National Aquarium, do so first. Then shoot straight to the **Top of the World**, 27 stories up at the World Trade Center (see page 279). The kids will get a literal overview of Baltimore and a real introduction to the city's history.

10 A.M. Even if you encounter lines at the **National Aquarium** (see page 272), it's well worth the wait. You and your children will spend two hours

immersed in life underwater.

Noon Head to **Harborplace** for lunch (see page 277). Afterward, watch the street performers at the plaza in front.

2 P.M. Walk two blocks to **Port Discovery**, Baltimore's new children's museum (see page 273).

5 P.M. Go back to **Harborplace**, where you can choose among seemingly endless eateries for dinner.

at the National Museum of American History in Washington. It's currently undergoing restoration, but you can see workshops on the restoration until the original is on display again. *At the east end of East Fort Ave., three miles southeast of the Inner Harbor, Baltimore; (410) 962-4290;* www.nps.gov/fomc

The Great Blacks in Wax Museum ★★★/$

Immortalizing the contributions of African Americans both to Maryland and to the United States, this museum features life-size replicas of Crispus Attucks, Frederick Douglass, and Sojourner Truth, as well as such modern heroes as Justice Thurgood Marshall, Martin Luther King, Jr., and Jesse Owens. One of the dioramas depicts the removal of Rosa Parks from a Montgomery, Alabama, bus—considered by many to be the event that sparked the modern Civil Rights Movement. *1601 E. North Ave., at N. Bond St., Baltimore; (410) 563-3404;* www.greatblacksinwax.org

★ Maryland Science FamilyFun Center ★★★★/$

This wonderful shrine to science not only offers lots of things to see—like an IMAX film and the planetarium—but also many things to do. And those hands-on activities are what really engage young visitors: children can practice landing the space shuttle in a mock-up of the

actual shuttle and participate in chemistry or electrical experiments in a supervised lab. Permanent exhibits cover energy, the Chesapeake Bay, space, structures, and the Hubble telescope. Don't miss the fabulous gift shop (as if the kids would let you!). *601 Light St., Baltimore; (410) 685-5225;* www.mdsci.org

★ National Aquarium FamilyFun ★★★★/$$

Among the most highly regarded aquariums in the country, this is also one of the Inner Harbor's most popular attractions. The architecturally notable building, with a 63-foot-long finback whale skeleton spanning the dramatic lobby, is home to more than 5,000 fish, birds, reptiles, sea mammals, and amphibians. Kids especially like Children's Cove, a hands-on area where they can hold horseshoe crabs, sea stars, and other small marine creatures. Bottle-nosed dolphins perform in the Marine Mammal Pavilion; unless you want to be as wet as the dolphins, don't sit too close to the pool. Also popular are the colorful residents of the multilevel Atlantic Coral Reef and the steamy South American Rain Forest. The aquarium supplies backpacks in which to carry your babies and toddlers, as the aquarium does not allow strollers. **NOTE:** Given the aquarium's popularity, consider buying timed-entry tickets in advance from Ticketmaster (*202/432-SEAT*). The best (least crowded) times to visit are early in the morning or on summer evenings, when the aquarium is open until 8 P.M. *Inner Harbor, 501 E. Pratt St., Baltimore; (410) 576-3800;* www.aqua.org

⭐ Port Discovery
FamilyFun Children's Museum
★★★★/$

Designed by Walt Disney Imagineering and a coalition of educators, this fast-paced, interactive children's museum encourages kids to explore and take risks by presenting them with a series of challenges. Probably the most popular exhibit is a simulated archaeological dig set in Egypt in the 1920s. Children are given clues for finding their way through an intricate maze to the pharaoh's tomb and also learn how to write their name in hieroglyphics. The galleries of the three-floor museum encircle a KidsWorks obstacle tower in which children climb, crawl, and scramble (little ones can get help from guides inside) their way to the top. If there's a downside to Port Discovery, it's that the high-tech equipment occasionally breaks down, leading to long lines. **NOTE:** Allow two to three hours—longer if it's crowded—to experience the 80,000-square-foot museum. Though the museum is geared to children ages 6 to 12, several activities keep preschoolers entertained as well. *34 Market Pl., in the historic Fishmarket Building, Baltimore; (410) 727-8120.*

DAY TRIP
Games, Trains, and Hard-shells

9 A.M. Eat breakfast at the hotel, then set out for the **Babe Ruth Birthplace** (see page 275), which opens at ten.

10 A.M. For many baseball fans, no player will ever surpass the Sultan of Swat. The Babe Ruth Birthplace is a shrine devoted to his career.

Noon If there's an afternoon baseball game, walk to **Orioles Park at Camden Yards** (see page 277). If a game isn't scheduled at Orioles Park, walk to the **B&O Railroad Museum** (see page 270) near Babe Ruth's birthplace. The kids will love to have lunch served in a diner car and will delight in the splendid collection of exquisite trains. Afterward, find solace for missing a game by walking to Orioles Park for a tour of the stadium and a visit to the Orioles Baseball Museum.

5 P.M. If crabs are in season, have a traditional Baltimore dinner at **Obrycki's** (see page 280). Ask the waitress to show your children how to crack a bucket of hard-shells.

USS *Constellation*
★★★/$

Permanently docked in the Fort McHenry shipyard after a recent $9 million renovation, the USS *Constellation* is one of the oldest surviving vessels of the Civil War era. Children will enjoy going aboard to investigate the guns and captain's cabin and will be entranced by the Ship's Company, a troupe of historical reenactors. Dressed as sailors from the Civil War period, the group presents demonstrations, drills, and musical entertainment on the *Constellation.* Guided tours are given daily; call ahead for reenactment dates and times. *Pier 1, off Pratt St., Baltimore; (410) 539-1797;* www.constellation.org

Walters Art Gallery ★★★★/$

This excellent art museum showcases pieces dating from ancient Egypt through the 20th century. Henry Walters donated the core collection to the city in 1931; it includes 19th-century art, porcelains from Asia, and Walters's home to house them. Children seem especially drawn to the armor and Egyptian artifacts exhibits; a docent-led children's tour helps them to enjoy even more. Theme-based programs start preschoolers down the art-appreciation path. A typical session might include a story about the four seasons, a chat about the seasons in art, and an opportunity for children to create their own artwork about the seasons. Make reservations if you want to get into a workshop (there's a charge for some, others are free). Troia, the gallery's Italian restaurant, serves lunch and dinner. *600 N. Charles St., at Mount Vernon Sq., Baltimore; (410) 547-9000;* www.thewalters.org

CRAB CULTURE

Baltimore's signature food is crab. Harvested in the Chesapeake Bay, the native crustacean is taken very seriously in this city and is eaten in every form: crab cakes, crab soups, soft-shells (crabs whose hard shells have molted), and the ever-popular hard-shells. Most kids will love being presented with a bucket of crabs, a mallet to crack them open, a dull knife—and the prospect of eating a meal with their fingers. But some young diners may balk at the thought of actually consuming the somewhat unattractive critters. Knowing how to approach crab eating (which is known around here as "picking") may make kids more open to this amusing and messy dining experience—or not.

First, a few useful terms: male crabs are called "jimmies," immature females are "she-crabs," and mature females are known as "sooks." Usually ordered by the

JUST FOR FUN

Babe Ruth Birthplace
★★★/$

After the Baseball Hall of Fame in Cooperstown, New York, this is the closest thing to a shrine that baseball fans have. If your kids still memorize statistics about who died years ago, they'll love seeing the memorabilia (balls, bats, uniforms, and trophies) that document not only the Babe's life, but also the history of baseball in Maryland. (Ironically, the Sultan of Swat never played for the Orioles.) A 25-minute film chronicles Ruth's life and career, which lasted from 1914 until 1948. Old-fashioned radios broadcast original tapes of announcers regaling fans with the legend's home-run highlights. If you plan ahead, you can have your child's birthday party in the museum—something especially popular during baseball season. *216 Emory St., Baltimore; (410) 727-1539.*

MUST-SEE FamilyFun MUST-SEE Baltimore Zoo
★★★★/$

Located within Druid Hill Park, a 650-acre recreational area created from a private estate, the zoo covers 160 acres and features more than 1,200 mammals, reptiles, and birds. Their home is currently evolving into a bio-park, where animals can roam in environments more closely resembling their natural habitats; the sprawling African Watering Hole already benefits resident zebras, pelicans, and rhinos. Your younger kids will love the Children's Zoo's 48 interactive exhibits that let them feel what it's like to be an animal: kids can sit like a frog on a giant lily pad, perch like a bird in an oriole's nest, poke their

dozen, crabs are priced according to the pound and size and served in buckets. They're boiled in seasoned water—which may taste rather spicy to finicky eaters—and eaten with the hands at tables covered with brown paper or newspaper.

When your bucket(s) arrive, put a crab on the table (you won't have plates or utensils) and pull off the claws, setting them aside to eat last. Turn the crab on its back and remove the "apron," a long thin piece of shell that divides the front shell detaching the top shell from the body. Remove the top shell and discard the gills (spongelike material). Snap the crab in two to reveal the white crabmeat and begin picking meat from the shells. After you eat the meat from the body, crack the claws and extract that meat.

As you'll discover, crab picking is not fast food. But now you're armed and ready to spend an evening over a few dozen hard-shells at one of Baltimore's esteemed crab houses (see Good Eats).

The Painted Screens of Baltimore

On a hot day in 1913, greengrocer William Oktavec found that his vegetables and fruit were wilting in the sun. He brought them inside his shop and painted groceries on his window screens to show what was available inside. Thus, a Baltimore folk-art tradition was born.

In this city of brick and concrete, where few row houses have front yards or shade trees, residents found that painted window and door screens gave them privacy and protection from the pounding sun while still allowing them to open their doors and windows. Polish, German, and Irish immigrants plied their trade throughout Baltimore's ethnic neighborhoods in response to the rising demand for painted screens—and in the process created a city trademark and a collage that brightens city streets even today. Popular motifs include village scenes, bucolic ponds with ducks or swans, and landscapes reminiscent of the European countryside left behind when families emigrated. Though few screen painters remain, and their art is vanishing with the popularity of air-conditioning, painted screens remain a charming reminder of Baltimore's ethnic heritage.

heads out of a hole like a woodchuck, or swing like a monkey across a bridge. Parents will be grateful for the tram that stops at all the zoo's main areas. Special activities are held for the Easter, Halloween, and New Year's seasons, and an educational summer camp is offered during summer. Druid Hill also has tennis courts, playgrounds, a late-19th-century greenhouse, picnic shelters, and an outdoor pool. *Druid Hill Park, Druid Park Lake Dr., Baltimore; (410) 366-LION;* www.wildearth.org

The Dime Museum ★★★/$

When was the last time your kids saw a stuffed and mounted unicorn, a mermaid, a double-faced calf, and the mummified remains of a giantess? Borrowing its name from the traveling American sideshows popular in the late 1800s, this recently opened museum displays these rather skillfully created curiosities—along with such other oddities as an entire village carved from human bones, delicate and intricate hair jewelry, a mammoth ball of string, and a mannequin covered in chewing gum. **NOTE:** It's clearly not to everyone's taste; skip it if your children are especially fearful or squeamish. But lots of kids love this stuff and are likely to giggle throughout. They may even leave with a newfound appreciation for the good ol' days before movies and television. Don't forget to pet the resident cats, Booger and Toots. Open Wednesday through Sunday, the museum admits children under 6 free. *1808 Maryland Ave., Baltimore; (410) 230-0263;* www.dimemuseum.com

Fells Point ★★/$

This lively waterfront community, founded in 1730, has recently been rediscovered and makes for a charming change of pace from the bustling Inner Harbor. Its famous shipyards turned out some of the best-known clipper ships of the 19th century. More than a century later, Fells Point has become a fashionable address that still retains its blue-collar roots. In addition to trendy shops and plenty of pubs, Fells Point is home to Broadway Market, the city's oldest open-air market. Look for the *Sleepless in Seattle* house at the water's edge. Children especially like the ride over in a water taxi; they leave from Baltimore's Inner Harbor.

Harborplace and the FamilyFun Gallery ★★★★/Free

Overlooking the Inner Harbor are Harborplace and the Gallery, three glass-paneled buildings housing more than 200 shops, stalls, and restaurants. Throughout the year, Harborplace hosts hundreds of family-friendly events on the plaza facing the harbor. Choral competitions, petting zoos, and concerts are big draws; but the best shows are given by imaginative street performers—jugglers, magicians, and acrobats—who often involve the audience in their stunts. Though all entertainment is free, buskers will pass the hat after performances. With its wide variety of eateries, this is a good place for lunch after a morning at the nearby National Aquarium. Parents can indulge in crab cakes or gyros, while kids grab pizza and ice cream. (Also see Good Eats and Souvenir Hunting.) **NOTE:** The pavilions can get crowded, especially on weekends. *At Pratt and Light Sts., Baltimore; Events hotline: (800) HARBOR-1; (410) 332-4191.*

Lacrosse Hall of Fame ★★/$

Kids in Baltimore generally start learning to play this fast-paced sport as soon as they can hold a stick. If your child is also a lacrosse player, you may want to pencil in a visit here. Otherwise, you can safely skip it. The lacrosse stars celebrated here will be unknown to all but the most enthusiastic fan. Still, your kids might become converts; the long history of lacrosse is depicted on a time line and memorabilia and photos are displayed. *113 W. University Pkwy., on Johns Hopkins University Campus, Baltimore; (410) 235-6882;* www.lacrosse.org

Orioles Park at Camden Yards ★★★★/$

Built on the site of a former railroad yard, this brick stadium has the feel of an old-time baseball park. It's the exclusive home of the

A Day of Art and Science

10 A.M. After a leisurely breakfast, arrive at the **Maryland Science Center** (see page 272); it opens at ten, noon on Sundays.

Noon Choose between two noted Baltimore museums: the **Walters Art Gallery** (see page 274) or the **Baltimore Museum of Art** (see page 269). Both have children's programs and workshops that introduce kids to their collections. Both also have restaurants that serve lunch.

4 P.M. Head back to the Inner Harbor to see the street performers at **Harborplace**. After two museums, your children will probably want a little unstructured time to decompress. Indulge in a little shopping or just watching the gulls in the harbor.

5 P.M. If everyone still has the energy, take a water taxi from the Inner Harbor to **Little Italy** for dinner. Eat early at one of the family-oriented restaurants crowding this small neighborhood; pick any one—it's hard to find bad Italian food here. Save room for dessert at **Vaccaro's** (see page 280).

Baltimore Orioles (nearby Ravens Stadium hosts Baltimore's football team) and, thanks to the hometown team's enthusiastic fans, games here are often sold out. If you can't get tickets at the box office, you may be able to buy some from the hawkers that congregate outside the park's main gate before each game.

Orioles Park offers some of the best food in baseball: crab cakes, barbecue, Polish sausage—all Baltimore specialties—as well as the ever-popular hot dog. A family picnic area lies beyond the outfield. For kids 14 and under, the park sponsors an Orioles Dugout Club: a $6 fee entitles members to discounted Orioles tickets, a T-shirt, a mascot photo, and baseball stickers. Tours (fee) of the park are given daily, except on game days. *Martin Luther King Blvd., within walking distance of the Inner Harbor, Baltimore; (410) 547-6234.*

The Power Plant ★★/Free
As its name implies, this retail complex was originally a power plant. It now contains Baltimore's Hard Rock Café, an enormous Barnes & Noble bookstore with a spacious children's section, and an ESPN Zone. Developed by Disney Regional Entertainment, the "Zone" is a sports-themed dining and entertainment complex that includes three areas: the Studio Grill restaurant; the Screening Room, which shows any game on the air; and the interactive Sports Arena, where budding

athletes can go up against cyberversions of famous pitchers in the batting cage or play arcade-style video games. Be forewarned: this can be an expensive afternoon. *601 E. Pratt St., Baltimore; Hard Rock Café: (410) 347-7625; Barnes & Noble: (410) 385-1709; ESPN Zone: (410) 685-ESPN.*

World Trade Center ★★★/$

Designed by I. M. Pei (who also designed the East Wing of the National Gallery of Art in Washington), the World Trade Center has become the most distinctive building on Baltimore's skyline. Kids will be intrigued to learn that it's also the tallest five-sided building in the world. From the 27th-floor observation deck, the entire family can take in wonderful views of Baltimore, the harbor, and the Chesapeake Bay Bridge. *401 E. Pratt St., Baltimore; (410) 576-0022; www.wtci.org*

BUNKING DOWN

Admiral Fell Inn
★★★/$$$

With fewer than 100 rooms, this small hotel in the Fells Point neighborhood used to be a vinegar factory. Now attractively restored and furnished with lovely antiques, it's a charming inn that welcomes families. Cribs and rollaways are available, and kids under 16 stay free. Request an interior room for quiet nights; breakfast is included in the rate. *888 S. Broadway, between Thames and Shakespeare Sts., Baltimore; (800) 292-4667; (410) 522-7377.*

Hyatt Regency Baltimore
★★★★/$$$

Right on the Inner Harbor, this glass-paneled, 487-room hotel has two restaurants and unparalleled views of

---

FamilyFun READER'S TIP

Road Scholars

As we were planning our family vacation to Colorado, my husband and I realized that our boys, Nicholas, 7, and Jason, 12, weren't as excited about the trip as we were. So my husband devised a fun pre-vacation research project. Each of the boys received questions two weeks before our trip. They were allowed to choose as many questions to work on as they wished (What's the tallest mountain in Colorado? What kind of animals live in Colorado and not Wisconsin?), and for each question answered, they received $4 of vacation spending money. The results were wonderful. Our children learned specifics about an unfamiliar part of our country and even came up with their own questions to investigate during our week in Colorado.

Diane Rush, Thiensville, Wisconsin

the harbor. Kids under 18 stay free, and a large, enclosed, rooftop swimming pool lets them splash away their excess energy. *300 Light St., Baltimore; (800) 233-1234; (410) 528-1234; www.hyatt.com*

Renaissance Harborplace Hotel ★★★★/$$$$

Adjoining Harborplace, this luxurious hotel with more than 600 rooms is conveniently located just minutes from the aquarium and Orioles Park. Families can take advantage of a pool, sauna, health club, two restaurants—and all that Harborplace has to offer. Children under 18 stay free. *202 E. Pratt St., Baltimore; (800) 468-3571; (410) 547-1200.*

Wyndham Baltimore Inner Harbor Hotel ★★★/$$$

Baltimore's biggest hotel (707 rooms) has two restaurants and a kid-pleasing outdoor pool. (Mom and Dad can use the health club across the street.) Children under 17 stay free. *101 W. Fayette St., Baltimore; (800) WYNDHAM; (410) 752-1100.*

GOOD EATS

Johnny Rockets ★★/$$

This Harborplace institution mimics a 1950s-style diner, serving great burgers, fries, and homemade ice cream. Your kids will probably be able to think only about the sun-

daes. *Light Street Pavilion, 301 S. Light, Harborplace, Baltimore; (410) 347-5757; www.johnnyrockets.com*

Obrycki's Crab House ★★★★/$$$

Families flock to this kid-friendly eatery, a favorite in a city of crab lovers. The large restaurant draws crowds for its communal dining experience and wonderful steamed crabs. Expect crowds and lines almost any time you go. Crabs are seasonal, so Obrycki's closes from December through March. (Also see "Crab Culture," page 274.) *1727 Pratt St., Baltimore; (410) 732-6399.*

Phillips Seafood Buffet ★★★★/$$$

This all-you-can-eat restaurant has a fixed-price buffet that includes the best of Chesapeake seafood. A less formal version of Phillips Harborplace, this location is much more kid friendly. *Light Street Pavilion, Harborplace, Baltimore; (410) 685-6600.*

Vaccaro's ★★★★/$$

Sumptuous Italian pastries and ice cream are available in one of Little Italy's best shops. Kids will have a hard time choosing between the array of cookies sold by the pound and the enormous ice-cream cones. Our choice: the cannoli, a pastry cone filled with whipped ricotta cheese. *222 Albermarle St., Baltimore; (410) 685-4905.*

SOUVENIR HUNTING

Big Dog Sportswear

Lots of T-shirts, most bearing the ubiquitous Big Dog logo, are the stock in trade here. Dog lovers will find it hard to choose just the right one. *Pratt Street Pavilion, Harborplace, Baltimore; (410) 528-0483.*

Dapy

The wacky gadgets here will delight your child's offbeat sense of humor. Kooky cookie jars, Lava lamps, a Mickey Mouse telephone, key chains with puzzles attached—you never know what will turn up here. *Pratt Street Pavilion, Harborplace, Baltimore; (410) 539-6771.*

The Discovery Channel Store

It's not just a store, but an environment that surrounds shoppers with the sights and sounds of the natural world—beneath the sea, in the rain forest, under the stars. You'll find lots of educational toys that let kids have fun while observing and experiencing our planet. *Light Street Pavilion, Harborplace, Baltimore; (410) 576-0909.*

DEM O'S

If Baltimore has a king, his name is Cal Ripkin and his cathedral is Orioles Park at Camden Yards. But even before the new baseball park was built, and before Ripkin began his illustrious career with the O's, baseball was revered in Baltimore. Home games often sell out, but if you can get tickets, a Baltimore Orioles game is a wonderful family activity.

Here are a few Baltimore baseball bits to toss around between innings:

♦ Cal Ripkin is not the most famous baseball player from Baltimore. Babe Ruth's home is near Camden Yards and the bar his father owned once stood right about where center field is today.

♦ Cal Ripkin's father, "Senior," was a member of the Orioles organization from 1957 to 1988. Though he spent his last year as manager, Senior was fired after only six games and rarely set foot in Orioles Stadium again—even to see his son play.

♦ As much as O's fans like Camden Yards, their previous home, Memorial Stadium, was revered and is now much mourned. It was nestled in a middle-class neighborhood, and nearby residents would rent out their driveways to fans coming to the game.

♦ The Orioles are known as a team that plays through personal injuries. This is epitomized by Cal Ripkin's "streak" (2,632)—despite recurring back injuries, he broke Lou Gehrig's previous record of playing 2,131 consecutive games.

Chesapeake Bay is home to a number of historic lighthouses, including Concord Point.

Maryland's Eastern Shore

WATER IS the element that unites the communities of Maryland's Eastern Shore. Bustling Annapolis, the capital of Maryland and home of the U.S. Naval Academy, is an 18th-century port with its historic district intact. The smaller towns along the Chesapeake—Oxford, St. Michael's, and Tilghman Island—move at a refreshingly slow pace, vestiges of a time when the Eastern Shore was so cut off from the rest of Maryland that it developed its own distinct speech patterns. Maryland's shore offers the honky-tonk excitement of Ocean City, with its carnival-like boardwalk, as well as the quiet solitude of Assateague, a haven for campers, ecologists, and fisherfolk. Since it's a mere two-hour drive from Annapolis to Assateague, the Eastern Shore of Maryland draws families who like a little variety in their vacation. For its part, Annapolis—once the capital of the United States—combines history, colonial architecture, and a front-row seat on glorious Chesapeake

THE FamilyFun LIST

MUST-SEE MUST-SEE

Chesapeake Bay (page 286)

Maryland State House (page 285)

Oxford (page 287)

St. Michaels (page 287)

Tilghman Island (page 288)

U.S. Naval Academy Museum (page 286)

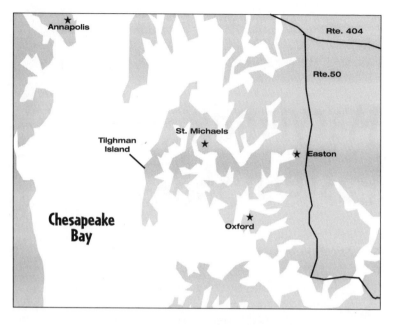

Bay. Only an hour's drive from both Baltimore and Washington, D.C., it seems a century away from both. Seventeenth- and 18th-century row houses line narrow streets that wind down to the Annapolis port, where sailboats bob on rolling waves. At one end of Main Street lies the harbor; at the other, the Maryland Capitol building, built in 1722, stands proud as the oldest legislative building still in use. Beyond Annapolis, the Chesapeake Bay has a series of charming small towns that draw families who enjoy fishing, boating, and other watery fun. Predating the American Revolution, many of these communities still retain their Colonial charm. Leisurely touring the Chesapeake

towns affords you a chance to while away a few hours on a boat ride, watching the waves lap ashore, riding bicycles through nearly traffic-free streets, and lingering over a family meal.

CULTURAL ADVENTURES

Historic Annapolis ★★★/Free

As you stroll through Annapolis, have the kids look for remnants of the 18th-century port—such as charming row houses, the central market, the old parks, the state house—which stand in stark contrast to the conveniences of a

21st-century town. The Historic Annapolis Foundation offers brochures and tapes for two self-guided tours: Historic Annapolis Walk with Walter Cronkite, and African American Heritage Walking Tour. For your own casual tour, start at the Maryland State House and head downhill toward the harbor. Historic buildings are marked with the Historic Annapolis Foundation Marker, an octagonal sign with a bas-relief of a tulip poplar. Many of the historic buildings are private homes or government offices that you can view only from the outside; exceptions include the **Williams Paca House and Garden** (*186 Prince George St.*), the **Hammond Harwood** House (*19 Maryland Ave.*), and the **Chase-Lloyd House** (*22 Maryland Ave.*). All three offer tours (best for older kids). **NOTE:** Be warned that Annapolis gets very crowded on weekends, and its brick sidewalks make for bumpy stroller rides. *Historic Annapolis Foundation, 77 Main St., Annapolis; (410) 268-5576 (for all three houses);* www. annapolis.com

Maryland State House
FamilyFun ★★★/Free

With architecture greatly influenced by the sea, the oldest U.S. state house in continuous use is topped by a dome shaped like a lighthouse. Your kids will be impressed by the building's rotunda—it has the largest wooden

Annapolis Calendar

History-rich Annapolis is a four-season vacation spot, where you'll find special events all year long. The festivities include traditional celebrations as well as some more unusual offerings. Here's a sampling:

JANUARY: Like many communities, Annapolis marks New Year's Eve with a family-oriented First Night celebration. There's music, dance, street theater, and more.

MAY: The Annapolis Waterfront Arts Festival brings crafts, food, and music to the city dock.

JULY-OCTOBER: Each Saturday and Sunday during this four-month period, the Maryland Renaissance Festival in nearby Crownsville entertains young knights and ladies, complete with food and entertainment. There are 200 performers, and there's a 5,000-seat jousting area.

DECEMBER: The Christmas Lights Parade sets Annapolis Harbor all aglitter. Boat owners deck their craft with lights and sing carols as they sail along the harbor, creating a delightful spectacle for those on shore.

dome built without nails. It's so big that the furniture looks tiny in comparison, almost child-size. Free tours are given daily. *91 State House Cir., Annapolis; (410) 974-3400.*

U.S. Naval Academy
FamilyFun Museum ★★★★/$
Founded in 1845 with seven teachers and 50 midshipmen, the U.S. Naval Academy is now over 4,000 strong. Students compete fiercely for a place in the Academy, and the campus—or the Yard, as it is called—is steeped in tradition. The visitors' center has an exhibit on the life of a midshipman, and you can take campus tours. Highlights include the crypt of Revolutionary War hero John Paul Jones, which lies beneath the Chapel. The reason for families to come here, though, is the Naval Academy Museum. The museum's incredible collection of ship models, navigational tools, and naval weapons will fascinate both you and your kids. The 11:45 A.M. tour might afford you a memorable glimpse of the midshipmen lining up for their noon meal formation in Tecumseh Court. *52 King George St., Annapolis; (410) 263-6933;* www.nadn.navy.mil

JUST FOR FUN

Chesapeake Bay
FamilyFun ★★★★/$$$
Most kids love boats, and there's no better way to experience the Chesapeake than from the water. You can take various tours—down the Severn River, which empties into the Bay, along Annapolis Harbor, past the Thomas Point Lighthouse, the Naval Academy, and the massive Chesapeake Bay Bridge.

The two best family tours are Watermark Cruises and those on the schooner *Woodwind.* Watermark runs 40-minute tours of the harbor, including the Naval Academy; the excursions depart from the city dock. The first cruise starts at noon and snacks are available on board. The schooner *Woodwind*, which leaves from the Annapolis Marriott (*80 Compromise St.*) four times a day, welcomes children over 5 on its two-hour cruise aboard a 74-foot classic wooden sailing yacht; snacks are provided. The cruises don't run in bad weather, so call ahead. *Watermark Cruises: (410) 268-7600; Schooner Woodwind: (410) 263-7837.*

Easton ★★★/Free
Founded in the mid-1600s, this sedate, slightly inland town is filled with a fine collection of lovingly restored, pre–Revolutionary War homes. Normally sleepy Easton wakes right up during the annual

Waterfowl Festival (*410/822-4567*), held the second weekend in November, when more than 450 artists display their works inspired by the wildlife of Chesapeake Bay. Your kids will likely shoot straight past the decoys and paintings on their way to the duck- and goose-calling contests and retriever and fly-fishing demonstrations. *Off State Hwy. 33.*

Oxford ★★★★/Free

FamilyFun Though once Maryland's biggest port, beautiful Oxford today is a tiny enclave with fewer than 1,000 year-round residents. Take a leisurely stroll to see its brick herringbone streets, lined with clapboard houses. Aspiring young seafarers might be interested in seeing how boats are maintained in Oxford Marina's dry docks. Come August, all kids will be enchanted by hundreds of sailboats—some very large and elaborate—parading along the shore in the Oxford Regatta. At water's edge, the historic Robert Morris Inn is an ideal vantage point for ogling boats cruising the Chesapeake almost any time of year (see Good Eats and Bunking Down). Near the inn, the **Oxford-Bellevue Ferry** (*410/745-9023*) carries passengers and fewer than a dozen cars on the 25-minute trip across the Tred Avon River to St. Michaels (*see below*). America's oldest (1683) privately owned ferry, it runs from March through November; there's a minimal fee. *Off State Hwy. 33.*

St. Michaels ★★★★/Free

FamilyFun One of the larger towns on the Chesapeake is also the one most geared to tourists—especially

---

DAY TRIP
Baywatch

9 A.M. Have breakfast at **Einstein Brothers' Bagels** (see page 290) along the Harbor before driving to the U.S. Naval Academy (see page 286). Tours are held year-round. Take the first walking tour of the day (9:30 in summer, 10 the rest of the year).

Noon Return to the harbor and pick up lunch at the **Crab Claw** (see page 290). Enjoy your picnic dockside.

1:30 P.M. If the weather is nice, cruise the Chesapeake aboard the schooner *Woodwind* (see page 286).

3:30 P.M. Return to **Annapolis** and spend a leisurely afternoon strolling its historic streets and exploring the myriad small shops.

5:30 P.M. Dine early dockside, pickin' and agrinnin' at **Buddy's Crabs and Ribs** (see page 290).

in summer, when Main Street's quaint shops draw an endless stream of visitors. Your kids will be more interested in the **Chesapeake Bay Maritime Museum** (*Mill St., 410/745-2916*; fee), housed in the 1789 Hooper Strait Lighthouse. The museum has several hands-on exhibits about boat building and highlights the Chesapeake's role in America's history. Youngsters will especially enjoy exploring the former lighthouse keeper's quarters and reading portions of his diary. Climb to the top of the lighthouse for lovely bay views. **Christmas in St. Michaels** (*888/465-5428*), held the second weekend in December, offers children the chance to have breakfast with Santa ($10 per child). There's also a Santa's Wonderland with games, activities, and photo ops with the big guy in red. *Off State Rd. 33; accessible by land, or ferry from Oxford; (410) 226-5111.*

Sailing on the Bay

There's no better way to see Chesapeake Bay than from a boat. The following companies offer a variety of bay tours. Be sure to call ahead, as many tours require reservations and most are seasonal.

Dockside Express: Two-hour ecotours. *St. Michaels; (410) 886-2643.*

Island Kayak, Inc.: Ecotours and kayak rentals. *Tilghman Island; (410) 886-2083.*

The Lady Patty: cruises on a restored sailing yacht. *Tilghman Island; (800) 690-5080; (410) 886-2215.*

Skipjack H. M. Krentz: *Tilghman Island; (410) 745-6080.*

Skipjack Rebecca T. Ruark: *Tilghman Island; (410) 886-2176.*

Skipjack Sailing Tours: *St. Michaels; (410) 745-6080.*

⭐ **Tilghman Island**
FamilyFun ★★★★/Free

The least spoiled of the Chesapeake Bay towns is reached via a drawbridge, which happens to be one of the busiest in the country. Another wonderful destination for kids and parents fascinated by boats, this working port is home to the last fleet of skipjacks, which are broad-bottomed sailboats used for harvesting oysters. Local full-time fishermen often can be seen tending their ancient boats, all of which are powered by sails. To see a working skipjack in action, take a cruise aboard the *Rebecca T. Ruark* (410/886-2176). Your children will be enchanted by the friendly captain's entertaining tales of oystering on the bay. Moms and Dads may enjoy the freshest oysters on the bay even more.

She Shows Seashells

My family loves to spend our vacations at the beach. We always collect many seashells that we think are pretty enough to frame so that we can make them part of our annual summer photo collage. Once we get home, Danielle, 9, and Tiffany and Stephanie, 7-year-old twins, pick out their favorite shells and glue them on the edge of an 8- by 10-inch frame. We cut up vacation photos and assemble the collage, then attach labels to caption the pictures. We hang the pictures proudly every year.

Lorene Hall, Starke, Florida

BUNKING DOWN

Annapolis Marriott Waterfront Hotel ★★★/$$$

This modern hotel offers great views of Chesapeake Bay. There's no pool or game room, but the in-town location, on-site restaurant, and over-sized rooms help to compensate. Children stay free in their parents' room. Schooner *Woodwind* tours leave from the nearby dock. *80 Compromise St., Annapolis; (410) 268-7555;* www.marriott.com

Historic Inns of Annapolis ★★★★/$$$$

You can make reservations for three lovely inns in the historic district at one central office. If you prefer to be near the State House, the Maryland Inn features the Treaty of Paris Restaurant. The Governor Calvert House, also near the State House, offers 54 inviting guest rooms. Overlooking the Governor's Mansion is the Robert Johnson House, which is actually three contiguous houses that have been integrated into one inn. At all three, guest rooms boast antiques and reproductions, which may make them too fancy for young children. The historic district location is fantastic. *Main office, 58 State Cir., Annapolis; (410) 263-2641.*

Robert Morris Inn/ Sandaway Lodge ★★★★/$$$

Open April through November, the historic Robert Morris Inn is the best place to stay in Oxford. Built prior to 1710 (and named for its former owner, who helped to finance the American Revolution), the inn has a private beach and some rooms with private porches. But families might prefer the larger rooms and slightly less formal atmosphere of its neighboring sister property, the Sandaway, whose grassy lawn stretches down to water's edge. *314 Morris St., Oxford; (410) 226-5111.*

The Tidewater Inn ★★★/$$$

This once-grand inn in the middle of Easton is starting to show its age, but its central location is ideal for strolling around town. There's a pool and restaurant. *101 E. Dover St., Easton; (800) 237-8775; (410) 822-1300.*

Wades Point Inn on the Bay ★★★★/$$$

Only five miles outside St. Michaels, this inn has guest rooms with bay views and kitchenettes. Children under 12 stay free. *St. Michaels; (888) 923-3466; (410) 745-2500.*

GOOD EATS

Buddy's Crabs and Ribs ★★★/$$

With 22 windows overlooking the city dock, this kid-friendly eatery is a great place to watch the goings-on on the Annapolis waterfront. Though the specialty is seafood, a children's menu—including macaroni and cheese, pizza, hamburgers, hot dogs, and chicken fingers—is geared to young palates. *100 Main St., Annapolis; (410) 626-1100; www.buddysonline.com*

Crab Claw ★★★★/$$

This very popular (hence, very busy) crab joint serves up every manner of crab to a faithful following. If your kids won't eat crustaceans, they can order from the kids' menu—chicken nuggets, hot dogs, hamburgers. *Navy Point, St. Michaels; (410) 745-2900; www.thecrabclaw.com*

Einstein Brothers' Bagels ★★/$

This bagelry near the city dock is a good spot for breakfast or lunch. Eat your freshly baked bagels with cream cheese, deli sandwiches, or soups here—or order them to go. *122 Dock St., Annapolis; (410) 280-3500.*

Harrison's Chesapeake House ★★★★/$$

A Chesapeake Bay standard, this no-frills restaurant serves excellent, fresh seafood. There's a kids' menu with a few nonseafood choices. *Chesapeake House Dr., Tilghman Island; (410) 886-2121.*

Middleton Tavern Oyster Bar and Restaurant ★★★/$$$

This 18th-century tavern serves traditional Maryland fare, including raw oysters and crab cakes. The sidewalk café is a good spot for people-

The Breaded Flounder Filet

In this ultimate kid-pleasing game, players hustle into the water, roll their wet selves in dry sand until completely breaded, race back into the water to rinse off, and race back to base. The winner gets treated to a round of sandy hugs before being buried to the neck in sand.

watching in summer and fireside chats in winter. *2 Market Space, Annapolis; (410) 263-3323.*

Robert Morris Inn ★★★★/$$$

Many places claim to have the best crab cakes on the bay, but the Robert Morris is renowned for its version. Casual enough for families, the inn is open for breakfast, lunch, and dinner. Kids can watch the Chesapeake boat traffic while they wait for their meals to arrive. *Morris St., Oxford; (410) 226-5111;* www.robertmorrisinn.com

SOUVENIR HUNTING

Annapolis Pottery

This pottery studio is especially popular with budding young artists. Your kids can sit on a set of bleachers and watch potters making stoneware. *40 State Cir., Annapolis; (410) 268-6153.*

Chesapeake Bay Maritime Museum Shop

Ideal for young salts, this shop stocks books, gifts, lighthouse reproductions, and food related to the history of the Chesapeake Bay. *Mill St., St. Michaels; (410) 745-2098.*

Crackerjacks

A fun stop filled with toys and children's books, it's right in the middle of historic Easton. *7 S. Washington St., Easton; (410) 822-7716.*

A Chesapeake Sampler

9 A.M. After spending a night in the Robert Morris Inn (see Bunking Down), ramble around **Oxford** (see page 287) or turn the kids loose to play on the inn's private beach.

11 A.M. Take the **Oxford-Bellevue Ferry**, then drive to nearby St. Michaels.

Noon Have lunch at the **Crab Claw** in St. Michaels (see page 290).

1 P.M. Spend an hour in the Chesapeake Bay Maritime Museum (see page 288).

2 P.M. Drive 12 miles south, and over the drawbridge, to **Tilghman Island** (see page 288).

3 P.M. Take a late afternoon cruise on a skipjack, preferably the *Rebecca T. Ruark* (see page 288).

6 P.M. Have dinner at **Harrison's Chesapeake House** on Tilghman Island (see page 290).

Load up on sunscreen, cotton candy, and coins for the arcade games, and head for the beach.

Ocean City

FOR MANY FAMILIES in the region, no summer would be complete without the traditional week or two in Ocean City. The original Ocean City beach town, now at the south end of the city, was composed of clapboard houses, small apartments, and boarding houses, some of which remain. But today's Ocean City has grown into a bustling seaside community, popular with college students and families who come for the clean (albeit crowded) beach and nonstop entertainment.

If you're seeking serenity and endless stretches of unspoiled beach, look elsewhere.

High-rise condos and hotels back up to a boardwalk lined with honky-tonk arcades, miniature-golf courses, water rides, and stands selling cotton candy, funnel cakes, and salt water taffy. There are amusement parks, water parks, and that one thing that amuses children above all else—the beach. So, if what you're looking for is non-stop fun and a place where we absolutely guarantee your kids will never get bored, well, this is it.

THE **FamilyFun** LIST

MUST-SEE
MUST-SEE

The Beach (page 294)

Ocean City Boardwalk (page 295)

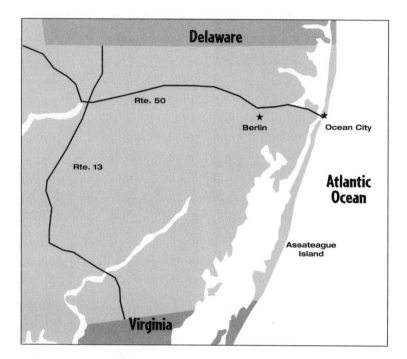

JUST FOR FUN

⭐ The Beach
FamilyFun ★★★★/Free

Sand, sand, and more sand. The Atlantic Ocean on one side and a lineup of hotels on the other—it's the making of a perfect summer vacation. *Ocean City.*

Frontier Town and Wild West Show ★★★/$

This is a throwback to the 1950s, when frontier towns and Santalands were all the rage for vacationing families. Never mind that it's actually in the East and no longer polit-ically correct, Frontier Town offers an afternoon's worth of kid-pleasing entertainment. There are bank holdups, a cancan show, stagecoach rides, and the like—all in the "small Western town" next to Ocean City. *Rte. 611, Berlin; (410) 289-7877;* www.frontiertown.com

Jolly Roger Amusement Park ★★★/$$

Ocean City's largest amusement park has huge roller coasters, a giant Ferris wheel, and water slides. Tons of stuff for toddlers, too. Need we say more? *30th St. and Coastal Hwy., Ocean City; (410) 289-3477;* www.jollyrogerpark.com

Ocean City Boardwalk
FamilyFun ★★★/Free

Your children won't know which way to turn: this wide, three-mile-long wooden expanse is an orgy of traditional beach junk food, dollar stores, T-shirt shops, and old-time carny attractions. Since it's likely to bring back wonderful childhood memories for many Moms and Dads, the whole family will enjoy the scene. *Ocean City.*

Splash Mountain Water Park ★★★/$$

Ten slides, two kiddie pools, and lots of water rides—including a log flume and submarine slide—are aimed at the 5-and-over set. Older kids can play water basketball and volleyball. *30th St. and Coastal Hwy. (next to the Jolly Roger), Ocean City; (410) 289-6962.*

BUNKING DOWN

Many realtors handle weekly rentals of Ocean City apartments, condos, and houses. *Contact Ocean City Visitor Information (4001 Coastal Hwy., Ocean City; 410/289-2800).*

Best Western Flagship
★★★/$$$

If you want to be right on the boardwalk, this is the spot. Families will also appreciate the spacious apartments, indoor and outdoor pools, and playground. *On the boardwalk, at 26th St.,* *Ocean City; (800) 837-3585; (410) 289-3384;* www.bestwestern.com

Holiday Inn ★★★/$$$

Located on the water, this 216-room property gives you a choice of hotel

Ocean City Escapades

10 A.M. Spend the morning on the **beach**.

Noon Cruise the **boardwalk** for typical beach fare—hot dogs, Thrasher's fries (with vinegar, not ketchup), funnel cakes, and ice cream.

1:30 P.M. Avoiding the beach at the hottest time of day, drop by an amusement park or one of the many **miniature golf** spots along the Coastal Highway. Each has a fun theme, such as Hawaii, Vikings, or Australia.

4 P.M. Return to the **beach** for an hour of winding down.

5:30 P.M. Eat an early dinner at **English's** (see page 296).

7 P.M. Bring your children out for a look at the Ocean City **boardwalk** scene at night.

rooms and efficiency units. The additional room and kitchen facilities in the efficiencies make them a good choice for families. Children under 19 stay free. *Oceanfront and 67th St., Ocean City; (800) 837-3588; (410) 524-1600; www.basshotels. com/holiday-inn*

Seabonay
★★★/$$

One block from the end of the boardwalk, the small (55 rooms) Seabonay has an outdoor pool. Another plus: children under 12 stay free. *Oceanfront and 28th St., Ocean City; (800) 638-2106; (410) 289-9194.*

GOOD EATS

English's Family Restaurant
★★★/$$

The all-you-can-eat menu and early-bird discounts make the two branches of this restaurant favorites of budget-conscious families. The place is famous for its fried chicken. *15th St. and Philadelphia Ave. (410/289-*

7333), and 137th St. and Coastal Hwy., Ocean City (410/250-1422).

Flying Fruit Fantasy
★★★/$

To offset beach junk food, buy the troops a nutritious fruit shake. Or just give up trying to eat right (it is vacation, after all) and order up ice cream or frozen yogurt instead. *On the boardwalk, between Second and Third Sts., Ocean City. No phone.*

Pino's Pizza
★★★/$

This pizza joint serves up the usual: buffalo wings, calzones, pasta, subs, and, oh yes, pizza. *96th St., in the Ocean Plaza Mall, Ocean City; (410) 723-FAST.*

SOUVENIR HUNTING

Candy Kitchen
Making candy since 1939, this sweet spot turns out Ocean City's famous saltwater taffy. *5301 Coastal Hwy., Ocean City; (410) 524-6002.*

Ocean City Beach Rules

♦ Ball or Frisbee throwing and other sports are not allowed while the lifeguards are on duty (9:30 A.M. to 5 P.M.).
♦ Surfing is allowed only in designated areas.
♦ Animals are not allowed on the beach at all.
♦ Bicycles and Rollerblades are allowed on the boardwalk at specific times. Check posted signs.
♦ Skateboarding is permitted only at the designated skateboard lot at Third Street and St. Louis Avenue.

FROZEN ASSETS

ICE CREAM novelties are a favorite kid treat, so show them how to re-create a boardwalk treat back home.

CHOCOLATE-CHIP ICE CREAM SANDWICHES

INGREDIENTS

2 1/3 cups all-purpose flour
1 teaspoon baking powder
1/2 teaspoon salt
1 cup (2 sticks) unsalted butter, softened
2/3 cup firmly packed brown sugar
1/2 cup granulated sugar
1 tablespoon vegetable oil
1 tablespoon light corn syrup
1 large egg
2 teaspoons vanilla extract
1 package (10 to 12 ounces) chocolate chips or M&Ms
3/4 cup chopped walnuts or pecans (optional)
5 to 7 cups vanilla ice cream

Preheat the oven to 325° F and adjust the shelves to the upper third of your oven. Lightly butter large baking sheets. In a large bowl, stir the flour, baking powder, and salt. In a separate bowl, combine the butter, sugars, oil, and corn syrup. Mix in the egg and vanilla extract until blended, then gradually add the flour mixture. Stir in the chocolate chips and nuts, if desired.

Pat 2 tablespoons of dough into flat circles on the prepared baking sheets, leaving two inches between them. Bake for 14 to 16 minutes, or until lightly browned. Remove the sheets to wire racks and cool for about 5 minutes. Using a metal spatula, transfer the cookies to racks and cool completely. Repeat until all the dough is used.

Let the ice cream soften in the refrigerator for 30 minutes. Spread 1/2 cup of ice cream on the bottom of one cookie. Place a second cookie on top. Wrap each sandwich in plastic wrap or foil and freeze for 2 hours, or until firm. If the sandwiches are too hard, let stand at room temperature before serving. Makes 16 to 20.

Washington,

THE MAJORITY of Americans go to Washington, D.C., twice in their lives. First, their parents take them to visit, then, as adults, they take their kids.

And indeed, the District of Columbia, one of the top family travel destinations in the country, is a place that the whole family will enjoy: the history buff awed by the halls of the Capitol building, the wide-eyed 3-year-old wowed by a stegosaurus in the Museum of Natural History, the young art lover wandering the splendid National Gallery of Art, the 10-year-old who yearns for a whole day in the Air and

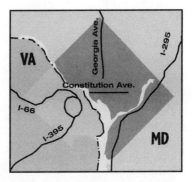

D.C.

Space Museum, and the preteen who wants to go shopping in Georgetown.

Which is to say, really, Washington has too much to do. You just can't see everything in the city in a typical three-day visit; don't even try. Doing justice to a family visit to Washington, D.C., is a perfect case of "less is more."

It's tempting to turn a Washington visit into one long history lesson. Don't do it. If you can blend culture with carousels and leave a lot for the next visit (you can be one of those families who visit *more* than twice), we guarantee you

a memorable trip—with your smiling troops asking when they can come back again.

ATTRACTIONS
$	under $5
$$	$5 - $10
$$$	$10 - $20
$$$$	$20 and over

HOTELS/MOTELS/CAMPGROUNDS
$	under $100
$$	$100 - $150
$$$	$150 - $200
$$$$	$200 and over

RESTAURANTS
$	under $5
$$	$10 - $15
$$$	$15 - $25
$$$$	$25 and over

***FAMILYFUN* RATED**
★	Fine
★★	Good
★★★	Very Good
★★★★	*FamilyFun* Recommended

At 6' 4", Abraham Lincoln was our nation's tallest president, so it is fitting that his Lincoln Memorial likeness also towers over the public. If the statue were able to stand, it would be 28 feet tall.

Washington, D.C.

A S YOU CAN SEE from the number of "Must-Sees" at the right, a visit to Washington, D.C., can be daunting. The nation's capitol has enough to please everyone in the family—and then some.

It's tempting to turn a visit here into one long history lesson. The Smithsonian Institution includes more than a dozen museums (listed separately); there are numerous private museums (two dedicated to children). Then you'll want to tour the White House and the Capitol, stroll through the Lincoln Memorial and the Vietnam Veterans' Memorial (among many other memorials). But there's more to the nation's capital than cultural pursuits. When you're all museumed out you'll still want to spend time in the spiffed-up downtown, with stores, restaurants,

THE **FamilyFun** LIST

MUST-SEE
MUST-SEE

Capitol Building (page 304)

Holocaust Museum (page 306)

Lincoln Memorial (page 310)

National Air and Space Museum (page 311)

National Gallery of Art Sculpture Garden ice-skating rink (page 326)

National Museum of American History (page 314)

National Museum of Natural History (page 316)

National Zoo (page 327)

Washington Monument (page 321)

The White House (page 323)

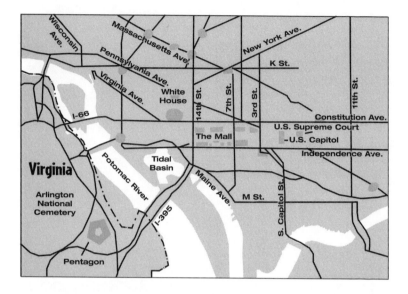

and a huge sports and entertainment complex, the MCI Center and Georgetown, a historic neighborhood with many restaurants and quaint shops (most, however, not for those on a budget). So hop on the Metro or one of the hop-on, hop-off open-air buses and enjoy. Your family is sure to give the capital its vote.

CULTURAL ADVENTURES

Arts and Industries Building
★★/Free
This fanciful redbrick building is the original home of the National Museum, which is now the enormous, multimuseum Smithsonian Institution. It stands next to the famous Smithsonian Castle, forming a wonderful Victorian duo. The Arts and Industries Building houses artifacts from the 1876 Centennial Exhibit, including fanciful and colorful horse-drawn carriages, farm and industrial machinery, silverware, and furniture.

Children will be most interested in the Discovery Theater, which offers a variety of short morning performances geared to the under-6 crowd (nominal fee)—puppet shows, plays, and other kid-pleasing shows. Check ticket availability early in the day; the theater often hosts groups from local schools. *900 Jefferson Dr., S.W., Washington, D.C.; (202) 357-1500;* www.si.edu/ai *Metro: Smithsonian.*

Bureau of Engraving and Printing ★★★/Free

Watching thousands of dollars roll off the press fuels the greediest fantasies of both children and adults. The Bureau of Engraving and Printing produces paper money, bonds, stamps, and White House invitations. (The kids will ask where coins are made: Philadelphia and Denver, at the government mints.) Every day, the bureau cranks out 22 million dollars in bills of every denomination (one-hundred-dollar bills are the largest denomination of U.S. currency). On the tour, you'll learn first about counterfeit money and the printing process, then move to the main show—watching that uncut currency roll off the press.

The most popular items in the gift shop here are shredded money and uncut bills (a little more expensive than the cut variety). And no, they do not give out free samples. Guided tours are available in the summer and self-guided tours are offered year-round. **NOTE:** This is a very popular attraction and requires tickets, most of which are gone by mid-morning. Plan your day accordingly. If you really plan ahead and contact the office of one of your senators or congressmen several months in advance, you can arrange a 45-minute personal VIP tour. *14th St., S.W., between Maine and Independence Aves., Washington, D.C.; (202) 874-3188; www.dep.treas.gov Metro: Smithsonian.*

Capital Children's Museum ★★★★/$

In an age of high-tech interactive children's museums, this place is a refreshing change. The converted convent is a low-tech, child-oriented experience that has kids learn by doing, not by watching. Of the five permanent exhibits, the best is the one on Mexico that is set in the building's former chapel. Children can make tortillas, grind their own hot chocolate, make large paper flowers, and try on traditional Mexican clothing. Cityscapes replicates the streets of Washington, D.C., complete with a mock Metrobus that children can "drive," sewers to climb in, and a firemen's pole to slide down. Young children will enjoy the maze; older ones will head for the manipulative puzzles and games and the

FamilyFun GAMES

What If?

Take turns answering these hypothetical questions and then invent some of your own:

♦ If you could live anyplace in the world, where would you live and why?

♦ If you could be the best on your block at something, what would it be?

♦ If you were stranded on a desert island and could eat only one kind of food for the rest of your life, what would it be?

computers. **NOTE:** The museum has no cafeteria. The closest restaurants are at Union Station, several blocks away. *800 3rd St., N.E., Washington, D.C.; (202) 675-4120; www.ccm.org Metro: Union Station.*

Capitol Building
FamilyFun ★★★★/Free

If the flag is flying over the Capitol Building, Congress is in session. The Capitol is on everyone's must-see list of things to do in Washington, but if your children are under 6, they may have a hard time understanding what makes it important or interesting. Children of any age can go to the House when it is in session; however, youngsters under 6 aren't allowed in the Senate when it is in session.

When planning your trip, contact your representative for tickets to the chamber galleries, which let you bypass the long lines of tourists. During the 45-minute (shorter in the summer) tour (tours depart the Rotunda every 15 minutes), you see the Rotunda, Statuary Hall, and the old Senate and Supreme Court chambers. Be sure to point out the frieze painted by Constantino Brumidi around the top of the Rotunda and see how many famous events in U.S. history your young history buffs can identify.

In Statuary Hall, kids will be intrigued by the acoustical design that allows whispers to be heard clear across the massive room. They'll also enjoy riding the tiny subway that connects the House and Senate offices to the Capitol building. The ride is free and is open to visitors—you might

THE METRO

D ON'T BE DAUNTED by the Metro system. Like Seattle's monorail and the Paris Metro, it's one of the most interesting aspects of traveling in the city. Another good thing about using the Metro is that you don't have to worry about driving and parking your car. Washington, D.C., police are notoriously vigilant about dispensing parking tickets. Most legal spaces are limited to one to three hours, and many unsuspecting tourists have

been caught in D.C.'s infamous tow-away zones.

Tips for tourists traveling on the Metro

♦ Fare cards can be purchased on the Washington Metropolitan Area Transit Association (WMATA) Web page: http://wmata.com
♦ One-day passes allow passengers to ride anywhere in the Metro system for $5. The pass is valid after 9:30 A.M. on weekdays and

even catch a glimpse of a senator or representative rushing to make a vote.

Stop at the Senate Dining Room (open to the public between 7:30 A.M. and 3:30 P.M.) for some of the famous Senate Bean Soup, on the menu since 1901 and a bargain at a dollar a bowl. *East end of the Mall, Washington, D.C.; (202) 225-6827; www.aoc.gov Metro: Capitol South or Union Station.*

It takes 570 gallons of paint to cover the exterior of the **White House.**

FBI Building ★★★/Free

This is one of the most popular tourist attractions in Washington, so be prepared for a wait (as long as two hours during the high season) for the one-hour tour. **NOTE:** To avoid the lines, write to your congressional representative in advance to arrange a time-specific tour. You can probably skip it if your kids are under 9—they'll have a hard time seeing above the plate-glass windows and an even harder time figuring out what the FBI does. Even if your children are older, you may want to think twice about visiting here—although our sample young visitors all loved this place. It's basically an advertisement for the FBI, with discussions of such topics as fingerprinting, blood sampling, and ballistic analysis. One room is filled with loot (jewels, furs, etc.) confiscated from drug dealers. Parents may be particularly concerned about the emphasis on guns—one room has over 5,000 guns, and the tour ends with a firearms demonstration. *10th St. and*

all day on weekends.

♦ Children ages 4 and younger ride free.

♦ Make a plan in case you become separated on the Metro. If a child gets lost, report immediately to the station manager.

♦ Take extra care on the escalators. A few children have been caught and injured when their hands or shoes became trapped in the machinery. If you have a stroller, take the elevator instead.

♦ Parking is free on weekends at Metro station parking lots, so you can park your car and ride into the city.

♦ Get a Metro Visitor's Kit. It contains maps, fare information, and two helpful brochures, *Take Metrorail to the Smithsonian* and *Metro's Family Guide to the Nation's Capital.* Call 202/637-7000 or log on to http://www.wmata.com to order your free copy.

Pennsylvania Ave., N.W. (entrance on E St. between 9th and 10th Sts.), Washington, D.C.; (202) 324-3447. Metro: Metro Center.

Frederick Douglass Historic Site
★★/Free

Frederick Douglass was the leading African American voice in the 19th century. Lecturer, writer, adviser to Lincoln, and outspoken proponent of human rights, Douglass was the son of a black slave woman and an unknown white man. For most of his career he lived in Rochester, New York, but after the Civil War he moved to Washington, D.C.—first to Capitol Hill and then to this beautiful Victorian home in Anacostia, where he died in 1895.

Children who know something about Douglass will be interested in the home, called Cedar Hill, which is run by the National Park Service and preserved just as it was in Douglass's time. A short film at the visitors' center explains the life and contributions of Douglass. If your kids like books, they'll be impressed by his remarkable library of 1,200 volumes, which remains intact.

The views from the lawn of Cedar Hill are unparalleled. Cedar Hill is off the beaten tourist track. The best way to get here is by car; the Metro stop is a few blocks away, but the neighborhood can be somewhat dangerous. Parking on the grounds is limited. *1411 W St., S.E., Washington, D.C.; (202) 426-5960; www.nps.gov/frdo/freddoug.html Metro: Anacostia.*

Historical Society of Washington ★★/$

A fanciful late 19th-century Romanesque mansion that was once the home of beer baron Christian Heurich now houses the Historical Society of Washington. Except for part of the second floor, which is now an extensive library of Washingtoniana, the house has been preserved as it was when Heurich and his large family lived here. Your kids may enjoy a glimpse into the life of a child in the late Victorian era, when children were meant to be seen and not heard. Take a picnic and lunch in the lovely garden behind the building. *1307 New Hampshire Ave., N.W., Washington, D.C.; (202) 785-2068; www.hswdc.org Metro: Dupont Circle.*

Holocaust Museum
MUST-SEE FamilyFun ★★★★/Free

MUST-SEE The Holocaust Museum is a memorial to the six million victims of the Nazi Holocaust. Although Jews were the primary victims, the Nazis also systematically exterminated Gypsies, homosexuals, the handicapped, and others. The permanent exhibit is divided into three sections, The Nazi Assault, The Final Solution, and the liberation of the survivors, The Holocaust: The Last Chapter, each occupying a separate floor.

Be advised: if your kids are under 11, much of the content will be too much for them. The Holocaust Museum is the most powerful museum in Washington—and perhaps in the world. Among the items on display are a boxcar used for transport to the death camps, piles of the victims' shoes, photos of whole villages that were exterminated, eyewitness testimonials by survivors, and moving examples of people who risked their lives to help those victims.

The genocide of millions of people is difficult for anyone to comprehend—many visitors look stunned as they move through the museum. Children 8 and older who have been prepared will get a lot out of a special children's exhibit on the first floor: Remember the Children: Daniel's Story relates the history of the Holocaust from the perspective of a young boy in Nazi Germany. Sensitively and carefully presented, it allows children to empathize with Daniel and learn about the Holocaust at a level that they are able to comprehend.

The second floor holds the Wall of Remembrance, 3,000 tiles painted by

The Presidential Tour

8 A.M. If you haven't acquired VIP tickets to the **White House** from your member of Congress, go to the visitors' center and get tickets. This probably means breakfast in your hotel before setting out. Getting tickets and taking the White House tour (see page 323) will take most of the morning.

Noon Reward yourself with lunch at the **Old Ebbitt Grill** (see page 333). Walk from the White House to the Lincoln Memorial, about a mile and a half. Or take the Metro from Farragut North to Foggy Bottom. The Metro route still involves a bit of a hike, but there are no Metro stops closer to the memorial.

1:30 P.M. Walk around the **Lincoln Memorial** (see page 310).

3 P.M. From the Lincoln Memorial walk across Independence Avenue to the Tidal Basin and the **Jefferson Memorial** (see page 308). Rent paddleboats at the **Tidal Basin** (see page 329) and spend a pleasant late afternoon on the water.

American children that commemorate the one and a half million children who died in the Holocaust. You need time-specific passes for the main exhibit, but not for Daniel's Story or the Wall of Remembrance. Advance passes are available from ProTix (800/400-9373) for a nominal service charge. Free same-day passes—available at the museum—are given out early in the day. The museum cafeteria is the only kosher restaurant on the Mall. *100 Raoul Wallenberg Pl., S.W., Washington, D.C.; (202) 488-0400; www.ushm.org Metro: Smithsonian.*

Jefferson Memorial ★★★/Free

When the Jefferson Memorial was completed in 1943, critics dubbed it Jefferson's Muffin because of the shallow domed roof supported by 54 columns that surround Jefferson's 19-foot-high statue. It's not as impressive as the nearby Lincoln Memorial (but what is?), although it has a beautiful view of the Tidal Basin. Children will appreciate the memorial more if they know a little about the man and his impact on America.

Inside the memorial are four panels of quotations of Jefferson, including one panel from the Declaration of Independence. The architects of the Memorial misquoted the Declaration, misspelling several words and changing the punctuation—intentionally, it turns out—so that they would fit more comfortably in the space. Ask your kids to find the errors. After vis-

The Smithsonian Museums on Foot

On a map, the Smithsonian looks like a compact complex of buildings. But it's a mile from the Washington Monument to the Capitol, a long, long way for little sightseers to walk. Here are some estimated walking times:

♦ Smithsonian Castle to American History Museum: **6 minutes**
♦ American History Museum to Natural History Museum: **5 minutes**
♦ Natural History Museum to Smithsonian Castle: **4 minutes**
♦ Freer Gallery to Air and Space Museum: **12 minutes**
♦ Air and Space Museum to American History Museum: **17 minutes**

iting the Memorial, rent a paddleboat and pedal around the Tidal Basin. *East Potomac Park, on the Tidal Basin, Washington, D.C.; (202) 426-6841.*

Kennedy Center for the Performing Arts ★★★★/Free

Perched right by the edge of the Potomac River, the John F. Kennedy Center for the Performing Arts houses a concert hall, an opera house, and the Eisenhower Theatre (plus a couple of smaller venues), where you can see bound-for-

Broadway or road productions of musical and dramatic plays, plus concerts, ballet performances, and films at the American Film Institute.

The building's mammoth Grand Foyer (longer than the length of the Washington Monument) is dominated by an impressionistic bust of President John Kennedy. Off the Grand Foyer is the Hall of States, which displays flags of all 50 states, and the Hall of Nations, which displays the flags of America's allies.

If you want to attend a production here, plan before you come—tickets are both pricey (think Broadway) and hard to come by. If the budget won't stretch that far, attend one of the informal concerts presented on the Millennium Stage in the Grand Foyer every evening at 6 P.M. The free, hourlong program differs every night, and showcases local, national, and international musicians who play all types of music. Listening to a live concert while watching the sun set over the Potomac is a relaxing way to wind down after a day of touring. Millennium Stage performances are advertised in the Style Section Guide to the Lively Arts in the *Washington Post*. Advance tickets are not necessary. Free tours of the building are available daily from 10 A.M. to 1 P.M. *New Hampshire Ave., N.W., Washington, D.C.; (202) 467-4600;* www.kennedy-center.org *Metro: Foggy Bottom/GWU.*

Library of Congress ★★★/Free

The Library of Congress is the largest library in the world. But your 8-year-

---

Sugar-coating History

My husband and I wanted our family trip to Washington, D.C., to be both educational and fun for our 9- and 11-year-old boys. However, we knew they might be less than enthusiastic about some of the historical tours we had planned. To engage their interest, we devised a game to play while sightseeing. Every morning I would give my sons three questions pertaining to the places we would visit that day. If they answered all three they could order the dessert of their choice at dinner. They could use any resource, including a plaque at the site, a tour guide, brochures, and the like. They thought it was great fun to win a dessert off Mom and Dad, and they were so successful that we bought a round every night. Websites and guidebooks were our sources for the questions. With that little bit of preparation, our kids ended up not only having a great time but learning a lot too.

Kathy Davis, Charlotte, North Carolina

old can't roam the stacks looking for his favorite Harry Potter book. It's a noncirculating library, and only serious researchers over the age of 18 can consult the seemingly limitless number of books, magazines, manuscripts, and photographs stored here. To get a taste of the Library of Congress that will satisfy adults and pique the interest of children, enter the Italian Renaissance Jefferson Building (the one with the dome) from the West Front entrance, across from the Capitol. Take a free, guided tour or simply go up the grand stairway to the Observation Gallery. This will give you a bird's-eye view of the recently restored Main Reading Room, one of the most dramatic and beautiful rooms in America. Tours are free but require a same-day ticket,

which are distributed at 10 A.M.; the library is closed on Sunday. *First St., S.E., Washington, D.C.; (202) 707-5000; tour information: (202) 707-5458;* www.loc.gov *Metro: Capitol South.*

MUST-SEE FamilyFun **Lincoln Memorial** ★★★★/Free

Looking at the Lincoln Memorial today, it's hard to imagine a more perfect expression of thanks from all Americans to the visionary president who led the country through the Civil War. Now how do you impress that on kids who would prefer to be in the Air and Space Museum? Advance briefings on American history help. But even very young children will also be impressed with the size of the Lincoln statue, which seems to be

Fun Facts About the Washington Monument

♦ The monument was almost not completed. The building was only half finished when the project ran out of money after the Civil War. Construction resumed in 1876 and was completed in 1886, but you can still see the change in the color of the marble marking where the first phase ended and the second began.

♦ The first president to go to the top of the Washington Monument was Harry Truman in 1946—60 years after it had been completed!

♦ The monument is made up of 90,000

tons of marble and granite—36,000 blocks in all.

♦ The stones at the base are 15 feet thick, while those at the top are 18 inches thick.

♦ The Washington Monument sinks a quarter inch each year.

♦ A 30-mph wind can make the monument sway an eighth of an inch.

♦ The top of the monument is capped with a nine-inch aluminum lightning rod.

♦ One aspect of the recent renovation was the installation of eight aircraft warning lights at the top.

barely contained in the temple. (If the statue were to stand, it would be 28 feet tall!) Read the inscription carved behind the solemn figure and then the Gettysburg Address carved on the south interior side wall. Ask the kids to imagine the area from the Lincoln Memorial to the Washington Monument filled with hundreds of thousands of people—they may have seen such scenes in the film *Forrest Gump* or in newsreels of Martin Luther King's March on Washington. (There's almost always someone yelling "Forrest!" by the side of the Reflecting Pool.) Then discuss the power that such groups have to implement change. *The Mall, 23rd St. between Independence and Constitution Aves., Washington, D.C.; (202) 426-6841; www.nps.gov/linc Metro: Foggy Bottom/GWU.*

Mary McLeod Bethune Home and Archives
★★/Free

This town house on Logan Circle was the home Mary McLeod Bethune, a civil-rights leader and educator; it will be of interest only to older kids who know something about—or have an interest in—black history. The child of freed slaves, Bethune founded a college for African American women in Florida and went on to become an adviser to Presidents Coolidge and Roosevelt. (She was part of Roosevelt's "Black Cabinet" that worked on minority issues.) She started and led the National Council of Negro Women, which now has its national headquarters here. The home has also been designated a national historic site and a center for black women's history. *1318 Vermont Ave., N.W., Washington, D.C.; (202) 673-2402. Metro: McPherson Square or McPherson Square/UDC.*

National Air and Space Museum
MUST-SEE FamilyFun MUST-SEE ★★★★/Free

The National Air and Space Museum is the most popular museum in the world. More than 175 million people have visited since it opened in 1976; its attendance figures surpass even those of the Louvre in Paris. Get to the museum early and immediately buy tickets to the Langley Theater, an IMAX theater that screens such films as *Blue Planet*, with breathtaking views of earth from space, and *To Fly*, which documents man's enduring fascination with flight. The films are short, and the special effects give audience members the sensation of flying themselves.

Start your tour at Milestones of Flight, the museum's main gallery as you enter from the Mall on Jefferson Drive. The most important objects in the history of flight are displayed or suspended overhead. Your kids will be fascinated at how small some of the planes are—not much bigger than a family minivan. Lindbergh's *Spirit of St. Louis*, in which he made

311

the first solo transatlantic flight, looks like a puddle jumper. The Wright brothers' 1903 Flyer, the first powered, heavier-than-air machine, looks about as sturdy as a balsawood toy. The Apollo 11 Command Module that carried astronauts Armstrong, Aldrin, and Collins to the moon is no bigger than a large trash container.

Mom and Dad may enjoy the early artifacts of flying like Amelia Earheart's jaunty red Lockheed Vega, the World War II fighter-er planes, and the early airmail biplanes, but the kids will want to touch the sliver of moon rock near the main entrance and then head for the space exhibits. Apollo to the Moon features Alan Shepherd's one-man Mercury Freedom 7, a full-size mock-up of a lunar module, and a Lunar Roving Vehicle. A new permanent exhibit, How Things Fly, helps demystify the science of flight with more than 50 interactive simulators. **NOTE:** The Air and Space Museum is being renovated through 2003 and about a quarter of the galleries will be closed at any one time. Don't miss the huge gift shop, which has lots of books, posters, and models. Buy astronaut ice cream for the kids; the dehydrated confection tastes remarkably like the real thing—minus the cold. There are two restaurants on the premises: the Flight Line cafeteria

Q: What does the G in G-Man stand for?
A: Government

and the more intimate (and expensive) Wright Place Cafe. *Independence Ave., S.W., on the south side of the Mall between 4th and 7th Sts., Washington, D.C.; (202) 357-2700; www.nasm.edu Metro: Smithsonian and L'Enfant Plaza.*

National Archives
★★★★/Free

Older children and their parents will grasp the importance of the country's most famous documents, the foundation of our system of laws, that are enshrined in the rotunda here. Younger kids may be more impressed by the fact that the documents are sealed in glass-and-bronze cases and lowered into a bomb shelter 20 feet below the ground for nighttime storage. The murals on the walls of the rotunda explain who wrote these documents and why they are important (a plus for you Moms and Dads who have grown a little rusty in American history). *Constitution Ave., between 7th and 9th Sts., N.W., Washington, D.C.; (202) 501-5000; www.nara.gov Metro: Archives/Navy Memorial.*

National Gallery of Art
★★★/Free

Your kids may balk at spending time in an art museum when Washington offers so many other attractions. Fortunately, the National Gallery, known for its unparalleled Impressionist collection and stunning works by Rembrandt and Raphael, has allures that will even tempt a 2-year-old. Start with the I. M. Pei–designed East Building, with its daring exterior architecture and a huge indoor atrium.

The knife-edge southwest exterior corner of the building bears the imprint of many small hands—little people can't resist touching it to see if it's really sharp (it isn't). Inside the soaring atrium is the magnificent Calder mobile, weighing several tons; it twists slowly overhead, mesmerizing even the most rambunctious toddler.

Connecting the East Building and the traditional West Building is a moving sidewalk that opens onto an indoor waterfall. Next to the waterfall is the National Gallery's Café/Buffet, an upscale cafeteria and a good place for Mom and Dad to rest while the kids try to figure out how the waterfall works (it's actually behind glass). A children's shop next to the café carries books, games, and puzzles. *Constitution Ave., N.W., between 3rd and 9th Sts., N.W., Washington, D.C.; (202) 737-4215; www.nga.gov Metro: Archives/Navy Memorial.*

National Geographic Explorers Hall ★★★/Free

The National Geographic Society was founded in 1888 and in 1964 moved into this modern building near Dupont Circle. The kids will

KIDS
in the White House

What's it like to live in the White House? Very few kids have gotten the chance to find out. The children of most U.S. presidents were already grown up by the time their parents moved to 1600 Pennsylvania Avenue. There have been a few exceptions.

Teddy Roosevelt had five young children when he was president. One son, Quentin, brought his pony up to the family quarters in the White House elevator. Fifty years later, John and Jacqueline Kennedy took up residence. In 1961, their daughter, Caroline, was 3 and their son, John, a newborn. Jacqueline Kennedy set up a small preschool in the White House for Caroline and a few other children, and the president often visited the class to play with the children. Like Quentin Roosevelt, Caroline had a pony whose name was Macaroni; he had the run of the White House Garden.

Amy Carter was 9 when her father, Jimmy Carter, became president. She was the only presidential child to attend public school in the District of Columbia. Chelsea Clinton, who was 12 when her father took office, went to the exclusive Sidwell Friends School in Northwest Washington. When she graduated from high school, President Bill Clinton gave the commencement address.

go for the first-floor museum—devoted to all things on land, under the sea, and in space—and its interactive exhibits. Young explorers can stick their hands into a wind tunnel that simulates a tornado, judge the size of a flying dinosaur by walking under a model of one, and find out about their environment from lots of interactive computer exhibits.

An 11-foot-tall globe is at the center of an interactive amphitheater in which visitors "travel" on a simulated flight around the earth. A "pilot" asks the audience questions that they answer from their seats; the correct answer is projected on a huge screen. The Explorers Hall is compact—plan on spending an hour here. But the kids may want to linger in the gift shop, which stocks atlases, videos, photographs, globes, and just about everything else related to geography. *1145 17th St., N.W., Washington, D.C.; (202) 857-7588;* www.national geographic.com/explorer *Metro: Farragut North.*

National Museum of African Art
★★★/Free

This is the only national museum devoted to African art. It's a good way to teach kids that Africa is not a country, but a collection of more than 900 diverse cultures. The collection of masks, figures, sculptures, and everyday objects will help children appreciate the diversity of these groups. Many of the items are accompanied by large color photographs that show how they are used in native cultures, and there are regular storytelling sessions, lectures, and musical performances. *Independence Ave., S.W., between 7th and 12th Sts., Washington, D.C.; (202) 357-2700;* www.nmafa.si.edu *Metro: Smithsonian.*

National Museum of American History
★★★★/Free

Unlike the other Smithsonian museums on the Mall that have a strong central focus, this museum has a little of everything—the popular exhibit of First Ladies' gowns; a complete rural post office; campaign buttons, posters, and other political memorabilia; early bicycles; and pop cultural artifacts like Dorothy's ruby slippers from *The Wizard of Oz* and the original Kermit the Frog Muppet. There are also musical instruments, hand tools, lithographs, pottery, a baseball autographed by Babe Ruth, a jersey worn by Michael Jordan, the original Star-Spangled Banner, ship models, cameras, coins—1.3 million artifacts in all. And it's not necessarily arranged logically. You can take the tour for an overview, but this is one attraction where parents have to do their homework and hone in on the exhibits that will engage their children.

The museum has two excellent

hands-on centers, one focused on science and the other on history. In the Hands on History Room, reproductions of artifacts give youngsters the chance to examine and use objects that they may have seen in other parts of the museum. They can choose from among the 30 activities, such as a highwheeler bike, trying on a pair of lady's stays or a gentleman's waistcoat, or sending a "message" by telegraph. The room is open noon through 3 P.M. Tuesday through Sunday; weekends get crowded, so try for a weekday. At the Hands On Science Center, kids can do safe, simple experiments—test for dyes and vitamins in different beverages, solve a crime by using DNA fingerprinting techniques, measure radioactivity with a Geiger counter, and use a computer to see how carbon dioxide affects global warming. The Hands on Science Center is open Tuesday through Friday from 12:30 to 5 P.M. and from 10 A.M. to 5 P.M. on weekends. At both hands-on rooms, children must be accompanied by an adult at all times, and free tickets may be required during busy times; ask for them at the information desk.

Other kid favorites at the

Traveling with Toddlers?

The Smithsonian offers the following suggestions for families with young children:

♦ The museums are usually less crowded on the weekdays right after 10 A.M.

♦ Ask Volunteer Information Specialists at the information desks (open 10 A.M. through 4 P.M.) to help you plan your visit. Many of the museums have information geared to children.

♦ Inquire about a highlights tour of each museum; ask for a floor plan and *What's New*, a listing of new exhibits.

♦ Visit the exhibits that the youngest children want to see first, since their attention spans can be short. When traveling with preschoolers, plan to spend no more than an hour in any one museum.

♦ Schedule frequent breaks: Stop at the museum shop. Get an ice cream at the Palm Court in the National Museum of American History. Stroll through one of the gardens (the Enid A. Haupt Garden behind the Castle and the Sculpture Garden next to the National Gallery of Art are good choices).

♦ Take a ride on the carousel across from the Arts and Industries Building.

♦ Visit a Discovery Room or a Hands-on Center.

American History Museum are the television artifacts (on the first floor near the escalator), including Kermit, Howdy Doody, Fonzie's leather jacket, and Edith and Archie's chairs from *All in the Family*. Kids can mail letters with a special-issue museum stamp and a Smithsonian postmark from the reassembled Headsville, West Virginia, country post office, then stop at the Palm Court, a re-creation of a Victorian ice-cream parlor, for a treat. The second floor has the First Ladies' gowns; From Field to Factory, an exhibit about African American migration from 1915 to 1940; and the Star-Spangled Banner lab and exhibit, which details how the tattered flag that flew over Fort McHenry in 1814 will be preserved and stabilized. On the third floor, children will delight in the giant dollhouse (near the escalator) and the ruby slippers worn by Judy Garland when she played Dorothy in *The Wizard of Oz. Constitution Ave., N.W., between 12th and 14th Sts., Washington, D.C.; (202) 357-2700;* http://american history.si.edu *Metro: Federal Triangle.*

National Museum FamilyFun of Natural History
★★★★/Free

Dinosaurs and bugs are beloved by most children—and this museum has lots of both. This is another place that may overwhelm you; let everybody pick his or her exhibit to visit. A particular favorite is the huge stuffed African elephant that dominates the museum's three-story rotunda. His footprint is 24 inches in diameter, only a little smaller than the height of some toddlers. Right next to the Rotunda is the Dinosaur Hall—a must-see for most families. The skeletons are displayed in their natural habitats; the bones of massive airborne reptiles hang from the ceiling.

In the second-floor Insect Zoo, your kids can watch a living bee colony (who can find the queen?), hold a Madagascar hissing cockroach (yuck!), and observe a working ant farm; children must be accompanied by an adult. At the Discovery Center, they can draw pictures of their favorite exhibits, work with microscopes, and handle fossils and arrowheads. Free passes are available at the exhibit door. The kids may be underwhelmed (it looks like colored glass to them), but Mom and Dad will want to see the Hope diamond, the centerpiece of the extensive gem exhibit and the largest blue diamond in the world. The museum also has a very popular IMAX theater (additional fee); get tickets early in the day if you want to see the film. **NOTE:** The National Museum of Natural History is undergoing a major renovation. Many of the dusty dioramas are being changed and updated. During the renovation there are no eating facilities on the premises.

10th St., between Madison Dr. and Constitution Ave., Washington, D.C.; (202) 357-2700; Metro: Federal Triangle or Archives.

National Postal Museum
★★/Free

Located next to Union Station, the National Postal Museum is a must for your young philatelist, although you can probably skip it if your family lacks such a person. Once Washington's main post office, it is now a Smithsonian museum devoted to mail, mail carriers, mail delivery, and stamps. The top floor of the museum is still a working post office, but the atrium has exhibits. If they're interested in mail at all, the kids will be fascinated by the various ways the mail was delivered in the early years of the United States—the mail sleds, stagecoaches, and, of course, the Pony Express. A mail railway car exhibit demonstrates how mail was sorted, delivered, and picked up, while the train barely slowed down at the station. *2 Massachusetts Ave., N.E., Washington, D.C.; (202) 357-2991;* http://web1.si.edu/postal *Metro: Union Station.*

Roosevelt Memorial
★★★★/Free

Washington's newest presidential memorial, which honors Franklin D. Roosevelt, has received mixed reviews from architecture critics. But it is the city's most child-friendly memorial,

A Day of History

8 A.M. Take the Metro to the Capitol South stop and walk to the Supreme Court (see page 319). If possible, let one person stand in line for tickets (and make sure you get them for the three-minute line) while the others go for breakfast at the Supreme Court cafeteria.

11 A.M. On the way to the Capitol, stop at the Library of Congress (see page 309).

Noon Walk to the nearby Capitol Building (see page 304). You might see a TV reporter and crew at work on the east side of the building. Go to the Senate cafeteria for lunch. If you haven't gotten VIP tickets from your Congressional representative, take an early afternoon tour.

2:30 P.M. Walk to Union Station, which is only three blocks from the Capitol (see page 329). By midafternoon, you'll be ready for a little rest. If the weather is warm, take the 90-minute D.C. Ducks tour, otherwise opt for the Old Towne Trolley tour, which also leaves from Union Station (see "Touring Washington," page 335).

5 P.M. Return to Union Station and head to the food court for an early dinner.

ROLLING ON THE RIVER

I T'S EASY to forget that Washington is a river town. The government dominates this city today, but it wasn't always this way. Settlers first came to Georgetown because it was on the Potomac and provided a good port. There are still plenty of river-related activities for families visiting Washington. And an afternoon on the Potomac is a good way to beat Washington's scorching summertime heat.

D.C. Ducks

tours begin with a traditional city tour—a good overview of what Washington has to offer—and then abruptly plunge into the Potomac. Your kids will love riding in the open-air World War II amphibious vehicle. Be prepared to get a little wet. Tours are only given in the warm-weather months and depart from Union Station. *(301) 985-3020.*

Spirit Cruises

offers both lunch and dinner cruises as well as a four-and-a-half-hour trip with a stopover at Mount Vernon, George Washington's estate. Costs vary according to the trip. *All boats leave from Pier 4 at 6th and Water Sts., S.W.; (202) 484-2320.*

Theodore Roosevelt Island,

an 88-acre nature preserve, is in the middle of the Potomac between Washington and Virginia. Named in honor of the great president/naturalist, it offers two and a half miles of trails that afford glimpses at a variety of plants, animals, and birds. Bring a picnic, but also bring bug repellent. You reach the island by a footbridge from the Virginia side of the river (also see page 345 in the Northern Virginia chapter of this book). *Follow the sign from the George Washington Parkway.*

Thompson's Boat Center

rents canoes, kayaks, and rowboats. It's also the boathouse for the area's sizable number of high school and college rowing crews. The students can be seen rowing the long, skinny boats on the Potomac in the morning and the late afternoon. *Thompson's is located at Rock Creek Parkway and Virginia Ave., N.W., next to the Kennedy Center on the Georgetown riverfront. (202) 333-4861.*

The Tidal Basin

is famous for its bounteous display of cherry blossoms in the spring, but your children will love renting a paddleboat for a leisurely spin around its calm waters (see page 329).

perfect for sight-seeing families. Located along the Potomac, the monument consists of four open-air rooms roughly divided by granite blocks. Each room represents one term of the Roosevelt presidency. Inscribed on the walls are quotes from the 32nd president, including, "The only thing we have to fear is fear itself" and "Among American citizens there should be no forgotten men and no forgotten races."

Few kids can resist dipping a toe into the enormous fountains of cascading water that grace each room. They may also like the many life-size statues depicting scenes from the Roosevelt era: a family listening to a fireside chat on the radio; a bread line from the 1930s (you won't be able to resist taking the inevitable photo of the kids standing at the end of the line); a life-size statue of Eleanor in old age, looking like a wonderfully accessible granny (this is the first presidential memorial to include a First Lady); and a larger-than-life seated statue of Roosevelt, with his beloved dog Fala by his side. (The Fala statue is as big as a lion, and his bronze head is already shiny from so much petting.)

Explain to children that polio left Roosevelt unable to walk, but he never appeared in public in his wheelchair. Located on seven and a half acres of land near the Tidal Basin, this memorial is a great place for families looking for space to run around, a hands-on activity, and perhaps even a cooling dip in the fountains. *900 Ohio Dr., S.W., Washington, D.C.; (202) 426-6841; Metro: Smithsonian.*

Supreme Court ★★/Free

The Supreme Court is at the top of most parents' "to do" list and at the bottom of most children's. Adults are fascinated by a firsthand look at the workings of the highest court in the land, but fidgety 6-year-olds and sullen 9-year-olds will be more bored than awed by the majesty of the Court. Luckily, there is a way to keep both generations (relatively) happy. Visitors to the court form two lines: one is for those who wish to observe an entire case, which takes exactly one hour; the other line is for folks who are satisfied with a three-minute glimpse of a session.

Coupled with the half-hour film about the history of the court, the three-minute option should give school-age children some sense of the importance of this judicial body. The court's hearings are open to the public Monday through Wednesday morning; the court is in session from the first Tuesday in October through April.

If the court is not in session, check out the short lecture on the workings of the court that's given every half hour starting at 9:30 A.M. The *Washington Post* lists the days in which the court is in session. **NOTE:** The Supreme Court cafeteria, located in the basement, is open to the public and serves excellent and inexpensive breakfast and lunch fare. Mom and Dad will get a kick out of seeing a Justice lunching with his clerks. *1st St., N.E., Washington, D.C.; (202) 479-3030; Metro: Union Station or Capitol South.*

Vietnam Veterans Memorial
★★★/Free

The design of this memorial has been as controversial as the conflict it represents. When it was first erected, this modern monument, designed by architect Maya Lin, was criticized for looking like a "scar on the earth." To satisfy those who wanted a less abstract memorial, a realistic statue of three battle-weary soldiers was later added nearby. But in the last 20 years, "The Wall"—(its two sides total 500 feet) a slab of reflective black marble on which the names of all of those killed in Vietnam have been carved—has become a national place of healing for veterans and their families. People take rubbings of the names, and leave notes, flowers, and even stuffed animals in remembrance of the dead soldiers. Some one and a half million people come to The Wall annually, making it the most visited of Washington's memorials and monuments.

Kids may find the powerful memorial inexplicable and even disturbing. Explain the purpose of the monument to your children ahead of time and prepare them for the solemn atmosphere and displays of emotion that are common here. Tell them to stay quiet and calm here— this is not a place for running around. For kids who are old enough to understand, this may be the most memorable experience of their visit. *On the Mall, next to the Lincoln Memorial, Washington, D.C.; (202) 426-6841;* www.nps.gov/vive *Metro: Smithsonian.*

Washington Dolls' House and Toy Museum ★★★/$

This museum is away from the Mall, only two blocks from the Maryland border, but it's worth the trip by Metro or car if you have a child who is infatuated with dolls and dollhouses. Tucked into a house, the museum is a carefully constructed collection of antique dolls, other toys, and miniature houses, including a set of Baltimore row houses, a Mexican dollhouse with an elevator and an aviary, and a Victorian Cape May–style hotel. The realism of the small structures is astonishing—telephones ring, lamps light, and elevators go up and down. The dollhouse maker's goal was not only to re-create in miniature, but

The White House has a variety of entertainment facilities on hand for the First Family, including a tennis court, jogging track, swimming pool, movie theater, and bowling alley.

also to preserve a bygone way of life. Although adults may appreciate the museum more fully than kids, youngsters will still get a kick out of the exhibits, which are at a child-friendly height for viewing. Seasonal displays celebrate Christmas, the baseball season, Halloween, and Easter. There are two gift shops, one for dollhouse collectors and the other a consignment shop for antique toys and dolls. There is no restaurant or snack bar on the premises. *5236 44th St., N.W., Washington, D.C.; (202) 363-6400; Metro: Friendship Heights.*

Washington Monument
★★★★/Free

This will probably be one of the first items on your children's "Washington Wish List"—and with good reason. With the possible exception of the Capitol and the White House, the 555-foot-tall monument is the most recognized symbol of the United States in the world. It is also one of the most visited of the national monuments, with 3,000 people each day waiting on long lines to go to the top. The notoriously balky elevator, whose breakdown has marred many visits, was fixed as part of a recent $8 million renovation. But the newly revamped Washington Monument attracts more crowds than ever, so you might want to make it your first stop of the day.

On the weekends you can take the 70-second elevator ride to the observation deck and then take a guided walk down (the guided walk is only conducted on weekends); the walk lets you see the inside of the memorial and its 188 memorial stones, commemorating important people and events in 19th-century America. The long lines are worth it. There is a gift shop in the monument and a snack bar. *On the Mall, 900 Ohio Dr., S.W., Washington, D.C.; (202) 426-6839;* www.nps.gov/wano *Metro: Smithsonian.*

Washington National Cathedral
★★★/Free

You may not want to mention this to your preschooler, but older kids may be interested to hear that this Episcopal cathedral began with a simple bequest by a child who died. According to legend, she left a box with $50 and a note that said, "Build a church on St. Alban's Hill." A century and a half later, one of America's only Gothic cathedrals towers above the Washington skyline. Although your youngsters might not be thrilled at the prospect of touring a church, the cathedral and its grounds are a welcome respite from the bustle of the Mall (although the two are not close together). Make the excursion into a game of "Can You Spot This?" Bring a pair of binoculars and ask your kids to find some of the funniest and most fanciful gargoyles ever carved; dragons, monsters, fierce lions, and even naughty children sticking their tongues out perch high above the nave. Kids may also like the Space Window, commemorating the flight of Apollo XI, which has piece of moon rock in its center.

In the back of the cathedral are statues of Washington and Lincoln with pennies and dimes embedded in the floor near the base. Kids also like the children's chapel; built to half scale, it has intricate kneelers decorated with baby animals and wrought-iron grilles adorned with imaginary beasts. If it's a clear day, take the free elevator ride to the top of the cathedral for an overview of the city. The top of the central tower is the highest point in Washington, 676 feet above sea level. It is a far bet-

DAY TRIP

Washington, D.C., with Older Children

8 A.M. Have **breakfast** in your hotel, then arrive at the Bureau of Engraving and Printing to get tickets for a morning tour. The first tours start at nine, but the tickets are often sold out early.

9 A.M. Tour the **Bureau of Engraving and Printing** (see page 303). The tour is only 20 minutes, but you'll want to stop at the gift shop and buy uncut or shredded money.

10:30 A.M. Walk from the Bureau of Engraving and Printing to the **Holocaust Museum** (see page 306). Entrance into the main exhibits requires tickets, but you'll probably want to limit your visit to Daniel's Story, a sensitive exhibit about the Holocaust designed especially for children, and the Hall of Remembrance, a nearly empty room meant for reflection. Neither requires tickets.

Noon Eat lunch in the Holocaust Museum cafeteria.

2 P.M. Spend the afternoon in the **National Museum of American History** (see page 314).

Evening If you have the energy to do something in the evening, select one of the following:

See the **free concert** on the Millennium Stage at the Kennedy Center (see page 308); performances take place at six each night.

In summer, see **women's professional basketball** at the MCI Center (see page 325).

Take a **tour of the monuments** at night. Old Town Trolley offers moonlight tours (see "Touring Washington" on page 335).

ter—and less crowded—view than the one from the top of the Washington Monument.

Back on the ground, let your kids run around a bit in the open Bishop's Garden while you take in a hilltop view of the city below. The cathedral grounds are the second-best place in the city (after the Mall) to see the fireworks on the Fourth of July. A small donation is requested for a tour. *Massachusetts and Wisconsin Aves., N.W., Washington, D.C.; (202) 537-6200; Metro: Cleveland Park or Tenleytown, both a mile away. The Old Town Trolley and the Gray Line also have stops at the cathedral.*

★ MUST-SEE FamilyFun The White House
★★★★/Free

★ MUST-SEE Parents and older kids will enjoy a visit to this, America's—and possibly the world's—most famous residence. But the long lines and the formal decor and architecture won't do much for the under-10 crowd. You're allowed in the public rooms on the first floor of the White House; the second floor is the First Family's private residence. The tour includes five rooms. The East Room is used for receptions, press conferences, and dances. (Tell your children that Teddy Roosevelt's rambunctious children used to roller-skate in this ornate setting.) The next three rooms are named for the dominant colors in their decor—the Green Room, the Blue Room, and the Red Room, all used for state occasions. The final room on the tour is the State Dining Room, where the president hosts formal dinners. If you take the guided VIP tour (*see below*) on your birthday, you may be invited to sit in the president's chair. (Photography is not allowed in the White House, but the tour guide agent may offer to take a picture using your camera.)

To make your family's White House visit as easy as possible, obtain VIP tickets ahead of time from one of your Congressional representatives. These tickets are free to constituents, but must be ordered as far in advance as possible. Members of Congress are given only a few tickets for each day, and they go quickly, especially for summer visits and from Thanksgiving through Christmas, when the White House is really gussied up for the holidays. VIP ticket holders still have to wait in line, but the line is shorter, and they are guaranteed entry. The VIP ticket also gets you a guided tour by a Secret Service agent. If you don't have VIP tickets, one person in the family can go to the White House visitors' center (*located in the Commerce Building between 14th and 15th Sts., N.W.*) and pick up same-day tickets, which are released at 8 A.M. and are often gone an hour later. With these, you can take a self-guided 25-minute tour. If you time your vacation right, and don't mind crowds, the most popular children's activity at the White House is the annual Easter Egg Roll, held on the White House lawn on the Monday after Easter. The White House is open Tuesday through Saturday. **NOTE:** The White House can be closed for official functions at any time, sometimes without prior notice; when this happens, even those with VIP tickets are out of luck. *1600 Pennsylvania Ave., Washington, D.C.; (202) 456-7041 for tour information;* www.whitehouse.gov *Metro: Metro Center.*

JUST FOR FUN

Georgetown ★★★/Free

Before there was Washington, there was Georgetown. Established in the 1600s as a port town, Georgetown was a quaint village of Federal houses and cobblestone streets that did not become part of the Federal City until the late 1800s. Georgetown still feels like a place apart, and is a nice place to take a break from culture. Kids might not want to spend much time looking at the neighborhood's many boutiques, tony restaurants, and historic homes, but they won't say no to a stop at FAO Schwarz in the Georgetown Park Mall. The store isn't as big as the one in New York, but the selection of toys is still staggering. Kids also enjoy an excursion along the C&O Canal, an

ANNUAL FESTIVALS AND EVENTS

T HE MALL is like a national playground. Many of the events that are held on the grassy expanse between the Capitol and the Washington Monument are especially geared to parents and children. Every four years, **the presidential inauguration** is accompanied by a variety of public events on the Mall and a terrific—but very long—parade down Pennsylvania Avenue. Dress warmly for this one, as temperatures are often well below freezing in late January (the 20th).

One of the most fun events on the Mall is the annual **Smithsonian Kite Festival in March**. The sight of hundreds of kites filling the early spring sky is breathtaking. From late June through the Fourth of July weekend, the Smithsonian hosts the **Festival of American Folklife**, which focuses on the crafts, music, stories, and food of one region in the United

architectural marvel built in 1828 to carry freight from Georgetown to Cumberland, Maryland, and now operated by the National Park Service. You can board a replica of a mule-drawn barge at 30th Street (*202/472-4376*) for a ride through the canal's working locks (there's a small fee). Rangers dressed in period costumes lead the group in song. You may also want to visit the **Old Stone House** (*3051 M St.; 202/426-6851*), reputed to be the oldest house in Washington. Its pleasant garden with fruit trees is a nice change from Georgetown's busy streets. The house, also run by the National Park Service, is open Wednesday through Sunday; there is no charge for admission.

When the troops get hungry, head for Martin's Tavern (see Good Eats). A family-owned place that has been the favorite of the Kennedys and many generations of Georgetown University students, it serves excellent burgers. **NOTE:** Georgetown does not have a Metro stop. Finding parking spaces is very difficult, and even if you find one, there's a two-hour limit for visitors.

MCI Center ★★★/$

The new MCI Center in downtown Washington has brought families back to the center of the city. The 20,000-seat arena hosts the NBA Washington Wizards (now owned and managed by Michael Jordan), the NHL Washington Capitals, the Georgetown University basketball team, and the WNBA Washington Mystics. Among the 200-plus other events held here each year are professional ice-skating shows and a variety of concerts. The best bets for family entertainment include Washington Mystics

States and one foreign country (the places change each year). Stages and tents offer food, dance exhibitions, and demonstrations of skills such as barn building and blacksmithing. For information on this year's festival, call the Smithsonian at (202) 357-2700.

On the **Fourth of July**, America throws a spectacular birthday party on the Mall. Yes, it's crowded, but thanks to the recent ban on alcohol, the crowd is friendly and family-oriented. Some people come just for the fireworks display at nine, but many make a day of it, camping on the Mall, listening to music from several concert venues, and generally enjoying a relaxed party. Ending the year is the **Pageant of Peace** on the Ellipse in December. The centerpiece is the National Christmas Tree, which the president lights every year. It is surrounded by 50 decorated trees, one for each state.

games, which take place during the summer months. Tickets to the professional women's basketball games are inexpensive ($8 and up), and you can buy them at the last minute.

The MCI Center is also home to the National Sports Gallery, where your kids can see such sports memorabilia as Babe Ruth's bat, Magic Johnson's Olympic jersey, and Mario Andretti's helmet. Also within the center is the American Sportscasters Association Hall of Fame; and about

40 interactive sports games. **NOTE:** The games are not included in the $5 admission fee, so if your kids are video-game fans, a visit to the National Sports Gallery can cost you lots of extra time—and chunks of change. *601 F St., N.W., Washington, D.C.; MCI Center: (202) 432-7328; National Sports Gallery: (202) 661-5133; www.mcicenter.com Metro: Gallery Place.*

National Aquarium ★/$

For a child who has seen the spectacular Baltimore Aquarium, just 45 minutes north of Washington, the National Aquarium will be a disappointment. Its 80 tanks house 1,200 freshwater and saltwater creatures, but the displays are uninspired, and the whole museum looks tired. One highlight is the touch tank, where children can get up close and personal with various marine animals. *Department of Commerce Building, 14th St. and Constitution Ave., Washington, D.C.; (202) 482-2826; Metro: Federal Triangle.*

National Gallery of Art Sculpture Garden ice-skating rink
★★★★/Free-$

This new addition to the Mall is a family-pleasing delight. In the winter you can go ice-skating (there's a fee) on a small round rink surrounded by huge modern sculptures. In the warmer months, the rink becomes a majestic fountain,

---

FamilyFun **TIPS**

A Visit to the National Zoo

- Get a preview of your visit through the zoo's Website: www.si.edu/organiza/muse ums/zoo

- Rent or bring a stroller. Even older children tire at the zoo.

- The best time to visit is in the morning. Animals tend to sleep at the hottest time of the day.

- The parking lot gets filled up early, and parking is scarce (and illegal) in the adjacent neighborhoods. Take the Metro.

- Wear comfortable shoes and use sunscreen.

- Set a realistic goal. You may not be able to see the entire zoo in the time you have allotted, so let each child pick the one thing they want to be sure to see.

- Bring a picnic. There are plenty of benches and grassy hills.

and the adjacent Art Nouveau pavilion becomes a café, a welcome respite from the heat of the Mall.

Children are intrigued and amused by the works of art that rim (but do not dominate) the garden. Roy Lichtenstein's House I looks like an almost life-size cartoon home, and Claes Oldenburg's giant typewriter eraser is sheer whimsy (though you may have to explain what a typewriter is). There's a fee for skating and skate rental. *Constitution Ave. N.W., between 7th and 9th Sts., Washington, D.C.; (202) 737-4215;* www.nga.gov *Metro: Archives/Navy Memorial.*

National Zoo
FamilyFun ★★★★/Free

Aside from the attractions on the Mall, this is *the* must-see for families visiting Washington, D.C. Its "biopark" combines natural history, botany, aquariums, and even art. Animals roam in environments that closely resemble their natural habitats. Plan on spending a full day if you want a thorough visit, though the zoo's five miles of winding, hilly paths can wear out small kids. (Single and double strollers are available for rental near the Panda Pavilion.)

Enter the main gates and head for the visitors' center on the left. Pick up a map and review the different walks, each marked by a distinct animal print. Also check the schedule of talks and feeding times on the zoo's map—the animals (like children) are at their most alert and animated when receiv-

ing food and attention.

Unfortunately, the most popular exhibit at the zoo lost its two stars. Ling-Ling and Hsing-Hsing, the pandas given to the United States by China, died; happily, two pandas have taken up residence here in their place.

Otherwise, your must-see list should include the following: the Think Tank features the zoo's innovative orangutan language project. Daily presentations demonstrate the success that trainers have had in teaching these large apes to communicate with humans. The interactive exhibits may get your kids thinking about instinct, thought, and the differences between the orangutans and humans. Check out the orangutans' cousins in the Great Ape House, which has a massive climbing area where the animals exercise.

Youngsters can also see a real dragon here—the zoo has the only Komodo dragons born in the western hemisphere. The huge lizards can grow to six feet in length! Don't miss the elephant-training demonstration in the Elephant House, which also contains giraffes, hippos, rhinoceroses, and pygmy hippos. Kids can also get surprisingly close to the lions

327

and tigers, which are contained by a small, but unbreachable, moat. Most striking are the pure white tigers, which look as if they'd leaped from an illustration in a book of fairy tales. Also fascinating is Amazonia, a simulated rain forest. As they make their way through the wet and humid habitat, your kids can look for poison arrow frogs, giant catfish, and colorful birds, though they must tread slowly and quietly to catch a glimpse of the well-camouflaged creatures.

The cafeteria-style Mane Restaurant is the only full-service restaurant in the zoo. It's open year-round, while the various snack shops are open in the warmer months (spring through fall). Don't miss the Zoo Bookstore in the Education Building near the main entrance, with its excellent selection of natural history books and gifts. **NOTE:** If you take the Metro, get off at the Cleveland Park Station and walk south to the zoo's main gates on Connecticut Avenue (it's half a mile downhill). On the way back, walk (also downhill) to the Woodley Park/Zoo stop. *3001 Connecticut Ave., N.W., Washington, D.C.; (202) 673-4800;* www.fonz.org *Metro: Woodley Park or Cleveland Park.*

Old Post Office ★/Free

Now administered by the National Park Service, the Old Post Office came within a whisker of being torn down. Built in 1899, the 12-story

---

DAY TRIP
The Best of the Smithsonian–East Mall

8:30 A.M. Have a leisurely breakfast at Sherrill's on Capitol Hill. Then take a hike (about a mile) to the National Air and Space Museum or take the Metro from the Capitol South station.

10 A.M. Arrive at the **National Air and Space Museum** (see page 311) as soon as it opens (at ten) and buy tickets for one of the IMAX films. Try to get an early afternnon show. Go across the Mall to the **National Museum of Natural History** (see page 316) to see the Dinosaur Hall and the Insect Zoo.

11:30 A.M. Take a break at either the **National Gallery of Art Sculpture Garden** (see page 326) or on the **Smithsonian Carousel** (see page 329).

Noon Return to the **National Air and Space Museum.** Have lunch before hitting the exhibits and seeing the IMAX show.

4 P.M. Go to the **Enid Haupt Garden** behind the Smithsonian Castle building. It's a peaceful retreat from the Mall and a good place to ask your kids about what has impressed them at the museums.

building was Washington, D.C.'s first "skyscraper"—and is still one of its tallest buildings. A group of preservationist-minded residents rescued it, and now it's been converted into a shopping mall with souvenir shops and fast-food outlets. But for families, the real attraction here is the observation deck, 270 feet above Pennsylvania Avenue. Second only in height to the Washington Monument (and with much shorter lines), it gives you a beautiful overview of the city. Be sure to walk through the clock tower to see the bells. *1100 Pennsylvania Ave., N.W., Washington, D.C.; (202) 289-4224; www.nps.gov.gov/opot/ Metro: Federal Triangle.*

Smithsonian Carousel ★★★★/$

Your kids under 4 may remember nothing about their first trip to Washington except that they rode on this antique carousel (nominal fee), accompanied by cheerful carillon music. It operates year-round, and parents might want to consider it a reward for children who behave well in museums. *On the Mall, near the Smithsonian Castle, Washington, D.C.; Metro: Smithsonian.*

Tidal Basin ★★★/Free

Surrounding the Jefferson Memorial, the Tidal Basin is most famous for its annual display of the blossoms on the Japanese cherry trees. In mid-April (the exact dates depend on the temperature and lots of other unpre-dictable factors), the Tidal Basin is ablaze with pink blossoms from the 600 trees that line the bank of an outpouching of the Potomac.

Many people time their Washington visit to coincide with the blossoming of the trees and the city's Cherry Blossom Festival, but if you're traveling with young kids, think twice before doing so. While the blooms are indeed spectacular, this is the Capital at its most expensive and crowded. Thousands of tourists descend on the footpaths of the Tidal Basin, and the streets are clogged with cherry-blossom-related traffic jams. If you go, wake up everybody at daybreak and cruise through in the very early morning. The Tidal Basin is a nice spot to visit other times of year, too. From April through October, you can rent paddleboats at a concession stand at the Tidal Basin (*202/484-0206*). Children love the pedal-powered excursions, and the park and the Jefferson Memorial look great from the water—even without the cherry blossoms. An easy walk from the Smithsonian museums, the park is also a terrific picnic spot. *Off Independence Ave., Washington, D.C.; Metro: Smithsonian.*

Union Station ★★/Free

Washington's refurbished Union Station is a wonderful reminder of the era of grand railway travel, when a conductor's cry of "all aboard!" started many family vacations. The magnificent marble building boasts huge columns, a vaulted ceiling, and ornate stenciling. It is now the main terminal for Amtrak and commuter lines to Virginia and Maryland. In addition, there are shops on the first and second floors, several full-service restaurants, and a food hall in the lower level that has offerings from almost every country (and something to please the pickiest eater). There's also a nine-screen multiplex cinema.

At Christmastime the station has an extensive miniature-railroad display, with trains chugging through an elaborate landscape complete with cars, houses, and villagers. Any time of year, check out the statue of Christopher Columbus in front of the station; the explorer is flanked by the figures of a European and a Native American, representing Europe and the New World. You pay for parking unless you have a stamped ticket from a shop or the movie theater. Union Station has a 1,400-car parking garage in back; it is also the departure point for Old Town Trolley and D.C. Ducks tours (see "Rolling on the River" on page 318). *Columbus Circle at Massachusetts Ave., N.E., Washington, D.C.; (202) 371-9441; Metro: Union Station.*

BUNKING DOWN

Embassy Square Suites Hotel
★★★★/$$$

All the suites have kitchenettes, making this a good bet for families in town for an extended stay. The property is in the Dupont Circle area, north of the White House, and is

Fun Facts About the Capitol Building

♦ Unlike New York or most other American cities, Washington has no skyscrapers. This is because in the 1890s Congress mandated that no building in the nation's capital could be taller than the seven-story Capitol building. This ensures that the Capitol dome will always dominate Washington's skyline.

♦ The sixth president, John Quincy Adams, suffered a stroke and died in Statuary Hall. A small gold star marks the spot where he fell.

♦ In the early part of the Civil War, the Capitol Building served as a field hospital for soldiers.

♦ About half of the country's state capitol buildings are modeled after the U.S. Capitol.

♦ The statue of Freedom on top of the dome has been hit by lightning many times. She has ten platinum-tipped lightning rods on her shoulders and her headdress.

convenient for sight-seeing. There's also a pool and a restaurant. *2000 N St., N.W., Washington, D.C.; (800) 424-2999; (202) 659-9000.*

Embassy Suites Hotel
★★★★/$$$$

With two-room units that accommodate up to six people, Embassy Suites hotels are very family-friendly. All the suites have kitchenettes, full breakfast is included in the room rate, and there's a pool and a game room for kids. It's also well-situated for your sight-seeing agenda. *1250 22nd St., N.W., Washington, D.C.; (800) 362-277; (202) 857-3388; www. embassysuites.com*

Holiday Inn on the Hill
★★★/$$

You can't beat this hotel's central location. And kids eat here for free! A few days before you go, check out their website for last-minute deals and you may save even more money. *415 New Jersey Avenue Northwest, Washington, D.C.; (202)638-1616; www.holiday-inn.com*

Hotel Harrington ★★/$

The oldest continuously run hotel in Washington, the 250-room Hotel Harrington is clean, comfortable, and not at all fancy; there's a restaurant, but no pool. Its location in the heart of downtown Washington can't be beat. *436 11th St., N.W., Washington, D.C.; (202) 628-8140; www.hotel-harrington.com*

Hotel Lombardy
★★★/$$$

This charming old-fashioned hotel is only three blocks from the White House. There are 127 rooms and 40 suites; most of the rooms have kitchenettes, and there are two restaurants in the building. *2019 I St., N.W., Washington, D.C.; (800) 424-5486; (202) 828-2600.*

Hotel Madera
★★★/$$$

A small simple hotel near Dupont Circle, north of the White House, it has a responsive staff. All suites have kitchenettes, another plus for traveling families. *1310 New Hampshire Ave., N.W., Washington, D.C.; (800) 368-5691; www.kemptongroup.com*

Hyatt Regency Capitol Hill
★★★/$$$

It's a typical Hyatt Regency hotel, with an elegant lobby, a swimming pool, and spacious rooms. Its major benefit is that children under 12 stay free; on the downside, there's not much in the neighborhood, and we don't recommend walking around here after dark. *400 New Jersey Ave., N.W., Washington, D.C.; (800) 233-1234; (202) 737-1234; www.hyatt.com*

Loews L'Enfant Plaza Promenade ★★★★/$$$$

You get a wide range of services at this luxury property. Kids will love the pool; Mom and Dad will appreciate the gym; and everyone will enjoy the family-friendly restaurant. But perhaps its biggest appeal is that it's the hotel closest to the Mall and the Smithsonian, making it easy for families to go back to their room during the day. *480 L'Enfant Plaza, S.W., Washington, D.C.; (800) 23-LOEWS; (202) 484-1000.*

J.W. Marriott
★★★★/$$$$
Near the National Theater and the White House Visitor Center, the Marriott is both convenient and comfortable. Children under 18 stay free. There's a pool and a restaurant. *1331 Pennsylvania Ave., N.W., Washington, D.C.; (800) 228-9290; (202) 393-2000;* www.marriott.com

Omni Shoreham Hotel
★★★★/$$$
This mammoth grande dame has just had an $80-million renovation. Guests in the 800-plus rooms enjoy every amenity, including an outdoor pool and a family-friendly restaurant. Another plus: it's a block from the Woodley Park Metro station and an easy walk to the National Zoo. *2500 Calvert St., N.W., Washington, D.C.; (800) THE-OMNI; (202) 234-0700;* www.omnihotels.com

The River Inn ★★★/$$$
This all-suite hotel (suites have kitchenettes) is in the quiet Foggy Bottom neighborhood between the White House and the Kennedy Center. There's a restaurant. Valet parking is available for a daily fee. *924 25th St., N.W., Washington, D.C.; (800) 424-2741; (202) 337-7600.*

GOOD EATS

Food courts in several of Washington, D.C.'s urban malls offer lots of choices, so if your family can't agree on one cuisine, try a place where each member can get his own. Food courts can be found in **Georgetown Park** (*at M St. and Wisconsin Ave.*), **Union Station** on Capitol Hill (see page 329), **Chevy Chase Pavilion** (*Wisconsin Ave. between Jennifer St. and Military Rd., N.W.*), and the **Old Post Office** (see page 328).

Government cafeterias also provide a varied menu at a very modest cost. There are cafeterias open to the public in the **Supreme Court building** (see page 319), the **Library of Congress** (see page 309), and the **Congressional office buildings** (*Rayburn Building, Independence Ave., between 1st St., S.W. and S. Capitol St.; Longworth Building, Independence Ave. and S. Capitol St.*).

Since the focus of the **National Air and Space Museum** is to preserve aircraft for future generations, planes and spacecraft obtained by the museum are never flown again. Aircraft at the museum are often the last remaining examples of their type.

America ★★★/$$

Something on the 200-item menu of American classics is going to appeal to your finicky eater. It's an easy and inexpensive choice—and the location in Union Station is a crowd pleaser. *50 Massachusetts Ave., N.W., Washington, D.C.; (202) 682-9555.*

Cactus Cantina ★★★/$

Huge portions of Tex-Mex dishes come with reasonable price tags. Children will like watching the tortilla machine as it churns out flat Mexican bread. There's a children's menu. In warm weather, dine on the delightful outdoor patio. *3300 Wisconsin Ave., N.W., Washington, D.C.; (202) 686-7222;* www.center stage.net/bars/cact.html

California Pizza Kitchen ★/$$

It's almost as common as McDonald's, but kids love this place. The specialty pizzas tend toward the trendy, but the good old tomato-and-cheese classics are here, too. *1260 Connecticut Ave., N.W., Washington, D.C.; (202) 331-4020.*

Hard Rock Café ★/$$

Yes, there's one in Washington, too. All-American classics like hamburgers and salads are accompanied by rock-and-roll videos and memorabilia. Your kids will love it. Be prepared to buy the Hard Rock Café Washington, D.C., T-shirt. *999 E St.,* *N.W., Washington, D.C.; (202) 737-7625;* www.hardrock.com

Martin's Tavern ★★★★/$$

The oldest family-owned restaurant in D.C. is in charming Georgetown. Ask to sit in the Dugout, a cozy room lined with sports memorabilia. Breakfast is excellent here, as are the burgers. At Christmas the restaurant is gaudily decorated inside and tied up in a big bow outside. *1264 Wisconsin Ave., N.W., Washington, D.C.; (202) 333-7370.*

Old Ebbitt Grill ★★★/$$

This is a Washington institution and an obligatory stop on many vacation itineraries. Expect crowds, but the burgers, seafood, and steak are worth it. *675 15th St., N.W., Washington, D.C.; (202) 347-4801.*

VACE Delicatessen ★★★/$

Not a restaurant (there's no seating), this Italian deli has the best and most reasonably priced submarine sandwiches and pizza in town. Other delicacies include fresh mozzarella, cold cuts, a variety of olives, and desserts. Take the Metro to Cleveland Park, pick up your picnic lunch here, and then walk to the zoo a half mile away. *3315 Connecticut Ave., N.W., Washington, D.C.; (202) 363-1999.*

The Wright Place ★★/$

Open for lunch only, this food court includes a McDonald's, a Boston

Market, a KFC, and the usual suspects for kids. It gets crowded, so plan to eat early. *On Independence Ave., N.W., between 4th and 7th Sts., Washington, D.C.; (202) 357-2700.*

SOUVENIR HUNTING

Animation Sensations

Here you can buy, if you can afford it, original cartoon art, including sketches and animation cels from famous cartoons. **NOTE:** Animation art is hot now, hence the high prices. *2914 M St., Washington, D.C.; (202) 337-5024.*

Another Universe

The Empire strikes back with comic books, action figures, and other collectibles from *Star Wars.* The intergalactic stock will also tempt your kids with Japanimation and various pop-culture icons. *3060 M St., N.W., Georgetown; (202) 333-8651.*

Chocolate Moose

This store will tickle everyone's funny bone. You'll find T-shirts, jewelry, practical jokes, candy, and, yes, a chocolate moose. Just a few blocks north of the White House, the shop also has hilarious greeting cards and postcards. *1800 M St., N.W., Washington, D.C.; (202) 463-0992.*

Fairy Godmother

This tiny independent book-and-toy store, on Capitol Hill, has unusual treasures, including children's books and tapes in foreign languages. *319 7th St., S.E., Washington, D.C.; (202) 547-5474.*

Made by You

Create a unique souvenir of your visit to Washington. This small shop has ceramic and glass planters, plates, bowls, mugs, and other items that your young artists can paint (ages 5 and older). Ceramic pieces won't be ready for four days and they don't ship, so stick to the glass work. *3413 Connecticut Ave., N.W., Washington, D.C.; (202) 363-9590.*

Political Americana

Only two blocks from the White House, this shop is a must for the American history buff. The store is divided into Republican and Democratic sides, and offers plenty of hats, buttons, T-shirts, mugs, and other items to show off your party affiliation. Even the baby can sport a bib that proclaims "Wee publican." *685 15th St., N.W., Washington, D.C.; (202) 547-1871.*

Tree Top Toys and Books

An independent store, it stocks high-quality toys, books, and videos. There's a wonderful selection of puppets and costumes. *3301 New Mexico Ave., N.W., Washington, D.C.; (202) 244-3500.*

TOURING WASHINGTON

There are many tours of Washington, some more appropriate for children than others. Read on—one is sure to please your crew.

Bike the Sites

runs a three-hour, eight-mile guided cycling tour that includes 55 major sites. The company provides 21-speed hybrid bikes, helmets, water bottles, and a handlebar bag. The tour is on paved paths and gravel trails and is geared to the "occasional" exerciser. Children must be over 9 years old. Guides comment on the history, architecture, and scandals of the nation's capital. Two-hour evening tours are offered during the summer. *(202) 966-8662.*

D.C. Ducks

uses recycled World War II amphibious vehicles—half open-air minibus, half boat—that tour the city streets, then plunge into the Potomac, cross the river to Virginia, and return over Memorial Bridge. It's a continuous 90-minute tour with no stops. Tours depart from Union Station; reservations are required. *(301) 985-3020.*

Gold Line/Gray Line

offers a nine-hour tour of Washington on large, air-conditioned buses. The buses have scheduled stops, but passengers must reboard the same bus. These tours are probably too long and too rigid for families with small children. *(301) 386-8300.*

Old Town Trolley Tours

offers a less inclusive tour of Washington. You can get off at different stops on the tour and reboard a later trolley (they're actually open-air buses), but if you stay on one bus, the loop of the center city takes two hours. The drivers deliver a lively commentary on the D.C. scene. *(301) 985-3020.*

Tourmobile

with its trademark open-air tandem buses, has the most flexible and comprehensive approach. Visitors can board and reboard any bus as many times as they like between 9 A.M.and 4:30 P.M. Twilight tours are also available. Stops are designated with blue-and-white signs. *(202) 554-7950.*

Virginia

BEACHES, MOUNTAINS, meandering rivers, and unparalleled sites from American history combine to make Virginia a vacationer's paradise, but a vacation planner's challenge. Its natural attributes—from the Shenandoah Mountains in the west to the Atlantic beaches in the east—would make the state a mecca for outdoor-oriented families. Then add its abundance of historic places, including Jamestown, the New World's first colony; Colonial Williamsburg; George Washington's home at Mount Vernon; Thomas Jefferson's

Northern Virginia

Fredericksburg and
Civil War Battlefields

Richmond ★

Williamsburg,
Jamestown,
and Yorktown

Western Virginia

Norfolk, Virginia Beach, and the Eastern Shore

Monticello in Charlottesville; Richmond, the capital of the Confederacy; and many of the important battlefields of the Civil War.

In fact, Virginia has too much to cover in a one-week vacation. Fortunately, its geography makes it easy to mix activities. For example, Williamsburg is right next to Busch Gardens Amusement Park; white-water rafting is plentiful not too far from Charlottesville; Virginia Beach is only 15 minutes from Norfolk; Kings Dominion is only half an hour from Fredericksburg.

Plan well, and you can be sure that your kids will remember this as their most awesome vacation ever.

ATTRACTIONS

$	under $5
$$	$5 - $10
$$$	$10 - $20
$$$$	$20 and over

HOTELS/MOTELS/CAMPGROUNDS

$	under $100
$$	$100 - $150
$$$	$150 - $200
$$$$	$200 and over

RESTAURANTS

$	under $5
$$	$10 - $15
$$$	$15 - $25
$$$$	$25 and over

***FAMILYFUN* RATED**

★	Fine
★★	Good
★★★	Very Good
★★★★	*FamilyFun* Recommended

Mount Vernon is a popular half-day detour for many D.C. tourists because of the intimate picture it gives of George Washington's life.

Northern Virginia

JUST MINUTES from Washington, D.C., the numerous attractions of Northern Virginia are a welcome change of pace for families seeking a respite from the monuments and museums of the nation's capital.

Arlington, which looks on a map like a little bite nibbled out of the southwest corner of Washington, D.C., is one of the capital's closest suburbs. But although largely residential, Arlington has several attractions worth a trip across the river to Virginia. Looking back: Arlington National Cemetery is the burial place of a quarter million soldiers, and both John and Robert Kennedy. Looking ahead: the Newseum is a museum of news and newscasters that will delight and educate both school-age kids and parents alike.

Northern Virginia is also the site of George Washington's beloved Mount Vernon. Accessible by car or boat (or bicycle, if you're ambitious), Mount Vernon is notable not only as the home of the nation's first president, but also as a remarkably

THE **FamilyFun** LIST

MUST-SEE
MUST-SEE

Mount Vernon (page 341)

Newseum (page 342)

Old Town Alexandria
(page 344)

Wolf Trap Farm Park
(page 342)

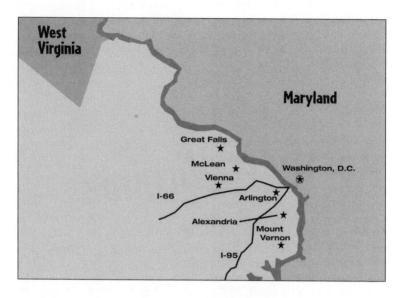

preserved 18th-century plantation.

Between Arlington and Mount Vernon lies the town of Alexandria. Old Town Alexandria, a village founded as a Colonial port in 1749, is a seaport of multicolored 18th-century town houses, brick sidewalks, cafés, and shops. Like Georgetown, Old Town Alexandria predates Washington, D.C. It also retains a flavor of the Old South—some of which can be experienced in the boyhood home of Robert E. Lee, the leader of the Confederate forces.

Other noteworthy Northern Virginia attractions include a colonial farm, an impressive waterfall, and an open-air performing arts center—to name a few. Plan on excursions to a few of these spots to add a bit of variety to your family's "grand tour" of Washington, D.C.

CULTURAL ADVENTURES

Arlington National Cemetery ★★★/Free

A cemetery may seem an odd choice for a family outing, but Arlington is an exception. Children old enough to understand something of Civil War history can appreciate the irony that the land used to bury the Union dead was acquired from the family of a Confederate general, Robert E. Lee. Younger children will simply be awed by the rows and rows of white crosses representing over a quarter-million soldiers who died in American wars—an impressive lesson in the consequences of conflict. Hike up the hill to the eternal flame marking President John F. Kennedy's grave; Jackie is buried beside him, and Senator Robert Kennedy is buried nearby. The view of D.C. from the Kennedy gravesite is breathtaking. Covering the cemetery on foot may be too much for your little kids, but you can hop on the Tourmobile (*202/554-7950*) for a guided tour that stops at various monuments and points of interest. *Directly across Memorial Bridge, Arlington; (703) 697-2131; www.arlingtoncemetery.com*

Mount Vernon
FamilyFun ★★★★/$

George Washington wrote of Mount Vernon, "No estate in United America is more pleasantly situated than this." As you and your kids stand on the porch of Mount Vernon and look down to the Potomac River, it's easy to appreciate Washington's satisfaction with his homestead. Whether you come by boat, Tourmobile, or car, it's about a half-hour trip from Washington, D.C. Get there early, as Mount Vernon draws about 6,000 tourists a day during the summer months.

Walk around the outbuildings first while it's still cool, then take a self-guided tour of the house. Docents in each room can answer questions about the furnishings, the history of Mount Vernon, and the Washington family. Approach Mount Vernon as both the home of a president and an artifact of plantation life, complete with slave quarters. Point out to your children that the kitchen is separate from the house to minimize the spread of any fire that might start from cooking, that Washington was so tall for his time (6 feet 2 inches) that he had to have a specially made bed, and that Washington's slaves were buried communally in unmarked graves with a simple stone memorial.

During the summer months, Mount Vernon has a hands-on History Tent (open from 10 A.M. to 1 P.M.) where children can card and spin wool, try on period clothing, and harness a (fake) mule. Also be sure to stop in the gift shop, which has a nice selection of reproductions of 18th-century children's toys. **NOTE:** A tour of the outbuildings and house should take about three hours, depending on the crowds. The grounds require a lot of walking, so be prepared to hike; it's stroller accessible—lucky toddlers. *George Washington Memorial Pkwy., eight miles south of Alexandria; (703) 780-2000; www.mountvernon.org*

Newseum
FamilyFun ★★★/Free

Across the river from Georgetown, via Key Bridge, is the only museum in the country devoted to broadcast and print news. It's also one of the most successful interactive museums in the area, appealing to both parents and children over the age of 6. You can see artifacts from the history of print, short films capturing some of the most famous moments in televised news, and studios where you can watch broadcasts being done. The Newseum also deals with the ethics of reporting and poses questions to children about what they would do if they were editor of a newspaper. The most popular exhibit is a simulated broadcast studio where your children can be videotaped reading news, sports, or the weather. Available for purchase, the tapes make a fun souvenir. *1101 Wilson Blvd., Arlington; (703) 284-3700*; www.newseum.org

Torpedo Factory Art Center
★★★/Free

During World War II, a mammoth building was constructed at the Old Town Alexandria waterfront to make war materials. After the war, the Torpedo Factory was no longer needed, but rather than tear it down, in the 1970s Alexandria converted it into studios for 150 artists who create pottery, sculpture, fabric art, glass, and musical instruments.

Families can wander around the glassed-in studios and watch the artists at work. Kids find the creation process fascinating, and many of the artists are happy to chat about their work. Most studios are also shops, and you can buy pieces from the artists. Free docent-led tours and self-guided tour brochures help make this spot even more appealing for children 6 and over. Reminders of the factory's original mission include torpedo casings and the industrial shell of an old munitions factory. *105 N. Union St., Old Town Alexandria; (703) 838-4565.*

Wolf Trap Farm Park
FamilyFun ★★★/Free-$$

Pack a picnic, pick an event, and spend an evening at this 117-acre-park, just 20 minutes west of Washington and home to a popular open-air performing arts center. Events range from touring Broadway shows, ballet, and opera to rock, reggae, and zydeco concerts (fees). The main draw is the setting: built on a natural slope, the Filene Center has 3,500 protected seats and another 3,000 on the lawn. A year-round education program, the Wolf Trap Institute for Early Learning Through the Arts, offers classes for preschoolers through adults and preperformance lectures (fees).

The biggest attraction for families is the annual two-day International Children's Festival. Held in mid-

September, it presents songs, dance, costumes, and crafts from around the world. Reservations and tickets are required for all presentations. You can buy a picnic box at Wolf Trap; *call (703) 519-3505. 1551 Trap Rd., Vienna; (703) 255-1900;* www.wolf-trap.org

JUST FOR FUN

Claude Moore
Colonial Farm ★★/$

This authentic pre–Revolutionary War farm offers children an amazing look at a simple Colonial farm family's everyday life. Kids can watch costumed workers do their daily chores—spinning, churning, breaking flax, harvesting—on a farm that has pastures, an orchard, and tobacco fields. In contrast to George Washington's more comfortable Mount Vernon home, this farm has a one-room house. All work is done with reproductions of period tools. Open Wednesday through Sunday, the farm has special events and educational programs for children; call for a schedule. *6310 Georgetown Pike, McLean, about 20 minutes from Washington; (703) 442-7557;* www.nps.gov/gwmp/clmo.htm

Great Falls
National Park ★★★/$

Children may be frightened by the 76-foot Great Falls as the Potomac thunders past them. And their fear

DAY TRIP
Follow in George Washington's Footsteps

8 A.M. Have an early breakfast at the hotel and arrive at **Mount Vernon** (see page 341) as close to the 8 A.M. opening as possible. Spend a leisurely three hours exploring the buildings and grounds.

Noon Drive the eight miles from Mount Vernon to Old Town Alexandria for lunch at the **Food Pavilion** next to the Torpedo Factory (see page 346).

1 P.M. Spend the afternoon in **Old Town Alexandria** (see page 344), sight-seeing or simply strolling.

5 P.M. Stop in at **Gadsby's Tavern Museum** (see page 346) to see where George Washington used to dance.

6 P.M. Have dinner at **Gadsby's Tavern** (see page 346), where the staff dresses in period costume, musicians entertain, and a town crier reads the news of the day.

is justified: every year, people drown when the swift current pulls careless climbers and waders into the torrent. But if you stay clear of the rocks and shallows near the falls, you'll find much to enjoy around these magnificent falls, whose water volume is greater than Niagara Falls (although the drop is not as precipitous).

A hike along the well-marked trails affords spectacular glimpses of the wildlife and seasonal blooms that thrive along the river. A visitors' center has exhibits about the area, and park rangers are eager to answer your kids' questions. **NOTE:** The Great Falls National Park on the Maryland side of the Falls has a different view of the same Falls, as well as of the C&O Canal. *9200 Old Dominion Dr., Great Falls, about 20 minutes from Washington; (703) 285-2965*; www.nps.gov/gwmp/grfa

BILLBOARD POETRY:
Take turns picking out four words from road signs. Give the words to the other players who have one minute to turn the words into a four-line, rhyming poem using one word per line.

GUESS MOBILE:
Name a guessmaster—the person who poses a guessing challenge. He or she could ask passengers to guess the color of the next passing car, or how long before you get to the next town. Or, with three clues, what it is that someone else sees.

Old Town Alexandria
★★★★/Free

Take your family for a trip back in time. Thanks to determined citizens who want to preserve Old Town Alexandria's charm, this place has been spared the sprawl of much of the rest of Virginia. Old Town is not an attraction like Colonial Williamsburg, but a modern town with a well-preserved history. Its main streets, lined with centuries-old redbrick homes, were named before the Revolution and maintain their royal titles—King, Queen, Prince, and Duke Streets. Old Town also has a decidedly Southern feel, perhaps because it was the home of Robert E. Lee. School-age children might be impressed by how close Old Town—a bastion of the Confederacy—was to Washington, D.C., the capitol of the Union.

A variety of historic homes in Old Town include the **boyhood home of Robert E. Lee** (*607 Oronoco St.*); the **Lee-Fendall House and Museum** (*614 Oronoco St.; 703/ 548-1789*), with a large collection of antique dolls and dollhouses; and the **Stabler-Leadbeater Apothecary Shop and Museum** (*105 and 107 S. Fairfax St., 703/836-3713*), which was a drugstore once used by George Washington. (Washington often came from his Mount Vernon plantation to sell his produce at the town market and to socialize in the taverns.)

Among other local attractions is

the Torpedo Factory Art Center (see page 342). Active families may want to bike the excellent trail (11 miles, one way) from Old Town Alexandria to Washington, D.C., which goes along the river past Ronald Reagan Washington National Airport. But you and your children also will enjoy simply walking the town's streets, savoring ice-cream cones, sitting in a café, or strolling near the harbor. *Ten miles south of Washington, D.C.; Metro stop: Alexandria.*

Theodore Roosevelt Island
★★★/Free

Named after the great president and naturalist Teddy Roosevelt, this small island in the Potomac has pleasant hiking trails that lead to a small memorial. Run by the National Park Service, the island's 88 acres shelter a surprising amount of wildlife, including hawks, fox, and ground-hogs. Trails stretch for two and a half miles around the island and are an easy walk, but bring plenty of bug spray. Technically, Roosevelt Island is part of Washington, D.C., but it's only accessible by car from Virginia; from the parking lot, you get to the island by walking across a footbridge. If your family is into canoeing, you can canoe to Roosevelt Island; rent a craft at Thompson's Boat House *(202/333-4861), near the John F. Kennedy Center for the Performing Arts in D.C. George Washington Memorial* Pkwy., *Arlington; (703) 289-2500*; www.nps.gov/this/

BUNKING DOWN

Embassy Suites Hotel
★★★★/$$$

Right across from the Alexandria Metro stop and a few short blocks from the center of Old Town Alexandria, this all-suite hotel is ideal for families, who'll appreciate the full kitchen and separate living room. There's also an outdoor pool, and children under 18 stay free. *1900 Diagonal Rd., Alexandria; (800) EMBASSY; (703) 684-5900*; www.embassysuites.com

Holiday Inn of Old Town
★★★/$$

In the center of Old Town, the 227-room Holiday Inn has an attractive brick facade. You can rent bicycles and hit the indoor pool for some diversion. Children under 18 stay free, and a complimentary continental breakfast is served each morning. Better still, you can bring Kitty or Spot—small pets are welcome. *480 King St., Alexandria; (800) HOLIDAY; (703) 549-6080;* www.basshotels.com/holiday-inn

Key Bridge Marriott
★★★/$$$

Just over the river in Virginia, this 586-room, 12-suite Marriott is within walking distance of George-town and the Newseum and offers wonderful views of Washington, D.C. Children under 12 stay free.

1401 Lee Hwy., Arlington; (800) 228-9290; (703) 524-6400; www.marriott.com

Ritz-Carlton Pentagon City
★★★★/$$$$

This sumptuous choice is located on a Metro line and connected to the Pentagon City Fashion Mall. Among the upscale amenities here are a fitness center, an indoor lap pool, and shuttle service to Ronald Reagan Washington National Airport. But the kids will probably be happier about the adjacent shopping center, which has a food court offering their fast-food favorites. Up to two children can stay in the same room as their parents at no additional charge. *1250 Hayes St., Arlington; (800) 241-3333; (703) 415-5000.*

GOOD EATS

Ben and Jerry's
★★★★/$

There's nothing quite like an ice-cream cone and a stroll along Old Town's waterfront. *103 S. Union St., Alexandria; (703) 684-8866*; www.benjerry.com

The Food Pavilion ★★/$

Located next to the Torpedo Factory Art Center, this collection of ethnic food kiosks is sure to have something that will please every palate. Children will also like the big gumball machine. *5 Cameron St., Alexandria.*

Gadsby's Tavern
★★★★/$$$

The premier tavern of the late-18th century, Gadsby's hosted George Washington's birthday parties in 1798 and 1799. Everything here—the menu, the servers, the decor—still evokes that period; they also try hard to accommodate a child's palate—and the desserts are superb. Children will enjoy the entertainment, usually a fiddle player or a crier who tells the news of the day—a day in the 1700s. A museum on the premises features period furnishings and the ballroom where Washington once danced. *138 N. Royal St., Alexandria; (703) 548-0363.*

Generous George's Positive Pizza and Pasta Place ★★/$

This places offers pizza and pasta in one dish: the Positive Pizza Pie is topped with a mound of spaghetti. The place is noisy and crowded and virtually kid-proof. *3006 Duke St., Alexandria; (703) 370-4303.*

Red Hot & Blue
★★★/$$

Barbecue is standard Southern fare, and this joint has some of the best in the area. Chicken, pulled pig, slaw, and baked beans are menu mainstays; the kids have their own menu. This place is very popular, so try to arrive early. *1600 Wilson Blvd., Arlington; (703) 276-7427.*

South Austin Grill
★★★/$$

One of the best Tex-Mex places in the Washington area serves tasty fajitas, burritos, chili, and other classics in a casual, colorful dining room with huge copper animal sculptures. No fewer than three salsas are set on each table, and there's a menu featuring the usual kid-friendly suspects. *801 King St., Alexandria; (703) 684-8969.*

SOUVENIR HUNTING

A Likely Story
Children's Bookstore

This shop is a treasure trove of children's books; there also are tapes, puppets, puzzles, and games as well, and parenting and foreign-language tomes are also stocked. *1555 King St., Alexandria; (703) 836-2498.*

The Disney Store

Located in the Pentagon City Mall, this is a feast of all that's Disney: stuffed animals, videos, jewelry, costumes, and games. A big screen plays scenes from famous Disney cartoons and may distract young buyers (fleetingly) from their shopping spree. *1100 S. Hayes St., Arlington; (703) 418-0310;* www.disney.com

One Two Kangaroo Toys

The specialty here is educational toys for children of any age. Brio, Thomas the Tank Engine, and Playmobil top the charts. *4022 28th St. S., Arlington (off the Shirlington exit of I-395); (703) 845-9099.*

George Washington: Fact and Fiction

Children who have learned about the first president in school might be interested to learn that the two most popular stories about George Washington are probably more grounded in myth than reality.

The anecdote about George chopping down his father's cherry tree? Most historians believe that the story has been exaggerated over the years. It is thought perhaps that young George may have struck the tree with his ax a few times (called barking), but did not actually chop it down.

The story that Washington threw a silver coin across the Potomac River? Unlikely. First of all, currency was very rare when George was a boy; tobacco certificates were traded. Secondly, historians say George would never have wasted any money he was fortunate enough to have earned. It is possible that George and his cousin were tossing stones across the Rappahannock River, near his home in Fredericksburg, when one landed on the other side. If you visit George's childhood home in Fredericksburg (see Ferry Farm on page 351), see if anyone in your family can throw a stone across the river.

If you're lucky, you may see foxes and beavers wandering through the many trees and wildflowers at Ferry Farm, George Washington's childhood home.

Fredericksburg and Civil War Battlefields

REDERICKSBURG sits halfway between Washington, D.C., and Richmond, Virginia. Lacking the glitz of its larger neighbors, the city is in some ways the forgotten middle child of this tourist region. But Fredericksburg, happily, is also free of the problems inherent to a major metropolis; instead, this gracious town offers a respite for travelers. Families visiting Fredericksburg will find a quaint 40-block historic district graced with more than 350 buildings dating back to the 18th and 19th centuries. A stroll down these pear-tree-lined streets conjures vivid images of the area's rich history—from Colonial times through the Civil War. In fact, it would not be unusual to pass a tavern waitress dressed in a period frock on her way to work or a gentleman in soldier's garb reenacting times passed.

THE FamilyFun LIST
MUST-SEE · MUST-SEE

The Battlefields (page 350)

Ferry Farm (page 351)

Hugh Mercer Apothecary Shop (page 352)

Kenmore Plantation (page 352)

Rising Sun Tavern (page 353)

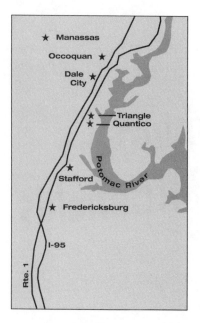

Museums, antiques shops, monuments, and restored homes add substance to the charm of this Southern-paced community. Preserving history is a top priority here. The four battlefields surrounding the city look much as they did when Confederate and Union soldiers fought upon them. For a peek into our country's more recent past, families can pop into a 1950s-style pharmacy, where an old-fashioned soda fountain still serves up the town's best milk shakes (see Good Eats). Movie theaters, department and chain stores, and large entertainment venues have been carefully placed so as not to disturb Fredericksburg's historic appeal.

Several of the town's parks offer shade in the summertime—when Fredericksburg (and indeed, the entire region) can be very humid—and plush grass on which to picnic. George Washington, James Monroe, and Thomas Jefferson, each of whom lived in or visited Fredericksburg, likely trod the same pathways and got their toes wet in the Rappahannock River, which surrounds the city. In season, the river now attracts a host of fun seekers—fishing, swimming, tubing, canoeing, kayaking, and generally staying cool. You and your children, no doubt, will want to join them.

CULTURAL ADVENTURES

The Battlefields
FamilyFun ★★★★/Free

Although their place in history is well established, the four area battlefields are places best visited with older children with an interest in history. The battlefields—Fredericksburg, Chancellorsville, Wilderness, and Spotsylvania—were sites of some of the bloodiest engagements of the Civil War. On these grounds, more than 100,000 men were wounded, killed, or captured. In December 1862, Confederate General Robert E. Lee overtook Union General Ambrose E. Burnside in Fredericksburg. The following spring, Confederate General

Stonewall Jackson assisted Lee in Chancellorsville, where the two Confederate factions beat General Joseph Hooker's Union troops.

Although they won the battle, the Confederates also suffered a devastating casualty, when Stonewall was accidentally shot by his own men and subsequently died of pneumonia. In May 1864, the two sides collided at Wilderness, where Lee and Union General Ulysses S. Grant battled to a draw. That same month, the armies fought again at Spotsylvania Court House. Park historians lead tours on a seasonal basis (spring, summer, fall) from the Spotsylvania or Fredericksburg visitors' center; at other times, tours are self-guided (fee for audio tape). *Fredericksburg/Spotsylvania National Military Park, 120 Chatham La., Fredericksburg; (540) 373-6122; (540) 786-2880.*

Following her service during the Civil War, Clara Barton went on to found the **American Red Cross** in 1881.

Belmont ★★/$

The guides at the former home of American portrait painter Gari Melchers are friendly and spend at least part of the tour speaking directly to the children present. If you choose to tour on your own, keep the kids interested by having them search the rooms for objects that appear in Melchers's paintings. *224 Washington St., Fredericksburg; (540) 654-1015.*

Chatham ★/Free

Owned and operated by the National Park Service, this Georgian-style mansion should be the jumping-off point for your tour of Civil War battlefields. It was used as a Union headquarters during the Battle of Fredericksburg; your would-be nurses will be interested to hear that Clara Barton had the challenging task of stabilizing the condition of many wounded soldiers here. Admission includes a seven-day park pass to the four area battlefields. *120 Chatham La., Fredericksburg; (540) 371-0802.*

Ferry Farm ★★★★/$

MUST-SEE
FamilyFun
MUST-SEE

George Washington was only 6 years old when his family moved to Ferry Farm. Although none of the property's current structures belonged to the Washingtons, archaeological digs are continually recovering family artifacts. The visitors' center contains information about the family and fragments of some possessions. Behind the center, a Children's Garden is being cultivated to grow a variety of 18th-century crops. Take a walk down to the river and see if your child can throw a stone to the other side (see "George Washington: Fact and Fiction," page 347). *268 Kings Hwy., outside of Fredericksburg in the county of Stafford; (540) 370-0732.*

Fredericksburg Area Museum and Cultural Center ★★/$

Originally the town hall, this museum covers area history from the 18th to the 20th centuries, including rotating exhibits on the first and third floors. A number of interactive exhibits geared to children cover topics like fossils, the Civil War, and 19th-century life. *907 Princess Anne St., Fredericksburg; (540) 371-3037.*

MUST-SEE FamilyFun MUST-SEE Hugh Mercer Apothecary Shop ★★★★/$

Once your children finish ogling the leeches in a jar at this 18th-century pharmacy, a living-history interpreter will regale them with stories of how the slimy critters were used in Colonial times. Yucky descriptions of early amputations and bleeding methods (enter the leeches) will help your kids appreciate the practices of their own family doctor.

Visitors also learn how Dr. Hugh Mercer used herbs and remedies to treat such Colonial maladies as colds, stomach upset, and sleeping problems. As you take the self-guided tour upstairs, see if your child can figure out why one of the doors has a round opening in it. (Answer: before leaving, patients would stick their heads through it so slaves could attend to their wigs.) *1020 Caroline St., Fredericksburg; (540) 373-3362; www.apva.org/apva/hugh.html*

James Monroe Museum ★★/$

School-age children learning about U. S. presidents may be interested in this small museum, which is on the site of James Monroe's first law office. In a back room, a display containing books, games, and trivia questions is set up for youngsters. *908 Charles St., Fredericksburg; (540) 654-1043;* http://jamesmonroe museum.mwc.edu/

MUST-SEE FamilyFun MUST-SEE Kenmore Plantation ★★★★/$

This home once belonged to George Washington's only sister, Betty, and her husband, Fielding Lewis. The house then became a hospital, in which more than 100 Union soldiers died. Today, evidence of cannonball damage to the building is obvious inside and out (see which family member can spot the holes first). The house is best toured when George Washington's Fredericksburg Foundation is hosting one of its hour-and-a-half-long Discovery Workshops for children. The workshops bring history to life through archaeological digs, Colonial games, and other activities. Complimentary tea and ginger cookies are included. *1201 Washington Ave., Fredericksburg; (540) 373-3381.*

Mary Washington House ★★/$

Built by George Washington in 1772 for his mother, Mary Ball Washington, this house is one place that grown-ups will like more than children do. But with a little effort young visitors can be kept interested and entertained, too. Challenge your kids to spot the animals carved into the furniture, to find the chamber pots, and to look for a rattrap in the kitchen. Behind the house, see if they can tell time on the sundial. *1200 Charles St., Fredericksburg; (540) 373-1569; www.apva. org/apva/mwash.html*

Rising Sun Tavern
MUST-SEE FamilyFun ★★★★/$ MUST-SEE

George Washington's youngest brother, Charles, built his home in Fredericksburg in 1760, when the town was the tenth-largest port in the colonies. In a later incarnation it became a "high" tavern, from which ladies could leave with their reputations intact. Today, this living museum has costumed "wenches" who pretend your family has just arrived by coach and plans to spend the night. Kids will be highly amused when the rules of the tavern are explained (women and men sleep in separate rooms; gentlemen eat in separate quarters from commoners). *1304 Caroline St., Fredericksburg; (540) 371-1494.*

Offbeat Touring

Looking to add a little spice to your sight-seeing? Try seeing Fredericksburg on a tour with a twist.

Fredericksburg Carriage Tours
Get a quick overview of Fredericksburg and its history in an appropriately old-fashioned way—while riding in a horse-drawn carriage. The tours, offered Monday through Friday, are a comfortable 45 minutes long. *(540) 654-5511.*

Friends of the Rappahannock
Ecotours are all the rage, and this one doesn't disappoint. Older children will be thrilled at the chance to explore the river by canoe. From March through October, you can also take half-day tours with an interpretive guide. Life jackets are provided, but all participants must be able to swim. *(540) 373-3448.*

Living History Company
The one-hour Phantoms of Fredericksburg tour will please big kids, as storytellers spin tales under the shadow of moonlight. (It all might be a bit too spooky for tiny tots.) Bring your camera and try to catch a ghost in action—we dare you! *(540) 899-1776.*

Trolley Tours of Fredericksburg
If your group is too big to fit into a carriage, try the trolley, another way to get the feel of yesteryear. You can take the 75-minute tour daily April through November. *(540) 898-0737.*

BUNKING DOWN

Hampton Inn Fredericksburg
★★/$$

Within minutes of the historic district, this economy-minded, 166-room property helps families cut costs by including complimentary continental breakfast in its rates. Another money-saver: children 17 and under stay free with a paying adult. Kids will like splashing in the outdoor pool. *2310 William St., Fredericksburg; (800) 426-7866; (540) 371-0330;* www.hampton-inn.com

Holiday Inn Select ★★★/$$$

Located in Central Park, this property has undergone a $6 million renovation, updating the 194 rooms. Each is now equipped with a Nintendo game, among other amenities. The property also offers an outdoor pool and two restaurants with children's menus. Kids under 18 stay and eat free when accompanied by a paying adult. *2801 Plank Rd., Fredericksburg; (800) 682-1049; (540) 786-8321;* www.basshotels.com/holiday-inn/

GOOD EATS

Carl's ★★★★/$

Even during thunderstorms, there's a line in front of this popular ice-cream stand. Kids love to watch the creamy custard—in your choice of chocolate, vanilla, or strawberry—as it slides down a silver chute and into a cup or a cone. The wait, which is rarely more than a half hour, will be the best spent of your visit. The stand is open from February through November. *2200 Princess Anne St., Fredericksburg. No phone.*

Goolrick's Drug ★★/$

This is the pharmacy of choice for locals suffering from milk shake cravings. The selection of seven flavors includes the usual vanilla, chocolate, and strawberry, plus cherry, mocha, root beer, and coffee. Promise the kids one of these sweet treats, and you may be able to squeeze one more historic tour into your day. *901 Caroline St., Fredericksburg; (540) 373-9879.*

Spanky's ★★★/$$

Grab one of the town's best sandwiches here; service is slow, so arrive before hunger strikes, then let your children explore the hundreds of odd items and photographs clogging every inch of this place. Children's options include grilled cheese and pizza. *917 Caroline St., Fredericksburg; (540) 372-9999.*

Tia's Tex-Mex ★★★/$$$

This chain restaurant, which serves fresh Mexican-style dishes, pleases young guests by handing them a hunk of tortilla dough to play with in addition to the usual crayons and coloring mats; or take the kids to the observation window in the back, where they can watch the cooks make tortillas. Ask to be seated on the patio during warmer months. *2931 Plank Rd., Fredericksburg; (540) 785-4487.*

Virginia Deli ★★★/$$

If your children are in the midst of an American history meltdown, treat them to a picnic instead of eating in a restaurant. Place your sandwich order here and head for a nearby park. *101 William St., Fredericksburg; (540) 371-2233.*

SOUVENIR HUNTING

Downtown

Nearly 40 antiques shops can be found on ten streets in the historic district, with the lion's share located on Caroline, Sophia, and William Streets. Many are stocked with old toys, games, and dolls that the kids will like, but beware that glassware and fine china may be stacked just inches away. Pick up a guide to these storehouses of the past at the Fredericksburg Visitors Center. *706 Caroline St., Fredericksburg; (540) 373-1776.*

It's Time to Play!

When everyone has had their fill of sight-seeing, hop in the car and head beyond **Fredericksburg**'s historic district for more active diversions.

Much of the city's recent development has been confined to an area known as Central Park on Route 3, a few miles from the historic district. There you'll find places perfect for a few hours of cut-loose activity.

Up the road apiece, the **Cavalier Family Skating Center** (*1924 Jefferson Davis Hwy., Stafford; 540/657-0758*) has a family roller-skating session on Sunday afternoon.

Fredericksburg Ice Park (*540/786-0809*) has year-round ice skating. **Fun Land** (*540/785-6700*) offers rock-wall climbing, laser tag, bumper cars and boats, go-carts, miniature golf, and video games—along with a massive complex of tubes for children to crawl through, climb over, and slide down. Even kids over 5 will find this one challenging. The play area for toddlers has a pretend grocery store and office, Moon Bounce, and ball pit.

And, for another kind of play, **The Riverside Center Dinner Theater** (*95 Riverside Pkwy., Fredericksburg; 540/370-4300*), a few blocks off Route 17, stages a Children's Lunch 'n' Show Theater every Saturday. Showtime is at 1 P.M. from June through August and at 11 A.M. the rest of the year.

Jabberwocky

If your child likes to read or be read to, stop by this bookstore brimming with the best titles for youngsters. Everything sold here is handpicked by the owners, including an assortment of toys, puzzles, and games with either educational or developmental merit. *810 Caroline St., Fredericksburg; (540) 371-5684.*

Occoquan

More than 140 stores line this town's historic district and riverfront. Browse the duplex shopping center on Mill Street, which houses crafts, specialty, and gift shops. Then walk across the footbridge to even more shops. *From Fredericksburg, take I-95 North to Occoquan/Rte. 123, exit 160; (703) 491-4045.*

Potomac Mills

More than 220 outlets and stores are divided into nine neighborhoods at this massive mall. Young children will be drawn to the Lego and Disney Catalog outlets as well as Toy Liquidators. The megamall also boasts a movie theater, arcade, and indoor arena for in-line skating and skateboarding. *From Fredericksburg, take I-95 North to Dale City, exit 156; (703) 643-1770.*

Quilts 'n' Treasures

This store is brimming with names like Brio, Playmobil, and LGB. The toys are top-notch—and so are their price tags. Consider giving children a spending limit before going in. *721 Caroline St., Fredericksburg; (540) 371-8166.*

Rocking Horse Gallery Inc.

Although clear visions of rocking horses fill your head, this store is actually filled with teddy bears, from the kind your kid can drag around the playground to the expensive collector's breed. *803 Caroline St., Fredericksburg; (540) 371-1894.*

REWARD GOOD BACKSEAT BEHAVIOR

Backseat squabbles were a big problem for the Niehues family of Red Wing, Minnesota, on long car trips. "Four kids can find a lot to fight about!" says mom Mary. Now, though, Mom and Dad give each of the kids a roll of quarters at the beginning of the trip. Every time they have to correct a child's behavior, the culprit forfeits a quarter. But any quarters still remaining at the trip's end are the child's to keep.

Manassas and More

JUST AN HOUR NORTH of Fredericksburg, Manassas shares a rich history and cultural heritage. **NOTE:** This outing is best appreciated by kids 9 and older; little ones will be b-o-r-e-d!

8:30 A.M. Arrive at the **Manassas Battlefield Visitor Center** (*6511 Sudley; 703/361-1339*) and pick up a map for the driving tour, which takes approximately two hours, as well as directions to the downtown area. Watch the 13-minute slide show that covers both battles; explore the grounds where they actually occurred and then drive to the Stone Bridge.

11 A.M. Head south for about five miles to the downtown area for lunch. Try either the **City Tavern Grille** (*9405 Main St.; 703/330-0076*) or **Okra's Louisiana Bistro** (*9110 Center St.; 703/330-2729*). Before leaving the downtown area, stop by the **Whimsical Gallery** (*9700 Center St.; 703/369-3400*); they have crazy hats, stuffed animals, puzzles, diaries, gel pens, and more.

1 P.M. Go to the **Manassas Museum** (*9101 Prince William St.; 703/368-1873*), which covers the history of the Piedmont region. Your school-age kids will be fascinated by the exhibits detailing daily life from the perspectives of a slave, a wealthy child, and a soldier (the gift shop sells boy and girl cloth dolls representing these personalities).

2:30 P.M. Choose one of the following sites, depending on when you're in town. The **Manassas Volunteer Fire Company Museum** (*9322 Centreville Rd.; 703/368-6211*) has antique equipment and is open Sunday only, April through October. The **Freedom Museum** (*10400 Terminal Rd.; 703/393-0660*) pays tribute to those who have fought wars in the name of freedom and is open Monday through Saturday year-round. The open-air **Manassas Industrial School/Jennie Dean Memorial** (*Wellington Rd.; 703/368-1873*), open daily, employs a kiosk and plaques to chronicle the founding of a Northern Virginia school for African Americans.

3:30 P.M. From Manassas, take I-95 South to Triangle, exit 150. Follow signs to the **Quantico Marine Corps Base.** Ask the soldier on duty at the gate for directions to the **Marine Corps Air-Ground Museum** (*703/784-2606; closed Monday*), where two hangars are filled with aircraft and armored vehicles from pre-World War II through Korea. The massive machinery will awe girls and boys alike.

Kid activities in Richmond include hundreds of hands-on exhibits at the Science Museum of Virginia.

Richmond

RICHMOND is defined by both its geography and history. Packed into only 62 square miles, it is a relatively compact city. In fact, in just two or three days your family will probably feel right at home in this commonwealth capital.

To the south, Richmond is bordered by the James River, which, in part, was responsible for the city's early prosperity. Before his presidency, George Washington was instrumental in developing a canal system from the river through the city. The canal fostered the shipping of tobacco, cotton, coal, and ore (see "Cruising Along" on page 365). Soon after, warehouses, taverns, and banks sprang up.

Today, you can visit some of those same riverside buildings in their new incarnations as modern

THE **FamilyFun** LIST

MUST-SEE MUST-SEE

Children's Museum of Richmond
(page 360)

Maymont (page 361)

Meadow Farm Museum
(page 361)

Metro Richmond Zoo
(page 364)

Science Museum of Virginia
(page 363)

Shockoe Slip and Shockoe
Bottom (page 367)

Virginia Historical Society and
Museum (page 363)

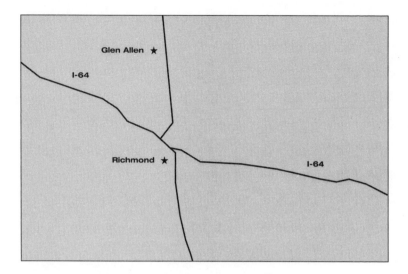

restaurants, shops, and tourist attractions. Unfortunately, many of Richmond's original structures were burned down during two devastating fires. The first occurred during the Revolutionary War, when Benedict Arnold ransacked the city. Confederate soldiers set the second fire; sensing defeat at the end of the Civil War, they torched much of the land in an effort to keep Union soldiers from gathering more provisions.

As your family tours this richly historic area, encourage your children to think about what it really must have been like to live in those times. Discuss what the city might have been like 100 or 200 years ago. Many of Richmond's museums are interactive, so your kids can also get a feel for our nation's early history.

CULTURAL ADVENTURES

Children's Museum of Richmond
★★★★/$

A real kid pleaser, this 42,000-square-foot learning center has something for everyone, from babies to preteens. Kids can run through an oversized mouth and crawl through a stomach in the exhibit on the digestive system; visit a pretend grocery store and apple orchard; explore a thrillingly dank, dark cave; and observe a stream bed with running water. They can also see solar-powered equipment, try the hands-on technology, and create something in the art studio. Toddlers have their own tot-size play area, too. Kids get

a kick out of standing between the silver disks outside and whispering secrets to people standing several feet away. *2626 W. Broad St., Richmond; (877) 295-2667; (804) 474-2667; www.c-mor.org*

Edgar Allan Poe Museum ★★/$

Older kids who have studied "The Raven" in school will find this museum intriguing. Although Poe never lived in this house, which is the oldest standing building in Richmond, it is thought that he lived nearby. Literature lovers will probably recognize the Enchanted Garden, which is modeled after Poe's poem "To One in Paradise." The tour guides know a lot about Poe's life, and you can see some of his possessions on display. *1914 E. Main St., Richmond; (888) 213-2763; (804) 648-5523.*

★MUST-SEE★ Maymont
FamilyFun ★★★★/Free (donations suggested)

Some places are designed for adults, others for children. Maymont defies the norm by presenting, in a clean and friendly manner, pleasures for both. Parents will enjoy a quick tour of the 33-room Romanesque Revival–style home and a stroll through nearby herb and botanical gardens. The kids will head for the numerous outdoor animal habitats, where black bears, bobcats, foxes, and bison live. Other popular attractions include the aviary; the Nature and visitors' center, with 13 aquariums, two playful river otters, and a 20-foot waterfall. The younger ones will go for the Children's Farm, where between noon and 3 P.M. they can feed donkeys, goats, and sheep. Children also enjoy the garden—its flat stepping-stones allow them to hop their way over to a long and narrow island. Best of all, you don't have to worry about tired toddlers: Five and a half miles of stroller-accessible walking paths connect all of these treasures. *2201 Shields Lake Dr., Richmond; (804) 358-7166; www.maymont.org*

When it was built in the late 1800s, **Maymont** included some amazing modern conveniences, including an elevator, electric lights, and central heat.

★MUST-SEE★ Meadow Farm
FamilyFun Museum ★★★★/Free

On selected weekends, your family can visit the past here, as interpreters reenact middle-class farm life as it was in the 1860s. Depending on the weekend, the kids may get to watch demonstrations of sheep shearing, open-hearth cooking, gardening, needleworking, and candle dipping. If you visit when no special program is scheduled, you can still tour the farmhouse, which was once owned by a doctor and his family. Children enjoy walking by the pens that hold chickens, turkeys, pigs, cows, horses, and

sheep. *3400 Mountain Rd., Glen Allen; (804) 501-5520.*

St. John's Episcopal Church ★★/$

Stop here if you have some real history buffs in the family. The short tour of this 18th-century church will reveal tricks used by past parishioners to keep warm (fire-heated coal or bricks) and a time line of the revolutionary Patrick Henry's life. At 2 P.M. on Sundays in the summertime, a reenactor delivers Henry's famous "Give Me Liberty or Give Me Death" speech, delivered in 1775. A map of the church cemetery shows where Elizabeth Arnold Poe, Edgar Allan's mom, is buried. *2401 E. Broad St., Richmond; (804) 648-5015; www. historicstjohnschurch.org*

DAY TRIP
A Paramount Adventure

LESS THAN a half hour from Richmond, **Paramount's Kings Dominion** (PKD) will win kudos from kids and parents alike. The 400-acre theme park features more than 200 rides, shows, and attractions.

Unlike most amusement parks, this family entertainment venue has intelligently placed all of its preschool attractions close together. Result: no long walks with whiny, tired children. Theme areas for little ones include KidZville, with more than a dozen rides and a massive play area; Nickelodeon Splat City, where pipes sputter green slime; and Nickelodeon Central, with characters and scenes from *Rugrats, Blue's Clues,* and *CatDog.* There's even an air-conditioned diaper-changing/nursing facility. A little-tykes water park has a very shallow pool with mushroom-shaped fountains and five Lilliputian-size water slides. Older thrill seekers will be wowed by the park's ten roller coasters, including the world's fastest suspended coaster and the world's only looping coaster with an underwater tunnel.

Beyond what's in the park, PKD has a 16-acre WaterWorks park, which opens when the weather heats up. They recently added four enclosed water slides, one of which is the world's tallest, fastest, darkest, and totally enclosed free-fall slide. Awesome! Other splashy highlights are a 650,000-gallon wave pool, a play area with more than 50 interactive water features, and two inner-tube rides. Open daily Memorial Day through Labor Day; weekends only April through May and Labor Day through early October. *From Richmond, take I-95 North 30 miles to Doswell, exit 98; (804) 876-5000;* www.kingsdominion.com

Science Museum of Virginia ★★★★/$

MUST-SEE FamilyFun MUST-SEE

The signs should say PLEASE TOUCH here. Your kids get to fool around with more than 300 hands-on exhibits, complemented by demonstrations and special events, at this very touchable museum. Subjects include aerospace, computers, crystals, electricity, illusions, chemistry, physics, and life sciences. You can see a planetarium show, too, for no extra fee. A best-value pass also includes an IMAX movie; among the films that have been screened here are *Michael Jordan: To the Max* and *Dolphins and Amazing Journeys. 2500 W. Broad St., Richmond; (800) 659-1727; (804) 864-1400.*

Virginia Aviation Museum ★★/$$

It's a bird, it's a plane. . . . This aviation showcase will wow children who have never seen a grounded airplane. (Some will be surprised to learn that they're a whole lot bigger than they look when they fly by in the sky.) More than 20 historic aircraft are on display, including an SR-71 Blackbird and a World War I SPAD VII. Call ahead to find out whether a special 20-minute children's tour and storytime is being offered. *5701 Huntsman Rd., Richmond; (804) 236-3622;* www.smv.org/wavmhome.html

Virginia Historical Society and Museum ★★★★/$

MUST-SEE FamilyFun MUST-SEE

Kids and their parents will learn more about Virginia and the nation it helped shape at this museum, set in an 1825 building. After you view the 12-minute video presentation, pick up the complimentary phonelike audiotape players at the front desk so your children can hear fascinating details as they walk through selected exhibits. Kids will especially like the Conestoga wagon, one of Richmond's first electric streetcars, a 1950s-style television set with rabbit ears, a canoe carved from a log, spears, and a dollhouse-size model of the historic Wilton House. With plenty of drawers to open and close, buttons to push, and Colonial clothes to try on, we guarantee your youngsters won't get bored. Before leaving, your budding historians can challenge themselves with a computer quiz. *428 North Blvd., Richmond; (804) 358-4901.*

JUST FOR FUN

Lewis Ginter Botanical Garden ★★★/$

Unlike many botanical gardens, this colorful fiesta is open year-round to display its many textures and

A Child's Dream Day

8:30 A.M. Have breakfast at the River City Diner (see page 366). Give each child a handful of quarters for the tableside jukebox.

9:30 A.M. Spend two hours at either the **Science Museum of Virginia** (see page 363) or the **Children's Museum of Richmond** (see page 360). Purchase tickets for a planetarium or IMAX show at the Science Museum for later in the day.

11:30 A.M. Head to either **Shockoe Slip or Bottom** (see page 367) and have lunch at one of the eateries.

1 P.M. Take a canal cruise or a walk along the floodwall (see "Cruising Along" on page 365).

2 P.M. Let the youngest child in your family pick the next destination. Options can include **Maymont** (stop at the Children's Farm area first, then visit the bears and other creatures; see page 361); **Meadow Farm** (skip the house tour; see page 361); **Metro Richmond Zoo** (don't forget the animal feed; this page); and **Three Lakes Nature Center** (watch the fish, then hit the playground; this page).

5 P.M. Grab a fast-food dinner on your way to the **planetarium** or **IMAX show**.

shapes. The kids will keep busy with a seasonal scavenger hunt as they search for rabbits, turtles, and ducks, while you pause to appreciate the foliage; regardless of when you visit, get the brochures at the visitors' center—they offer suggestions for walks. The koi ponds are favored by youngsters, too.

At the Children's Tropical Greenhouse, kids get a lesson in practical science with exhibits that match plants to the everyday products—such as dish soap and shampoo—that they are used to make. *1800 Lakeside Ave., Richmond; (804) 262-9887; www.lewisginter.org*

Metro Richmond Zoo
FamilyFun ★★★/$

MUST-SEE · MUST-SEE

Have you ever hand-fed a giraffe? What about a camel or a llama? This 35-acre zoo is no ordinary animals-behind-bars type of place. A few of the 400 animals that live here are in cages, but many are within reach—either behind fences or wandering freely. Be sure to buy some of the animal feed (25 cents a handful, $2 per cup). There's a concession stand and a gift shop. Open year-round. *8300 Beaver Bridge Rd., about a half hour southwest of Richmond; (804) 739-5666.*

Three Lakes Nature Center
★★★/Free

Look, listen, and explore are the words for this nature-oriented fantasyland. A 50,000-gallon aquarium gives a kids'-eye view of fish that live in the park's three man-made lakes. Chalkboard, stamps, stencils, and other hands-on materials will keep them happy at the interactive displays. Outside, an amazing playground is divided into areas for curious toddlers, energetic children, and adventurous preteens. The 117-acre park is open Tuesday through Sunday from March through November, and weekends the rest of the year. *400 Sausiluta Dr., Richmond; (804) 261-8230.*

BUNKING DOWN

Crowne Plaza Hotel Richmond
★★★★/$$$
Overlooking the James River, this upscale, 300-room property has valet service (welcome after a day of touring) and an indoor pool (always welcome as far as kids are concerned). Triangular-shaped suites offer expansive views of the river and the city and have kitchen facilities (a small refrigerator, sink, and microwave) that off-

set some of the cost of staying here. The staff goes out of its way to inform families about special events around town. Children under 18 stay free. *555 E. Canal St., Richmond; (800) 227-6963; (804) 788-0900.*

Embassy Suites Hotel
★★★/$$$
This all-suite property in a suburban setting has an indoor pool, a daily two-hour reception with soda and snacks for children, a cooked-to-order complimentary breakfast in the atrium each morning, and an on-site restaurant. Another big plus: all rooms have kitchen facilities—and two TVs. *2925 Emerywood Pkwy., Richmond; (800) 362-2779; (804) 672-8585; www.embassysuites.com*

Radisson Hotel Historic Richmond ★★★/$$
The rooftop pool will please the kids, while Mom and Dad will appreciate the complimentary shuttle service to the downtown area from this 230-room property. Children under 17

Cruising Along

Weather permitting, take a ride on a flat-bottomed canal boat. The excursion, offered by **Kanawha Cruises** *(804/649-2800)*, allows passengers to see the confluence of three centuries of transportation methods: an 18th-century canal, a 19th-century train track, and a 20th-century highway. George Washington designed Richmond's canal system, which today is protected by a floodwall. The tour guides are informative and funny; and your kids will be entertained by the turtles, waterfowl, and fish swimming for the half-hour ride. Fare at press time was $5 per adult, $4 for kids 5 to 12, and free for youngsters under 5. The boat departs from *1701 Dock Street.*

stay free. *301 W. Franklin St., Richmond; (800) 333-3333; (804) 644-9871*; www.radisson.com

GOOD EATS

Bottoms Up Pizza ★★★/$$

It's always nice to find a pizza place that understands that parents might want some interesting choices even as they surrender to the pleas for pizza. This Richmond landmark, where you can dine inside or on the deck, serves up to 1,200 people on a typical weekend day, so you know the dough is delicious. *1700 Dock St., Richmond; (804) 644-4400.*

River City Diner ★★★★/$$

This retro-1950s diner has an old-fashioned soda fountain, jukeboxes at each table, and deliciously hearty meals. The Rochester Garbage Plate includes two hot dogs, chili and cheese, baked beans, home fries, coleslaw, and potato salad for $6.99. Among the other comfort-food choices are meat loaf, pork chops, deli sandwiches, and breakfast items served all day and into the night. *1712 E. Main St., Richmond; (804) 644-9418.*

SOUVENIR HUNTING

17th Street Farmers' Market

On the first Saturday of each month, this produce market in Shockoe Bottom hosts Arts on the Market. Handmade crafts are sold while clowns, musicians, and others entertain. There are usually contests and art projects, such as making T-shirts.

Richmond's African American Roots

Richmond has a wealth of sites to pique your older kids' interest in African American history.

The Black History Museum and Cultural Center of Virginia

(804/780-9093) at Clay Street has exhibits on the Jackson Ward neighborhood, which was Richmond's African American business and entertainment district in the early 20th century. You can also see the works of some African American artists. To make your visit more interesting, call ahead to arrange a personalized family tour.

Richmond's **St. Luke Penny Savings Bank** was the first bank opened by a woman in the United States. The story is even more amazing when you learn that Maggie L. Walker was an African American and that she opened the bank in 1903.

The Maggie L. Walker National Historic Site *(600 N. 2nd St.; 804/771-*

At 17th and Main Sts., Richmond; (804) 780-8597.

⭐ Shockoe Slip and Shockoe Bottom
FamilyFun

Snuggled against each other, close to the James River, Shockoe Slip and Shockoe Bottom are newly renovated neighborhoods that are ascending the trendiness scale. The Slip boasts many small boutiques and specialty shops. The Bottom has a variety of restaurants as well as some artsy stores that you can probably skip if you have little kids. *Shockoe Slip: 13th to 15th Sts., along E. Cary St., Richmond. Shockoe Bottom: 15th to 25th Sts., along E. Cary, E. Main, and E. Franklin Sts., Richmond.*

Toymaker of Williamsburg
Traditional playthings—soldiers, dolls, games, and puzzles—stock most of the shelves at this Shockoe Slip toy store, but give your kids a few bucks and they'll have a blast getting inexpensive trinkets such as key chains, finger puppets, and miniature cars. *1215 E. Cary St., Richmond; (804) 783-1744.*

World of Mirth
The nine-block Carytown section (along Cary Street, from Nansemond to Boulevard) is known for its eclectic shops, and this one is made for kids. There are marionettes, puppets, mustache kits for dress-up, and lots of crazy hats. Faced with 30,000 items jammed into a 3,500-square-foot space, the kids will have a hard time choosing that essential item. *3005 W. Cary St., Richmond; (804) 353-8991.*

2017) details Walker's life and the journey that led to her success. It may prove inspiring to the would-be businesswomen in your family—and give a little lesson on how far both African Americans and women have come since 1903.

If you've got theater buffs along, stop at the corner of Adams and Leigh Streets, where there's a monument to theater legend Bill "Bojangles" Robinson.

Also worth a visit is the 131-year-old **Sixth Mount Zion Baptist Church** *(14 W. Duval St.; 804/648-7511),* where the charismatic preacher John Jasper gave his famous speech, "The Sun Do Move." A small museum contains some of Jasper's personal effects; tours should be prearranged.

The **Elegba Folklore Society**
(101 E. Broad St.; 804/644-3900) at times schedules cultural programs and special events related to African American heritage; the gallery has fine art, crafts, and artifacts.

Your kids may get to help historical interpreters at Jamestown Settlement with Colonial activities such as making tools from bone, shooting a bow-and-arrow, and hauling cargo aboard a ship.

Williamsburg, Jamestown, and Yorktown

S ITUATED ON a flat peninsula wedged between the York and James Rivers, the three Virginia towns of Williamsburg, Jamestown, and Yorktown are linked by geography as well as by the prominent roles they played in American history. Jamestown is the site of the first permanent English settlement in America; Williamsburg is a re-created Colonial town; and Yorktown is the site of the last battle of the Revolution. Together, they form a popular tourist area known as the Historic Triangle.

Captain John Smith—almost all grade-schoolers know who he was—established Jamestown on the western shore of the peninsula in 1607. By the end of the 17th century, Williamsburg—at the top of the triangle—had overshadowed Jamestown, which had grown weary from battling disease, starvation, and the native Indians. It survived and thrived longer, and with little effort, it stole the title of Colonial capital from Jamestown, becoming a meeting place for political and social notables.

THE **FamilyFun** LIST

MUST-SEE
MUST-SEE

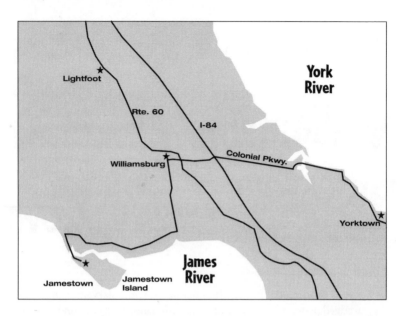

Yorktown, in the southeast corner, earned its place in the spotlight when the Revolutionary War ended on its fields. It again made history nearly a century later, when Union troops descended on the area, forcing the outnumbered Confederate soldiers to retreat to Williamsburg.

Today, take your kids to the Historic Triangle and you'll find activities so captivating that youngsters will forget that it's the 21st century. It's possible for a family to make a quick but not thorough swing through this important trio in as little as a weekend, but it is best to plan at least a four- or five-day excursion.

Hairpieces were very much in fashion during Colonial times. Wigs made of goat, horse, yak, and human hair were sold in towns like Williamsburg.

That way, you can schedule in some playtime at Busch Gardens Williamsburg or Water Country USA. If you have more time, you can see some of the handful of lesser-known attractions and outlet centers worth a stop. If you only have a few days, though, you'll probably want to spend as much time as possible exploring the Historic Triangle, knowing that you and your children will acquire an unforgettable education.

The sites of the Historic Triangle are connected by a well-maintained 23-mile roadway called Colonial Parkway (*757/898-2410*). Numerous scenic lookouts, plus a few beach areas dot the route. Have your children watch for wildlife—herons, bald eagles, osprey, and deer live here—as you make your way from one town to the next.

CULTURAL ADVENTURES

MUST-SEE Colonial Williamsburg
FamilyFun ★★★★/$$$

MUST-SEE The historic area called Colonial Williamsburg encompasses 88 original 18th-century structures plus hundreds of reconstructed buildings (flags hang in front of the buildings to indicate that they're open to the public). First, head to the visitors' center to pick up a copy of *Visitor's Companion*, which contains a map of the Colonial area and a weekly list of special and regularly scheduled events. Take note of the Colonial smiley faces, which indicate child-friendly attractions, then make a family plan for your visit. Although three sites are highly popular—the Governor's Palace, the Capitol, and the Courthouse—kids usually prefer the trade shops—printer, bookbinder, grocery, milliner, silversmith—along Duke of Gloucester Street and the scattered pastures where rare farm animals graze.

Families should also spend some time in the rural trade complex off North England Street, where children can make bricks by kneading

clay with their feet. The nearby Market Square, with its stockade and imposing magazine, is perfect for photo ops.

Keep in mind that popping in and out of historic buildings does not rank at the top of most kids' list of fun stuff. Get the kids involved by having them compare life today with Colonial life, and help your children talk with the historical interpreters. Several hands-on programs also help bring history to life; for example, your child can participate in one of the free arms lessons at the military encampment. If your budget allows, rent one of the colonial outfits for $20 at the booths on Market Square—they're a big hit with "dress-up" fans. **NOTE:** A bus circumnavigates the area and makes numerous stops, helpful when everyone's feet get tired. *Visitors' center: Colonial Parkway, off U.S. 60 Bypass, just east of Va. 132; (800) 447-8679; (757) 220-7645;* http://www.colonial williamsburg.com/

MUST-SEE Jamestown Island
FamilyFun ★★★/$$

MUST-SEE This small island in the James River is where Captain John Smith established the first permanent English settlement in the early 1600s. While you're at the visitors' center deciding which ranger-conducted tour to take, your children can try on some Colonial clothes or figure out the contents of a few mystery bags. Enroll your school-age kids in the Junior Ranger Program.

It's inexpensive ($1.50), and if they complete the workbook (by watching a film, attending an interpretive program, and identifying historical sites here), they get a certificate and a badge. The self-guided tour around the ruins and monuments in both the Old and New Towne sections takes approximately 40 minutes. **NOTE:** Watch your little ones carefully by sites five, six, and eight, where the retaining wall along the river is low enough for them to step over. At the Pocahontas statue (on the tour), talk with your children about how the settlers' actions affected Native Americans. After your walking tour, explore the island by car. Loop Drive has three- and five-mile options that pass 1,500 acres of wildlife, woodland, and marsh, much like the landscape that the settlers would have inhabited. *Visitors' center: western end of Colonial Pkwy., five miles southwest of Williamsburg; (757) 898-2410; www.apva.org/tour*

Jamestown Settlement ★★★★/$$

This settlement, which contains a museum and living-history areas, tells the story of the first Colonists to reach Virginia and the Powhatan Indians they encountered. The museum isn't worth much if you have little kids—navigation and coat of arms are the only touchable exhibits. The charm of this place lies in the village, fort, and three ships behind the museum. In the village, which is made up of four reed-covered houses, your kids may scrape a deerskin, pound corn, help make tools out of bone, climb into a canoe, and practice bow-and-arrow skills using corncob darts. In the fort, they can try on armor or play a game of ninepins (Colonial bowling). A blacksmith demonstrates the heating and forging of tools. On board the ships, ask the kids whether they'd have made the journey to the New World in the cramped and primitive cabins that these Colonists called home for so many months. *Colonial Pkwy., at Rte. 31; (888) 593-4682; (757) 253-4838.*

Watermen's Museum ★★★★/$

How many ways are there to catch a fish? Your kids will find out at this small museum overlooking the York River. Indoor exhibits include model boats, a whale's jawbone, an aquarium, and drawers of shells. At the exhibit on the beach behind the museum kids can tong for oysters. Take a minute to dip your toes

into the salty river water and search for shell fragments. The gift shop is jammed with reasonably priced toys, T-shirts, shells, and children's books. *309 Water St., Yorktown; (757) 887-2641; www.watermens.org*

★MUST-SEE★ Yorktown Battlefield
FamilyFun ★★★★/$
★MUST-SEE★ The visitors' center at this battlefield has a 70-foot-long replica of an 18th-century British warship. It's one-fourth the size of a real frigate, but the kids will still enjoy a wonderful perspective of life on board. Beyond the ship, a children's exhibit features three dioramas; the narration tells the (fictional) story of a 13-year-old boy who sneaked into the army during the Revolutionary War. Consider enrolling your school-age child in the Junior Ranger Program (see Jamestown Island, page 371). The seven-mile driving tour of the battlefield takes approximately 45 minutes. A ranger-led Siege Walk lasts about 35 minutes; recommended for kids 5 and older. *Visitors' center: at the eastern end of Colonial Pkwy., about 14 miles northeast of Williamsburg; (757) 898-2410.*

★MUST-SEE★ Yorktown Victory
FamilyFun Center ★★★★/$
★MUST-SEE★ This highly interactive museum covers the history of the area. The over-5 set will like the many exhibits with buttons to push and questions posted on plaques. Some exhibits have television

When the Lights Dim

Nighttime entertainment in Williamsburg ranges from comedy shows to off-Broadway performances. The following are two of the more family-friendly venues.

The Music Theater of Williamsburg ★★★/$$$
School-age kids love this wonderful toe-tapping revue, especially if they're interested in dance or music. The two-hour show features pop and show tunes from the 1940s through the 1960s. Reservations are necessary. *7575 Richmond Rd., Williamsburg; (888) 687-4220; (757) 564-0200.*

Mystery Dinner Playhouse ★★★/$$$$
A four-course dinner complements this comedy/murder mystery show. Be prepared to get involved, as the actor-waiters expect audience members to help solve the evening's crime. This two-and-a-half-hour extravaganza is best for children ages 8 and older. *5351 Richmond Rd., Williamsburg; (888) 471-4802; (757) 565-2000.*

sets showing reenactments that complement the written descriptions. If you're traveling with younger kids, you may want to proceed directly to the Children's Kaleidoscope Room, where they can see Colonial clothing, a mancala board (an African game played with smooth stones), mystery boxes, a hornbook to practice writing, wood rubbings, books, Colonial games, and computers for testing kids' historical knowledge. Good photo op: a small table with Colonial cooking utensils. Outside the museum, a military encampment and 1780 farmstead have demonstrations of candle dipping (in the winter), open-fire cooking, tobacco farming, and gardening, presented on a rotating basis. *Colonial Pkwy., at Old Rte. 238, Yorktown; (888) 593-4682; (757) 253-4838.*

JUST FOR FUN

Busch Gardens Williamsburg
★★★★/$$$$

This huge theme park has distinguished itself by creating nine hamlets—Banbury Cross, Heatherdowns, San Marco, Festa Italia, Oktoberfest, Rhinefeld, New France, Aquitaine, and Hastings—that feature rides, shows, restaurants, and shops. Each hamlet is designed to replicate the atmosphere of a town in England, Italy, Germany, France, or Scotland. Walkways, a train, and

a sky ride help connect the hamlets, which are spread out over 100 acres.

If your preteens are mature, consider renting a pair of two-way radios ($10) at the Emporium Gift Shop in Banbury Cross to keep in contact with those old enough to explore on their own while Mom and Dad stick with their younger siblings. You can then head in opposite directions (clockwise and counterclockwise), planning to meet in either Oktoberfest or Festa Italia halfway through the day. Preteen favorites at the park include five roller coasters, one of which has nine drops and reaches speeds of 73 mph. Vroom!

Although most of the hamlets have a few rides for little ones, parents of preschoolers should start their day in Rhinefeld's Land of Dragons. The walk from Banbury Cross, near the entrance, is the start of a skyride that covers a distance tiring for little legs. There's a spectacular three-story tree house, complete with a water-play area; a Captain

Kangaroo show that ought to keep them happy at the Land of Dragons, plus five rides: a mini-flume, a Ferris wheel, and three others that go round and round. An antique carousel is nearby.

Then cross the river to Heather-downs to see the world-famous Clydesdales. If your babes are not too tired, continue on to San Marco, Festa Italia, or Oktoberfest for most of the remaining kiddie rides. **NOTE:** At press time, parking cost $7 per car, though $10 will get you a "preferred" (closer) parking space, which you may be willing to spring for after a long day in the park. *From Williamsburg, take Rte. 64 East to Rte. 199 to Rte. 60 East; follow signs; (800) 343-7946; (757) 253-3350; www.buschgardens.com*

Water Country USA
★★★/$$$$

Three miles west of Busch Gardens Williamsburg, this big, wet playground features a new toboggan-style flume, one- and two-person flumes, two family-raft rides (anyone afraid of the dark should skip this one), and numerous slides. The children's area has slides, spray jets, a waterfall, a heated pool with interactive activities, and a watery obstacle course. The Caban-A-Rama Theater has an aquatic and gymnastic athletic show. The Minnow Matinee Theater hosts a musical review. Swim diapers are required for kids not yet potty trained; you can buy them at the park's WC Duds shop for $12.99 each. Six eateries throughout the park will keep tummies full. *From Williamsburg, take Rte. 64 East to Rte. 199 to Rte. 60 East; follow signs; (800) 343-7946; (757) 253-3350; www.revolution aryfun.com/water.html*

BUNKING DOWN

Holiday Inn Downtown
★★★/$$

This 137-room, Colonial-style property has lots of kid-pleasing amenities, including an indoor pool, shuffleboard, and putting green. Ledo's Pizza and Pasta Restaurant, renowned for its square pizza, is on the premises. Kids age 12 and under stay and eat free with a paying adult. *814 Capitol Landing Rd., Williamsburg; (800) 368-0200; (757) 229-0200; www.basshotels.com/hol iday-inn*

Kingsmill Resort
★★★★/$$$$

Look no farther if you want to be pampered. This luxury villa resort is both kid-friendly (game room, and indoor and outdoor pools) and has lots of extras for adults (three championship golf courses, a spa, tennis courts, a sports club). The Kingsmill Kampers Program (fee) has age-appropriate activities for 3- to 12-year-olds, including arts and crafts, games, and sports. The Kid's

Night Out program allows parents to have a relaxing dinner; baby-sitting is also available for children 3 and older. A complimentary shuttle takes guests to Colonial Williamsburg and Busch Gardens. *1010 Kingsmill Rd., Williamsburg; (800) 832-5665; (757) 253-1703.*

SpringHill Suites by Marriott
★★★★/$$$

The lion's share of accommodations can be found on Richmond Road in Williamsburg, including this all suite-property, which has plenty to lure families. The 120 suites, which sleep up to six, have separate dining, sitting, and sleeping areas. In-suite kitchens have a refrigerator, microwave, sink, and coffeemaker. The kids will like the spacious indoor pool. Perhaps one of the best features is a lavish complimentary breakfast: cereal, bagels, toast, muffins, pastries, and more. A television in the lobby often plays cartoons for kids. *1644 Richmond Rd., Williamsburg; (888) 287-9400; (757) 941-3000;* www.marriott.com

GOOD EATS

Applebee's ★★★/$$$

A chain restaurant, yes, but the kids may be glad to see the familiar menu, especially if they're picky eaters. Crayons, a coloring mat, and a sheet of stickers will please preschoolers. For the grown-ups, steak, chicken,

Colonial Clothing

Today's fashion-conscious kids may be intrigued by the clothes of yesteryear. Ask them to put themselves in a Colonial child's shoes: what might be some of the pros and cons of wearing these typical Colonial outfits?

BOYS: long shirt, stockings, breeches, shoes, waistcoat, straw tri-corner hat.

GIRLS: shift, stockings, petticoat, dress, apron, cap, shoes, straw hat.

seafood, and pasta dishes are served in sizable portions. A children's menu carries the usual suspects: hot dogs, pizza, and burgers. The kitchen will even prepare a meal not listed if you have a really picky eater. *1640 Richmond Rd., Williamsburg; (757) 564-7261;* www.applebees.com

Carrot Tree Kitchen
★★★/$

This is the place to pick up box lunches for a picnic. If you'd rather eat on the premises, there's a small café. *1782 Jamestown Rd., Jamestown; (757) 229-0957.*

Colonial Williamsburg Taverns

Each of the four taverns listed below is open for lunch and dinner, offers inexpensive kids' menus, and has a costumed waitstaff and strolling balladeers. All require dinner reservations, but make them in person at Josiah Chowning's. *For all four: (800) 828-3767; (757) 229-1000.*

Christiana Campbell's Tavern
★★★/$$$

Seafood is the specialty here. *Waller St., between York and Nicholson Sts., Williamsburg.*

Josiah Chowning's Tavern
★★★/$$

Beef and pork are the specialties here; it's also slightly less expensive than the others. *Duke of Gloucester St., next to Courthouse, Williamsburg.*

King's Arms Tavern ★★★/$$

Come here for hearty beef and lamb dishes. *Duke of Gloucester St., between Betetourt and Blair Sts., Williamsburg.*

Shields Tavern ★★★/$$$

Right next to the King's Arms, this spot has the biggest menu of the four taverns. *Duke of Gloucester St., between Betetourt and Blair Sts., Williamsburg.*

Nick's Seafood Pavilion
★★★/$$$

Seafood is the specialty here, especially soft-shell crabs and broiled lobster tail, but there are nonseafood items on the menu, too. The children's menu is sure to please. *Water St., Yorktown; (757) 887-5269.*

Outback Steakhouse
★★★/$$$

You'll almost always have to wait a little while to be seated at this steak joint, but it's perfect for families tired from a day of touring. Parents need not be concerned about noisy children, as this place has a din of its own. While you wait, preschoolers can play with the chalkboard and large bead toy in the waiting area. If they're really having a blast, ask for a small bead toy to take to the tables. Ask your server for some warm bread and butter for the kids to munch on until your meal arrives. The children's menu features chicken tenders, ribs, and macaroni and cheese. *3026 Richmond Rd., Williamsburg; (757) 229-8648; www.outback.com*

SOUVENIR HUNTING

Outlet shopping is abundant in the Historic Triangle, with huge depots dedicated to such items as Christmas ornaments, kitchen utensils, sneakers, fine china, and electronics. The following are a few of the most popular factories in the area. If you go on weekdays, you can visit the observation rooms where you and your kids can watch the workers create the products.

A LONG-WEEKEND ITINERARY

Day One: Jamestown

9 A.M. Start your day at **Jamestown Island** (see page 371).

10:30 A.M. On your way out, stop by the **Glasshouse**, near the entrance to Jamestown: the Original Site. Listen to the audio message that explains the significance of the glassblowing industry during Colonial times. Around the bend, watch craftsmen blowing glass the same way they did nearly 400 years ago.

11:30 A.M. If you are visiting Tuesday through Sunday, order a box lunch for $5 to $7 from **Carrot Tree Kitchen** (see page 376) for a quick tailgate lunch before heading to the Jamestown Settlement. You can eat at the small café on the premises.

Noon Explore the **Jamestown Settlement** (see page 372), where kids can pretend to be either Captain John Smith or Pocahontas.

3 A.M. Visit one **factory outlet** (see Souvenir Hunting on page 379). Reward good behavior (your child's, that is!) with some spending money.

Day Two: Colonial Williamsburg

8:30 A.M. Stop at the **Colonial Williamsburg visitors' center** (see page 371). Pick up a copy of *Visitor's Companion*, buy admission tickets, and make reservations for dinner.

9 A.M. Take the **red line bus** (free for ticket holders) for a three-minute ride to the entrance of the historic area. At this bus stop, the red line also connects with the blue line bus, which circumnavigates the area and makes numerous stops, one of which may be the closest to your first stop.

9:15 A.M. Begin your tour of the historic area.

11 A.M. Visit the **Play Booth Theater**, if they have a child-friendly event on the schedule.

Noon Go to the **Capitol Yard** for the firing of the cannon. Plug your ears and open your mouth to help lessen the effect of the boom.

12:30 P.M. Visit the **Gaol** (jail to us) and speak to the prisoners.

1 P.M. Have lunch at the nearest tavern (see Good Eats on page 376).

2 P.M. Head to the **Military Encampment** for a lesson in arms (most kids are delighted when the sergeant booms orders at them).

2:45 P.M. Continue your tour of the historic area.

Day Three: Theme Parks!

10 A.M. Spend the day at either **Busch Gardens Williamsburg** (see page 374) or **Water Country USA** (see page 375). For lunch, you can choose from among cafés and vendors serving typical park fare.

Day Four: Yorktown

9 A.M. Start your day at the **Yorktown Battlefield** (see page 373). Enroll your school-age child in the Junior Ranger Program. Go on a ranger-led Siege Walk.

11 A.M. Visit the **Watermen's Museum** (see page 372), where your child can try to pull up a few oysters using tongs.

Noon Walk around the historic town and have lunch at **Water Street Landing** (*757/886-5890*), overlooking the York River from Water Street. Midday fare includes pizza and sandwiches.

1:30 P.M. Explore the **Yorktown Victory Center** (see page 373), especially the Children's Kaleidoscope Room. A cannon is fired daily at 2:35 P.M.; in May, a military drill takes its place.

3:30 P.M. Visit one **factory outlet** (this page). If your kids have been good, treat them to a souvenir.

The Candle Factory Outlet Shop

Children will enjoy seeing candles being mass-produced (at a rate of six million per year), while their parents shop for candles and soaps. A small selection of shaped soaps will fit most kids' budgets. *7521 Richmond Rd., Williamsburg; (757) 564-3354.*

Williamsburg Doll Factory

The temptation is difficult to resist, but kids still can't touch the porcelain beauties perched daintily throughout the store. **NOTE:** Do not enter with impulsive toddlers, or you may have to make an unexpected (and costly!) purchase. Children who can follow the rules are invited to watch the artisans paint faces and apply hair to the pretty dollies. *7441 Richmond Rd., Williamsburg; (757) 564-9703.*

Williamsburg Pottery Factory

With more than 70,000 items for sale in 22 buildings, this retailer is one of the largest in the region. Kid favorites: the complexes containing dolls (Solar 1) and toys (Building 21). Craftspeople can be seen working on traditional salt-glazed pottery (Ceramic Building), lamps, floral arrangements, and cement garden fixtures. *Seven miles west of the historic area. Rte. 60 W., at Lightfoot Rd., Lightfoot; (757) 564-3326.*

After touring the Luray Caverns and Thomas Jefferson's Monticello, your family can make camp in Shenandoah National Park.

Western Virginia

I N Western Virginia the history of Charlottesville and the natural wonders of the Shenandoah Mountains join forces to make this a good place for a family vacation.

Charlottesville *is* history. Did you know that our third, fourth, and fifth presidents were friends and neighbors—all with homes near this beautiful university town? Of the trio, Thomas Jefferson had the strongest influence locally, for he not only built his plantation, Monticello, just outside of town, but he also planned the resident University of Virginia. James Monroe lived just a couple of miles from Monticello in a country retreat called Ashlawn-Highland. Montpelier, once the home of James Madison, is some 35 miles north of town. (Also see "Charlottesville's Presidential Past," page 388.) All three presidential homes are open to the public, and each reveals a different aspect of our nation's early years. It's pretty heady stuff for kids, although grade-schoolers will be okay if you deliver it in manageable doses, heavily laced with some real kid pleasers—like the Virginia Discovery

THE FamilyFun LIST

MUST-SEE
MUST-SEE

Luray Caverns (page 385)

Monticello (page 383)

Skyline Drive (page 387)

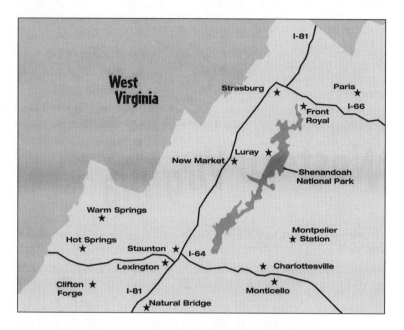

Museum and Michie Tavern.

When your family has had its fill of history and indoor attractions, turn to the Shenandoah Mountains, perhaps the most beautiful range this side of the Rockies. (You can see the mountains on the horizon in Charlottesville; it's 21 miles to the entrance of Skyline Drive.) Unlike their western brethren, the Shenandoahs brim with deciduous trees that burst with patches of yellow, orange, and red each fall. Much of the Shenandoah Valley is made up of national parks where your family can hike, raft, and otherwise enjoy the great outdoors. And sprinkled throughout the mountains are small towns like Lexington that retain an old-fashioned flavor.

CULTURAL ADVENTURES

Ashlawn-Highland
★★★/$

President James Monroe purchased this property—which he liked to call his "cabin castle"—in part to be near his friend Thomas Jefferson. Monroe's first guests here were James and Dolley Madison. Monroe planned it as his retirement haven, but he ended up selling it when financial troubles hit. You can now tour the restored working plantation—the elegantly furnished home—and watch demonstrations on tinsmithing, open-hearth cooking, and cattle raising. Have the kids see how far they can roll hoops on the expansive lawn. *1000 James Monroe Pkwy., two and a half miles southeast of Monticello, Charlottesville; (434) 293-9539.*

★★★★/$ **Monticello**

MUST-SEE

FamilyFun Although he designed his magnificent home using classical building principles, Thomas Jefferson also incorporated many modern innovations in Monticello, which he dubbed his "essay in architecture." Point out to the kids that Jefferson's grand home had a primitive form of air-conditioning and a copying machine. Your preschoolers will probably be pretty bored here, but grade-schoolers will enjoy such things as the visitors' center's 38-minute film *Thomas Jefferson: The Pursuit of Liberty.* **NOTE:** Lines for the tour of Monticello form early, so it's best to try to get the 8 A.M. tour.

Afterward, your family can stroll through the grounds and gardens and discuss what you've seen. (Be prepared to answer some of the inevitable tough questions about Jefferson's life, like the contradiction between having a slave as a common-law wife and promoting democratic principles.) Be sure to pick up the free *Monticello Gardens Children's Guide* (available on-site), which contains activities for parents and children, a history of the gardens, and plant-related word games. Kids ages 6 to 12 will go for Monticello's Family Workshops

(*434/984-9828*), held on Saturday morning; they'll learn something about charting family histories and marbleizing paper. **ANOTHER NOTE:** To do Monticello justice, allow about three and a half hours. *Rte. 53, two miles southeast of Charlottesville; (434) 984-9822;* www.monticello.org

Montpelier ★★★/$

About 35 miles north of Charlottesville, this rather modest home once belonged to James Madison and his wife, Dolley. In 1900, the du Pont family bought it and made several additions, including an Art Deco lounge that looks like a set for a Fred Astaire movie.

Unlike Monticello, Montpelier is

FamilyFun GAME

One Minute of Words

Everybody gets a pencil and paper. Someone has to be the timekeeper. The timekeeper picks a letter, tells it to everyone else, and shouts "Go!" Players write as many words as possible that start with that letter. When a minute is up, the timekeeper says "Stop!" and all the players put down their pencils. Whoever has the most legitimate words wins. Decide in advance whether you can finish writing a word you've already started when the game ends. Now, give yourself one more minute to write a sentence with as many of the words as you can.

still being restored, offering a glimpse into how preservationists painstakingly research the history of an old house. Older kids with a historical bent will find this behind-the-scenes look fascinating. Both James and Dolley are buried in the family cemetery here. The kids can run around in the beautiful gardens and blow off some steam. *11407 Constitution Hwy., Montpelier Station; (540) 672-2728.*

University of Virginia (UVA)
★★★/Free

Thomas Jefferson built Monticello high on a hill so that he could look at this, his other glorious creation. One of America's oldest universities and one of its most prestigious state institutions, UVA is the embodiment of Jefferson's philosophical and architectural ideals. Its Great Lawn is a sweeping expanse of green surrounded by student rooms and capped by the Jefferson-designed Rotunda. Older children who were captivated by Monticello—and impressed with Jefferson's great breadth of knowledge—will enjoy a visit to the University of Virginia. Free 45-minute campus tours are available. *University Ave., Charlottesville; (434) 924-0311;* www.virginia.edu

Virginia Discovery Museum
★★★/$

With its emphasis on art and history, this hands-on children's museum in downtown Charlottesville will spark your kids' imaginations. Kids can dress up as modern-day grown-ups in modern-day jobs or go back in time and pretend they're living in Colonial Virginia. It's all high-concept, but fairly low-tech—sketch in an arts-and-crafts studio, participate in a giant game of checkers, dress up as a firefighter or police officer, see an active beehive. *East end of the downtown mall, Charlottesville; (434) 977-1025;* www.vadm.org

JUST FOR FUN

The Jefferson Pools
★★★/$$

Legend has it that these therapeutic hot springs were originally discovered by a young Native American. In 1766, George Washington designed a men's bathhouse to stand above the pools; 70 years later, a women's bathhouse was added next to it. Both structures are still in operation—and still segregated. Only 20 feet in diameter and less than five feet deep, the pools are not for swimming, but for soaking (by the hour).

For children, the appeal here lies in the natural buoyancy of the mineral-rich water. (Older kids may like the buildings' history and architecture.) If you forget your swimsuit, you can rent a handmade bathing costume (kid sizes, too) designed in the 1930s. (Younger family members will surely get a kick out of seeing Mom or Dad in the old-fashioned attire.) Open daily mid-April through October. *Rte. 220, Warm Springs. No phone.*

Lexington ★★★/Free

Once home to Stonewall Jackson and Robert E. Lee, who are both buried here, this town seems frozen in the 19th century. It has changed so little since the 1800s that the 1993 Jodie Foster and Richard Gere movie *Sommersby*, set in the post–Civil War era, was filmed here. Downtown is a warren of interesting shops and restaurants, but the best way to explore Lexington with kids is on the evening Ghost Tour ($$). From May through October, the 90-minute guided tour through Lexington's alleyways regales your family with tales of the former residents who purportedly still haunt these streets. (The not-*too*-scary excursion is appropriate for all but the most impressionable little ones—or kids of any age who conk out early.) Meet outside the Lexington Visitor Center (*106 E. Washington St.; 540/463-3777*); tours depart at 8:30 P.M. *On Slate Rd. 60, near the junction of U.S. 64 and U.S. 81.*

Luray Caverns
FamilyFun ★★★★/$$

All along Route 81, giant billboards advertise the Shenandoahs' many caverns, of which Luray is surely the best. Discovered in 1878 by a tinsmith and a local photographer, it's now the most commercial

Shenandoah Park and Luray Caverns

9 A.M. Enter Shenandoah National Park (see page 386) at the park's northernmost entrance in Front Royal. Drive to the Dickey Ridge Visitor Center near Mile 4 and pick up a self-guided map of Fox Hollow Nature Trail.

10 A.M. Walk **Fox Hollow Nature Trail** (at Mile 4.6) to the Fox family's old home site, where remnants of old farm fences still stand, and a family cemetery remains. The one-and-a-fifth-mile trail, rated "Easy," takes about one and a half to two hours to complete.

Noon Drive to the **Panorama** stop near Mile 33. Have lunch in the restaurant.

1:30 P.M. Leave the park on Route 211 and drive to **Luray**, a short distance away.

2 P.M. Spend the afternoon touring **Luray Caverns** (this page).

4:30 P.M. Return to Shenandoah Park and continue south on Skyline Drive for about ten miles. Spend the night at the **Skyland Lodge** (see page 390), the highest point in the park.

of the local caves—but also the most accessible and fascinating to children. One-hour guided tours follow paved, well-lighted walkways through cathedral-size chambers filled with stalactites and stalagmites. Children are especially drawn to formations like the "fried eggs," which look like the real thing, but are made of limestone. Culminating the tour is the Great Stalacpipe Organ, which actually makes music (hammers strike stalactite formations throughout the cave). *Exit 264 off I-81, Luray; (540) 743-6551.*

Natural Bridge ★★★★/$
In 1774, Thomas Jefferson purchased what he called "the most sublime of Nature's works" from King George III. Your kids may be less awestruck by Natural Bridge, but it has spawned a cottage industry in the Shenandoah Valley, and a visit here now encompasses not only the bridge, but a cavern tour, a wax museum, and an evening light show called Creation. At 90 feet long and 215 feet above Cedar Creek, the limestone bridge was once a holy place for the Monocan Indians—which did not keep the federal government from building a road on top of it. Cedar Creek Trail, a nature walk underneath the bridge, makes a nice hike. Combination tickets are available for several attractions. *Rte. 11, Natural Bridge; (800) 533-1410; (540) 291-2121;* www.natural bridgeva.com

Shenandoah National Park ★★★★/$-$$
About a billion years ago the forces

The Shenandoah Valley's State Parks

THOUGH Shenandoah National Park is justifiably the most famous and most visited park in Western Virginia, the region has several noteworthy state parks, too. *For information on camping and cabin reservations, call (800) 933-PARK.*

lake. Two furnished lodges have a total of 11 private bedrooms with shared kitchens; shared bathrooms; and common living rooms, each with a telephone and TV/VCR. *Exit 27 off I-64 to Rte. 629, then seven miles north to near Clifton Forge; (540) 862-8100.*

Douthat State Park
One of Virginia's oldest state parks has mountain scenery, special interpretive programs, a restaurant, 40 miles of trails, and a 50-acre stocked

Shenandoah River Raymond R. Andy Guest, Jr., State Park
Situated on the shores of the Shenandoah River, Virginia's newest state park opened in 1999 with 13

of shifting tectonic plates, wind, and water molded the spectacular scenery of this national treasure, part of the Blue Ridge Mountains. English settlers explored the Shenandoah region before the Revolutionary War and, by the late 1800s, nurtured a few settlements and small industries like mining.

Designated a National Park in 1925, with many of the rest stops and the Skyline Drive created during the following decade, the park was instantly popular and continues to draw millions of tourists. Some visitors simply view it from Skyline Drive (*see below*), others stay for weeks to hike part of the Appalachian Trail. The park's dramatic rock formations, spectacular fall foliage, and year-round natural beauty will wow all but the most jaded preteen. Look, too, for remnants of the homes mountain people were forced to sell to consolidate the park. The park and Skyline Drive have four main entrances: *Front Royal on U.S. 340 near the junction of I-81 and I-66; Thornton Gap, 33 miles south of Front Royal on U.S. 211; Swift Run Gap, 68 miles south of Front Royal on U.S. 33; and Rockfish Gap, 105 miles south of Front Royal at I-64 and U.S. 250; (540) 999-3500; www.nps.gov/shen*

Skyline Drive

MUST-SEE FamilyFun ★★★/Free

If you don't have time to hike or camp in Shenandoah National Park, the next best thing is to drive historic Skyline Drive, the 105-mile road that stretches across the entire length of the park.

miles of trails for hiking, biking, and horseback riding. Families who want to overnight can try one of the ten primitive campsites (equipped with fire rings, picnic tables, and portable toilets). *Off Rte. 340, between Front Royal and Luray; (540) 622-6840.*

Sky Meadows State Park

On the eastern side of the Blue Ridge Mountains, this park features pastures, woodlands, and plenty of scenic vistas—plus access to the Appalachian Trail. Families might enjoy a walk to Mount Bleak House, a reconstructed house of a middle-class family from the 1850s. *Two miles south of Paris, take Rte. 50 to Rte. 17 south; (540) 592-3556.*

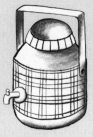

Without stops or traffic you can complete the drive in about three hours, but with 75 designated overlooks affording breathtaking valley views, you'll never be able to do it justice in just one day. The winding road can induce car sickness, too, so try driving it in pieces and stopping often. Snack bars, souvenir stands, and waysides are frequent on the drive (many of the picnic areas and rest stations were built by the Civilian Conservation Corps during the 1930s, when the drive was built). You can buy a

National Park Service audiotape that relates the history and geology of the park. **NOTE:** Traffic jams are common during the peak fall foliage period in October. The park and Skyline Drive have four main entrances: *Front Royal on U.S. 340 near the junction of I-81 and I-66; Thornton Gap, 33 miles south of Front Royal on U.S. 211; Swift Run Gap, 68 miles south of Front Royal on U.S. 33; and Rockfish Gap, 105 miles south of Front Royal at I-64 and U.S. 250; (540) 999-3500; www.nps.gov/shen*

Charlottesville's Presidential Past

CHARLOTTESVILLE lays claim to three of the most influential men—friends and neighbors, all—in American history. **Thomas Jefferson**—lawyer, architect, academic, musician, writer, and third president of the United States—built Monticello high atop a hill so that he could gaze upon his magnificent University of Virginia. Jefferson's genius was so great that John F. Kennedy later remarked to a gathering of Nobel Laureates at the White House that they were the greatest collection of talent ever assembled "since Thomas Jefferson dined alone."

Neighbors **Dolley and James Madison** expanded their once modest home, Montpelier, with Jefferson's advice. James Madison, the fourth

president, is considered the "Father of the Constitution." Dolley Madison was famous for fleeing the White House, under siege by the British during the War of 1812, with the Gilbert Stuart portrait of George Washington.

The fifth president, **James Monroe**, was a master of foreign policy; he carved out the Western Hemisphere as the infant United States' province. Monroe's plantation, Ashlawn-Highland, also benefited from his friend Jefferson's advice. Unfortunately, Monroe's mounting debts forced him to sell the estate.

Be prepared to answer every child's question about these brilliant statesmen: if they were so smart, why did they have slaves?

BUNKING DOWN

Camping families will find innumerable sites at private campgrounds and state and national parks. Information on national park accommodations is available through the National Park Reservation Service (*P.O. Box 1600, Cumberland, MD 21502*; http://reservations.nps.gov). *For information on private campgrounds, call (540) 740-3132 or write the Shenandoah Valley Travel Association (P.O. Box 1040, New Market, VA 22844).*

The Boar's Head Inn
★★★★/$$$$

This large (175 rooms) complex at the University of Virginia replicates a Colonial inn—albeit one that has been conveniently modernized with four swimming pools, a health club, bicycle rentals, tennis courts, and jogging trails. There's plenty here to keep an active family busy. Most of the nearly 200 rooms are furnished with antique reproductions (preferable to the real thing for parents with little ones). An uplifting plus: hot-air balloon rides (for a fee) are available from the inn's extensive grounds. *200 Ednam Dr., Charlottesville; (800) 474-1988; (434) 296-2181.*

Hampton Inn and Suites
★★★★/$$$

Especially appealing to families are the 75 suites at this new hotel just east of UVA's campus. The privacy of a separate bedroom and the convenience of a complete kitchen come at reasonable rates. Breakfast is included, another plus. *900 W. Main St., Charlottesville; (800) HAMPTON; (434) 923-8600;* www.hampton-inn.com

The Homestead
★★★★/$$$$

In 1993, this venerable 440-room resort was a frayed dowager. But a dazzling renovation turned it into a nationally renowned vacation spot. Founded in 1766 at the site of natural, therapeutic hot springs, it's now a four-season resort with golfing on world-class courses, skiing, tennis, mountain biking, hiking, swimming in two spring-fed pools, and a spa. The brand-new KidsClub program has both indoor and outdoor activities—science and art projects inside; ice-skating, hiking, and swimming outside. The camp-like program (fee; included in some hotel packages) is divided into two age groups, 3 to 7 and 8 to 12, and there's one counselor for every six children. Still looking for something to do? Try fishing, bowling, horseback riding, carriage rides, a game room, and a choice of two evening movies. *Hot Springs; (800) 838-1766; (540) 839-1766.*

Hotel Strasburg ★★★/$$

In the middle of quaint Strasburg, this old charmer is filled with antiques, but the atmosphere isn't so refined that it puts parents on edge and intimidates children. There's a wonderful, family-friendly restaurant on the premises. *213 Holliday St., Strasburg; (800) 348-8327; (540) 465-9191.*

Luray Caverns Motel West ★★★/$$

Owned and operated by Luray Caverns, this established, well-run motel is just across from the entrance to the caverns. *Rte. 211 Bypass, Luray; (540) 743-4536.*

Skyland Lodge ★★★★/$$

Built in 1894 at the highest point on Skyline Drive, this lodge has reasonably priced accommodations, including 177 motel rooms, six suites, and 20 cabins. Guest rooms are comfortable, though not lavish, and the views are spectacular. *Mile marker 41.7 of Skyline Drive, Shenandoah National Park; (800) 999-4714; (540) 999-2211.*

GOOD EATS

The Hardware Store ★★★/$$

Yes, it was once a hardware store and still features the interior of its former identity. The large portions of hearty American fare are meant to satisfy the hungriest college student. *316 E. Main St., Charlottesville; (434) 977-1518.*

Manhattan Hot Dog Company ★★/$

Fast food goes gourmet here—you can sit down or take out. The menu includes wraps, fresh bagels, and Nathan's hot dogs and is sure to satisfy young customers. *3 W. Nelson St., Lexington; (540) 464-1501.*

Michie Tavern ★★★★/$$

Once the center of Charlottesville social life, this historic tavern now serves hearty Colonial food for lunch. Kids love the fried chicken and sweet

Water Adventures

The South Fork of the Shenandoah River is popular for all kinds of water sports. Families with older children may want to try **white-water rafting**. **NOTE:** Age 6 is usually the lower limit for kids taking short trips; age 12 for daylong rafting, but the rapids are also classed by category—IV or V is probably too rough for children under 12. Even if your family isn't up to tackling the white water, there's plenty of fun to be had on the river. Try **canoeing, or rent an inner tube** and spend a lazy afternoon floating downstream. Try the **Front Royal Canoe Company** *(540/635-5440)* for kayaking, rafting, canoeing, and tubing; **Downriver Canoe Company** *(800/338-1963; 540/635-5526)* for canoeing, rafting, kayaking on a flowing mountain river, and tubing; or **Shenandoah River Outfitters** *(800/6-CANOE-2; 540/743-4159)* for canoeing kayaking, and tubing. All require reservations.

desserts, all served by people in period costume. After lunch, visit the tavern's general store, stocked with crafts, traditional food, and Virginia wine. *683 Thomas Jefferson Pkwy., Charlottesville; (434) 977-1234.*

Mrs. Rowe's Family Restaurant and Bakery ★★★★/$

Though people come from miles around for Mrs. Rowe's famous pies, the traditional Southern-fried chicken is also justifiably famous. *Richmond Rd., Staunton; (540) 886-1833.*

Waterwheel Restaurant ★★★/$$

One of five restored buildings at the Inn at Gristmill Square, this old mill has been converted to a restaurant, but not gussied up. Though the menu is limited, the staff is accommodating to young guests. Be sure to ask how the mill worked. *Country Rd. 645, Warm Springs; (540) 839-2231.*

SOUVENIR HUNTING

The Hobby Horse at the Homestead

Children will love the toys, books, and clothing in this shop at the Homestead resort. Little girls in a "mommy" stage will long for one of the astonishingly realistic baby dolls. *Hot Springs; (800) 838-1766; (540) 839-1766.*

Leave No Trace

The National Park Service has developed a policy to minimize the visitors' impact on the park environment. Called "Leave No Trace," the policy aims to promote and inspire responsible recreation through the following guiding principles:

- Plan ahead and prepare.
- Travel and camp on durable surfaces.
- Dispose of waste properly.
- Leave what you find.
- Minimize campfire impacts.
- Respect wildlife.
- Be considerate of others.

Leave No Trace symbols (a purple circle with a green wave) are on trails and overlooks throughout Shenandoah and other national parks. Think of it this way: anything you took in with you, you also have to take out, even if it's trash now.

Sunday's Child

This charming shop in downtown Lexington carries toys and gifts. The store motto: "In a learn-to-play-again setting, your wishes are fulfilled." *14 W. Washington St., Lexington; (540) 463-1786.*

Young girls tend to love Chincoteague and Assateague, not just for the beaches but for the wild ponies running along them.

Norfolk, Virginia Beach, and the Eastern Shore

A TRIP TO EASTERN Virginia means lots of shoreline—along the rolling Atlantic as well as the calmer Chesapeake. But that's about all the communities here have in common.

Norfolk, a city forged by the U.S. Navy, has rehabilitated its once sleazy, sailor-friendly waterfront, adding, among other attractions, a kid-pleasing maritime center.

Norfolk's downtown has also been revived with chic restaurants and luxury condominiums.

A 15-minute drive south of Norfolk, the city of Virginia Beach reigns over a very popular and crowded four-mile stretch of sand along the Atlantic. The thriving vacation spot also sports high-rise hotels, pulsating nightlife, and plenty of rainy-day fun for young families.

At the other end of the activity spectrum are Chincoteague and Assateague Island. Located at the northern end of Virginia's eastern shore, these serene spots grace pristine seashore with only the waves for company. The children's book *Misty of Chincoteague* has made this quiet community a special favorite with kids, and, yes, the famous ponies really do exist. For a step

THE **FamilyFun** LIST

MUST-SEE ★ MUST-SEE

Chincoteague and Assateague (page 394)

Tangier Island (page 395)

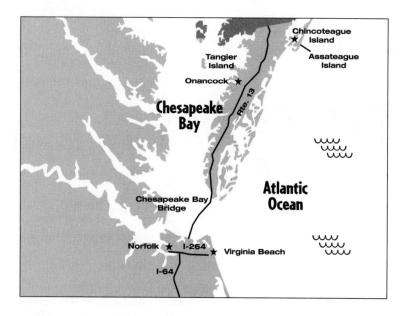

back in time, remote Tangier Island—where residents speak a dialect close to 17th-century British English—offers a glimpse of life that is fast disappearing. Your children, who may have to strain to understand their hosts, may be convinced that they've landed in a foreign country. In many ways they have.

JUST FOR FUN

Chincoteague and FamilyFun **Assateague**
★★★★/Free

Come for the miles of unspoiled beaches and the lure of wild ponies, which, legend has it, are descendants of Spanish horses shipwrecked on America's shores. Assateague Island (the larger of the two) is a barrier island to Chincoteague Island. While all of Chincoteague Island is owned by Virginia, half of Assateague Island is in Maryland and half in Virginia. Assateague Island (the Virginia side) is a national wildlife refuge called the Chincoteague National Wildlife Refuge; it's for day use only and is completely unspoiled. There is no place to stay here (however, camping is permitted on the Maryland side of the island). Chincoteague Island has motels and beach homes and restaurants.

The wild ponies are located on Assateague until they are rounded up and swim across the Chincoteague Channel to Chincoteague (the town).

The swim takes place the last consecutive Wednesday and Thursday in July. The ponies swim over on Wednesday morning and back on Friday morning. Chincoteague Island is seven miles long and a half mile wide and was settled as a fishing village in the 1600s by the British. There are no ocean beaches on Chincoteague, but there are 37 miles of unspoiled ocean beaches on Assateague. A bridge connects the two islands. To get to Chincoteague, take Ocean Highway Rte. 13 on Virginia's Eastern Shore Peninsula to Rte. 175 toward Chincoteague Island.

That Assateague doesn't have enough marsh grass accounts for the ponies' extra-small size. They are so hardy, though, that the herd has to be culled annually. Immortalized in the book *Misty of Chincoteague*, the horses are the stuff of legend that thoroughly enthrall children; practice saying, "No, we can't buy one and take it home." Aside from the horses, the beach is the thing here. There's lit-

tle else in terms of entertainment in Chincoteague, a community geared more to fishing than to tourism. For many families, that's this area's big attraction. Contact the **Chincoteague Chamber of Commerce**, *P.O. Box 258, Chincoteague; (757) 336-6161;* www.assateague.org *or* www.chinoteaguechamber.com

MUST-SEE FamilyFun MUST-SEE **Tangier Island**
★★★★/Free

A day trip to this little island in Chesapeake Bay is nothing like a day in old-time Williamsburg. Tangier is a real place, somewhat rough around the edges, where the fishing life has changed little since the island was first populated in 1608. To get a sense of life here, your family should stroll along unpaved lanes, sample the seafood in an out-of-the-way café, and try to engage locals in conversation. Ask your children to consider what it would be like to live on the island, where there's no doctor and virtually

T Squares

My son, Jason, age 10$^{1}/_{2}$, has a number of T-shirts from sports teams he's played on, camps he's gone to, and places we've visited. Jason's aunt, Linda, came up with a creative way to preserve those memories after he has outgrown the shirts. She cuts a section from the front and back of each shirt, sews them together, and lightly stuffs them to make mini-pillows. She then sews the pillows together to make a soft and comfortable quilt. It's a great keepsake, and as Jason gets older and taller, the quilt just grows with him.

Debbie Emery, Northboro, Massachusetts

no crime; where everyone knows everyone (most of the 850 residents have one of four surnames); and where very little changes from century to century. Cars aren't allowed on Tangier, so park in Onancock, Virginia (*on the Eastern Shore; U.S. 13S to Rte. 179W; look for signs*), and board the ferry (*757/891-2240*); *Ferries run from Memorial Day through October 15.*

Sculpt a Dune Buggy

Here's a beach craft your kids will really get into. This two-seater dune buggy has all the options: sand dollar headlights, a Frisbee steering wheel, a driftwood windshield, and a pebble license plate.

Help your kids pile up a big mound of sand and pack it down firm. Start sculpting the body. Keep in mind the old artist's trick: working from the top down, carve away anything that doesn't look like a dune buggy.

Round the car's hood and trunk, carve fat tires into the sides, and dig out a seat, a slanted dashboard, and a hole where the driver's and passenger's feet fit comfortably.

Once the basic shape is in place, your kids can add the trim: tire treads, driftwood windshield and bumpers, a shell hood ornament, a beach grass antenna, a towel seat cover, or whatever else they dream up.

As a last step, they can fill 'er up with shell gasoline.

Norfolk
★★★/Free

Follow the fleet to Norfolk: for years, the town's claim to fame was as a port of call for thousands of U.S. sailors—a somewhat seamy reputation. But the waterfront community has since cleaned up its act and now has several family attractions. The biggest is **Nauticus, the National Maritime Center** (*One Waterside Dr., Norfolk; 757/664-1000*). Resembling a warship, the battle-gray building has six theme areas where children can learn about nautical navigation, the Navy, sea creatures, and the aquatic environment.

Kids especially enjoy the bridge of the USS *Preble*, which has been installed on site. They can also re-create a naval battle by computer or experience what it's like at the bottom of the sea. Two working submarines are usually docked nearby and you can board them. If your kids have a real interest in things naval, you may want to tour the world's largest naval base. The base for the Atlantic Fleet, **Norfolk Naval Base** (*9079 Hampton Blvd; 757/444-7955*) is home port for more than 100 ships and 130,000 employees. Free guided tours meet at the naval base tour office, with the last one leaving at 2 P.M. Call ahead for tour details.

When you're ready for a bite to eat and a little souvenir shopping, head for the Waterside Festival Marketplace, with 120 shops and restaurants. On the first weekend in June, families flock here for **Harborfest** (*757/441-2345*); the annual event features musical performances, tall-ship tours, a sailboat parade, and aerial stunt flyers. Norfolk is 190 miles southeast of Washington, D.C. I-64 runs from Richmond to Norfolk. *For more information, contact the Norfolk Convention and Visitors Bureau at (800) 368-3097 or (757) 441-1852.*

Virginia Beach ★★★/Free

Though the beach itself is long (20 miles) and lovely, the town of Virginia Beach itself is abuzz with activity. Vacationers pack high-rise beachfront condos and hotels (which unfortunately block ocean views) and throng a boardwalk lined with T-shirt shops, video arcades, and restaurants. Biking is not allowed on the boardwalk, but an adjacent path accommodates both cyclists and skaters.

When you're ready for a break from the sand and surf, take your kids to **Ocean Breeze Amusement Park** (*849 General Booth Blvd.; 800/678-WILD; 757/442-4444*), where a go-cart track, miniature-golf course, batting cages, and a wave pool will keep them entertained for hours. Unless you want to be overwhelmed by partying college students, it's best to avoid Virginia Beach during spring break period (mid-March through mid-April). *Follow I-64 to Va. 44, 17 miles from Norfolk. Visitors Information Center: (800) 446-8038.*

Virginia Beach Fesivals

For complete information on special events throughout the year, call Virginia Beach's Visitor Information Center at *(800) 446-8038.*

Early May Held at the Oceana Naval Air Station, **Race at the Base** is a three-day weekend event with vintage race cars from the 1950s through the 1970s.

Mid-May Beach Music Weekend kicks summer into high gear with free performances of now-classic beach music.

Mid-June The Virginia Beach **Boardwalk Art Show** is the East Coast's largest outdoor art show.

Mid-September The Neptune Festival bids farewell to summer with entertainment and a huge sand-sculpture competition.

Mid-November through January 1 Holiday Lights at the Beach sets the boardwalk aglitter with 250 festive displays.

BUNKING DOWN

Maddox Family Campground ★★★/$

Rent a campsite and hookup—kids will make a beeline for the pool and playground. *6742 Maddox Blvd., Chincoteague; (757) 336-3111.*

Norfolk Waterside Marriott ★★★★/$$

Located near the Waterside Festival Marketplace, this member of the national chain makes for a nice location; complimentary continental breakfast is a family-friendly plus. *235 E. Main St., Norfolk; (800) 228-9290; (757) 627-4200;* www.marriott.com

Quality Inn Virginia Beach Oceanfront ★★★★/$$$

As far as kids are concerned, this hotel has three things going for it: it's right on the boardwalk, it has an indoor pool, and it has an outdoor pool. Kids under 12 stay free. *Eighth St. and Atlantic Ave., Virginia Beach; (800) 228-5151; (757) 428-8935.*

Vacation Cottages

Furnished cottages in Chincoteague can be rented by the week, month, or season. Prices for accommodations vary greatly, depending on size, quality, location, and season. *4405 Depot Rd., Chincoteague; (800) 457-6643; (757) 336-3720.*

GOOD EATS

AJ's by the Creek ★★★/$$

Children who like seafood will be happy here. For those who turn up their noses at anything with a fin or shell, AJ's serves up pasta dishes as well. *6585 Maddox Blvd., Chincoteague; (757) 336-5888.*

Hilda Crockett's Chesapeake House ★★★★/$$$

Feast on a traditional Tangier Island lunch of fresh bread and seafood at this inn. Crab cakes are a house specialty. *Tangier Island; (757) 891-2331.*

Waterside Festival Marketplace ★★★/$$$

With 30 restaurants and food stands, this place has something for everyone. Two places stand out: **Il Porto** (*757/627-4400*) serves Mediterranean fare and has a children's menu; **Schooner's Harbor Grill** (*757/627-8800*) has seafood, huge sandwiches, and burgers. *Waterside Dr., Norfolk; (757) 627-3300.*

SOUVENIR HUNTING

Learning Express

About a mile from the boardwalk, the shop carries educational toys by Brio, Playmobil, Thomas the Tank Engine, and other top brands. *752 Hilltop North Shopping Center, Virginia Beach; (757) 425-2377.*

THE CIVIL WAR IN VIRGINIA

SOME OF THE BLOODIEST battles of the Civil War were fought in Virginia, along the corridor from Manassas south to Williamsburg. The Confederate and Union Armies were locked in a fight for their respective capitals—Richmond in the South and Washington in the North—separated by only 120 miles. Fredericksburg, Manassas, Richmond, Chancellorsville, and Williamsburg saw monumental conflicts and the loss of thousands of men on both sides.

More than a century later, it's difficult to imagine the magnitude of the struggle, especially for youngsters who are unfamiliar with the history of the Civil War. Children look at the national military parks and see rolling hills, fields, perhaps a reconstructed house. For preschoolers, that's probably enough. Young grade-schoolers can learn more about the devastation inflicted by the Civil War, especially on the South, with the help of a knowledgeable park ranger.

But if your children are a bit older and you would like them to better understand this chapter in history that saved our nation, you may want to attend a **Civil War battle reenactment**. Members of innumerable reenactment organizations, associated with the military companies of both the North and the South, regularly stage these mock battles on or near the original battlefields. The reenactors wear faithful copies of original uniforms, carry weapons (that shoot blanks), sleep in tents, and enjoy music from the Civil War era—and they're often accompanied by their wives and children, also in period costumes. The reenactments may last several days. Contact the battlefield park you wish to visit for a schedule of reenactments or search the Web under the name of the battle, the battlefield, the name of the company involved, or Civil War Reenactments in Virginia.

Index

Also from FamilyFun

FAMILYFUN MAGAZINE: a creative guide to all the great things families can do together. Call 800-289-4849 for a subscription.

FAMILYFUN.COM: visit us at www.familyfun.com and search our extensive archives for games, crafts, recipes, and holiday projects.

FAMILYFUN COOKBOOK: a collection of more than 250 irresistible recipes for you and your kids, from healthy snacks to birthday cakes to dinners everyone in the family can enjoy (Disney Editions, 256 pages; $24.95).

FAMILYFUN CRAFTS: a step-by-step guide to more than 500 of the best crafts and activities to do with your kids (Disney Editions, 256 pages; $24.95).

FAMILYFUN PARTIES: a complete party planner featuring 100 celebrations for birthdays, holidays, and every day (Disney Editions, 224 pages; $24.95).

FAMILYFUN COOKIES FOR CHRISTMAS: a batch of 50 recipes for creative holiday treats (Disney Editions, 64 pages; $9.95).

FAMILYFUN TRICKS AND TREATS: a collection of wickedly easy crafts, costumes, party plans, and recipes for Halloween (Disney Editions, 98 pages; $14.95).

FAMILYFUN BOREDOM BUSTERS: a collection of 365 activities, from instant fun and after-school crafts to kitchen projects and learning games (Disney Editions, 224 pages; $24.95).

FAMILYFUN HOMEMADE HOLIDAYS: A collection of 150 holiday activities, from festive decorations and family traditions to holiday recipes and gifts kids can make (Disney Editions, 96 pages; $14.95).